Teddy Roosevelt
at San Juan

TEXAS A&M UNIVERSITY
MILITARY HISTORY SERIES
54

Teddy Roosevelt

AT SAN JUAN

THE MAKING OF A PRESIDENT

by Peggy Samuels and Harold Samuels

Texas A&M University Press
College Station

The paper used in this book meets the minimum requirements
of the American National Standard for Permanence of Paper
for Printed Library Materials, Z39.48-1984.
Binding materials have been chosen for durability.

Library of Congress Cataloging-in-Publication Data
Samuels, Peggy.
    Teddy Roosevelt at San Juan : the making of a president /
by Peggy Samuels and Harold Samuels. — 1st ed.
        p.   cm. — (Texas A&M/military history series ; 54)
    Includes bibliographical references and index.
    ISBN 0-89096-771-7 (alk. paper)
    1. Roosevelt, Theodore, 1858–1919—Military leadership.
2. Presidents—United States—Biography. 3. San Juan Hill,
Battle of, 1898. 4. United States. Army. Volunteer
Cavalry, 1st. 5. Spanish-American War, 1898. I. Samuels,
Harold. I. Title. III. Series: Texas A&M University
military history series ; 54.
E757.S19   1997
973.91'1'092—dc21   97-9903
                                                        CIP

There never was another such body of men under arms. Their opportunity came, and they rose to it, and they stand ensconced in the gilded pinnacle of fame; but they know now, and admit it sadly among themselves, in the little groups that still cling together, that the Rough Riders can never follow their old Colonel again. They will mount and ride no more. There is nothing left but to talk it over.

—Broughton Brandenburg,
"The Rough Riders Ten Years Afterward"

Contents

CONTENTS

Illustrations

MAPS

Acknowledgments

Graham A. Cosmas, chief, General History Branch, U.S. Army Center of Military History, Washington, D.C., read the manuscript before publication and made valuable suggestions concerning the military.

Michael E. Pilgrim, Military Archives Division, National Archives, Washington, D.C., and Wallace Finley Dailey, curator of the Theodore Roosevelt Collection, Harvard College Library, Cambridge, Massachusetts, were most helpful when we began our research in 1982 and 1983.

*Teddy Roosevelt
at San Juan*

Chapter 1

The Beginning

This is a look at one brief, jubilant episode in the energetic, exciting life of Theodore Roosevelt. The time is one o'clock on the afternoon of July 1, 1898, during the Cuban phase of the Spanish-American War. Roosevelt is a thirty-nine-year-old colonel of volunteers. He is preparing to advance at the head of his Rough Riders, the most colorful regiment in the American V Army Corps.

The overall military objective is the capture of the city of Santiago de Cuba. The immediate target is the central sector of the fortified San Juan Heights to the left of El Camino Real, the muddy trail that two divisions of American soldiers took to march into battle. Capturing the blockhouse on San Juan Hill is the key to breaching the Spanish defenses on the heights above the city.

Roosevelt and his Rough Riders are positioned as reserves in the rear of two regular regiments on the right side of the trail. The Rough Riders are facing the lower and poorly defended hillock called Kettle Hill, rather than the steeper and more bristling San Juan Hill. This is the remote location that Roosevelt's superiors appear to have chosen to preclude him from engaging in any rash action.

As the only soldier on horseback among the American attackers, Roosevelt is the most visible man on the field. Suddenly he initiates an unauthorized charge. While he is racing up the slope, his horse is halted by a wire barricade. He leaps off the horse to climb through the strands on foot and run ahead of his men. Panting, he reaches the

Col. Theodore Roosevelt of the Rough Riders. *Harper's Pictorial History of the War with Spain* (New York: Harper and Brothers, 1899), p. 330.

crest of Kettle Hill. His young troopers fall in behind him as he revels in the exultation of the moment.

Afterward, Roosevelt called this his "one crowded hour." At the end of the fighting, he described his perceived role to his faithful chronicler Richard Harding Davis, the most celebrated of the Spanish-American War correspondents. Through Davis, Roosevelt became recognized by the press as the U.S. Army's paramount hero of the day. The journalists' job was to create heroes where necessary to sell newspapers and Roosevelt was clearly the most promotable actor of the campaign. His feats were magnified countless times in popular prose, poetry, and paintings. These interpretations of his charge at San Juan depicted a singular personal success—partly fictitious but wholly triumphant.

Roosevelt's selection as nonpareil was not without foundation. There was no denying his fearlessness. His bravery and achievements in the fighting were no greater, however, than the courage displayed and elevations captured by the regular soldiers on the more important left side of the same arena. The tale he told Davis about his part in the assault exaggerated what he had done, at the expense of the regulars.

Three years later when he was sworn in as the twenty-sixth president of the United States, Roosevelt credited his political success to what was then known by most Americans as his legendary charge up San Juan Hill. He had conveniently forgotten that he had topped the more modest Kettle Hill. Even after he became a sophisticated international statesman, his wife Edith warned that this august civilian personage still embraced the impetuous cavalryman within him. He gloried in memories that altered the facts of his short wartime connection with the Rough Riders.

Roosevelt was born in 1858 and he died in 1919. He was one of the best known men in the world during and after his two presidential terms which lasted from 1901 to 1909. His popularity has never ended. Even today, political scientists consider him to have been among the ablest of American chief executives.[1]

Despite his elitist background as the older son of a rich and socially prominent Dutch family in New York City, Roosevelt's exuberant love of outdoor life and his broad intellectual interests came to exemplify the American ideal of the period. He was an ornithologist of note in his youth, a member of the scholastic honor society at Harvard, the youngest New York state legislator, a boss stockman in Dakota Territory, a big-game hunter, an author of historical nonfiction and outdoors books, a municipal and federal civil servant, a military man, and governor of the state of New York. He also was a deputy sheriff who tracked and captured bad men across the expanse of the Old West. All of this was accomplished before he was forty-one. After leaving the presidency, he killed African lions and quarreled with the Italian Pope.

His career was the realization of the daydreams of thousands of action-oriented American boys. His varied experiences made him the symbol of masculinity for his day, but he was probably not someone people would enjoy meeting at close quarters. Admiration at arm's length would have been a more prudent response. He was too combative in seeking his ends to let anyone relax with him, too self-centered to listen, and too vindictive when crossed to permit chancing a spontaneous reply. He was bigger than life. His daughter Alice claimed that he wanted to be the bride at every wedding and the corpse at every funeral.

The focus of this report is on the charge Roosevelt initiated at San Juan, to explain what he did and why he did it. The story unfolds on two separate tracks. The main track starts with the formation of the Rough Riders and carries the action along in chronological chapters. Alternating with the chapters that move the story forward are subsidiary chapters that function as flashbacks. This provides a succinct "Looking Back" at elements of Roosevelt's earlier life to supply the reasons for his performance in storming the hill. The subsidiary line continues until Roosevelt is ready for his "one crowded hour."

There is also a message for today. A persuasive politician who is genuinely liked by the electorate is seldom discountenanced by the disclosure that the experiences propelling him into office were overstated.

Chapter 2
The Cowboy Cavalry

Unintentionally, Melvin Grigsby made it possible for Theodore Roosevelt to become colonel of the Rough Riders. Grigsby was South Dakota's state attorney general in 1898. He wanted to serve as an army officer in the anticipated hostilities with Spain, but his governor would not provide him with the prerequisite, an appointment to the state militia. Roosevelt had the same problem in New York and like Roosevelt, Grigsby was not a man to quit.

In late March, Grigsby and dozens of other militant westerners sent telegrams offering their services to President William McKinley's secretary of war, Russell Alger. Grigsby also suggested that cowboys would be desirable recruits for a proposed U.S. Volunteer Cavalry. To bypass his governor and gain the preferment he wanted, he went to Washington on his own in mid-April to lobby for legislation authorizing the cowboy cavalry.[1]

At the capital, Grigsby found that Judge Jay Torrey of Wyoming had already persuaded Wyoming's Sen. Francis Warren to introduce a bill in Congress providing for a cavalry regiment of one thousand Wyoming cowboys to serve as volunteers for two years. As a substitute for the Warren bill, lawyer Grigsby wrote a more sweeping provision specifying that "the President may authorize the Secretary of War to organize regiments [of riders] possessing special qualifications, not to exceed three thousand men." Special qualifications meant cowboys who could ride and shoot. The provision was enacted on

April 22 as part of the bill creating a wartime army, two days after the president signed the congressional resolution of war against Spain.

Six days after the Army bill passed, Secretary Alger issued regulations providing for "three regiments of cavalry to be composed exclusively of frontiersmen." Giant athletes, Indian braves under Buffalo Bill Cody, outlaws led by Jesse James's brother Frank, and Colorado cowgirls volunteered. They were not deemed to be covered by the provision and they were not accepted. The three units of "horsemen and marksmen" were to constitute the entire Volunteer Cavalry for the Spanish-American War.

While lobbying to get the cowboy legislation through Congress, neither Grigsby nor Torrey had contacted an obvious source of assistance, the bellicose Theodore Roosevelt who was assistant secretary of the navy. The reason was that the two westerners wanted no competition from him in securing their commands. They were disappointed when Roosevelt was advised of the regulations on April 23, before they were told. As the only member of the McKinley administration who could even remotely be described as a frontiersman, Roosevelt was closeted with Alger before the regulations were published. Alger was the solitary jingo in McKinley's cabinet, so he was predisposed favorably toward the vehemently interventionist assistant secretary. In contrast, Roosevelt had reservations concerning Alger's ability as an administrator. Fortunately, he had kept his doubts to himself for once.[2]

In their meeting, Alger offered Roosevelt the post of colonel of the initial cowboy cavalry regiment. He was amused when the New Yorker responded oratorically for the historical record, "I have done more perhaps than any one man in bringing on this war, and I feel it my duty to go out in the field, if I have to leave my body there. My country is first."[3]

Informally, Roosevelt later confided that he believed

Secretary Alger was fond of me personally. He liked my attitude on Cuba. Accordingly, he offered me command of one of the regiments of the National Volunteer Cavalry. I told him that after six weeks' service in the field I would feel competent to handle the regiment, but I would not know how to equip it or how to get it into the first action. If he would make Leonard Wood colonel, I would accept the lieutenant colonelcy.

Alger thought this an act of foolish self-abnegation. He told me to accept the colonelcy, make Wood lieutenant colonel, and Wood would do the work anyway, but I answered that I did not want what I did not earn. He laughed at me a little, but he promised to do as I wished. Wood instantly began the work of raising the regiment. I continued as Assistant Secretary of the Navy, trying to plan and also being used by Wood to finish getting equipment.[4]

Wood accepted the command as his due, although he had been a doctor in military service, not a field officer. The appointment changed his life, too, putting him in position to become an army general with a national reputation.

A Military Hero

Born in New Hampshire in 1860, Leonard Wood was two years younger than Roosevelt. His father had been what today is a rarity, an impecunious physician. Because of his father's profession, he was accepted by Harvard Medical School at the age of twenty, although he lacked a college degree.[5]

In 1885, Wood began practice as an army doctor in Arizona where he was described as not handsome or popular but self-reliant, clever, and "ambitious enough to want to be President of the United States." He earned a Medal of Honor for bravery in chasing the Apache chief Geronimo, saved Gen. Nelson Miles's leg from amputation after a riding accident, and on November 18, 1890, married into a prominent Washington family. On that same day, the ill-fated battleship *Maine* was launched.[6]

In 1895, Wood was transferred to Washington as assistant attending surgeon with the military rank of captain. His patients included President Grover Cleveland. When McKinley was elected president the following year, Mrs. McKinley became Wood's charge. She was a chronic invalid who was convinced that Wood was helping her. He also treated Alger, the secretary of war.

Roosevelt met Wood at a Washington dinner party in June 1897, less than a year before the cowboy cavalry was organized. The combative Roosevelt was impressed with Wood because he was a decorated military hero. The pair proved to be compatible. Philosophically, both were jingoes. They agreed wholeheartedly on the need to oust European powers from colonies in the Western Hemisphere and on the benefits that would flow from American imperialism. Roosevelt was an aristocrat, a fact that made the association flattering for the homespun Wood.[7]

Physically, both took strenuous exercise which they considered essential to health. They rode or walked together almost every day. While they strode along, they planned such exotic ventures as selling reindeer meat in the Yukon during the Gold Rush. Roosevelt backed out of the project because he was afraid of missing the invasion of Cuba. McKinley referred to the pair jocularly as "the War Party." When Wood came to the White House to treat Mrs. McKinley, the good-natured president always asked him, "Have you and Theodore declared war yet?"[8]

Wood was essential to the McKinleys' welfare. Roosevelt, however, was excluded from the residential quarters of the White House. His loud incessant speech, his violent gesticulating, and the force that radiated from him even in repose upset Mrs. McKinley's precarious emotional balance. His mere presence disturbed her.[9]

One Man in a Thousand

When Roosevelt told Wood about his arrangement for a regiment they would share, Wood responded ungraciously. He had "understood from Alger that his proposition was to give each of us one of the new regiments, but your action rendered it unnecessary, even if he had contemplated doing it." There were only two other voluntary cavalry regiments, though, and Torrey and Grigsby had earned those.[10]

Wood's pique at being cast in his natural role as second fiddle to a dominant individual such as Roosevelt was already threatening "the War Party." What saved the relationship was the lower-keyed Wood's ability to play the waiting game. He knew that after the regiment was organized, he and not his lieutenant colonel would be in charge.

Roosevelt, though, was a hard man to keep down. He had already advised friendly newspapermen concerning his apparent magnanimity toward Wood. The journalists wrote that, "when the facts concerning Roosevelt's appointment come to light, he has shown a deference to military experience and a modesty" in making way for Wood "which might possibly be observed in one man in a thousand."[11]

In truth, though, while Roosevelt would be second in command at the outset, he had managed to make himself outstanding in every other organization he had ever joined. He knew that he would eventually take over the regiment, too. In substantiation, the article which praised his deference already was calling the troopers "Roosevelt's Rough Riders," not "Wood's Rough Riders."

As assistant secretary of the navy, Roosevelt had catered to the press much as he had done in previous positions. He opened his office to reporters and cheerfully granted every request. Secretary of the Navy John D. Long noticed that Roosevelt's "room in the Navy Department bubbled over with bright young fellows." They were mainly newspaper correspondents looking for feature material from the most engaging source.[12]

The leading correspondent was Richard Harding Davis. Roosevelt had originally mistrusted him as an un-American Anglophile. During Roosevelt's stint as New York City police commissioner, however, Davis made midnight forays into the streets with him and was invited to dine with the Roosevelt family at home.[13]

Despite Davis's pretentious manner, his peers respected him for his ability. After war was declared, Davis asked Roosevelt for permission to go aboard a warship assigned to the naval blockade of Havana. He bragged to his mother that "Roosevelt telegraphed me the longest and strongest letter on the subject, instructing the Admiral to take me on as I was writing history." Without telling Davis, Roosevelt also provided the same type of letter for rival reporters. He wanted newspapermen to be obligated to him.[14]

Roosevelt's solicitude for members of the press was rewarded. In the normal course of journalistic operations, the label affixed to a man when he first appears in the headlines usually sticks forever. In 1882 when he was a state legislator, Roosevelt had been described as a dude misplaced in politics. This characterization could have lasted, but instead Roosevelt was able to improve his image as he matured. No one referred to him as a dude in 1898. Newspapermen stressed his determination and his gusto, giving Roosevelt a positive national image. Articles on him and his new regiment were uniformly laudatory.[15]

Harper's Weekly editorialized that "Theodore Roosevelt deserves respect from his countrymen. He is a man of courage and intelligence. We know he has the honor and welfare of his nation in his mind and heart."[16]

Davis's *New York Herald* added, "It is a dashing thing, and a happy combination has been struck in selecting Mr. Roosevelt—a man whose gallantry and spirit are unquestioned, who has roughed it with the cowboys of the plains, and who is thoroughly qualified to handle the soldiers. Mr. Roosevelt has written to plainsmen suggesting they enter his regiment."[17]

The *New York Times* pointed out that "the men he will lead are ready the moment they enlist. They have their own mounts, their own arms, and know how to fight all the time." As far as the American people could tell, Roosevelt was in command of the cowboy regiment and not Wood who seldom was mentioned.[18]

In addition to securing this personal approbation, Roosevelt found another means to attract attention. He had obtained Alger's approval to include mounted New York City policemen in the cowboy regiment. If he could also enlist eastern society types, he would have an irresistible melange of tough West and effete East, much like his own mixed background that so attracted newspapermen. He wrote to college athletes and city clubmen he knew, telling them to be prepared. "It may very well be that we can use your company," he advised. "You must have everything ready so I can slash you in."[19]

He was involved in the regiment with all his heart. There was no question in his mind that he was doing the right thing by quitting job and home for a turn at soldiering. In his passion to fight, civilian responsibilities were thrown aside. He was eager to get moving. "This is going to be a short war," he asserted prophetically. "I am going ashore with my troops, get into the first fight, and keep going until it is over."[20]

He began the leave-taking in Washington with notice to his diffident boss, Secretary Long. Long's April 25 diary entry was prescient:

My Assistant Secretary, Roosevelt, has determined to go into the Army. He has been of great use; a man of unbounded energy and force, and thoroughly honest—which is the main thing. He has lost his head to this folly of deserting the post where he is of the most service and running off to ride a horse and, probably, brush mosquitoes from his neck on the Florida sands—and yet how absurd all this will sound, if by some turn of fortune he should accomplish some great thing and strike a very high mark.

Long recognized that Roosevelt was by nature a risk taker and not one who would be satisfied to remain a career bureaucrat.[21]

Like Long, Roosevelt's friends thought he was making a foolish move for a thirty-nine-year-old with a sick wife, six children, little money in the bank, and a job as an influential administrator in the Navy Department. The clever John Hay wrote, "Theodore Roosevelt, that *wilder werwegener* [adventurous savage], has left the Navy where he had the chance of his life and has joined a cowboy regiment."[22]

The enlistment was not seen as shrewdness in laying the groundwork for political advancement. Rather it was viewed as an expression of irresponsible immaturity. Winthrop Chandler remarked, "I think Roosevelt is going mad. The President has asked him twice as a personal favor to stay in the Navy Department, but Theodore is wild to fight and hack and hew. It is really sad. Of course this ends his political career. Even Cabot says this." The jingo Sen. Henry Cabot Lodge had been Roosevelt's mentor.[23]

Most of the men closest to Roosevelt regarded him as having been an unpopular politician in previous positions, a failed ranchman, and only marginally successful as a writer. In their opinion, with no other career open to him and no reservoir of money, he was lucky to be in the Navy Department. He was supported mainly by Edith, his patient, devoted, ailing wife. She was willing to have him fight in Cuba because that was what he wanted, despite the problems he was leaving her to handle at home.

Roosevelt was oblivious to his friends' concerns. He was certain that by entering the army he was furthering his aspirations. He expected to become a hero, capable of being elected to any office.

A Secondary Role

Alger sent telegrams to the governors of Arizona, New Mexico, Oklahoma, and the Indian Territories on April 25, advising them "the President directs that Captain Leonard Wood, U.S.A., be authorized to raise a regiment of Cavalry as mounted riflemen, and to be its

Colonel, and has named Hon. Theodore Roosevelt as Lieutenant Colonel. All the other officers will come from the vicinity where the troops are raised. What can you do for them?" The Northwest was left to Torrey and Grigsby.[24]

In Arizona, enlistment of volunteers had already started. In New Mexico, recruitment began quickly in response to Alger's telegram. Albuquerque's weekly newspaper proclaimed that "rough riders and crack shots are wanted. If you want to lick Spain, come to the front." Similar appeals were made in Oklahoma and the Indian Territories.[25]

The Southwest was the section of the country where Wood had tracked Geronimo to win the Medal of Honor. His feats were remembered favorably by local citizenry, but regular army officers refused to join Wood's regiment. Professional soldiers would not serve under a doctor.[26]

On the other hand, Roosevelt had chosen Wood as colonel because of organizing skills he knew Wood had learned in the service, doctor or not. This was the only time Roosevelt had willingly adopted a secondary role. He needed to avoid making the kind of mistake in mustering in and early handling of the regiment that might diminish his political chances after the war. He could not risk ridicule.[27]

As Roosevelt recognized, Wood was a methodical and private man. Concentrating on planning, he left public relations to Roosevelt, even though newspapers wrote that "Colonel Wood is lost sight of entirely in the effulgence of Teethadore."[28] Wood derived satisfaction from sitting three regular army cavalry sergeants at tables in his Washington medical office to make out the hundreds of requisitions and orders necessary to organize and equip a regiment of cavalry from scratch. He told Roosevelt that supply officers were upset by his requests. One quartermaster complained, "I had a magnificent system here. My department was in good working order, and this damned war comes along and breaks it all up."[29]

To Wood, getting the regiment prepared for combat was an exciting covert competition with other volunteer cavalry and infantry regiments. "First one ready, first one in" was his motto. He expected his unit to have the best equipment and to lead those going to Cuba.[30]

The U.S. Army had modern Krag-Jorgensen rifles and carbines for the regulars, while most volunteers received outmoded Springfield rifles with carbon-powder ammunition. Carbon powder was a hazard in battle because it smoked when fired, disclosing the soldier's position. Wood understood that regular cavalry regiments would not willingly be brigaded with volunteers who were a danger to their neighbors because they were using black gunpowder in obsolete weapons. He insisted on receiving the Krag-Jorgensen carbines employing smokeless cartridges and he knew how to exert influence on General Flagler who was in charge of distributing the limited supply of carbines. Securing the modern Krag carbines was Wood's major achievement in outfitting the Rough Riders.[31]

When the quartermaster general told Wood that regulation blue woolen uniforms were not available for the regiment, Wood requisitioned coarse brown canvas "fatigues" that were intended for work in the stables. He would not wait for the correct uniforms while there was an alternative. By choosing the stable garb, he gained credit as a strategist. Regulation uniforms were heavy and dark, while the canvas uniforms were light in weight and color and thus more appropriate for the tropics. The outfits gave his volunteers an advantage over the regulars.

When cavalry sabers were not to be had for enlisted men, Wood located a New England manufacturer of tools for Cuban plantations. He ordered machetes, even though they were not army issue. Here again he enhanced his reputation. Sabers were not suited to fighting where there would be no hand-to-hand combat, whereas machetes could be used to clear brush as well as to fight.[32]

Finally, Wood selected San Antonio as the assembly point for the regiment because the Texas city was almost as hot and humid as Cuba. Also, San Antonio was near Fort Sam Houston and its storerooms, where he might be able to obtain things he had failed to request or that did not arrive on time.

In a record three days, Wood had his requisitions and orders ready to enroll men, organize the regiment, and procure equipment. He put the papers in a huge folder, walked over to Alger's office, and sat there for hours while Alger signed each document to make it official. Next Wood appointed jack-of-all-military-trades Lt. Tom Hall as regimental quartermaster to oversee receipt of the materials. Wood entrained for San Antonio with Hall on May 2 to greet the newly enlisted troopers from the Southwest.[33]

Wood sent no formal purchase orders to suppliers, just telegrams, and he retained no copy of the telegrams. He was a man in a hurry, traveling light while prevailing over army red tape and shortages. He kept Roosevelt in Washington to expedite the requisitions on the Ordnance and Quartermaster departments while winding up his duties as assistant secretary of the navy.[34]

Wood had been a splendid choice for colonel. His careful preparations were successful in getting the regiment ready expeditiously. Despite the regulars' prejudice against volunteers, he made Roosevelt confident of being set for the first embarkation for Cuba.

Participation in the invasion was critical to Roosevelt for financial as well as patriotic reasons. He was habitually short of funds, and a book publisher, the Frederick A. Stokes Company, had written to him, "Your record of stirring occurrences will be of intense interest, and we should like to become its publishers, on your own terms, when your war duties are concluded."[35] Unhappily for Stokes, the canny Roosevelt already had promised the rights to Scribner's which published both a magazine and books. He warned Scribner's that, in addition to Stokes, "the *Century* people and the *Atlantic Monthly* have also been writing me." He noted, "If I do the job at all, I am going to do it thoroughly. Possibly I could make some such arrangement (provided neither the yellow fever nor a Mauser bullet catches me) as I have made before, namely, to have the thing appear in magazine form, that is, in popular form, first, yet when it comes out as a book to be in shape as a permanent historical work." That proposition offered the potential of two printings of the same material—and for two payments.

Uncle Sam's Brownies

Mild-mannered as Wood generally was and obligated as he was to Roosevelt for putting him in command, he firmly rejected the nickname "Rough Riders" for the regiment. The term rankled because it fit Roosevelt so well. "Wood's Rough Riders" was not as trippingly said as the alliterative "Roosevelt's Rough Riders."[36]

Roosevelt professed to hate the nickname, too. He explained caustically from his navy office that the original Rough Riders had been the Pony Express. Later, however, the name had been cheapened by dime novels and Buffalo Bill's Wild West Circus. He insisted that people who thought his regiment was to be "a hippodrome affair" comparable to Buffalo Bill's would be making a mistake. "The regiment may be one of rough riders," he asserted with his habitual earnestness, "but they will be as orderly, obedient, and well-disciplined a body as any in the service. They go out for business and when they do business no one will entertain for a moment the notion that they are part of a show."[37]

For a short time the press humored Roosevelt by referring to the 1st Volunteer Cavalry not as "Rough Riders" but as "Teddy's Terrors," "Teddy's Holy Terrors," "Teddy's Tarantulas," "Teddy's Cowboy Contingent," "Teddy's Canvasbacks," and "Uncle Sam's Brownies." The last two names fit visually because the men wore the brown canvas jackets and pants and brown leggings to go with regulation blue shirts, black shoes, and gray-brown campaign hats. They looked mostly brown, while the regular cavalry was mostly blue.[38]

Despite other nicknames such as "Roosevelt's Rough 'Uns," "Roosevelt's Wild West," "Roosevelt's Regiment," the "Fighting First," the "Cowboy Cavalry," and the "Mounted Rifle Rangers," Roosevelt held his ground. "Don't call them rough riders, and don't call them cowboys," he insisted. "Call them mounted riflemen." That was how they had been described by Alger, but the secretary's designation lacked color. Newspapers preferred the alliterative "Roosevelt's Rough Riders," and that was the name used in headlines: "Roosevelt's Rough Riders Will Be the Finest," "Roosevelt Informs His Rough Riders," and "Enlists in Roosevelt's Rough Riders."[39]

Soon Roosevelt himself began referring to "the regiment of rough riders." He could not resist the alliteration, either, although he was circumspect enough to avoid adding his own name. The public quickly adopted the moniker "Roosevelt's Rough Riders." So did the army, informally, and Wood was stuck with a nickname that boosted his second in command, not him.

The Fifth Avenue Boys

Three regiments of cowboy volunteers had been formed. The limit on the number of men was 3,000, with 1,000 enlistments available for each regiment. The initial enrollment that was authorized for the Rough Riders, however, was only 780, so Roosevelt had to ask Alger for permission before increasing the upper limit of the regiment to 1,000 troopers.[40] Then, before notifying Wood, Roosevelt sent telegrams to his eastern friends and acquaintances who were waiting to be contacted about enlistment. He told them to come on the double and to "bring on your men." Because the recruits were well-known blue bloods and amateur athletes, the Washington press corps covered their arrival as front-page news.[41]

The group was labeled "the Fifth Avenue Boys, the most disparate of the republic's adventurers, coming from the scholastic seclusion of Harvard, from gilded clubs of the metropolis, from splendors of millionaires' palaces." Some were even "from the wild life of the plains," purportedly just like real cowboys. Despite being gentlemen and thus natural leaders in their own eyes, they were supposed to serve in the ranks with the common cowboys rather than as officers. Roosevelt claimed they were "gentleman rankers," the poor little lambs of the Kipling poem reborn as ordinary soldiers.[42]

The "Fifth Avenue Boys" included

> *Messrs. Woodbury Kane, Reginald Ronalds, William Tiffany, and Craig Wadsworth, a very deplorable depletion of the New York dandies. All are intimate friends of Mr. Roosevelt, an "old chappie." Each of the four took a servant with him. One or two took golf clubs and polo mallets. Such expedients have been the making of many a cavalry regiment in the British service.*
>
> *Mr. Woodbury Kane has been a polo player. Mr. Craig Wadsworth has been a leader in the Genessee Valley fox hunt and has led many a good german dance in New York ballrooms. Mr. William Tiffany spent several years on the plains of Montana, playing cow-boy. Mr. Reggy Ronalds played tackle at Yale. Nobody who knows them will doubt they will honor their breeding.*

As his motivation for enlisting, Basil Ricketts of Princeton confessed, "I just couldn't be happy while the war was going on." Percival Gasset of Harvard declared, "I had raised a troop of 75 polo players but I couldn't get them in the Army. I knew Mr. Roosevelt and admired him and thought I would rather go in his regiment." A. M. Coville admitted that "I hardly know whether genuine patriotism or love of adventure offers the leading stimulus. I am dead anxious to go and am gloriously happy."[43]

The immediate outcry from skeptical reporters was that the recruiting of "Teddy's Gilded Gang" instead of more cowboys represented favoritism. The *New York Post* referred to the society men as merely those "with the swellest names." Roosevelt tried to squelch the accusation by announcing that "they are mostly men born in the Southwest or who have lived there a great deal." This was not true, but it deflected the complaints while Roosevelt repeated that they were "real Americans, going as troopers, to be exactly on the same level as the cowboys. The best man is to be advanced."[44]

Regimental Quartermaster Tom Hall knew better about the expectations of promotion after he saw the contents of the Fifth Avenue Boys' trunks. They contained expensive "Cravenetted" uniforms tailor-made by Brooks Brothers in New York City, like those of Roosevelt and Wood. The waterproofed khaki-type jackets and trousers gave the society men away as having been promised, or at least as having anticipated, appointment as commissioned officers. Gentlemen they were. Rankers they did not expect to remain for long.[45]

Roosevelt brought this first group of Fifth Avenue Boys, "the very inspiration of young manhood," to Washington on May 5. He gathered them together in the recruiting room of the army's dispensary building. Standing in the center of the group, he made a dramatic speech. The alerted reporters took notes.[46]

"You have reached the last point," he cautioned. "If any man doesn't mean business, let him say so. An hour from now it will be too late. Once in, you've got to see it through. You've got to perform without flinching whatever duty is assigned to you, regardless of the difficulty or the danger attending it. No matter what comes, you mustn't squeal. Think it over, and if any man wishes to withdraw he will be gladly excused, for hundreds are ready to take his place."[47]

Thaddeus Higgins was not one of the "Boys." He had been a noncommissioned officer in the regular 6th Cavalry before becoming a New York City mounted policeman. As acting sergeant, he marched the volunteers upstairs in columns of twos to take the oath. No one backed out. There had been six thousand applicants for enlistment in the Rough Riders, and more mailbags of requests were arriving daily. The final count of applications was over twenty thousand.

Sergeant Higgins told the press that the men of the regiment were the equals of the legendary Irish Rangers. "They are ready to storm the gates of Hell," he contended. "Every man would rather die on the battlefield than come back without serving in battle. Surely I would.

This is no picnic but it is better for we will do the hardest fighting of the war." Higgins was Roosevelt's kind of fire-eater.[48]

The next day, this eastern contingent of the Rough Riders assembled near Roosevelt's Navy Department room. They were on time, puffed with newspaper praise that they were "all carefully picked men. They have hearts of flint, muscles of iron. Every man of them means to return wreathed in laurels."[49]

Roosevelt then dispatched them to the railway station in carriages, en route to San Antonio, Colonel Wood, and the westerners in the regiment. They had been sworn in as troopers. Wood would have to accept them. How the authentic westerners would react to Reginald and Percival was a different question.

Scourges on Settlements

The combination of Roosevelt, the frontier, and Fifth Avenue caught and held the imagination of the American public. More newspapermen were assigned to report on the Rough Riders than on all of the regiments of regulars combined. The premise was that the Rough Rider "regiment will make itself famous if an opportunity presents itself. They are not to be let loose as scourges on settlements, but where they strike they will leave a mark." The *Denver (Colo.) Field and Farm* advised, "Keep an eye on Teddy's Terrors. They are the stuff from which came the knighted chivalry of old."[50]

As soon as the regiment was formed, Roosevelt wrote to Gen. Fitzhugh Lee who was thought likely to head a division in the expeditionary force. "Get our regiment with you when you go to Cuba," he pleaded. "They won't be well trained at first, but by George! they will be good for outpost work from the beginning."[51]

Instead of being teamed with Lee, however, the Rough Riders were intended to have a role in Cuba as singular as their makeup. Alger advised Roosevelt that, as soon as the Rough Riders were "perfectly organized, they would go immediately to Cuba and act under orders independent of those to the Regular Army." Embarkation would be from Galveston, Texas, along with the first force of regulars to leave.[52] According to the *New York Herald,* the Rough Riders were to cooperate with rebel General Máximo Gómez on a roving assignment in the coastal area west of Havana. They were to "go where danger is the greatest."

Roosevelt was so excited at this answer to his dream of leading a cavalry charge in enemy country that he could hardly contain himself. At a reception he attended in Washington, a visiting French woman was backed against a wall by his flailing arms during a fervent discussion of war strategy with another bureaucrat. When she could retreat no farther, a button on his sleeve accidentally ripped a silk rose from her shoulder strap. He apologized profusely in broken French, omitting the nouns in his haste. She liked his sincerity.[53]

Secretary Long made no concession to Roosevelt's war fever. He confided to his diary on May 5 that in an argument with a New York vendor, an agitated Roosevelt "shouts at the top of his voice. His forte is his push. He lacks serenity." Long valued politeness above strong objections to a contractor's shoddy performance.[54]

Serenity was at the bottom of the list of what Roosevelt thought he needed. He was being goaded to his limit by naval, personal, and Rough Rider problems. His brother-in-law demanded that Roosevelt come to New York City to review his slim financial portfolio before serving in a war where he might die. Roosevelt refused to go until he was told that his wife would be required to attend in his place. She was recovering from an operation, accepting an occasional dinner invitation but not yet well, so he went grudgingly.[55]

Then at last, on May 6, Roosevelt was sworn in as lieutenant colonel of the 1st Volunteer Cavalry Regiment by Adj. Gen. Henry Corbin, the strong man of the War Department, and he handed in his resignation as assistant secretary. He intended to leave for San Antonio that night. Scores of friends and acquaintances came to the Navy Department to wish him luck during a day-long departure celebration. Appreciative naval employees joined to buy him a fine cavalry saber as a parting gift.[56]

Even his political adversary Sen. Mark Hanna appeared in the department. Hanna, who privately ridiculed him as "that cowboy," declared, "Roosevelt, I bid you good-bye. I wish you a successful venture, and a safe return. I feel perfectly sure that if there is any fighting in Cuba, you will be in the thickest of it."

The farewell, however, turned out to be premature. Roosevelt complained that Wood telegraphed him to "stay until the early part of next week, to keep things moving. So I shall have to stay." He replied to Wood that he "hated hanging around here with you in all the turmoil. I shall wire you this afternoon, hoping you will allow me to start tomorrow." On May 10, he was still grumbling, "It will be two or three days before I get off."[57]

Didn't Dewey Do Well

Long sighed with relief when Roosevelt resigned. The secretary had been disturbed by the lack of clarity about the end of Roosevelt's tenure. He hired a crony of his as a less glamorous assistant secretary and then because Roosevelt lingered on, had to find a temporary office for him. When news broke of one of the biggest naval triumphs in the nation's history, the supposedly departed Roosevelt remained on the scene, hogging the credit.[58]

Just a week after war was declared, Adm. George Dewey destroyed the Spanish Asiatic fleet on Manila Bay in the Philippines. The victory was the American entree to the Orient, although McKinley confessed, "When I received the cable from Admiral Dewey telling of the taking of the Philippines, I could not have told where those damned islands were within 2,000 miles." In a salute to the admiral, Old Glory flew from every Washington staff, and steam sirens screamed on the river. Crowds gathered before newspaper bulletin boards and sang patriotic songs.[59] It appeared that the war with Spain would be short. McKinley was now confident that Spanish forces in Cuba would surrender before an American army could get there.[60]

According to Roosevelt, only he in all of Washington had been prepared for a Pacific triumph of that magnitude. He let everybody know his contribution. "Didn't Admiral Dewey do wonderfully well?" he rejoiced. "I got him the position out there in Asia last year, and I had to beg hard to do it; and the reason I gave was that we might have to send him to Manila. And we sent him—and he went!"[61]

It was also Roosevelt, not Long, who provided the press with the summation: "Evidently the boys have done the job. The trouble with Spain is that they are 200 years behind the times. It is impossible to get ahead of Yankees. We still have Cuba and Porto Rico to attend to, and we will have avenged the *Maine*." The *Maine* was the battleship that had exploded in Havana harbor on February 15, 1898. "Remember the *Maine*" was the slogan that helped to precipitate the war.[62]

When Long announced that he would give out an important dispatch just received from Dewey, Roosevelt casually preempted the secretary's press conference by releasing the cable himself to the fifty reporters who were waiting in the Navy Department hallway. A humorous cartoon in *Life* magazine portrayed Long as having been merely Roosevelt's silent partner.[63]

Roosevelt finally left for San Antonio at 10 P.M. on May 12. He was accompanied by Edward Marshall, a Navy Department coachman. The *New York Times* reported that Marshall was a veteran soldier who had served two hitches in the all-black 10th Cavalry. He "secured a leave of absence from the Navy Department and insisted on going with Lieutenant Colonel Roosevelt to serve in the regiment of mounted riflemen."[64]

There was, however, no integration in the U.S. Army. Except for a tinge of Indian red and a few Hispanics, the Rough Riders were as racially pure as custom demanded in all-white units. Marshall went with the regiment as Roosevelt's body servant, a valet paid and equipped by Roosevelt, not "to serve in the regiment" as an enlisted man.[65]

To close the Roosevelt era in the Navy Department, Long penned a peevish postscript concerning his assistant's outstanding performance. The secretary told his diary that "the credit for the readiness of our Navy belongs neither to Mr. Roosevelt or myself. I get some credit because I am at the head; Roosevelt, because he was such an active fellow in other things. The whole credit belongs to the Chiefs of the Bureaus." He failed to mention that the chiefs had been directed by Roosevelt.[66]

Long added that "Roosevelt had push, but he had a tendency to disorder and rush and tempestuousness." The secretary at last was showing his resentment at the aggressiveness of his former assistant.

Chapter 3
Looking Back at "Teedie"

The eager Theodore Roosevelt who was on his way to boot camp at San Antonio in mid-May 1898 had a split genealogy. His ancestors were both merchants and warriors. As a consequence, he was both sophisticated and impulsive.

His father, a seventh-generation New Yorker, was an even more complex personality. He was an icon of masculine perfection for adoration by his wife and children, a reluctant shirker of military service in the Civil War, and an unconscious competitor with his young son for the attention of the beautiful mother. His was the commercial side of the family, the side that provided the models for his son's bureaucratic bent. Over the course of more than two centuries, the Roosevelt men had progressed from farming to trapping to retail hardware to imported plate glass and, most recently, to the intangibles of banking and brokerage. They were among the leaders of the city's financial, cultural, and social affairs.[1] Oddly, it was the gentle mother's people who were gallant fighters.

The younger Roosevelt was named after his father, with no middle name and no designation as Junior. He was a Wednesday's child, born October 27, 1858, under the astrological sign of Scorpio, the arachnid that presaged his power and appeal. His birthplace was a comfortable brownstone in a fashionable Manhattan neighborhood.[2]

Great Heart

The original Theodore was a gentleman and a sportsman. He was one of the first to drive a four-in-hand carriage—that is, one drawn by four horses in tandem. Big, virile, and handsome, he had a strong face framed by a full beard. A millionaire but not as rich or patrician as the Astors or the Vanderbilts, his vocation was charity. His family called him Great Heart after John Bunyan in *Pilgrim's Progress*. For kindness and morality, vigor and elegance, he was a hard act to follow. Yet he was not a prig.[3]

In 1853, the senior Theodore married Martha Bulloch who was called Mittie. She was the daughter of a Georgia planter. Back when Theodore's great-grandfather was a shopkeeper, her great-grandfather was the first governor of Georgia. His family members were pedestrian, prosperous, and sometimes dull. Hers were aristocratic, mercurial, martial, and land-poor. The Bullochs sold four slaves to pay for Martha's wedding party.[4]

After the birth of baby Theodore in 1858, Martha developed postpartum blues. She remained in her bedroom for three months, retreating from her husband while keeping with her the son she favored over first-born Anna who had a spinal curvature. Her pet name for the son was Teedie.[5]

A third child, Elliott, was born in 1860. The intimate contact between Mittie and Teedie abruptly ceased, and his care was left to nursemaids. Within a year, Teedie was as "full of woe" as his Wednesday birth had predicted.

The Allotment Commissioner

The Civil War began when Teedie was two-and-a-half years old. The senior Theodore claimed that he felt an obligation to serve the North as a soldier. His wife was dedicated to the Confederate cause, however, so he compromised. He became a civilian allotment commissioner in late 1861, working without compensation to induce federal soldiers to set aside part of their pay for the benefit of their wives and children. He wrote Mittie from the front, "I cannot help feeling it would be my duty, unless this had turned up, to be away altogether by joining the army."[6]

With Theodore absent, Mittie described Teedie as her "little berserker," a counterpart of the Norse warriors who fought in a frenzy. Although Teedie would go to any length to gain her attention, he was frustrated in his rivalry with handsomer Elliott and a fourth child, the cuddlier Corinne. Mittie wrote that "Elliott came into my bed and fell asleep while I was stroking his ears." Teedie was already in her bed and was "miserably jealous about Elliott's sleeping by me."[7]

In a letter dated December 5, 1861, Mittie told her husband that "Teedie was very unwell last night." From then on, her references to Teedie were of colds, fevers, bronchitis, vomiting, and diarrhea.[8] Soon, Teedie started to experience tightness in his chest, making it difficult for him to draw a deep breath. The sound of Teedie in a night attack was the wheeze of a child seemingly close to death. The special bond between Teedie and Mittie was restored, as she devoted herself to his relief. The course of the family's day was dependent upon Teedie's asthma.

Theodore returned home in November 1863. He saw in Teedie a skinny, slow, patiently suffering five-year-old invalid who confessed to feeling "doleful" before attacks of suffocation and terror. Theodore's response was to step between Mittie and Teedie. Most spasms came at night when Theodore and Mittie might otherwise have been together. Instead, Theodore would pick Teedie up and walk the floor for hours. Sometimes he would have the carriage brought to the door and take Teedie for a long ride in the park. The asthma did not improve.[9]

Abraham Graf

Under the 1863 Conscription Bill, a well-to-do draftee could hire a substitute to avoid serving in the army. The legislation was highly unpopular. Rioters protested the contrast between "the rich man's money and the poor man's blood."[10]

Theodore had not volunteered for military service in 1861 or 1862. When he received his draft notice in 1863, he went to a reputable broker. For one thousand dollars he was furnished with Abraham Graf to serve in his place. A slight, fair, blue-eyed thirty-six-year-old German just off the boat, Graf was paid a bounty of thirty-eight dollars to enlist in the 7th New York Infantry for three years. Within two months, Graf was captured, paroled, and hospitalized. He died

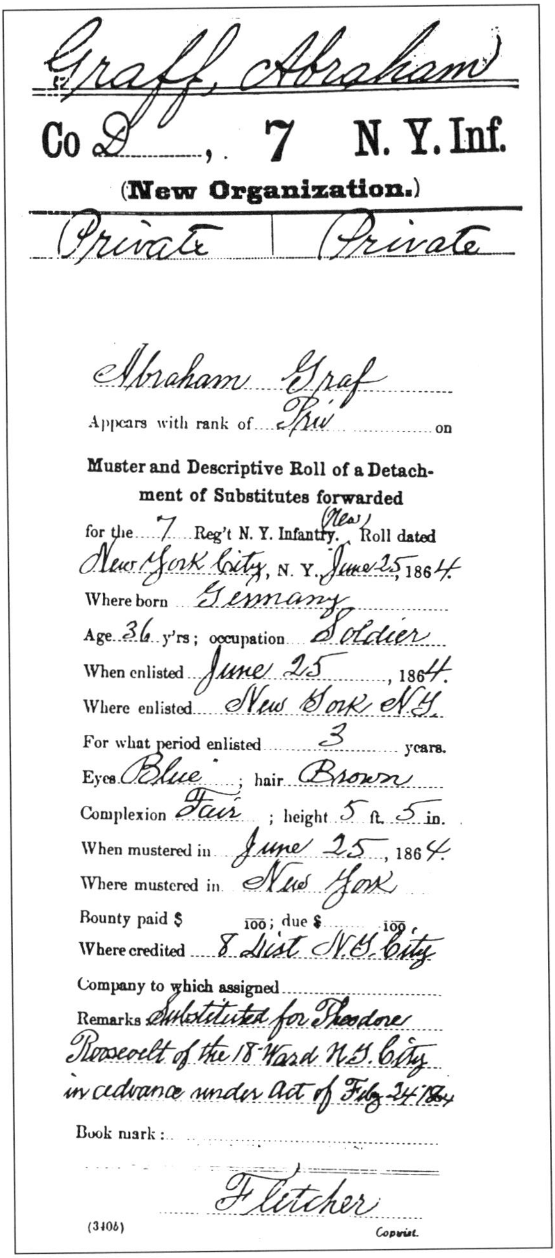

Graff, Abraham

Co D, 7 N. Y. Inf.

(New Organization.)

Private | Private

Abraham Graf

Appears with rank of ... Priv .... on

Muster and Descriptive Roll of a Detach-
ment of Substitutes forwarded
for the 7 Reg't N. Y. Infantry. (New) Roll dated
New York City, N. Y. June 25, 1864.
Where born Germany
Age 36 y'rs; occupation Soldier
When enlisted June 25, 1864
Where enlisted New York N.Y.
For what period enlisted 3 years.
Eyes Blue; hair Brown
Complexion Fair; height 5 ft. 5 in.
When mustered in June 25, 1864.
Where mustered in New York.
Bounty paid $ 100; due $ 100.
Where credited 8 Dist N.Y. City
Company to which assigned
Remarks Substituted for Theodore
Roosevelt of the 18 Ward N.Y. City
in advance under act of Feb 24 1864

Book mark:

Fletcher

(3406) Copyist.

The mustering in of Abraham Graff (also spelled Graf and Graft),
who was a hired substitute for the senior Theodore Roosevelt in the
Civil War. National Archives.

No. 2.

RECORD OF DEATH AND INTERMENT.

Abraham Graff

Name and number of person interred.
Number and locality of the grave . .
Hospital number of the deceased . . *6135*
Regiment, rank, and company . . . *Private Co. "D" 7th N. Y. Vols*
Residence before enlistment . . . *None, enlisted immediately on coming*
Conjugal condition, (and if married, } *to this country*
  the residence of the widow) . . }
Cause of death . . . . . . } *Intermittent Fever, Quotidian Type,*
                               2. Scurvy
Age of the deceased *38*
Nativity . . . . *Switzerland*
References and remarks . . . . }
Date of death and burial . . . . *March 31st* , 186*5*.

[A duplicate of this Record has been forwarded to the Sexton, and another remains at this Hospital.]

To *Brig General L. Thomas*
       Adjutant Genl. U.S. Army

SIR:

    It becomes my duty to inform you that the person above described died at this Hospital as herein stated; and that it is desired his remains should be interred with the usual military honors.

                Respectfully,

                             C. Slotten Vol.
                                  Surgeon U. S. Army.

MILITARY HOSPITAL. *Pt Lookout Md*

This copy of Record is to be transmitted to the Adjutant General at Washington immediately after the place of burial and the number of the grave have been ascertained and registered. The above notification is to remain attached.

Effects of Abraham Graff Co. D 7th N. Y. Vols
One Knapsack One Shirt
One Haversack One pr Drawers
One Woollen Blanket One Towel
One Knife one Fork One Spoon

The record of Graff's death in a military hospital, showing the wrong birthplace while inventorying his sparse effects (no money, no pants). National Archives.

the next year from fever and scurvy. No one claimed his scanty effects. Theodore had never met him.[11]

All of the able-bodied male Bullochs fought for the South. No Roosevelt took up arms, but at their social level, no disgrace was attached to the employment of a proxy.

Theodore was Great Heart personified. He made no enemy in a life marred only by one flaw that he and later his older son deeply regretted. He failed to respond in person to his country's call.[12]

Chapter 4
The Making of a Soldier

Roosevelt wore his tailored Brooks Brothers uniform proudly during the two days on the train to San Antonio in mid-May 1898. He carried himself squarely, like an officer in the regulars, although he had to explain to cavalry aficionados why his jacket and trousers were not regulation royal blue like his shirt. Instead, the uniform had been billed to him as "fawn Cravenette with canary yellow trimmings" to approximate the brown of the Rough Riders' stable garb.[1]

For a decade he had yearned to be a combat officer in the U.S. Army. Seven years earlier, he had been rabid about an inconsequential incident with Chile. At that time, statesman John Hay wrote to his friend Henry Adams, "For two nickels, Teddy Roosevelt would declare war himself and wage it solo."[2]

In 1895 he had advocated an aggressive stance against Great Britain. He remarked to Lodge that "the clamor of the peace faction has convinced me the country needs a war." He told his brother-in-law, "If there is a muss, I shall try to have a hand in it myself for the conquest of Canada."[3]

Later the same year, he began to look to Cuba as his destined arena. He advised the governor of New York that "I must have a commission in the force that goes to Cuba." He added, "I am a quietly rampant 'Cuba Libre' man," but he was far from quiet. Consequently, the reply he received was negative. All of the New York commissions already had been assigned to the governor's patrons.[4]

Long before the war with Spain, Roosevelt had announced with his usual bravado that he would "willingly give ten years of life for the right to wear the veteran's button that shows a man has done his part in bearing arms for his country."[5] Wearing the insignia of a lieutenant colonel in the U.S. Volunteer Cavalry pinned to his tunic was even better than sporting a veteran's button. He was finally compensating for the one blemish on his father's record.

All Could Ride

At 7 A.M. on Sunday morning, May 15, Roosevelt stepped briskly down from the Southern Pacific Railroad's Pullman car onto the San Antonio platform. The sign on the station building read, "This Way to Camp of Roosevelt's Rough Riders."

He had in his hand a slim book, *Drill Regulations for Cavalry, United States Army, 1896,* that he had been studying. Behind him was his valet Marshall, lugging three heavy suitcases. They took a horse-drawn cab to the Menger Hotel where Roosevelt registered and left Marshall to put the accommodations in order. Roosevelt went into the dining room and ate a hot breakfast.

While Roosevelt was getting settled, Colonel Wood was at the Rough Riders' camp in Riverside Park, just beyond the San Antonio city limits. He was attired in a carefully pressed light brown uniform similar to Roosevelt's, with indicia of rank on the high collar and silver eagles on the shoulder straps.

In the ten days Wood had been in camp, he had worn only casual military dress while receiving recruits from the four southwestern areas and assigning them places. Orderly Jim Brown from Oklahoma Territory was surprised to find him formally outfitted this morning. When Brown was told to "get the phaeton," the light two-seater carriage with an open top, he knew that an important event would occur.[6]

"Take me to the Western Union telegraph office," Wood commanded in his soft voice. He descended there to pick up a handful of incoming wires. Then he directed Brown, "Now to the hotel on the Plaza." Roosevelt was waiting in the shade of the Menger Hotel doorway. He strode quickly across the sidewalk while Wood sprang down to meet him. They embraced, much to the embarrassment of the orderly, who never before had seen two unrelated men hug each other in public. The two officers climbed into the phaeton and began to

An Evening at the Hotel. W. Nephew King, *The Story of the Spanish-American War* (New York: Peter Fenelon Collier and Son, 1900), p. 129.

talk so intently that they did not notice they had started back toward camp.[7]

Brown drove on, watching the fringe swing from the carriage rails. He listened to the excited conversation coming from the rear seat until Wood remembered convention and remarked to his companion, "This is James Brown, one of our troopers." Roosevelt leaned forward, examined the driver's insignia, smiled confidently, and assured the trooper, "We shall get along well together, Bugler Brown."

With strangers, Wood was reserved, not talkative but a listener. With Roosevelt, however, he expressed himself fluently. While Roosevelt could recount only his frustrating experiences with the Quartermaster and Ordnance departments in Washington, Wood had 850 recruits in camp. He was optimistic about every one of them, predicting that in ten days the regiment would be ready to embark for Cuba to join the insurgents.[8]

While they bounced along in the carriage, Wood pointed out that the tents, carbines, fatigue uniforms, and saddles that Roosevelt had been expediting had all been delivered late. Wood had made do in every instance. At first, there were no new blankets. The men had to sleep on the floor of the Exposition Building, which was infested with scorpions. The more fortunate troopers bedded down two to a blanket borrowed from the pack mule outfit and returnable each morning for use on the animals. No one complained. Wood was sure that the regiment was weeks ahead of other volunteer cavalry and infantry units.[9]

In the beginning, Wood said, a more diverse bunch would have been hard to find. The men were Texas Rangers and New York policemen, the mayor of Prescott, Arizona, and the marshal of Dodge City, Kansas, five Baptist and Presbyterian ministers, lawyers from small towns, outlaws unable to enlist under their right names, a Yale quarterback and a Princeton tennis champion, Harvard and Columbia crew captains, miners, and dandies from the Social Register. There were even some cowboys to uphold the well-publicized image of the regiment.[10]

The easterners were Roscoe and Percival, Winthrop and Woodbury, Dudley and Guy, while the westerners were Smokey and Rocky Mountain Bill, Bronco George, Dead Shot Jim, Fighting Bob, and Rattlesnake Pete. The press had categorized the troopers as

> *Rich man, poor man, Indian chief,*
> *Doctor, lawyer, not one thief,*
> *Merchant, sheriff, artist, clerk,*
> *Clubman, quite unused to work,*
> *Miner, hunter without peer,*
> *Broker, banker, engineer,*
> *Cowboy, copper, actor, mayor,*
> *College athletes, men of prayer,*
> *Champion amateur sports to boot—*
> *And all of them could ride and shoot!*[11]

One of the Fifth Avenue Boys Roosevelt had mustered in was Hamilton Fish who had previously distinguished himself not as a frontiersman but by fighting with policemen in New York City's Tenderloin, punching Bowery waiters, and riding hard on the bare backs of harnessed Central Park cab horses. Even Fish, Wood acknowledged, was showing leadership qualities. Wood's driver heard Roosevelt's approving replies as a repetition of "Bully! Bully!"[12]

Wood also told Roosevelt about Mickey O'Hara who had been boss packer during Wood's rigorous Geronimo campaign. O'Hara's current pack train of 189 mules and three horses was the first Rough Rider unit to arrive in San Antonio. Presuming on the past relationship, O'Hara borrowed thirty dollars from Wood, got drunk, and would remain drunk as long as the money lasted. That was when Bugler Brown noted Roosevelt's new military laugh. While smiling, Roosevelt uttered "Hah! Hah!" with his teeth clenched and his incisors bared.[13]

"These troopers," Wood maintained, "are the best men I have ever seen together." When the Arizona contingent arrived, he said, they had willingly drilled on foot with wood slats in place of missing carbines. As more troops reached camp, they drew their uniforms in installments and wore whatever they received, just to encourage themselves by showing something military. Their one goal was to get to Cuba. Each additional piece of uniform or equipment made them believe they were that much closer.[14]

When their horses were delivered to the holding pens at the railroad station, there was still no saddle or bridle in camp. Riding bareback with rope halters, the Rough Riders herded the unbroken horses through San Antonio's main streets. They gave "exhibitions equal to anything Buffalo Bill's Wild West Show put on for $1.00."[15]

A few of the easterners were dissatisfied. They found camp food nauseating and manual labor too hard. They missed valets, urban cuisine, soft beds, hot baths, and clean underclothing. Despite their grievances, they were assigned to round out the numbers in the westerners' troops. By the time all of the pieces of the brown stable uniforms were issued, no one could tell one recruit from another by appearance.

I Shall Spend Your Lives

Wood and Roosevelt were still talking animatedly when they reached the main gate of Camp Wood, the title the Rough Riders had given their village of army tents. Rumors of Roosevelt's arrival had spread among the westerners. They had been warned that the man whose family name was part of their informal regimental designation was only a New York City cop with a lot of inherited money.

To see Roosevelt in person, the troopers lined both sides of the road inside the camp. When he appeared, the men were noticeably disappointed. They had been hoping for a commander who was a big tough scrapper. He was of only medium size. He wore glasses like a tenderfoot and was smiling broadly like a big-city politician. Despite the letdown, the westerners ran through the gate in good spirits, glad for the break in routine. They unhitched the horses and pulled the phaeton to Wood's headquarters tent. One trooper found a wooden box, and the men yelled, "Speech, Colonel Roosevelt! Speech!"

Roosevelt stood on the box and responded by emphasizing in his assertive manner that they were soldiers now and Rough Riding was not a lark. The troopers fell silent and dispersed quickly after the concluding sentence, "Men, I shall not hesitate to spend your lives as I spend my own." They understood for the first time that war was really at hand. Roosevelt would lead wherever there was fighting. Some of them would surely die.[16]

It was still Sunday morning, and Roosevelt accompanied Wood to religious services in the large canvas pavilion at the Exposition Building. Bishop James Johnston of the West Texas Protestant Episcopal Diocese gave the sermon. "We should not feel we are fighting for revenge," the bishop preached, "for revenge belongs exclusively to the Almighty, but you should feel that you are warring to redress wrongs." This admonition recalled President McKinley's humanitarian rationale for the war. The message was too insipid for Roosevelt, though he sat quietly.

At the end of the service, Roosevelt had a practiced two-fisted greeting for each of the dozens of troopers who pressed forward to grasp his hands. Then he retired to his tent next to Colonel Wood's quarters near the wooden buildings on the right side of the line of officers' tents.

Quartermaster Hall had been promoted to adjutant and was occupying the tent temporarily. Although Hall expected to be evicted and to sleep on a table in his office, Roosevelt insisted on sharing the space. Hall later described Roosevelt as "the most remarkable man I ever met." After Hall ran away from the first battle, Roosevelt's characterization of him was unprintable by the standards of the day.[17]

Although there were hundreds of telegrams and letters for Roosevelt to answer, he was distracted by ten thousand curious Texan visitors, "the fair sex being in the majority." Most of the visitors had boarded San Antonio trolleys featuring canvas banners, "Take This Car for the Exposition Grounds Where Roosevelt's Famous Rough Riders Are Camped."[18]

The streets of the camp were filled with civilians peering at the famous soldiers. Roosevelt was besieged with callers. One was the celebrated Texas Ranger Lee Hall who asked for a chance to command a squadron as a major in the Rough Riders. Roosevelt recognized competition and put Hall off. There was room for only ten troopers, he replied. Even then, he admonished Hall, "I want crackerjacks, though."[19]

After the close of a sparsely attended concert in town, the orchestra conductor, Professor Beck, took his military band to the camp in carriages for an evening musicale. The band surrounded Roosevelt's tent, playing patriotic songs such as "Yankee Doodle." Troopers and visitors demanded another speech.[20]

Roosevelt had been waiting for an opportunity to take issue with the benign bishop. The explosion of the battleship *Maine* in Havana harbor in February 1898 continued to preoccupy him. He stepped out of his tent and up on the box, ignoring the visitors to address the troopers directly. "When we get to Cuba and get to the Spaniards, I want your watchword, my men, to be 'Remember the *Maine*,'" he exhorted. "And you shall avenge the *Maine!*" Roosevelt implied that a muscular Almighty intended to use the Rough Riders as His bludgeon in a holy "eye-for-an-eye" war.[21]

The War May Develop a Hero

The next morning, Wood turned the training of the troopers over to Roosevelt. This was as much to make the second-in-command ready for combat as for the benefit of the men. Roosevelt's brief experience as a captain in the New York National Guard was of no value in Camp Wood. The Guard had followed infantry procedures and had been lax at those. As new leader, he had to drill troopers according to the cavalry manual both on horseback and on foot.

To free his time, Roosevelt had Marshall brought out to the camp. Regular officers generally chose orderlies from the ranks as their servants. A soldier assigned as an orderly was the responsibility of the government, not the officer, and could be returned to the ranks for any reason. Roosevelt's inexperience had led him to bring Marshall to Camp Wood. He then had a valet whose civilian status, color, and lack of familiarity with Roosevelt's privileges created problems, despite previous cavalry service.[22]

Officers had to supply their own gear. Regular officers and knowledgeable orderlies knew how to buy bucket packs of agate-wear pots, plates, and tableware for $4.17 from Ettenson Woolfe. Marshall did not. Consequently, Roosevelt used the same mess kit the quartermaster issued to enlisted men. Also, while regular officers acquired collapsible canvas cots for use in the field, Roosevelt slept on a rubber mattress on the ground "like being on the roundup again." When he ate in his tent, the meal was served on a makeshift platform of stacked boxes instead of on a folding mess table.[23]

One thing, though, Roosevelt took care of in advance, in addition to his tailored uniform. Officers furnished their own mounts so he had written from Washington to a hunting companion in Texas, asking to purchase two horses that would be spirited yet gently broken to the saddle. As soon as he could get away from camp on Monday, he went to inspect the mounts that were waiting for him at the San Antonio livery stable.[24]

One horse was a small bay stallion he named Texas in honor of its state of origin. He tried Texas out by riding up and down St. Mary's Street in the heart of the business district. Scores of onlookers admired the popular military figure seated comfortably on his prancing cow pony.[25]

Crowds and publicity were Roosevelt's meat. He complained in a letter to his second son Kermit that "photographers swarm in camp and are a great nuisance for they are always taking pictures or asking to take pictures." His grumbling was only an affectation. He was the camp soldier most wanted for photographs and interviews, and also the most willing. He made time available whenever he was asked anything by newspapermen. When he was not sought out, he volunteered background data and opinions.[26]

Suddenly, a specific new need arose for all the favorable attention he could get. After seventeen years of ups and downs as a politician, his future was brightening unexpectedly at a time when he was concentrating on his military rather than his political fortunes.

The "easy boss" Sen. Thomas Platt had loosed a thunderbolt from

Roosevelt's home state of New York. During a casual press conference, Platt stated flatly that the Republican renomination of sitting Gov. Frank Black was in doubt because of pervasive scandals in the administration. "McKinley and Congress have declared war on Spain," Platt remarked. "That war may develop a hero. Popular sentiment may force the nomination of that hero for Governor of New York. Theodore Roosevelt has just resigned as Assistant Secretary of the Navy and is drilling his Rough Riders in the West. General Francis V. Greene and Colonel Frederick D. Grant have volunteered their services. Any one of them might come out of the war adorned with such laurels as to compel his nomination." Platt had opposed the war with Spain.[27]

Roosevelt did not see the bland Greene or Grant as competition. Someone else more credible could easily turn up, however, so he instituted an even closer relationship with the journalists to foster the "popular sentiment" Platt had mentioned.[28] He knew that the governorship of New York would be the right postwar position for him. To pursue that goal, he made the Rough Riders a reporter's dream of access and information.

The Damndest Ass

Wood was aware that in the press, the Rough Riders were Roosevelt's regiment, not his. The implied aspersion bothered him, yet he took no action until his friends back home plagued him with adverse comments about Roosevelt's continual self-aggrandizement. "The New York newspapers keep talking about Roosevelt's regiment," one advocate pointed out. "Give the reporters discipline and have things called by the right name."[29]

Wood had been warned many times that there would be difficulty with Roosevelt who had played his own hand in every other post he had held, without regard for his superiors. In San Antonio, however, the only problem Wood had was the excessive citing of Roosevelt in the press. There was no complaint about Roosevelt's conduct. In camp there was no question at all about who in fact was the regiment's superior officer.[30]

Nevertheless, whenever Roosevelt in his earnest manner now said something in Wood's presence about "my regiment," Wood became hostile. He remarked in an icy tone, "I am still commander of this regiment." Wood looked for opportunities to put the lieutenant colonel down in public.[31]

Roosevelt's custom was to read the *Drill Regulations* as he walked alone in camp. He would scan a page and hold the book behind his back while he thought about what he had read. Then he would give the orders aloud, oblivious of troopers passing by. His problem was in applying the text. His first attempt to command a mounted squadron was a garbled order impossible to perform. He saw the troops circle in confusion and had to call the squadron's major to take over.[32]

After the poor start, though, he regained his composure. He and the troops did well. In appreciation, he ordered a halt that afternoon at Quinn's little brewery in the woods near the camp's rear gate. There he bought a big mug of beer for each of the three hundred troopers. It was a memorable reward for the men on a hot day.

In the evening, an officers' training class was in session when Wood entered the tent. He had heard about Roosevelt's enhanced popularity with the troopers because of the beer. In a short talk, he discussed the matter of officers fraternizing with enlisted men. Naming no name, he finished by asserting that an officer who would take a squadron out for practice and then drink beer with the men was unfit to hold a commission.[33]

There was a dead silence in the tent. The disconcerted group broke up at once. How the impulsive Roosevelt would react to the reprimand was the subject of intense discussion among the other officers. Most thought Roosevelt would either resign or use his Washington connections to force Wood out.

According to Wood, the censure that seemed intended was meant in jest. "I went to my tent," he recalled. "In a few minutes, I heard the quick pattering walk of the Lieutenant Colonel coming up. He scratched on the fly of my tent and said, 'I would like to speak with the Colonel.' I looked at him, trying to keep a stern face. He said, 'I want to talk with you, sir. I agree with every word you said. I wish to say, sir, that I consider myself the damndest ass within ten miles. Good night,' and off he went." Roosevelt accepted the rebuke as justified, ending the speculation among his fellows. He never would have resigned when the regiment was this close to Cuba.[34]

Quinn, who ran the small brewery, was a patriot as well as a merchant. The next morning he sent a message to Roosevelt, offering to donate two kegs of beer for the rest of the men. Roosevelt declined. "Beer," he exclaimed, "is a subject I never want to hear about again."[35]

The interplay between Wood and Roosevelt was watched closely by the troopers. Sgt. Dave Hughes of Arizona described Roosevelt as "one of the biff-bang-do-it-right-now-cannot-put-it-off-another-minute sort, with ambition, energy, and power. Wood was more reserved, cool, cautious, and exacting. Wood was the regular soldier, the backbone. Roosevelt was the volunteer, one of ourselves. Wood organized, trained, commanded, and was admired. Roosevelt preached, exhorted, scolded, encouraged, and was adored. They worked together in harmony."[36]

Wood generally displayed a poker face, hard to read. Roosevelt was a man of nervous strength rather than grace. He did everything with ferocious earnestness. Even if he did not know how to do something, he would expend every effort to get it done, one way or another. Roosevelt stood by the men he liked, although he was intolerant of the few he did not care for.[37]

Wood was gentle ordinarily. In extreme excitement, he was stern. The men said that Roosevelt behaved in the same energized manner all the time, except for acts of calculated showmanship. Wood was diplomatic, Roosevelt direct. Wood asked for advice, seldom for information. Roosevelt wanted information, never advice. He decided everything by himself.[38]

Wood was sensitive to men as individuals. For Roosevelt, the privileges of rank outweighed consideration of individuals' feelings. At Camp Wood, mosquitoes were fierce. Men suffered from multiple bites. Wood did not sleep under mosquito netting because he did not think it would look right to the enlisted men who had no netting. The other officers did not use netting because Wood did not. When Roosevelt arrived, he slept under mosquito netting without noticing how the men or the officers made up their beds. The rest of the officers then slept under netting, too.[39]

Despite his sometimes lordly manner, Roosevelt was a much more attractive figure than Wood. He was admired even by those who distrusted his impulsiveness as a leader. He was a real man, the Rough Riders remarked, if not the soldier Wood was. Yet the troopers already recognized that he was going to take over as colonel some day soon. The promotion was predestined.[40]

In response to the palpable devotion and dependency that flowed to him from the troopers, Roosevelt sensed a growing power in himself to manipulate their emotions and deeds. Before San Antonio, he had been a legislator, reformer, and bureaucrat in positions where he had been a potent force, but he had never been the commander of a large body of men. His overriding daydream had been of heading some stupendous martial adventure such as a major cavalry charge. His reality, however, had been a seat at a desk.[41]

Now he was in a situation where he could act out his innermost visions for the first time. He had the followers and the horses. When he spoke, hundreds of eager faces turned toward him and attuned themselves to his magnetism, waiting for his words.

He rejoiced as he explored and perfected this new strength while he carried on the daily routine of getting himself and his men ready for the ultimate exploit. He would be taking the cavalry to the front in a battle to be fought on behalf of his country.

Ornery Afoot

Sunday mornings were reserved for the religious services that were accompanied by a cowboy choir. In the afternoons the troopers boiled their uniforms and underclothes to kill body lice. Dressed in odds and ends, they wrote letters and gossiped with visitors.[42]

During the week, distractions were avoided. Wood had a sign posted at the main gate, "All Civilians, Except Reporters, Prohibited from Camp." Roosevelt described the daily drilling as "incessant and the progress of the regiment wonderful."[43]

Training began an hour before sunrise with grooming and feeding the horses and ended at sunset when the horses were settled down. In between, the duties were heavy. The horses were watered after the men ate breakfast. Next came the mounted drill that had begun as an impromptu rodeo. "Just imagine the men forking wild ponies on those dinky little army saddles," an Arizonan remarked. Breaking the horses sent four men to the hospital and one to his grave.[44]

The weather was clear. Walking, trotting, and galloping the horses raised dust clouds so dense that men sometimes could not see the horse in front. Regardless of the animal's color, its haunches would be stained dark brown with sweat and dirt.[45]

After cleaning the horses and themselves, the men ate their midday dinner. Roosevelt went to his contrived mess table where he propped a copy of *Wagner's Organization and Tactics* against a pitcher while Marshall served food purchased in the city to supplement rations.[46]

At 2 P.M., there was dismounted drill. The men did not appreciate Wood's choice of Central Texas to approximate the Cuban climate. The normal afternoon temperature was 97 degrees. The humidity was above 80 percent in the morning and dropped only to 50 percent in the afternoon. Westerners complained that pitching hay on the ranch had not brought out half the amount of sweat raised by foot drills in San Antonio.

Drilling dismounted was not successful. "We sure did appear ornery afoot, out of line, out of step," one westerner confessed, "and when we wheeled we must 'er looked like a rattler. When we drawed up before Colonel Roosevelt, he says, 'Well boys, well boys, I've seen better marching than that, but I'll be damned if I ever saw worse.' We threw our hats in the air and laughed. The Colonel laughed, too."[47]

Roosevelt dismissed dismounted drilling as physical exercise, not as a true military requirement. The Rough Riders were going to Cuba to be irregular cavalry, he contended, not infantry. Why should cowboys practice walking in step when being on foot was unnatural for them?

Despite Roosevelt's observation that "the Harvard and New York men are getting on capitally with the cowpunchers," journalists hunted for newsworthy altercations between West and East. They found few. Marshall asked to remain with Roosevelt, but the valets of the Fifth Avenue Boys were sent home. Civilian clothes were donated to an orphan asylum. Kane dug a ditch. Wadsworth carried wood. Goodrich learned to throw a lariat. The press was compelled to admit "there were no laggards" among the New York recruits. The *New York Herald* reported pretentiously that "the bonhomie that exists between the Rough Riders of Arizona and their Eastern comrades speaks well for the esprit de corps."[48]

Except for one Yale student who was promoted to lieutenant, the

Fifth Avenue Boys were still privates on May 17. At this point the financier John Jacob Astor offered to join the regiment as a major and bring with him a battery of six Maxim field guns. Despite pressure from the War Department to accept the proposal, Wood turned Astor down. The excuse was that Maxims were made in Germany. Replacement parts were not readily available.[49]

Instead, Fifth Avenue Boy Woodbury Kane presented the regiment with a pair of American-made Colt rapid-fire guns that cost eight thousand dollars. The Colts were accepted, even though additional ammunition for them would be available in the field only if bullets could be captured from Spaniards who used Mauser rifles of the same caliber.[50]

Kane was one of their own. The day the guns arrived, he was promoted to first lieutenant. Goodrich became a second lieutenant. Hamilton Fish was made sergeant. So was Tiffany. Wadsworth was appointed corporal.[51]

The Arizonans resented these promotions and asked Wood to advance one of their troopers to lieutenant. Wood replied that the westerners had elected their officers before leaving Indian Territory. He was appointing the collegians only as additional officers in expanded troops, he explained, not as replacements. Fortunately for the "esprit," the westerners recognized the prerogatives of social class. Except for one resentful private from Indian Territory who "called down" Tiffany for giving an order improperly, the men agreed to the distinction. The private was sustained by a commissioned officer also from Indian Territory. The contretemps faded in the excitement of the approaching expedition to Cuba, although Tiffany was "wroth."[52]

A bard among the cowpokes who had expected to dislike the easterners admitted that at first

> we was somewhat disappointed, I'll acknowledge, fur to see
> Sich a husky lot o' fellers as the dandies proved to be
> An' the free an' easy manner in their bearin' that they had
> Sort o' started the impression that they mightn't be so bad.
> There was absence o' eye-glasses, an' o' center parted hair,
> An' in social conversation they was expert on the swear,
> An' the way they hit the grub-pile sort o' led us to reflect
> That our previous impression mightn't prove so damn' correct.[53]

Ready

Wood had instructed the recruiters to "take no man whose belly is bigger than his chest." That order had generally been complied with. The troopers started in reasonably good physical condition and benefited from rigorous drills and plain food.[54]

By May 22, the Rough Riders' organizational chart was complete. As specified by the secretary of war, the regiment contained one colonel and one lieutenant colonel, plus their headquarters staff. Each of the three squadrons was led by a major. There were four troops to a squadron. Each troop had a captain, junior officers, and fifty-five to fifty-nine enlisted men.[55]

Every trooper eventually received the new bolt-action Krag carbine and a small McClellan saddle, eleven to fourteen inches in size, depending on the quartermaster sergeant's estimate of the dimensions of the man's seat. The carbine was packed in stiff protective cosmoline grease that had to be removed manually with rags. The leather accouterments required saddle soap, oil, and plenty of rubbing before use.[56]

That was for ordinary men. Celebrities like Roosevelt received fine weapons as gifts. The Winchester Arms Company presented him with an 1895 model carbine with a specially finished nickel steel barrel and English walnut stock. He did not take this showpiece to Cuba.[57]

The day after the completion of the organizational chart, the adjutant general in Washington sent Wood an economical telegram asking, "When ready for service?" Wood replied at once, "Ready. Don't forget we want to go with the first party."[58]

The expectation was that the regiment would soon "march" more than two hundred miles to Galveston, Texas, where steam lighters would put the men, horses, and supplies on ships to transport them to Cuba. The *New York Herald* reported "scenes of riotous joy, and if the regiment can make as much noise in the face of the enemy, it will win without firing a shot." The roar erupted although the telegram had indicated only that Washington was aware the Rough Riders were completing their training.[59]

In truth, Wood was exaggerating the preparedness of his Fifth Avenue Boys. The regiment had formed as a mounted unit for the first time that day. Bugler Brown blew "Boots and Saddles" to start the drill and "Wadsworth's mustang got the bit in his teeth. When the band struck up, the horse ploughed its way through a crowd of spectators and came near overturning Colonel Roosevelt's tent. Tiffany made a bungle at fastening his horse's girth and tumbled off while passing in review. Ronalds made the acquaintance of the business end of his bronco and as a result has his leg bandaged. Fish was a bit too gay and was sent to the rear."[60]

The quality of the drill did not bother Roosevelt. Instead, he was concerned because there had been no order to move the Rough Riders physically into the expeditionary force. It was not his nature to sit back and wait. He wrote first to his friend Senator Lodge on May 25: "If they begin to send troops to Cuba, I shall wire you to see that we go. We are all ready now to move. I hope no truce will be granted."[61]

He addressed President McKinley on the same day: "This is just to tell you that we are in fine shape. Wood is a dandy Colonel, and I think the rank and file of this regiment are better than you would find in any other regiment. In fact, in all the world there is not a regiment I would so soon belong to. The men are picking up the drill

Major-General Shafter, Commanding the First Expedition to Cuba. *Neely's Panorama of Our New Possessions* (New York: F. Tennyson, 1898).

wonderfully. They are intelligent, and, rather to my surprise, they are very orderly—and they mean business." Businesslike was his most frequent approbation for the troopers.

"We are ready to leave at any moment," he added, "and we hope we will be put into Cuba with the first troops; the sooner the better; at any rate, we do want to see active service against the enemy. Pray present my warm regards to Mrs. McKinley and tell her that she will never have cause to fear being ashamed of the First Volunteer Cavalry, which is, in a peculiar sense, her regiment." What the connection was with the invalid Mrs. McKinley, only Roosevelt knew.[62]

Remarkably, in view of the burdens of his office in wartime, the President received Roosevelt's letter and read it. On May 30 he instructed his personal secretary to advise the secretary of war, "If the regiment is ready, why not order them to the front at once."[63]

The secretary of war had anticipated the president by three days. The Rough Riders already had been "directed to proceed to Tampa and report to General Shafter."[64] Possessing influential friends such as the president, the secretary of war, and the senator had paid off. The regiment was instructed to depart for Florida, where the Rough Riders would be brigaded with regulars under Gen. William Shafter for the first expedition to Cuba.

Joining the regulars in Tampa was not as exciting a prospect as the previous reference to embarking via Galveston to ride with the Cuban insurgents as irregulars. However, it was literally a step in the right direction—east.

Chapter 5
Looking Back at Body Building

At first, some of the westerners among the Rough Riders were put off by the nose glasses Roosevelt called *pince nez*. Once the troopers got to know him, though, they idolized him. They even mimicked the way his head thrust combatively forward from his bull neck, the way his heavy lower lip was drawn down to display the gleaming teeth that were his pride, and the way his jaw muscles contracted and released rapidly when he was excited, which was much of the time. The troopers watched him bustle resolutely out of his tent, half trotting on his toes like a child, and they thought they could sense a field of electrical energy surrounding him.[1]

When Roosevelt took his glasses off, the troopers could see two different personalities peering out of his gray-blue eyes. The familiar one was primitive, eager, and candid. In an unguarded moment, though, he might look more sophisticated, mature, and feline.

His persuasiveness as a leader was due in large part to his absolute sincerity. The troopers were awed by this straightforward dynamo who claimed that whatever an individual wills himself to be, he can be. He spoke of himself as a common man raised to a higher power by his own determination. When the men wrote home, they declared that he was one of the wonders of America, as turbulent and as terrific as Niagara Falls. They would never have believed what a weakling he had been as a child.[2]

A Lesser Person

In 1866 when Teedie was eight, his illnesses were no longer life threatening. His father provided strong black coffee and medicinal cigars as effective homemade remedies for the asthma. Yet Teedie felt himself to be a lesser person, small, clumsy, timid, and already nervous about his future. He was a thin, bookish, wheezing boy who now, out of devotion to his father, chose to sign himself Theodore Roosevelt, Junior.[3]

Mittie was proud of her son, despite his ailments. She remarked on "his quiet patrician air with his large blue eyes not looking at anything present." In turn, he told his diary, "I read until Mama came in and then she lay down and I stroked her head and she felt my hands and nearly cried because they were feverish."[4]

By 1870, the junior Theodore was called Teddy. His father urged him to build his puny frame through dedicated physical training. Once Teddy began to exercise, body tone and confidence improved quickly. To develop his thin legs, he skipped rope. In addition, his awkwardness was discovered to be the result of extreme myopia. Corrective eyeglasses helped. By 1875, he could hold his own in running and jumping with his peers. His asthma continued to diminish as he grew older.[5]

By the time he left for Harvard in 1876, he was the star among the family children. He proved to be very different, however, from his classmates in Cambridge. He was quick, abrupt, and intense, while they affected the air of perpetual boredom they had acquired in preparatory schools. When he saw that his lineage and wealth allied him with the fashionable clique, he joined them. Later, they would be the Fifth Avenue Boys.[6]

He made himself into a dandy. He was vain about his little hands and his size-five feet that were dainty enough to fit snugly inside his mother's slippers. He also compared other people's ears unfavorably with his own, which were small and set close to his head. By the end of his first year in Cambridge, he was wearing a beaver hat and sporting an English cane to go with his tailored English clothes.[7]

The Passing of Great Heart

Roosevelt recorded joyous episodes in his diary until February 9, 1878, when his father died from cancer of the stomach. Then he wrote, "I felt as if part of my life had been taken away. With the help of my

God I will try to lead such a life as he would have wished." After four months, he began to deal with the loss: "Father was so cheerful it would be *wrong* for me to be gloomy. How I wish I could do something to keep up his name."[8]

When the will was read, Roosevelt noted that "I am left about $8,000 a year, comfortable although not rich." In comparison, the salary of Harvard's president was $5,000 a year. The amount of the principal of the inheritance was $125,000, held in trust.[9]

Soon after Roosevelt returned to Cambridge for his junior year, he met "Miss Alice Lee, one of the most ladylike girls." Fifteen months later, he confessed that it had been "a real case of love at first sight—and my first love too." Alice was a Brahmin of Boston. He saw in her the same qualities he adored in his mother. Alice was passive, impractical, and childish, brought up to be cherished.[10]

The engagement was announced in March 1880. "Thank Heaven," Roosevelt exulted, "I am absolutely pure. I can tell Alice everything I have ever done." He expected the same from her, although he did not disclose that the doctor at Harvard had advised him that his heart was weak. His tremendous energy and addiction to risk were from then on due partly to his conviction that he would die sooner than the average man because he came from a short-lived family.[11]

At noon on his twenty-second birthday, he married Alice Lee. He told his self-edited diary that their "intense happiness is too sacred to be written about."[12]

Horse-Car Conductors

Roosevelt replaced his father at the head of the dinner table in Mittie's Gotham mansion where Alice and he lived. In discussions, his sympathies were with Democratic party principles. As he explained, though, "It is Democratic practice that I object to. Besides, I am neither of Celtic descent nor yet a liquor seller."[13]

In February 1881, Roosevelt abandoned the Democrats to join the 21st District Republican Association which met over the bar at 59th Street and Fifth Avenue. The district included residences similar to his mother's as well as West Side tenements, but the club was run by "saloon keepers, horse-car conductors, and the like," rather than by society types. He persevered in order "to belong to the governing, not the governed class." At loose ends, he also enrolled in a graduate course at Columbia with Professor John Burgess. The Anglo-Saxon origin of American social institutions was a Burgess tenet.[14]

Because of his Knickerbocker name, Roosevelt was nominated for election to the New York State Assembly in October 1881. He was twenty-three years and one day old. Reform was fashionable that year, so Roosevelt was elected with the aid of supporters whose names were included in the *Banker's Directory* and the *Social Register*. He was the third Roosevelt to serve in Albany and the youngest assemblyman ever.[15]

When Roosevelt appeared in the legislature for the first time, the professional politicians considered him to be "a joke, a dude, the way he combed his hair, the way he talked—the whole thing!" He spoke "as if he had an impediment, sort of tongue-tied. He would often open his mouth and run out his tongue." In a month, however, he was called "the Scotch Terrier" because of his slight figure and aggressive manner. His targets were the "guilty and criminal rich" who abused public trust.[16]

In three months, he was receiving attention in the press. The *New York World* described him as "chief of the dudes." He "bowed his acknowledgments. His trousers were so tight that in making gyrations he only bent the joints above the belt. When Mr. Roosevelt finished, the other dudes took the tops of their canes out of their mouths and tapped the floor with the other end, and then they lighted cigarettes."[17]

After the assembly adjourned in May 1883, Alice became pregnant with their first child. Roosevelt bought acreage in Oyster Bay on Long Island and committed seventeen thousand dollars to construct a twenty-two-room mansion to shelter the large number of offspring he expected to procreate.[18]

A Curse on This House

Under stress in Albany, Roosevelt wheezed again and suffered from diarrhea. A former naval commander he met suggested that he visit southwestern Dakota Territory to recover his health.[19]

On September 8, he descended alone from a Northern Pacific train into the darkness of the Little Missouri station. Within two weeks he killed his first bison, giving the guide a hundred-dollar tip and inventing the war dance he connected with all kinds of killings from then on. In another four days, he bought the Maltese Cross cattle ranch that utilized free government range. Cowmen told him that the enterprise would require an additional forty thousand dollars for stock. "This is what I was like," Roosevelt bragged later, "when I had the bark on."[20]

He returned east with his health restored and his pocketbook depleted. During the legislative term he remained in Albany, living in a hotel and taking the train to the city on weekends. Alice was with Mittie in the Manhattan mansion. The baby was due in mid-February.[21]

Roosevelt was in New York City for the weekend of February 9. By Monday he was restless and Alice told him to go back to Albany. Although his mother was ill and Alice was close to the time for delivery, he convinced himself easily that his duty was to return to the legislature.

During the early morning of February 13, a page handed Roosevelt a telegram. A baby girl had been born the night before. Alice was doing "fairly well." In mid-morning, however, a second telegram arrived, advising him that Alice's condition was deteriorating. He rushed for the next train south. He reached home before midnight, in time to hear his brother exclaim, "There is a curse on this house." Roosevelt's mother died at noon on February 14, St. Valentine's Day. Alice died in Roosevelt's arms two hours later.[22]

Roosevelt never mentioned Alice again. He even avoided the baby because he saw a resemblance to his dead wife. Three days after the funerals, he left his child, went back to Albany, and took up pending assembly business. He was able to divorce himself from urgent personal demands to concentrate on long-term career goals.[23]

I Ceased to Be Afraid

Roosevelt helped to start an independent Republican movement in New York for the 1884 presidential election. The campaign began his alliance with Henry Cabot Lodge of Massachusetts who was methodical and restrained, a counterbalance for the impulsive and intuitive younger man. They were described as dudes who "had their hair parted in the middle, banged in front; wore an eyeglass, rolled their R's and pronounced 'either' with the I sound." When they were pleased they applauded "with the tips of their fingers, held immediately in front of their noses." He was a long way from being able to serve as the bloodthirsty colonel of the tough Rough Riders.[24]

In June, Roosevelt returned to the Maltese Cross ranch. Strenuous physical exertion relieved his melancholy. He wore "a broad sombrero, silk neckerchief, fringed and beaded buckskin shirt, sealskin chaparajos, alligator cowboy boots, with braided leather bridle and silver spurs, a pearl-hilted revolver and a beautifully finished Winchester rifle." Killing big game and taking impulsive financial risks soothed him. He said he slept well at night for the first time since the deaths of his mother and wife.[25]

He remarked that "at first there were all kinds of things" in the West "of which I was afraid, from grizzly bears to 'mean' horses and gunfighters, but by acting as if I was not afraid I gradually ceased to be afraid."[26]

When he went back to New York to spend Christmas with the depleted family, he brought along his western duds and gear. He posed in his Dakota costume before a big city photographer, standing manfully on imitation grass in front of a painted backdrop.[27]

Chapter 6
The Trip to Tampa

When Colonel Wood read the May 27, 1898, telegram from the War Department directing the Rough Riders to report to Gen. William Shafter in Florida, his expression did not change. He turned and calmly handed the wire to Roosevelt.

Equally in character, Roosevelt read the message, shrieked a war whoop, and went into the mock Indian dance that had ritualized his killing big game for fifteen years. The troopers followed Roosevelt's example. They were volunteers, yet due to Wood's managerial ability, Roosevelt's influence, and their own spunk, they were scheduled to be part of the first expeditionary force. That called for letting off some steam.[1]

The order to pack up in San Antonio arrived just in time, for the troopers and for the city. The men were almost fully equipped, they were as well versed in mounted drill as they thought they had to be to ride in Cuba, and they treated dismounted drill as a joke. They were bored with training routines and considered themselves ready for a little fun before heading to a prompt embarkation.

The war was simply not being taken seriously in the ranks. Spain and Spanish soldiers were the announced enemy, and Anglos from the Southwest tended to be condescending toward all "Spaniards"—European, Caribbean, and American. They lumped "the Dons" with poor Mexicans they knew at home, and they were convinced that "them Cubians ought not to be hard to lick. Greasers mostly. Greasers fight like sheepherders." There were few among the troopers to

The Rough Riders in Tampa, Packing for Santiago de Cuba. Stereopticon view. (New York: Underwood and Underwood, 1898).

refute the vilification of Spaniards in general or the deprecation of Spanish soldiers as fighters.[2]

Rough Riders of Latin descent were rare. Even in New Mexico where the people were predominantly Spanish speaking, most of the troopers had been chosen from the Anglo minority. The one Latino officer was Capt. Maximiliano Luna. The insurance agent from Santa Fe was unhappily aware that his ancestry made people suspect him of having secret Spanish sympathies. He had to work harder at being accepted.

Because of the overconfident denigration of "greasers" and the perceived overwork in drills, discipline was failing. Rough Riders who were refused passes to hike to San Antonio at night squeezed under the fence around the camp after taps and went without leave. Guards did not try to stop them.

Twenty troopers from Indian Territory brutally beat the Chinese proprietor of a city restaurant and demolished his building for an imagined slight. The Chinese restaurateur received no compensation, although the men were tried in the local court and convicted. Sentences were suspended and fines were remitted so as to make sure that there would be nothing to keep any of the brawling troopers in town after the regiment moved to Tampa. The westerners among the Rough Riders had quickly become undesirables in San Antonio.[3]

Two days before the telegram from Washington arrived, Professor Beck's band played what proved to be the final concert in honor of the Rough Riders. Half the regiment attended the evening performance in the park next to Camp Wood, along with hundreds of San Antonio residents. The men were mostly from Oklahoma and Indian Territory and were looking for more sport than could be expected from a family-style musicale.

The audience sat in the open under glowing electric light bulbs strung for the occasion through the park and in the pavilion. The featured musical number was "The Cavalry Charge." Professor Beck had stationed a dozen picked troopers in front of the band so they could fire pistols in the air to provide verisimilitude.

After the pistol volley was fired on cue, however, a trooper in the back of the audience yelled, "Help 'em out, boys!" The shooting became contagious as the men discharged their pistols into the night sky until they exhausted their ammunition. Another trooper cut the electric cable. All the lights in the park went out. The audience panicked, and women were injured in the rush to escape. Wood and Roosevelt hurried to the park, but in the dark they could not gain control. There was no way to discover who the instigators were.[4]

The riot was widely publicized in the national press. The regiment's rowdy aspect was emphasized across the country and people were led to fear the Rough Riders. To most of the journalists, however, the men's varied backgrounds, their enthusiasm, and their colorful leadership were still positive features. Regardless of whether they were undisciplined cowboys or trained cavalry, the regiment and its lieutenant colonel remained eminently newsworthy.[5]

Down the Dusty Pike with Darwin

Tampa had been selected as the port of embarkation because it was both secure from Spanish naval attack and closer to Cuba. Although the city was on the western side of the Florida peninsula, the distance from Port Tampa to Cuba was less than from other comparable American harbors. Moreover, the city's docks were at the inner end of Tampa Bay's thirty-mile channel to the Gulf of Mexico. Vessels in Port Tampa were presumed to be safe from Spanish marauders.[6]

The ships to serve as transports for the expedition had begun to arrive in Port Tampa by the end of April, while Roosevelt was still assistant navy secretary in Washington. Regular infantry regiments reached Tampa on May 10, and regular cavalry and artillery units arrived on May 25. The thin peacetime ranks of these regular regiments had been supplemented with recruits.[7]

President McKinley started pressing General Shafter to ship the army to Cuba before Roosevelt sent the appeals to him and to Lodge. The Rough Riders were not even in Shafter's plans until serious deficiencies in supposedly trained manpower were noted in the assembled regiments. Only then did Shafter order the Rough Riders to Tampa. Wood and Roosevelt were unaware of how much they owed to Shafter's failure to resolve his initial logistical problems.[8]

To carry out Shafter's directive, Wood relied upon Adjutant Hall to enter into passenger and freight contracts with connecting railroads. Hall was a novice at the job and the men suffered.

In contrast, regulars like the 10th Cavalry knew the ropes. Its adjutant specified exact times and conditions for railroad compliance. The food to be eaten during the trip was obtained by telegraphing ahead to vendors at each stop and also by providing the men with money to buy coffee. In addition, its quartermaster supplied rations of canned corned beef, canned beans, and hardtack for emergencies en route. The 10th was black and could not expect as much as a free drink of water from white southerners along the way.[9]

The Rough Riders, however, were innocents in the hands of the railroads. The rumor was that the regulars in Tampa were ready to board the transports, so speed was essential. Wood and Roosevelt were openly worried about the slightest delay. They were willing to put up with any inconvenience to get to the port on time.[10]

Planning for the Rough Riders' trip eastward along the Gulf Coast seemed simple. The regiment that now numbered one thousand men, the thirteen hundred horses and mules, the ordnance, and the supplies were divided to fit into seven long trains of up to eighteen cars each. Wood was in charge of the first three trains, Roosevelt the latter four. The trip would commence on Sunday, May 29, and take two days. Canned rations for six meals would be issued to the troopers at the start. That was all the food they would have. There was no provision for additional food or coffee. There was no allowance for contingencies.[11]

Trouble began immediately. The originating Southern Pacific Railroad failed to supply the ramps needed to lead the animals into the stock cars. Wood improvised inclines, but getting the horses on board took all morning. Boss packer O'Hara's mules were loaded, too, while O'Hara remained drunk. Wood's three trains did not depart until after 1 P.M. Half a day had elapsed.[12]

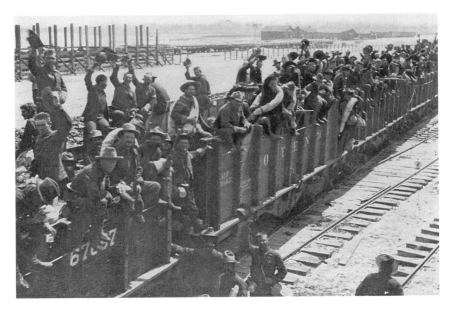

How the Rough Riders Rode Roughly to Port Tampa. *Harper's Pictorial History of the War with Spain* (New York: Harper and Brothers, 1899), p. 314.

Roosevelt led the remaining troops to the railway yard on the run and hurried the loading of the rest of the animals, trying to make up for Wood's lost time. Before the task was finished, though, a few men despaired at the backbreaking work. There was no Sunday Closing Law in San Antonio, so they disappeared into town to patronize what the good citizens called "vile drinking booths."

By the time sergeants rounded up the drinkers, Roosevelt had discovered that coaches for the troopers would not be shunted onto the siding until morning. Guards were posted to prevent further wandering, while the tired troopers bivouacked on the ground beside the track. The animals were left in the cars. The officers were too weary to punish slackers.[13]

Roosevelt's first train started at 8 A.M. on May 30, almost a day late. Some of the men were crowded two to a single seat in the coaches. As soon as the train was in motion, however, happy troopers began singing

> We thud-thud down the dusty pike,
> We jingle across the plain,
> We cut and thrust, we lunge and strike,
> We throttle the sons of Spain,
> Going to Cuba with Roosevelt.

The lieutenant colonel gave his berth, the only one on the train, to a trooper with a suspected case of the measles, and he took a coach seat. He began reading a book he had brought from home, Demoulin's *Superiorité des Anglo-Saxons,* an excursion into Social Darwinism. Roosevelt endorsed the book's thesis, the racial inferiority of Latins, but he employed descriptions more polite than his men's references to greasers.[14]

Roosevelt simplified his brand of Darwinism for the attentive Rough Riders who clustered around him. "Through all nature," he expounded, "it is a case of the survival of the fittest. Look at the magnificent trees along the river. The ones that started crooked were crowded out and died. The strong and the straight saplings appropriated all the food."

Then he moved from plants to creatures. "It is the same with wild animals," he pointed out. "The cripples and the inefficients that cannot support themselves are killed off."

Next were the humans: "You never see blind or maimed China-men. They are quietly sent to join Confucius." The white race, he explained to the troopers, was too tenderhearted: "We allow degenerates to keep on breeding degenerates instead of eliminating them, or at least sterilizing them."

"Physical monstrosities and babies that are plainly abnormal are nursed with great care," he declared, "instead of being given a whiff of chloroform at birth. We build great institutions to confine the hopelessly insane, when everyone would be better off if these incurable patients were put out of the way."

From this extreme stand he backed off a little, to acknowledge to the men that "the blind and the crippled of course must be provided for." He then concluded his sermon about the human condition by asserting that "every able-bodied man who produces nothing has no place in the world." Women's roles were a different story. He simply did not believe in woman's suffrage.

Finally, he took up government's function in the natural order by trotting out laissez-faire economic doctrine. "We are complicating things, too, in the way of legislation," he observed. "The best governed nations have had the fewest laws." He finished with an example the westerners appreciated. "The old Vigilantes in Montana did not have a single law," he asserted, "but they did have a simple wholesome code which everyone knew. Life and property are secure as a consequence."[15]

By the time he completed the synopsis of his personal concepts of Anglo-Saxon supremacy and the white man's burden, as he had adapted them from Professor Burgess, Demoulin, Capt. Alfred Mahan, and Rudyard Kipling, Roosevelt had dealt the full deck of what he called "expansionism." The troopers loved the discourse, both because of the intimacy with Roosevelt and because it helped to pass the hours.

I Took Charge

Roosevelt's train reached Houston, Texas, the first planned stop, after progressing only two hundred miles in twelve long hours. Although it was night, the depot was crowded. City dwellers and farmers had read about New York society doings in their newspapers for years. They flocked to the railroad yards to peer at the scions of the rich, the broad-shouldered athletes, and the bow-legged cowboys. They could not tell one grimy soldier from another.[16]

In front of this appreciative audience, the inadequate unloading facilities forced the weary troopers to give the equivalent of another Buffalo Bill rodeo. Then they watered, fed, and rested the animals the same way that the farmers who were watching did every day at home. When the troopers finished the feeding, they were inundated with flowers, fruit, and milk. Some were offered hard liquor and quickly started to get drunk, as they did whenever there was a long enough delay near friendly civilians.[17]

The next night the train reached New Orleans, after traveling an additional 350 miles. Roosevelt stood astride the roof of a stock car that was switched over the Mississippi River at 2 A.M. Then he hastened to the pens to see the fatigued men water and feed the horses again. A regular cavalryman from a troop in the train ahead had passed on the dubious warning that five horses had been "hamstrung by a Spanish sympathizer" the previous night. Roosevelt posted a double guard around his horses, with orders to shoot to kill.[18]

The city streets were mobbed with sightseers in the middle of the night. "Best of all," Wood had noted when he passed through, "was an American flag in the hands of all. We are indeed once more a united country."[19]

Young women drove to the yard in carriages to wave miniature flags and beg for buttons from the troopers' uniforms. The Rough Riders from New Mexico had been warned in Santa Fe that each lost button would cost them fifty cents, but they could not resist the local belles who would have the buttons made into stickpins. Adjutant Hall remarked that he "would not like to guess at the number of buttons missing," especially after the troopers discovered that horseshoe nails could be bent into adequate replacements. The men also exchanged names and addresses with the young women, despite the barrier of different regional accents.[20]

The local press reported that before noon on June 2, "the Rough Riders went out over the Louisville & Nashville Railroad. College men, frontier characters, New York society men, Cherokees, Chocktaws, cowboys, and millionaires were side by side and seemed to relish it. Every member of the troop refers to 'Teddy' Roosevelt in the highest terms."[21]

From then on, the schedule broke down completely. The two days planned for the journey stretched into four. The men were up every night tending to the animals. Roosevelt wrote Lodge that "when the delay grew past bearing, I took charge of the train myself." His taking over accomplished nothing.

When the rations that had been issued were exhausted, no more were available. The self-sufficient Rough Riders roped domestic chickens, pigs, and geese through coach windows, pulled them inside, gutted them, and cooked them on the floor of the moving train. Roosevelt did not stop the men because there was no other food. Not until Tallahassee, Florida, did they get a square meal. They ate fresh beef donated by residents and cooked over camp fires. The officers were entertained in private homes.[22]

Wood's contingent had arrived in Tampa on the evening of June 2. The men tied the animals to picket lines before they camped for the night in the field beside the track. Meanwhile, Wood walked two miles to the Tampa Bay Hotel in town to clean up and report to Generals Shafter and Nelson Miles. He was overjoyed to learn that Shafter had definitely selected the Rough Riders for the first expedition to Cuba. Four hundred of the one thousand troopers would make the initial voyage.[23] Some regiments of regulars were also cut back, to eliminate unready recruits.

The next morning, June 3, Wood returned to the bivouac to march his troopers through Tampa and then a mile and a half past the hotel to West Tampa where they were guided to the assigned campground. On the way, the regiment was cheered by soldiers of the 71st Volunteer New York Infantry who were standing on top of freight cars. The applause was intended for the missing Roosevelt.[24]

The lieutenant colonel arrived with his troops later in the day. He was furious, castigating "the railway system as in the wildest confusion." Dumped off the train at Ybor City, eight miles from the encampment, he had seized wagons to carry the regiment's baggage. No rations were available, so the officers spent seventy-two dollars of their own to supplement the men's food. Roosevelt snarled at the army quartermasters, who were no better organized than the railroads.[25]

He was as tired and dirty as the troopers, yet he was elated at having completed the trip from San Antonio without loss of man or animal. His delight vanished after he spoke to Wood. Because Wood was taking only four hundred men to Cuba, Roosevelt would have to remain behind, waiting for a second expedition, if there ever was one. Four hundred men constituted merely an enlarged squadron calling for one major in addition to Wood, not a lieutenant colonel.[26]

Wood ignored Roosevelt's panic. He was absorbed with his own complaint. He felt he had overcome tremendous obstacles to get the horses to Tampa, and now the troopers would be dismounted because they were replacing a volunteer infantry regiment that was not combat ready. Roosevelt did not give a damn about the men's horses at this moment. He would have crawled to go with the first force. His pride required it and his future depended on it. When Wood would not help him, he went to the hotel to plead with Miles and Shafter.

Fortunately for Roosevelt's state of mind, another volunteer regiment had proved to be partially unfit. The embarkation orders were being revised to take two Rough Rider squadrons instead of one. The revision meant that Roosevelt could be included in the first expedition, along with Wood and six hundred troopers, as long as two majors were left behind. Roosevelt knew he could convince Wood to make that much of a concession.[27]

The regiment still was to be sent dismounted. This was both for lack of transport space for the horses and because Miles visualized the invasion as proceeding through dense inland jungles that cavalry could not penetrate. Now that Roosevelt was part of the expedition, however, he could safely press the generals to reinstate the regiment's animals. He asked Lodge to use his influence to "have the horses sent to us very early." He had to have a horse to fulfill his vision.[28]

Four Lovely Days

Before he left San Antonio, Roosevelt telegraphed his second wife, his childhood friend Edith Carow, to join him in Tampa. His sister stayed with the children in Oyster Bay while Mrs. Roosevelt took the train on June 1. She arrived in Tampa the night of June 3, soon after a joyous Roosevelt had resolved his problem with Shafter and Wood.[29]

His wife's visit was good for Roosevelt. He had been a closet worrier since his early wheezy days. Now he was fretting once again. He was concerned about getting the Rough Riders to Cuba with the first regiments, about his capacity for command, about what his behavior would be under fire, and about his ability to make a personal triumph out of the war. His first wife had been "Baby." She had needed him to take care of her. Edith Roosevelt was mature, his sustainer as well as his lover. She gave him confidence.[30]

He said that they had "four lovely days" together. The setting was the Tampa Bay Hotel with its surprising silver minarets and Moorish arches. The rest of the city consisted of wooden houses stripped of outside paint by windblown sand that crept around window frames and under doors.[31]

Two regimental bands played in the hotel after sunset. The rotunda was alive with uniformed officers of the army and navy, foreign attachés in exotic dress, popular correspondents in eccentric field outfits, and stylishly coiffured and costumed women. Wood gave Roosevelt leave to be with his wife from dinner through breakfast each day of her visit. Two enlisted men who were old friends ate with them one evening, scandalizing correspondent Richard Harding Davis who frowned on any kind of "fraternizing."[32]

Edith Roosevelt was driven "out to the camp and saw it all—the men drilling, the tents in long company streets, the horses being taken to water, the little horse Texas, and finally the [regimental] mascots, the mountain lion and the jolly little dog Cuba." This was the first mention of the lion and the dog.[33]

Only two women gained access to the Rough Riders' camp in Tampa. A Fifth Avenue Boy's wife entered with Edith Roosevelt, eliciting more complaints about favoritism. No action was taken.[34]

His Moment Was Close

The Tampa encampment was comprised of nearly thirty thousand regulars and volunteers who were living in tents on a great sandy treeless plain. The weather was hot and the atmosphere was highly charged. Tempers were on edge. Black cavalrymen were encamped twenty-five miles east in rural Lakeland, to isolate them from contact that might result in trouble with white soldiers and white civilians.[35]

More than 150 correspondents had been in Tampa for weeks, waiting for war news. Big city papers had six or eight journalists and photographers under the direction of a bureau chief. The Associated Press had twelve people in Tampa, plus eight more in outlying areas. The *New York Herald* paid fifty dollars an hour to lease a telegraph wire to New York City. Major papers also maintained dispatch boats ready to cover the embarkation and invasion. The Associated Press had four boats under contract.[36]

So far, however, the reporters had been compelled to reconcile themselves to what Davis labeled "the rocking chair stage" of the campaign. Novelist Stephen Crane remarked that the newspapers should have sent playwrights to create news because otherwise none existed.[37]

By the time Roosevelt and the Rough Riders arrived, correspondents were desperate for legitimate material. Writers, illustrators, and photographers hurried to obtain passes from Adjutant Hall to interview the Rough Riders. Such journalistic luminaries as Davis, Crane, John Fox, Jr., Caspar Whitney, and Frederic Remington were received with open arms. At last the press had fresh copy.[38]

The Rough Riders were praised as the most picturesque regiment ever to serve under the American flag. The positive attitude of every trooper was said to be evident in his face. Each man was in Tampa for personal accomplishment, determined to be ahead of his fellows. According to the correspondents, each expected to be most prominent in the war.[39]

The press in Tampa ignored the rowdyism that some of the westerners had displayed. Instead, the Rough Riders were described as imbued with the true-blue quality of pure amateurs. The Fifth Avenue Boys were applauded for relinquishing Wall Street stock tickers and polo mallets. They were making the greatest financial sacrifices. The regiment as a whole was commended for embracing different cultures allied only through overriding patriotism. To illustrate the diversity, Davis joked about the easterners' complaint that there were too many beans in the diet, while the westerners claimed that they never got enough beans.[40]

In other volunteer regiments in Tampa, the undistinguished sons of notables strutted around as colonels wearing unearned eagles. In the Rough Riders, men famous because of their civilian accomplishments were eagerly serving as ordinary troopers under Wood and Roosevelt. Correspondents found the attitude of these "gentleman rankers" most refreshing.[41]

Roosevelt was the symbol of the Rough Riders. Davis referred to him in print as "the biggest thing here and the most typical American living," an officer "with energy and brains and enthusiasm enough to inspire a whole regiment." Davis had already decided on the lieutenant colonel as the soldier most likely to become a hero in the combat. Other correspondents followed Davis's lead.[42]

Wood was becoming increasingly resentful of the emphasis on Roosevelt. He deprecated his subordinate and denied that Roosevelt had contributed to getting the regiment ready. He told his wife that "by the time Roosevelt came down [to San Antonio,] we were in pretty good shape." Although this was an exaggeration, he had become aware "not long after I had been joined by Roosevelt that if this campaign lasted for any considerable length of time I would be kicked upstairs to make room for the promotion of Roosevelt." Like Davis and Navy Secretary Long, he had come to believe in the inevitable ascent of Roosevelt's star.[43]

On the first full day in Tampa, June 4, Roosevelt drilled the Rough Riders on foot because the horses were tired. The second day he held mounted drill, although the performance was ragged because of stage fright in front of regular Army officers and overseas experts. The third day, the drill was "very good and much admired by foreign attachés," according to Roosevelt who insisted that "we are doing as well as the regular regiments." English and German observers in Tampa maintained that the Rough Riders had the most soldierly camp.[44]

Naturally, the regular cavalrymen were jealous. They resented the Rough Riders, insinuating that Roosevelt's regiment was "not so warm" and that the cowboys were in Tampa only because of "a big pull in Washington." In mock seriousness, the suggestion was offered that the regiment be broken up as the best device to make real soldiers out of poorly trained volunteers.[45]

In addition, the regulars delighted in initiating rumors that the Rough Riders would be left behind when the regulars embarked for Cuba with Shafter. The jesting ended when the regiment officially was assigned to the Cavalry Division's 2nd Brigade under Brig. Gen. S. B. M. Young.[46]

Tampa residents agreed with the regulars in disparaging the Rough Riders. They were afraid of the cowboy volunteers. The Floridians had read about the musical "Cavalry Charge" in San Antonio, about criminal convictions, and about roping pigs and chickens en route to

Tampa. They regarded the entrepreneurial Rough Riders as a threat to civic decorum, and they petitioned Wood to confine his troopers to the encampment. When Wood refused, the *Morning Tribune* ran articles about Rough Riders who engaged in brawls in the streets and in houses of prostitution.[47]

The Rough Riders were only a small percentage of the soldiers in the encampment, yet frightened citizens of Tampa stayed indoors after dark in a self-imposed curfew. Some residents carried guns to defend themselves as vigilantes. The people even formed a committee to ask the army paymaster to refrain from making disbursements to the Rough Riders while they were in Tampa. That way, they would have less money to spend on whiskey, women, and gambling, and there would be less violence. The romantic aspect of the Rough Riders seemed evident only to civilians who were far away from them.[48]

Although the Rough Riders had not received a cent since they were mustered in, the paymaster agreed with the townspeople. He refused to make any disbursements to the men, so Wood appealed to Washington, over the heads of Miles and Shafter. When the paymaster was ordered to comply, he delayed by asking for muster rolls. The regiment had not been that formal under Adjutant Hall. Now lists of troopers and service dates were made out in a hurry. Mistakes in records that became permanent were inevitable.[49]

At six o'clock in the evening on June 6, the Rough Riders lined up for a hot and sandy march to the Tampa Bay Hotel. Alongside the hotel's indoor swimming pool, the men were compensated for services during May. Some men were shorted. Trooper Arthur Cosby received only $2.10 for the month. Then the men marched back to camp, arriving at 10 P.M., only to be told to prepare to embark the next day. The Rough Riders had been paid and the citizens had been protected, all at the same time.[50]

Edith Roosevelt took the train for home the morning of June 7. Her husband was ready for the embarkation to begin. He knew that his greatest moment was nearly at hand.[51]

Chapter 7
Looking Back at the Westerner

When Roosevelt left New York City for Dakota Territory in mid-April 1885, he was pale after a winter spent writing a book about his own hunting trips as a ranchman. His spare frame had "a general look of dyspepsia," and he still spoke in the languid, drawn out, yet shrill tones he had picked up at Harvard. He told his foreman Merfield who met him at the Little Missouri station, "Bah Jove! Aw, ahm ahl tiahed out, yieu knaow."[1]

He joined the regional spring roundup and helped to stop a stampede of cattle by wild riding in rough terrain at night. He accepted that the cowboys who rode with him might be his equal in that kind of daring the job required, but he insisted upon recognition that they were not his equal in social standing. When a fellow rancher born in the West addressed him as Roosevelt without the Mister, he turned truculently to demand, "What did you say?" From then on, the rancher called him Mr. Roosevelt, just as everyone else did.[2]

By June 20 he had been on the roundup for almost two months, covering thirty to forty miles a day on horseback. After a steady diet of steak, beans, and dried apple pie that was the chuck wagon fare two or three times a day, he was no longer slim. He was becoming barrel-chested, thick-necked, brawny, and burned walnut brown. Thirty pounds heavier than he had been in college, he was finally achieving the physical development his father had encouraged.[3]

He acknowledged that "ranch life had been the making" of his body. On his first trip to the Badlands in 1883, the sheriff had thought "by his looks" that he was "some kind of a tin-horn gambling outfit." When Roosevelt was interviewed on his way east by rail at the end of June 1885, however, the reporter in St. Paul saw him as "rugged, bronzed, and in the prime of health. There was little of the dude in his rough and easy costume, with a big handkerchief tied about his neck." Roosevelt's speech had changed, too. "The slow, exasperating drawl and the unique accent have disappeared, and in their place is a nervous, energetic manner of talking with the flat accent of the West." His voice was now powerful enough to be heard in the midst of a cattle drive.[4]

He had quit politics, so ranching and writing about his experiences as stockman and hunter were what he had left. His literary subject was man versus nature, with the West as his backdrop. He was among the earliest authors to take the cowboy seriously, crediting the cowpuncher as well as the hunter and the settler with self-reliance, stoicism, audacity, manliness, morality, and rugged strength. Those were the same traits he saw in himself.

On August 25, he was back again in his room at the ranch, ensconced with his books and his little rubber bathtub. Within the week, a French marquis who was an expert duelist issued what could have been taken as a challenge. Roosevelt responded in an ambiguous manner, and the Frenchman chose to accept Roosevelt's reply as a satisfactory explanation. That ended the issue.[5]

Roosevelt later changed the story by telling eastern guests that the Frenchman had actually challenged him. He said he chose shotguns loaded with buckshot as weapons for the duel, making it inevitable that both men would be killed or disfigured. The marquis apologized to him, he claimed, rather than face buckshot.

In Finnegan's Wake

After Roosevelt returned to the ranch in March 1886, he found that three petty criminals led by Mike Finnegan had stolen the boat the ranch hands used to cross the river. The thieves set off downstream, thinking themselves safe because there was no way to pursue them on horseback while the Dakota Territory was still snowbound. The chase had to be by water, and there was no other boat.

A prudent man would have let the thieves keep the thirty-dollar craft. Not Roosevelt, a sometime deputy sheriff. He responded by having a rough scow constructed quickly. The night before the scow was ready, a guest from Boston overheard Roosevelt in his room, rehearsing what he would say when he confronted the thieves: "I've got the gun on you! I know you stole my boat, and I'm here to claim it!"[6]

After extreme hardship on the river, the capture took place just the way Roosevelt had visualized it. Vigilantes might have hung the thieves on the spot. Instead, he left the recovery of both boats to his men, and with his rifle at the ready, he walked alone behind the three disarmed outlaws to conduct them to the nearest town with a jail. He went thirty-six hours without sleep and trudged forty frigid miles on foot through snow and mud, ending as "the most bedraggled figure ever seen" in Dakota. To cap it all, he claimed he kept awake by reading the two-pound Russian novel *Anna Karenina* at rest stops and by firelight.[7]

Roosevelt admired the ranch hands as practitioners of the Protestant work ethic, but his appreciation was limited by the conventions of his class. A letter he wrote to his sister was apologetic concerning the men: "If we can arrange a visit from you, I dread seeing you at table, for we have no social distinction and the cow boys sit down in their shirt sleeves."[8]

These were the Dakota cowboys who later volunteered to serve as cavalrymen in regiments that never reached Cuba.

Hero or Coward

Roosevelt remained in Dakota through the early summer of 1886 to give the Fourth of July oration. Afterward, the editor of the *Bad Lands Cow Boy* newspaper predicted that Roosevelt would eventually be elected president of the United States. Roosevelt's considered reply was, "If your prophecy comes true, I will do my part to make a good one." He was twenty-seven.[9]

Later in July he returned to New York City where he was offered the presidency not of the nation but rather of the city's Board of Health. He declined, based on Senator Lodge's advice that the office was beneath his dignity, and he went back to Dakota. He had already killed deer, elk, antelope, cougar and other big cats, timber wolf, grizzly and other bears, and buffalo. The heads were mounted as trophies in his summer place on Long Island. He had never, however, shot the rare white "antelope goat" native to the Coeur d'Alene Mountains in Montana Territory.[10]

By September, he was deep in the mountains with his foreman and the Montana hunter Jack Willis. When at last he shot a prize specimen of white goat, he went into his Indian war dance to ritualize the killing. The following day he chanced a solitary climb on a mountain ledge, slipped from an overhang, fell sixty feet into the soft top branches of a pine tree, and descended unharmed. He told this tale frequently, needing to confirm his fearlessness over and over.

When he wanted a photograph of an uncharted three-hundred-foot waterfall, he had himself lowered two hundred feet into the gorge at the end of two lariats tied together. The two men at the top could not pull him back up, so he hung there, swinging calmly for hours while the hunter worked his way to the bottom of the gorge and signaled the foreman to cut the dangling Roosevelt loose. He fell safely into deep water, still clutching the camera.[11]

Roosevelt was again showing that his pluck could not be questioned. To him, a man was either a hero or a coward. As a potential hero, he was cocky, self-important, and oblivious to the needs of people around him. It had taken a long time for him to start to come to terms with his feeling of guilt at having abandoned his father, mother, and first wife, the three who had meant most to him, when they needed him most.

Western trips provided risks to relieve what remained of his fading anguish. If he could survive the severe self-testing, he could expect to live his full span of years and prosper, even though a full span for a member of his family might be relatively short.

The Cowboy Candidate

At the ranch he sat in a rocking chair while he read or talked. The chair oscillated according to the intensity of his feelings. When he was excited, the chair traveled rapidly across the floor until the runners hit an obstacle. Then he changed direction and started rocking again.[12]

He was rocking across the room and reading the *New York Times* in late September when he suddenly ceased the forward movement, hunched his shoulders, and set his jaw. He had made a decision. The *Times* he was reading reported that he was being mentioned as Republican nominee for mayor of New York City. Surprisingly, he was favored by both the independents and Boss Platt. He started east at once to offer himself as "the Cowboy Candidate," the youngest candidate ever.[13]

The campaign lasted only three short weeks. On November 1, he looked to be the winner. In the last few days before the election, however, the Democrats persuaded New Yorkers that at twenty-nine, he was too inexperienced for the office. After he lost, the editors of *Century* magazine which published his outdoors articles, tried to console him by pointing out that "you were talked about for the Vice Presidency before you reached the age of eligibility." "Oh no, no," he lamented. "This is the end of my political career." He was despondent. He had been close to a victory that would have validated his larger goals.[14]

In mid-April 1888, he faced economic tragedy. He lost three-fourths of his cattle in an incredible Dakota blizzard of the sort that occurs only once in a hundred years. There would be no further earnings from cattle sales, and, as he had squandered his inheritance, his income was insufficient to support his lavish style of living. With no alternative, he gave up his New York City residence and moved to his summer place, Sagamore Hill on Long Island. As a literary gentleman, he relied on a large output of writing, emphasizing quantity rather than quality.[15]

Politics, however, remained his first love. On May 11, he was exhilarated by being named the Young Republican Independents' principal guest at a New York reception. Perennial party toastmaster Chauncey Depew quipped that other orators for the evening had submitted their texts to Roosevelt for clearance so as not to embarrass him "when he runs for President." The *New York Sun* added that, "due to circumstances beyond his control, he will not be able to take the office of President of the United States before 1897," the first term when he would be eligible under the constitutional age limitation.[16]

Politicians and the press recognized Roosevelt's promise, while he professed to see the world as having passed him by.

Be Not a Butcher

Roosevelt's second wife Edith assumed responsibility for their children and for the Long Island house and grounds. He avoided domestic problems. When he needed fresh material for his writing, he took another western trip where he was alone except for a guide. Since he already had bagged trophy heads of every American creature he coveted, shooting was limited to bigger trophies or food to be eaten.[17]

His Montana guide hunted wild animals for their skins. The reformed Roosevelt admonished him, "That is wholesale murder and you must stop it. You are a Christian at heart. Be a sportsman and not a ruthless butcher of defenseless animals."[18]

The guide was fascinated by his patron. He observed that Roosevelt took off his glasses to read around the campfire, although "at ten feet he could not recognize a friend without them." He sat up late with books, then woke with a smile. The fastidious Roosevelt shaved every morning, spent a lot of time brushing his teeth, and took a bath every day, even when the water was icy. He ate fish but never went fishing. Catching trout on a delicate fly was not a blood sport.[19]

Despite what he told the guide about butchery, he loved strenuous stalking of large animals, loud explosive sounds, stricken targets, and rich red stains. Writings about his hunting experiences sold readily to popular magazines and to publishers of outdoors books. In addition, shooting big game was a realizable peacetime substitute for the dream of leading his all-out cavalry charge in a killing war.

Chapter 8
Starting Toward Cuba

After the Rough Riders arrived in Tampa on June 3, Roosevelt discovered that the V Army Corps was being grossly mismanaged by Shafter's quartermasters. Even at this late date, many of the regulars were poorly equipped and fed and were inappropriately dressed in the heavy regulation blue uniforms. Surprisingly, the bungling had not been exposed by correspondents who were clearly hungry for news.[1]

These regular regiments were the heart of the army, but they had been maintained for years at greatly reduced manpower levels. Now the ranks had to be augmented at once with raw recruits who decreased the regiments' readiness. At least, though, the regular regiments were relatively close to being fit for duty. In contrast, most of the volunteer regiments in Tampa remained hopelessly untrained and lacking in uniforms or weapons other than black-powder Springfield rifles.

The stumbling blocks had been President McKinley, Secretary of War Alger, and decades of congressional neglect. Over the years since the Civil War, Congress had reduced the army to 27,500 men who were now supposed to be able to lead in conquering Cuba, Puerto Rico, and the Philippines. There were 196,000 Spanish soldiers in Cuba alone.[2]

For his part, the president had been telling Secretary Alger for months to expect a settlement with Spain rather than war. No preparation for an invasion by the army was necessary yet, he had advised. Further, his strategists had determined that if war did come, the primary responsibility would fall on the navy. Getting the navy ready to attack Havana was essential. The condition of the army was important, but congressional authorization for mobilization of the army was delayed.[3]

The secretary added his own blunders. He thought that Spain would surrender without a fight if war were declared. Also, he knew that if an invasion of Cuba was ordered, the surgeon general would discourage an embarkation close to the summer rainy season when diseases could take a heavy toll. Consequently, the secretary ordered only limited military preparedness in April and early May.

Unexpectedly, the navy achieved a tremendous coup by bottling the Spanish fleet inside Santiago de Cuba's deep harbor at the eastern end of the island. The result, however, was that both naval forces were immobilized. Shore batteries prevented the American fleet from entering the harbor to attack the Spaniards, so the Americans could not get in and the Spaniards could not get out.

To end the stalemate, the navy demanded emergency assistance from the previously ignored army. As long as the Spanish warships could not escape from the harbor to maneuver in the open ocean, the navy pointed out, an American invasion fleet would have safe passage. The need was to take the forts guarding the mouth of Santiago Bay by an immediate land attack on the city and the adjacent shore, thus enabling the American fleet to steam in. Action was needed quickly because a storm might blow the American squadron away from the mouth of the harbor, freeing the Spanish fleet.[4]

To oblige the navy, the president overruled the surgeon general. He ordered the unprepared army to embark for Cuba in the few weeks left before summer officially started. Although he had fought in the Civil War and understood battle conditions, McKinley persuaded himself that even after the beginning of the rains in Cuba, soldiers who ate appropriate food, drank boiled water, camped on high ground, and kept themselves clean and dry would stay healthy despite the history of disease on the island.[5]

The sanitary standards he set were impossible to achieve. Even if his regimen had been realized, however, it would have been largely ineffective. Medical science learned later that yellow fever and malaria were spread by mosquitoes which multiplied during the rainy tropical summer, rather than by a lack of personal hygiene.

The War Department did not start ordering war goods from vendors until just before the regular regiments were directed to report to Florida in early May. Purchases were shipped to Tampa by rail, but no one thought to note the contents of the freight cars on the outside of the cars or in the bills of lading. A needed article could be in any one of scores of unmarked cars.[6]

Compounding the disorganization, incoming freight cars were routed from the Tampa rail yard directly to the transports at Port Tampa. The only railroad from the Tampa main line to the port was a single privately-owned track ten miles long. Cars could move along this roadbed in only one direction at a time. Army trains shared the track with gaily decorated coaches carrying paying passengers who were looking forward to a day at the harbor so that they could watch the brave soldiers prepare to sail to romantic Cuba. The single track soon became overburdened, and hundreds of loaded freight cars, unable to reach the transports, swamped the Tampa yard.[7]

The public was unaware of the fiasco in Tampa because informal military censorship had been imposed on the journalists. Although the ostensible reason was to withhold information that might benefit the Spaniards, the restraint also prevented exposure of army shortcomings.[8]

Poultney Bigelow reported the truth about the army in *Harper's Weekly* and was denounced as a traitor. Davis joined the attacks on Bigelow, but privately he too despaired of army inefficiency. So did Roosevelt in his letters and diary. "No plans, no staff officers, no instructions to us," he complained. "Each officer finds out for himself and takes his chances."[9]

Roosevelt did not go public with protests, though. As long as he was to be on one of the transports, he wanted the invasion at any price. Besides, colonels seldom felt the effects of managerial neglect the way their subordinates did.

"I Organized This"

When Roosevelt was assistant navy secretary, he bought or leased for the navy the best commercial vessels available. Few suitable ships remained for the army quartermasters to rent for the voyage to Cuba. Only three were passenger liners, and they had limited accommodations. Most were freighters. Others had been used to transport cattle. Several were barely seaworthy. Even so, there was a severe shortage of ships.

Because the voyage was expected to be short, civilian contractors were instructed to put haste and quantity before comfort in converting the rented boats into transports for the crossing. Carpenters installed rough and crowded wooden bunks with inadequate ventilation, insufficient toilets, and no cooking facilities for the men. Despite the closeness of the undersized bunks, however, the converted transports had room for only sixteen thousand men, rather than the twenty-five thousand General Miles judged necessary to defeat the Spaniards in Cuba. The difference was a blow to Miles and Shafter but a boon to Alger. He had to provide nine thousand fewer volunteers who were ready for battle.[10]

The transports were moored outside the port, along a narrow tongue of land that bordered the dredged channel. By May 31, the vessels were provided with coal and water. The loading of rations, guns, ammunition, wagons, and supplies continued for another week. Then the time came for horses and men to go on board. The Rough Riders' pack train was led onto a transport with other animals.

Wood and Roosevelt were still restricted to two squadrons of dismounted Rough Riders and had selected 560 men from eight of the twelve troops. Four hundred twenty would stay behind, including a sad Maj. Henry Hersey who was held back to make room for Roosevelt. Fifth Avenue Boys who were scheduled to be left in Tampa offered five hundred dollars to troopers who were willing to exchange assignments, but the embarkation rosters were set. Nine troopers who had been passed over deserted.[11]

Among the men Wood failed to take along was the sergeant major who maintained regimental records for the adjutant. From then on, irregular field reports were the only official Rough Rider papers documenting the Cuban experience. Many were composed casually and long after the event.

Roosevelt assured the men remaining in Florida that they would miss nothing. To raise their hopes, he rashly gave his word that "I organized this as a mounted regiment. There will be no fighting until I get the rest of the men and horses over." In last-minute preparations, he hired a black cook for the officers' mess, sent his valet Marshall ahead to the port with the officers' horses, and laid in treats for his own table.[12]

After the Rough Riders were officially reclassified as foot soldiers, a squad of regular infantrymen was detailed to show them how to prepare blanket rolls to be carried on their backs instead of on the mule train. The regiment's dog tents sheltered two men, each with a half to button to his mate's half. The horseshoe-shaped roll was made by wrapping one half of a canvas tent around a man's blanket and necessaries to form a cylinder. The ends were fastened together, and the roll was thrown over the trooper's head, over his left shoulder, across his chest, and under his right arm.[13]

Officers such as Roosevelt were not burdened with blanket rolls. Their baggage remained on the pack train with the regimental stores.

Sail at Once

On June 7, President McKinley directed Shafter to "sail at once with what force you have ready." His patience with the general had run out as the time for summer's dread diseases approached and the Spanish fleet threatened to escape.[14]

Shafter had no precedent to follow. No American army officer had ever managed an overseas expedition of this magnitude. He was not a theorist but a practical man, and the logistics of the embarkation were too complicated for him and his staff. Nevertheless, the president was the commander-in-chief. To comply with the president's directive, Shafter relied upon the enterprise of his line officers. During the evening of June 7, he sent aides to direct the regimental commanders to move their men the ten miles from the Tampa campground to the troopships in Port Tampa harbor. The officers were given specific routings and warned that "those who are not on board by daybreak will be left behind."[15]

The commanders promptly had the men take down the tents, make up their packs, load the wagons, police the camp, and head for the assigned train siding or the one treacherous wagon trail over the sand. Shafter's staff had estimated that 2,500 soldiers an hour could be moved to the port by train and wagon, but only the first few regiments got through by the designated means. The track and the trail were soon gridlocked.[16]

To facilitate the movement of the rest of the units, the allowance for officers' baggage was decreased from 250 to 80 pounds. Next, only six horses were permitted per regiment for officers' use. Nothing broke the impasse, however, until desperate regimental commanders exercised their own initiative rather than relying on Shafter's routings.[17]

The 71st New York Volunteers seized at bayonet point an engine and flatcars not assigned to them. The 9th Infantry stole wagons from a rival regiment. The 6th Infantry appropriated stock cars and stood in manure. The all-black 10th Cavalry made its way the longer distance from Lakeland. Only the 2nd Massachusetts started a little late. Its men had discovered bottled beer in an unmarked freight car.[18]

The leaders who were most effective were the aggressive ones like Roosevelt. As soon as Shafter's instructions arrived, he realized that wagons were needed to haul matériel to the train siding to be indicated by the corps quartermaster. He directed three officers to obtain wagons by lease or purchase, advancing the money from his own pocket.[19]

By the time wagons were borrowed from the 2nd Cavalry which still had its pack train, the Rough Riders chosen for Cuba were ready. At 10 o'clock, the two squadrons began marching in the dark toward railroad cars assigned to them for the ride to the port. The troopers were in high spirits.

When the men arrived at the siding, however, they found that a regular cavalry regiment with the same routing, an earlier notice from Shafter, and its own wagons had taken possession of all the cars. Wood was advised by a staff officer that another train would be backed from the port for the Rough Riders, although a regular cavalry officer who was standing triumphantly alongside the cars told Wood that he "needn't worry" about getting to the port. "Your regiment is not going," the officer sneered. "You're not wanted."[20]

Wood retained his composure. He had the men unload the wagons in the dark to be ready to board the next train. Then they stretched out in ranks to rest. After three hours, another staff officer ordered the regiment to move to a different siding. Wood had the men load the matériel back on the wagons and march to the designated switch. There they lay on the ground again, their heads on their blanket rolls.[21]

At 6 A.M., the morning was clearing as Shafter's hour for sailing approached. The Rough Riders were disappointed, stiff, tired, disgusted, and hungry, until they saw that their perambulations during the night had brought them back close to the camp where they started. Their mates who had remained behind cooked them a quick breakfast of bacon with hardtack and coffee.

The promised transportation never arrived. While the Rough Riders were finishing their sparse meal, though, a train with a baggage car and a string of empty coal gondolas started to roll slowly past them, backing from the port to the city of Tampa after a final fueling of the transports. On his own authority, Roosevelt halted the train and, as he bragged later, "by various arguments persuaded the engineer" to allow the men aboard.[22]

Some troopers contended that the "arguments" involved threats of force. Others claimed bribery. In any event, the troopers were glad to throw their supplies and blanket rolls into the dusty cars and climb in after them. Anything that would carry the regiment to the transports was acceptable.

In half an hour, the coal train with the blackened but cheering Rough Riders pulled into the Port Tampa yard. The infantrymen of the 71st New York Volunteers were sitting on flatcars on a parallel siding. They had been proud of being among the first to arrive at the port, beating regular regiments, but they were still awaiting further orders as the Rough Riders inched past, shouting

Rough, tough,
We're the stuff,
We want to fight,
And we can't get enough![23]

The infantrymen recognized the Rough Riders by their unique stable uniforms and the blue polka-dot bandannas that contrasted with the solid red neckerchiefs of other regiments. The infantrymen called for an appearance by their fellow New Yorker, the popular lieutenant colonel who had once been a captain in the state militia. The demand was good-humored.[24]

Roosevelt was in the baggage car with the officers. He strode to the open door, grinned, and then bowed like the national celebrity he was. The infantrymen observed that the uniform of the usually dapper Roosevelt looked as if he had slept in it. He had.[25]

"We Seem to Have It"

While the Rough Riders were unloading regimental matériel from the coal gondolas at 8:30 A.M., they gazed around the busy port. They saw an impressive fleet of thirty transports in and about the channel beyond the docks. Thousands of soldiers were pouring into the harbor area. In the absence of instructions from Shafter's aide in charge of harbor assignments, officers were racing about trying to locate transports available for boarding.

For an hour, the Rough Riders stood alongside the track in the increasingly hot sun while Wood and Roosevelt searched for Shafter's aide. Wood complained that the scene was "confusion worse confounded. No head, no tail." Finally, he obtained permission to board the *Yucatan,* which had been leased from the Ward Line since coastal trade had been suspended for the duration of the war. The ship was among the faster transports, although it was a freighter.[26]

The *Yucatan* had also been designated for occupancy by three additional regiments, the 2nd Infantry, the 4th Cavalry, and the 71st Volunteers. The four regiments would have amounted to four times the number of men the ship was designed to accommodate, so Wood quickly commandeered a launch, was ferried to the transport where it was anchored in the channel, and induced the *Yucatan*'s captain to dock the vessel.

Meanwhile, Roosevelt had run back to the troopers. He left the stores under guard and quick-marched the two squadrons down the long slip to the *Yucatan*'s waiting gangplank and onto the ship. Four companies of the 2nd Infantry were already on board, along with their regimental band. So were 120 horses of the 4th Cavalry. With the addition of the Rough Riders, the *Yucatan* was loaded to double her capacity.

Anticipating boarding attempts by other regiments, Roosevelt put a guard at the gangplank. He allowed entry only to a pair of photographers from the fledgling Vitagraph Company who had movie cameras for making newsreel films. Publicity was always welcome.[27]

Roosevelt explained smugly that "the rest of the Second Regulars and the 71st arrived a little too late, being a shade less ready in individual initiative." When the 71st's Capt. Anthony Bleecker, who was a Manhattan Knickerbocker like Roosevelt, went to the *Yucatan* to negotiate, Roosevelt asked in apparent amity, "What can I do for you?" Bleecker replied, "That's our ship." "Well," Roosevelt remarked, "we seem to have it," and the 71st was routed by volleys of coal thrown from the *Yucatan*'s bunkers that had just been topped off.[28]

The *Yucatan* Carrying the Famous Roosevelt's "Rough Riders" to Cuba.
Stereopticon view. (New York: Underwood and Underwood, 1898).

The 71st was commanded by Col. W. A. Downs. He had replaced Gen. Francis Vinton Greene, the New Yorker who had turned down Roosevelt's application to join the 71st before war was declared. This was the same General Greene who was Roosevelt's potential rival for the Republican nomination for governor of New York. He was headed for the far-away Philippines with a different regiment, instead of coming closer to Cuba where most of the newspaper correspondents would be.[29]

While the Rough Riders shouldered their supplies the length of the channel from the railroad terminus to the *Yucatan*, Colonel Downs applied the lesson he learned from Wood and Roosevelt. He sent his lieutenant colonel onto the bay to seize the unoccupied *Vigilancia*, the newest passenger ship in the Ward Line and the finest in the transport fleet. The Rough Riders unintentionally had done the 71st a favor.[30]

There exist two less flattering versions of how Roosevelt boarded the *Yucatan*. Wood as usual downplayed Roosevelt's role in favor of his own. He claimed that before he appropriated the transport, he ordered Roosevelt and Captain Capron to march the squadrons of troopers to the pier. As he remembered it, the two units arrived at the gangplank at the same time and reported to him on the docked transport. He implied that none of Roosevelt's histrionics with the 71st happened, but Wood, like Roosevelt, was a self-serving witness. Capron died in Cuba before he could add his version. Bleecker survived but did not comment for publication.[31]

The quartermasters who were criticized by both Wood and Roosevelt responded with their own story. "I read with much amusement," one of their officers later remarked, "what our friend 'Teddy' had to say about Tampa. I have a distinct recollection of meeting with the wild and woolly Rough Rider at the foot of the gangplank as he was about to embark. I informed him that he was assigned to the transport before us and that he could march on at any time. The Rough Rider then galloped on board. There are a great many funny things testified to by various parties, and I don't know whether it is worthwhile to pay the slightest attention to them."[32]

Neither Wood's nor the quartermaster's version of the Rough Riders' embarkation was published at the time. Roosevelt alone had access to the press. He was credited in print with the Yankee gumption that carried the day for his regiment. Even in its infancy, the military legend of Teddy was hard to buck.

A Room with a View

The ranking army officer on the *Yucatan* was Colonel Wood, who looked forward to a relaxing voyage. He assigned staterooms and seats at table to the officers and had a room to himself with a porthole that opened. So did Roosevelt. Berths for the men were in the hold where the heat was permanently oppressive. There were no pillows, mattresses, or sheets for the men, and there was no need for the blankets they carried.[33]

Each bunk was designed for two occupants and their gear, in an arrangement similar to the pairing in the dog tents. The bunks were three tiers high, with two and a half feet between the tiers. The area was no bigger than the inside of a tent, and tall men could not lie straight. Floor space was equally tight. While settling in, men could just about move around. They were constantly bumping into each other, but they remained cheerful.

Despite the compact accommodations in the hold where closing the hatches during a storm could have caused mass suffocation, there were scores of men without berths. They slept in the open on the narrow upper deck, positioned crosswise. This did not permit any of them to stretch out. Yet no one grumbled. After all the doubts and delays, the Rough Riders were part of the first American invasion of Cuba. They would be going this way just once. They wanted only to get on with the voyage.[34]

By early afternoon on June 8, the *Yucatan* was stowed with all the soldiers and supplies the ship could safely contain. The other transports were fully loaded, too, and the expedition was about to start. Finally, the *City of Washington* steamed grandly down the bay at the head of the flotilla, just as the president had ordered. The *Washington* was the fast Ward Liner that had been moored next to the battleship *Maine* the night of the explosion in Havana harbor.

The beginning of the voyage was inspirational, in that it was shaped from what had appeared to be chaos. Right after the *Yucatan*'s engines were started, however, the captain received revised orders from Shafter via a megaphone in the hands of an aide standing on the deck of the little tugboat *Captain Sam*. In response, the *Yucatan*'s engines were switched off. The ship was moored again in the Port Tampa channel at half past three in the afternoon. So were twenty-eight other transports. No explanation was given.[35]

The *City of Washington* did not receive Shafter's recall. She had steamed off for Cuba by herself, loaded with soldiers and supplies, without knowing where landing would occur and without looking astern. The gunboat *Castine* was dispatched to bring the liner back but did not catch up until the Cuban coast was sighted. Three days elapsed before the gunboat and the transport returned to Port Tampa. The other twenty-nine transports were anchored approximately where they had been before the false start. The men remained on board.[36]

When the invasion was postponed, Roosevelt was distressed. He was sure that Spain had surrendered and the Rough Riders would be disbanded without seeing action. He wrote his ten-year-old son, "We are feeling rather blue, for it looks as if the war might end before we get a chance to do any fighting, so that all our work and sacrifice would go for nothing. However, it can't be helped; and we must do our duty, whether things go as we wish or not. We get no news here, and the confusion is great; all we can do is to keep ready and wait for whatever may befall us. If the chance comes, or if we can make it come, I believe we will do good work." Fortune had marched to his orders thus far in the war, and he hoped to continue his mastery.[37]

Other Rough Riders feared that the indefinite postponement of the expedition meant that the Spaniards under the redoubtable Admiral Cervera y Topete had already broken the blockade and had defeated the American battle fleet in the Caribbean. A naval loss like that would have constituted a major personal blow to Roosevelt. Destruction of the warships would end plans for the invasion and perhaps even result in peace. Peace would mean the end of his aspirations. He would never be able to make his mark in combat.[38]

The Phantom Fleet

The reason finally given for postponing departure was naval caution. Two American gunboats converted from millionaires' yachts during Roosevelt's navy tenure had reported seeing two Spanish cruisers and two Spanish torpedo boats on the well-publicized route that the American transports would follow along the northern coast of Cuba. Although all Spanish cruisers known to be in the Caribbean were blockaded in Santiago harbor, the Naval War Board recommended that President McKinley defer the expedition until sighting of the enemy warships could be verified. The transports were brought back inside Port Tampa Bay under the dubious protection of one obsolete field gun at the end of the dock.[39]

This was the threat of "the phantom fleet." The *New York Times* editorialized that "the Spaniard may have no navy or army, but he is expert at circulating rumors of the movement of ships he does not possess." More time had been lost in the effort to get the army to Cuba before the rains started.[40]

Cynics claimed that the expedition was held back because McKinley was apprised that preparations had been inadequate, rather than because of enemy ghost ships. Medical supplies critical to the invasion had been forgotten. Now Shafter was able to secure five additional transports and load them with more men and stores. Even the already overburdened *Yucatan* was backed up to the dock to receive two more carloads of cargo.[41]

In the interim, the most critical problem was what to do about the men on the transports. They could not be returned to the Tampa encampment which had already been occupied by newly formed volunteer regiments from the North. The men had to remain on board, where the crowded quarters prevented them from keeping clean and exposed them to communicable diseases. All that was done to compensate, however, was to give the men leave to go on shore for a few hours at a time and to permit swimming. Few men from the West could swim.[42]

The first night on the *Yucatan,* many bunks made of green wood joined by too few nails had collapsed. This was taken as a joke, and the next morning the lumber was rebuilt into solid platforms. There were, however, complaints about other aspects of the sleeping accommodations and about the food. The issue was fairness, from an odd standpoint.[43]

The officers paid a dollar a day to the Ward Line steward for three cooked meals. At midday the officers had hot soup, meat, vegetables, bread and butter, and dessert served on china dishes, followed by coffee in a china cup with cream and sugar.

In contrast, the men were handed hardtack and a chunk of cold beef out of a can at each meal. For dinner they also had cold beans or tomatoes, one can to a squad of eight, with each man taking a spoonful as the can was passed around. Occasionally, the men had both beans and tomatoes, with canned peaches for dessert. They squatted on the deck in the dazzling noon sunshine, juggling their mess kits and tin cups of coffee.[44]

The officers sat on chairs at a cloth-covered table in a private dining saloon, served by orderlies and by the black valets of the officers. When meals were finished, the valets ate the leftovers. After officers went to bed, the valets slept comfortably on soft couches in the dining cabin.[45]

The troopers did not complain about "upstairs-downstairs" differences. Rank had its privileges in the army. Some whites, however, felt an antipathy toward blacks. The feeling extended to the eating and sleeping advantages the valets had over the troopers, but Wood made no concession to the malcontents.

When Roosevelt invited "gentleman rankers" to dine with the officers, troopers' protests were effective. Money could always buy food from the officers' kitchen, however, if not a place at the officers' table. A Fifth Avenue Boy could lay down a dollar bill and say, "Give me something to eat." Men without money had no extra food.[46]

The worst blow to the enlisted men's diet concerned canned "fresh" beef. Canned roast beef and canned corned beef were precooked and palatable. The canned fresh beef, though, was raw and "horrible, nauseating, sickening in odor." As a former medical officer, Wood called the "fresh" meat a hazard to health and ordered it thrown overboard. The beef shortage never was remedied.[47]

In addition, Wood authorized the kitchen steward to sell iced water as an alternative to the stale and tepid water in the ship's tanks. Wood set no price and the steward asked seventy-five cents a glass. Even thirsty men were reluctant to spend that much money for water, so four tons of ice still remained in the ship's hold at the end of the voyage. On the other hand, beer, which was prohibited, was available clandestinely from soldiers on board. At twenty-five cents the small pint, beer was cheaper than iced water. At twenty dollars a gallon or a dollar a shot, "red rat poison" whiskey was more expensive.[48]

Fortunate men brought food from shore to relieve the sameness of the rations. They had boxes of specialty items such as pickles, sardines, and lemons. For them, the supplemented fare was not too bad. For officers, the food was fine.[49]

Healthy Looking and Rugged

Roosevelt made no attempt to ease the debilitating conditions of the men. Depressed by his own concerns over whether the Rough Riders would ever reach a battlefield, he wrote that "the tropical rain is very bad for men. We are all crowded so close together it is hard to move up and down the decks." He did not suggest offering more frequent leaves, improving the sleeping arrangements, or providing more varied food or cheaper iced water.[50]

Instead, he spent most of the time in his cabin, reading and worrying. He went to Port Tampa once in a while. Soldiers saw him sitting alone at a table in a little hotel near the pier, unable because of the shortages to buy delicacies he would have had at home. The occasional correspondent found him "sunburned, healthy looking and rugged, with a figure somewhat slighter." He was quoted as stating the obvious, that "there is not a man in the regiment who is not eager and anxious to get to Cuba."[51]

His spirits were boosted a little when *Harper's Weekly* magazine backed a movement among independents to run him for Congress from the 14th District in New York City as "an honest, intelligent, educated man." He knew, however, that the Republican machine would not consent to his nomination unless he could generate more leverage on "Easy Boss" Platt than was possible while sitting in a rickety Port Tampa hotel, looking at makeshift transports lying idle in the rapidly polluting channel.[52]

When Roosevelt's men took shore leave, though, they saw sights quite different from his sober outlook. There was a wooden sidewalk called Last Chance Street running for a mile beyond the pier where Roosevelt sometimes sat. The boardwalk usually was more crowded with soldiers than the *Yucatan's* deck. Temporary canvas booths offered a variety of articles and services for men who had money. There were specialty foods such as sausages, pies, and lemonade. Soldiers could have their hair shampooed and shingled and their faces shaved. In front of some of the tents, "a gent in a white shirt and no collar was the bartender, and behind each bartender was a woman, maybe two."[53]

After two days the channel was fouled with the transports' wastes, so the boats were moved into the bay where men could swim in cleaner water. Mornings and afternoons, soldiers made sure no female tourist was in sight before they stripped to the skin, dove from the decks, and swam from ship to ship, visiting. One Rough Rider was injured by a sting ray, but the principal worry was sharks. Hundreds of men were in the water on June 10, when, according to Roosevelt, "one big fellow came so close that the men got hastily back into the boats."[54]

The hours passed slowly. Roosevelt at last organized exercises to fit the limited space. He had troopers line up in single file, hands on the shoulders of the man in front, and tramp around the deck singing "Ta-Ra-Ra-Boom-De-Ay."[55]

In the evening, men gambled. Cash was plentiful at first. Professional sharpers among the troopers on the *Yucatan* ran chuck-a-luck, craps, and other betting games without regulation by the officers. Many a man who woke up with a twenty, it was said, went to bed insolvent. A gambler from Raton, New Mexico, wrote, "I won $200 last night and $400 the night before. There is money to burn on this boat. If Charlie will only send me the dice he promised, I will be well situated." Dice whose fall could be predicted were in demand.[56]

Then, on the night of Saturday, June 11, the tugboat *Captain Sam* approached the *Yucatan,* and Shafter's aide told the transport's captain to be ready to depart for Cuba at a moment's notice. On Sunday morning, however, they were still in Port Tampa. Religious services conducted by the 2nd Infantry's chaplain were held on the afterdeck. Roosevelt stood prominently next to the cowboy choir.[57]

In the afternoon, Roosevelt gave one of his characteristically inspirational speeches. "It is a great historical expedition," he preached to the troopers, "and I thrill to feel that I am part of it. If we fail, of course we share the fate of all who do fail, but if we are allowed to succeed—for certainly we shall succeed if allowed—we will have scored the first great triumph in what will be a mighty world movement." He was talking about American expansionism.

Roosevelt claimed that "all the young fellows here only dimly feel what this means." He would have been surprised to read Rough Riders' diaries repeating portions of his talk word for word as their own entries. They even copied his credo, "We are confident the nearing future holds for us many chances of death and of hardship, as well as honor and renown."[58]

Troopers who did not attend Sunday services were also on deck, passing a Bible around. When the book was returned to its owner, he discovered that the men had been making cigarette papers of Revelations and Saint Paul's Epistles. The Acts of the Apostles also had been consumed as wrappers, except for the first four chapters.[59]

On Monday morning, the *Yucatan* received another order to stand ready. Roosevelt immediately entertained the troopers with his impromptu war dance. He was not disconcerted by the presence of the few Rough Riders who were real Indians.

In the afternoon, the ship's funnels began to emit dense smoke. The *Yucatan* hoisted her anchors and moved slowly ahead. Piers were lined with spectators under a burning sun, bands were playing, flags were flying, and the rigging of the ship was filled with soldiers who were cheering and shouting.[60]

Blinded by mists rising on the bay, the *Yucatan* sideswiped a sand bar. Thrown directly into the path of the transport *Matteawan*, she did not respond to her helm. Only 150 yards separated the two ships when the captain blew his whistle and dropped the starboard anchor to retard the forward drift. When the ships were seventy-five yards apart, the *Yucatan* came under partial control but could not stop until only three yards remained between the ships. In the bow of the *Yucatan* were stowed thirty-five hundred pounds of dynamite. The close call reminded the men that this was the "hoodoo day," the thirteenth of the month. The eeriness was compounded when the sailing of the transports was postponed again. No reason was given.[61]

At noon on Tuesday, June 14, the expedition was finally set to leave Tampa Bay with fifty-three ships, including thirty-five transports, four auxiliary vessels to aid in debarkation, and fourteen warships to serve as escorts. After giving the signal to start, Shafter's flagship, the *Seguranca,* pointed her bow down the bay to lead the column. There was no band, spectator, flag, or other display of excitement on the ships or on the shore.[62]

Allowing three days for the voyage, the V Army Corps was expected to arrive at Santiago de Cuba by Friday. The *New York Herald* predicted that the weekend would see the American flag flying over Santiago's forts. According to the *New York Times,* the landing would be "tantamount to the liberation of Cuba from Spain and the extinction of Spanish authority in the Western Hemisphere."[63]

Roosevelt was again enthusiastic. The rocking chair part of the war was over. The American Army at last was on its way to Cuba to support the U.S. Navy in destroying the enemy's Caribbean battle fleet.

Chapter 9
Looking Back
at the Uncivil Servant

Roosevelt believed that it was his Dakota experiences as boss stock-man that had prepared him to command the Rough Riders. His only other executive roles had been in his bureaucratic days from 1889 to 1898, when he had held three consecutive appointive desk jobs. He had been a maverick in every one of them.

Roosevelt's mentor Lodge was reelected to Congress in 1888. As a supplicant, the young man made his plea to "Dear old Cabot": "I would like above all things to go into politics but in this part of the State that seems impossible, especially with such a number of wealthy competitors." He was pressed for money and looking for steady work in the federal government. Otherwise, he lamented, he would have to continue to "go in especially for literature, simply taking the part in politics that a decent man should."[1]

Roosevelt's preference was to serve as James Blaine's assistant secretary of state. Coincidentally, Blaine was approaching Lodge for a recommendation for the same opening. When Lodge suggested Roosevelt, however, Blaine replied that "my real trouble in regard to Mr. Roosevelt is, I fear he lacks the patient endurance required in an Assistant Secretary. Mr. Roosevelt is amazingly quick in apprehension. Is there not danger that he might be too quick in execution? Matters are continually occurring which require the most thoughtful concentration and the most stubborn inaction. Do *you* think Mr. Roosevelt's temperament would give guaranty of that course?"[2]

Lodge knew an accurate analysis when he heard one. He left Blaine and turned directly to President Benjamin Harrison on Roosevelt's behalf. The sole managerial opening that had gone begging in the new administration was one of the three Civil Service Commissioners. The position was open only because the Republican party did not consider it worth selling. The pay was merely $3,500 a year, residence in Washington was required, and the task was clerical.[3]

Nevertheless, Harrison resisted appointing Roosevelt to the commission, deeming him "somewhat impatient for righteousness" and therefore a potential troublemaker. Harrison gave in only after Lodge exerted pressure in behalf of the Independent Republican constituency and Roosevelt expressly promised the president to defer to authority. On May 3, two weeks later, Roosevelt had his first federal office.[4]

The Snivel Service

At that time, nominees for president of the United States were chosen by political bosses who represented the principal industrialists and financiers. The election of a president was held partially in order to determine which political party would control selection of jobholders in the federal government.[5]

Independents, including Roosevelt, had crusaded against this disruptive spoils system for twenty years. In 1883, a Civil Service Reform Act was passed by Congress, but the executive branch did not obey the law. When Roosevelt was appointed, the commissioners had been tools of the administration in power for six years. Reformers ridiculed the Civil Service Commission as the "snivel" service.[6]

Roosevelt made Harrison's misgivings come true. He quickly decided upon a combination of action and publicity. After all, he thought, the Civil Service Act existed. The law had simply not been enforced. Carrying out the law was his sworn duty as commissioner, even though the target would be his own party.

"I have always tried to put myself where things were likely to happen," he asserted. From the start, he took the lead in the commission by strength of personality. He opened his office door to the press and to complainants who naturally were dismissed Democrats.[7]

In two weeks he was bragging that "there is personal satisfaction in having shown that I did not intend to have the Civil Service Commission remain a mere board of clerks." In six weeks he was advised that Harrison intended to fire him. Lodge soothed the president, but Roosevelt was unruffled. In lieu of thanks, he remarked dreamily, "What funnily varied lives we do lead, Cabot! We touch two or three little worlds, each ignorant of the others. Our literary friends have but a vague knowledge of our political work, and a number of our sporting and social acquaintances know us only as men of good family, one of whom rides hard to hounds, while the other hunts big game in the Rockies."[8]

In 1891, the House Committee on Civil Service supported Roosevelt's charges that Republican bosses had knowingly violated the Civil Service Act. Because of the blatant illegalities, independent Republicans did not support President Harrison in the 1892 election. Their votes were the margin of victory for Democrat Grover Cleveland's return to the presidency. Roosevelt was vindicated, but the Republican party that had appointed him was turned out of office because of him. Cleveland then offered Roosevelt a new term as commissioner under the Democrats. Roosevelt accepted. He had no place else to go.[9]

When politics palled, Roosevelt sought the company of other writers. He met Richard Harding Davis at a British Legation dinner and described Davis as "so entirely unintelligent, it was a little difficult to argue with him. The man has the gift of narration, but when it comes to breeding, even Kipling could give him pointers."[10]

The English author Rudyard Kipling was an artist's son and not a gentleman by Roosevelt's standards. Kipling wrote to John Hay, "Roosevelt would pour out projects, discussions of men and politics, criticisms of books, in a full-volumed stream, emphatic and enlivened by bursts of humor. I curled up on the seat opposite, and I listened and wondered, until the universe seemed to be spinning and Theodore was the spinner."[11]

Haroun el Roosevelt

By mid-1894, Roosevelt had tired of the Civil Service Commission. Democrats in power obeyed the law. In March 1895, he secretly sent word to the liberal Mayor William Strong of New York City that he would welcome appointment as one of the three city police commissioners. Strong ignored the application because he had doubts about employing such a domineering and combative person. The mayor was turned down by the first two men he approached, however, and the Good Government party—the "Goo Goos"—swung behind Roosevelt as soon as his availability became known. The appointment was made in April for five years at six thousand dollars a year—a substantial raise in pay.[12]

The beginning of Roosevelt's tenure on the Police Commission was a honeymoon with the people of New York. He overshadowed everyone else in city government, including the mayor. His acts, dress, and opinions were reported widely in the news, satirized amiably in cartoons, and analyzed favorably in editorials.[13]

Police reporters trusted Roosevelt. They described him as "the biggest man in New York to-day. He has more callers than the President." Good Government officials told him, "You are doing the greatest work of which any American to-day is capable."[14]

After one month, he started taking reporters on unannounced midnight tours to check on patrolmen. "We would sit in a doorway," journalist Jacob Riis wrote, "and time how long police talked to each other. Then Roosevelt would hurry up to them, always asking first, 'What is your post?' Some men were scared."

The friendly press dubbed him "Haroun el Roosevelt," after Haroun el Raschid, the caliph of Baghdad who had walked incognito at night through the city on the Tigris a thousand years earlier. Roosevelt confessed to Lodge, "I am amused at the way I have become for the moment rather a prominent personage, but I am not deceived. There is nothing permanent in my hold, politically."[15]

Not Responsible for Rooseveltism

Roosevelt was right about the lack of permanence. After eight short weeks on the job, he admitted, "I have run up against an ugly snag, the Sunday Closing Law [for saloons]. I have no alternative save to enforce it, and I am enforcing it."[16]

When he refused to relent, the Republican party stated publicly that it "was not in any way responsible for Rooseveltism." He was denied the right to speak as a Republican. The Civil Service Act which he had successfully enforced in Washington had been directed against politicians. In New York City, however, he outlawed family-style beer gardens on the one day workers had off. A friend commented that only "a great and glorious war, for which he yearns, might give effective outlet to his inclinations." In the absence of a war, however, there was no other job he really wanted. Mayor Strong's request for his resignation met with a firm refusal.[17]

Off-year elections for city council were held in November 1895. Although the reform ticket lost because of voter reaction against Roosevelt, Lodge comforted him: "The day is not far distant when you will come into a large kingdom. I do not say you are to be President to-morrow. I do not say it will be—I am sure it may and can be. You so underrate your political strength, I fear you will miss the opportunity which will give you a big place in national politics."[18]

At that point, Roosevelt's popularity in New York City plunged even farther. The problem was Roosevelt's deprecatory attitude toward his fellow commissioners. From the first day in office, he had announced commission decisions as "my policy." He ran the department as if he were leading a cavalry charge, whooping and hollering out in the open where the journalists could see him.[19]

The other commissioners had suffered his capers grudgingly while his success reflected well on them. When he was in trouble, however, so were they, and for actions they had not approved. They became vocal and obstinate. The resulting impasse on the commission was demeaning to Roosevelt.

In November 1896, the Good Government party was swept out of office in New York City, in favor of Tammany. Mayor Strong was beaten badly in the reelection race, and Roosevelt was again held accountable. His resignation on April 17, 1897, was termed "a glorious retreat." In fact, though, New Yorkers were heartily sick of his contentiousness and were glad to see him go.[20]

Chapter 10
Landing at Daiquiri

For the Spanish gunboats thought to be free in the Caribbean, many opportunities existed to attack the transports. Even so, Roosevelt was unconcerned. The gunboat commanders were leaderless as long as Admiral Cervera was trapped in Santiago harbor. What he did fret about was precisely where the *Yucatan* was heading and what might happen to prevent him from landing in time to take part in the assault on the Spaniards.

As usual, Wood was calmer than Roosevelt. He wrote, "I am beginning to pick up sleep and feel more like a Christian." To avoid the transport's crowded decks, he remained in his stateroom with officers of the regular 2nd Infantry, "cussing out things in general."[1]

Roosevelt turned to officers of the Rough Riders for companionship. He relished discussions with Capt. Allyn Capron, the regular army officer on loan to the regiment who "knew, so far as white man could know, Apaches' ways of thought." As a part-time westerner, Roosevelt envied this alleged insight into primitive minds. He also spent hours with Capt. Buckey O'Neill, the former mayor of Prescott, Arizona, who "was bent on gaining high military distinction by risking his life." O'Neill's resolve was the same as the aims of many Rough Riders, including Roosevelt.[2]

The first days on shipboard were so alike that the calendar lost meaning for the troopers. The *Yucatan* was placed safely in the center of the first line in the second of the three groups of transports. Surrounded by the other vessels, Wood thought of the expedition as

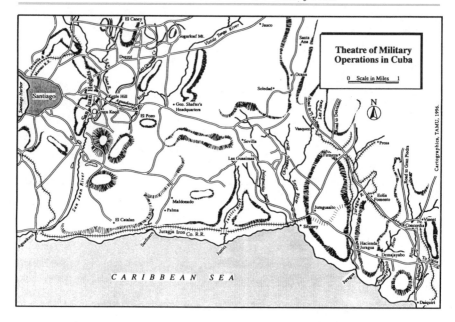

Theater of Military Operations in Cuba. Map adapted from R. A. Alger,
The Spanish-American War (New York: Harper and Brothers, 1901), facing
p. 182. Adapted by Cartographics Service Unit of the Department of
Geography, Texas A&M University.

placid: "painted ships in a painted ocean—imagine three great long
lines of steaming transports with a warship at the head of each line,
spaced 800 yards from each other on a sea of indigo blue as smooth
as a millpond. The trade wind sweeping through the ship has made
the voyage very comfortable." He did not venture into the hold where
the breeze did not reach.[3]

Roosevelt was more interested in the destination than in the details of the journey. He bragged that "we knew not whither we were
bound, Santiago or Porto Rico, but we were sure we would win."
According to the newspapers, the objective was Santiago, so the men
assumed that such a publicized terminus must be a ruse to fool the
Spaniards. They began to believe in Santiago after they found cargo
plainly stenciled "En Route to Santiago." They became positive days
later, when the *Yucatan* turned south around the eastern end of Cuba
and passed Guantanamo.[4]

During the day, the troopers' boredom was relieved by drilling, exercise, guard duty, dismounted cavalry schooling, and efforts to get clean. Each man had only one uniform. The seams had been infested with body lice since San Antonio. There was no way for the men to boil clothes on board ship, and they were annoyed when the soap designed for cold salt water did not lather. The Arizonans dragged their uniforms on ropes behind the ship to drown or dislodge the parasitic insects until the ship's propellers cut one of the ropes. The trooper whose uniform was lost stood naked and stunned while friends searched for replacement clothing for him.[5]

Because Roosevelt's valet was on another transport with the officers' horses, keeping his uniform clean was a problem for Roosevelt, too. He wrote to his younger son, "I have to get along without Marshall, so yesterday I had to wash all my clothes. They looked rather funny after I got through." Apart from the laundering, he was a seasoned ocean traveler. Some of the men were violently seasick or weakened by the heat in the hold. They lost weight quickly and fret-

Landing at Daiquiri. *Harper's Pictorial History of the War with Spain* (New York: Harper and Brothers, 1899), pp. 320–21.

ted about their ability to handle themselves physically in the land battles ahead.[6]

Troopers who were not bothered by the sea or the heat were hungry much of the time. Rations continued to be insufficient and repetitious, and prices for food from the officers' kitchen rose rapidly. The ship's baker was making two hundred dollars a day in tips from troopers for bread and pies. A few famished Rough Riders without money to pay for extras hid beside the door to the officers' dining saloon and grabbed plates being returned to the kitchen. They ate the scraps and licked the gravy.[7]

During the evening, the men listened to the 2nd Infantry band play concerts on the forward deck. After sunset, the ship became a blaze of illumination as men assembled in a festive atmosphere on the upper deck to sing such popular songs as "The Banks of the Wabash" and "Sweet Marie." At taps, the ship's lights were extinguished, except for a bolted-down soapbox standing on end at the stern. The open side showed a lantern flame for the transport behind to follow.[8]

Soon the men began to search the night skies for the fabled tropical constellation, the Southern Cross. On June 18, four days out of Tampa Bay, Roosevelt caught his first glimpse of the Cross overhead while he could still see the Big Dipper. He pointed the star configurations out to the troopers, but most were disappointed. They had expected brighter portents.[9]

Killed, Wounded, or Promoted

On the morning of Sunday, June 19, the Rough Riders' Chaplain Henry Brown of Arizona held nondenominational services on the afterdeck. The topic of his sermon was respect.

Next, Roosevelt gave an inspirational speech intended to reassure the Rough Riders about an unnecessary exposure to Spanish attack. The previous afternoon, Shafter had inexplicably ordered the *Yucatan* to drop out of the convoy and join the lonely *City of Washington* and her tow which were lagging far behind the long lines of protected ships. The commander's reasoning was incomprehensible to Roosevelt who privately categorized Shafter's order as "simply idiotic." This was an expression of disrespect that Chaplain Brown would have joined.[10]

The *Washington*'s great speed, demonstrated by her false start at

Tampa Bay, had been throttled back by tying her to a schooner filled with drinking water. The tow made the encumbered transport by far the slowest in the fleet. Guarded only by the gunboat *Bancroft,* the *Washington* and the wallowing dead-weight schooner had been alone on the open ocean, out of sight of the rest of the convoy. The *Yucatan* was now back with them, for no benefit anyone on board could see. The worried Rough Riders felt at hazard every time an unidentified ship came into view, yet neither Wood nor Roosevelt questioned the order publicly. This was no time to irritate Shafter.[11]

Correspondents on other transports were aware of the vulnerability of the *Washington* and the *Yucatan.* They could not understand why Spanish torpedo boats did not dash into the fleet and inflict mortal damage, at least to the stragglers like the *Yucatan.* The danger was most evident at night just before taps when the running lights were on and the men were singing. The correspondents concluded that no nation other than a weak and apathetic Spain would have permitted unmolested passage to such an exposed foe. Conversely, they believed that only an optimistic and vigorous people like Americans would have embarked upon the expedition at all.[12]

News dispatches reported only two alarms. A pair of Spanish gunboats approached the fleet boldly one morning, then turned tail when the cruiser *Osceola* steamed over to engage them. The second encounter took place on a foggy midnight when a Spanish torpedo boat unwittingly penetrated into the heart of the darkened fleet. The Spanish vessel was hailed in English and quickly responded with a breathless "Yes!" rather than "¡Sí!" before racing for the Cuban coast with American warships in vain pursuit.[13]

Humorous incidents experienced by the Rough Riders were few. Once the *Bancroft* raced alongside the *Yucatan* to inquire whether Roosevelt, the navy's favorite soldier, was on board. The sailors cheered when the lieutenant colonel took the rail to shout that he was indeed present. Later, another gunboat sped back to the *Yucatan* to offer armed support for Wood and Roosevelt. The notorious Rough Riders were falsely reported to have mutinied at being relegated to the rear of the convoy.[14]

At last, at 9 A.M. on Monday, June 20, anxieties about the destination of the voyage ended as the fleet came to a stop twelve miles off Santiago. When the *Yucatan* and the *Washington* steamed up to the end of the line, troopers could see the flagship *Seguranca* pulling close to shore. Shafter was on his way to a prearranged meeting with naval and insurgency officers to formulate a strategy for the Cuban landing.[15]

The transports had come through the journey without a casualty. There was bad news, however, in the loss of barges and tugs needed to unload soldiers, animals, artillery, and supplies at the beachhead. The fleet had started with an insufficient two barges and three tugs and arrived with only one of each.[16]

Except for the captain of the *Washington* who was intimidated by the angry response to his false start from Tampa, the independent captains in their privately owned transports had refused to tow auxiliary barges and tugs. Towing entailed uncompensated danger and was not required in the leases. One captain who was compelled to accept a tow because his lease was ambiguous was suspected of having cut the missing landing barge loose the first night out. The messenger tug *Captain Sam* had deserted. For reasons unknown, the third tug never arrived.[17]

The good news, Roosevelt observed, was that "we have just heard how a hundred marines landed and beat off a Spanish attack" at Guantanamo Bay, the first American foothold in Cuba. "We suppose," he added, "we shall land and have our share of the fighting right away."[18]

At the dining table in the officers' mess, an immoderate toast was drunk especially for the coming hostilities: "To the officers—may the war last until each is killed, wounded, or promoted." The troopers were more sentimental. "I cannot help but wonder," a Rough Rider from Harvard mused, "what the barren shore has in store for me, but am eager to land and get into a fight in order to find out what kind of stuff is in me." Privately, Roosevelt had the same concern.[19]

Hurrah for Erin Go Bragh

The transports drifted idly the rest of the day. They were still stationary on June 21. Roosevelt wrote that "far off on shore we can see the frowning Spanish batteries, and around us the great warships steam slowly, sullen and majestic." A sergeant from Tucson observed, "We can see Morro Castle as plainly as you can see San Xavier Mission from the schoolhouse."[20]

In the afternoon, the gunboat *Castine* approached the *Yucatan*.

Her commander yelled through a megaphone, "Be ready to land at daybreak. Good luck to you all, and regards to Colonel Roosevelt." Roosevelt was standing on the bridge with Wood and the *Yucatan*'s captain. He waved his hat, then broke into an Irish jig, chanting, "Shout hurrah/For Erin go bragh/And all the Yankee nation!" rather than his usual war whoops accompanying a mock Indian dance. Afterward he took Captain Capron by the arm, saying "Come along, you old Quaker. Let's go to supper."[21]

Once the time for the landing had been set for sunrise, the troopers were elated, too. They disassembled and oiled the carbines that had been supplied relatively late in their training. There had been no opportunity for target practice and most guns had not been fired.

Younger men listened respectfully to the *Yucatan*'s storytelling sailors as they warned against the perils of the Cuban jungle. Tarantulas were said to be particularly dangerous because their sting caused an uncontrollable desire to dance, followed by sudden stupor. More carefree men rolled up in their blankets on deck, enthusiastically singing, "I went to the animal fair/The birds and the beasts were there." Eventually they slept. A few introspective types lay by themselves. Like the Harvard alumnus, they had "often wondered how it would feel on the eve of a battle, but," they were surprised to discover, "it feels no different from anything else."[22]

Some troopers were still awake when the transport's bugler blew reveille at 3:30 the next morning as the ship steamed slowly eastward. A close, soft, sultry mist obscured the coast, despite a slight breeze. Fires blazing on shore were barely visible. Heavy gray clouds were reflected in the swells of a leaden sea while the men packed their blanket rolls for the landing. They fastened the wire bails of tin cooking cans to their loads and stowed three days' rations in extra haversacks. Mess kits, quart cups, and canteens filled with the ship's stale water hung from their belts.[23]

At five o'clock the sky brightened while the troopers ate the usual cold rations for breakfast. The morning turned cool, clear, and a little windy. The early light revealed a great semicircle of transports facing the village of Daiquiri from five miles at sea. Closer in were the warships, and between the two lines of vessels stood Shafter's flagship.[24]

Daiquiri was also the name of a narrow stream at the foot of the mountains, terminating in a slender half-moon cove eighteen miles east of Santiago. To some troopers, the scene was like the hills behind old San Francisco, while to others the mountains were replicas of the Catskills of New York State or the ranges of northern Arizona. There was a desire to make the coast's menacing aspect appear familiar, however remote the comparison.[25]

Machine shops of the Spanish-American Iron Company, a subsidiary of the Carnegie Corporation of Pittsburgh, were prominent in the village. A high steel pier ran into the bay for dumping ore into cargo ships. Beneath it was a shorter wooden dock of open construction forty feet long and twenty feet wide. The wood was smoldering. Between the pier and the shops, black smoke was rising from the huts of Cuban employees. Two sharp explosions were heard from gunpowder ignited in a flaming shed. The Rough Riders thought the bursts were cannon fire aimed at them.[26]

To the right of Daiquiri was Mount Losiltires, a thousand-foot sugar loaf. With a borrowed spyglass, Roosevelt could make out a blockhouse on the summit with a flagstaff at the side but no Spanish banner. Trenches had been dug halfway down the bluff and there was a barbed wire entanglement at the base. Additional blockhouses were on other high points.[27]

The defenses of Daiquiri were naturally strong and had been fortified against attack from the sea. For the invaders, the outlook was for a long, bloody day.[28]

See What We Can Do

At eight o'clock, three transports carrying Gen. Jacob Kent's infantry regiments broke away from the formation with an escort of warships to make a feint at a landing on the other side of Santiago. In a separate maneuver, warships also steamed nine miles toward Santiago. At nine o'clock, they began an unanswered bombardment of presumed shore batteries.[29]

At 9:40 A.M., the Spanish heliograph operator at a signal station on the mountain behind Daiquiri reported to Santiago headquarters that American naval broadsides had begun against fortifications guarding the village and the cove. The signal station was then abandoned.[30]

The Rough Riders had become impatient in the six hours since reveille, but now they were at the *Yucatan*'s rails cheering wildly. Explosions were spectacular as blockhouses took direct hits without responding. The mountainsides repeated the thundering salvos of the big guns while geysers of dirt spurted from shots into soft earth. Ragged figures ran from shelters.[31]

The officers on the *Yucatan*'s bridge watched shells strike for miles up the coast. Captain Capron was the son of an artilleryman. He acted like a happy boy. Roosevelt had arranged for the navy's target practice while he was assistant secretary. He was beaming with delight behind his spectacles. Turning to Capron, he yelled, "Now you see what we can do!" He identified with the gunnery officers on the warships.[32]

Forty-five minutes after the signal to start the attack had been fired from the flagship, the shelling ceased and Gen. Henry Lawton's infantry division began the invasion. The eager soldiers climbed down cargo nets hung over the transports' sides and stepped into one of fifty cutters manned by the navy's two hundred sailors who were assisting in the landing. Each boat held sixteen soldiers. Soon the sea was streaked with strings of these small boats pulled by steam launches. Lawton was in the first cutter, controlling operations. Field officers like Lawton who led advances were expected to suffer casualties, but Lawton survived this day.[33]

Roosevelt hopped around the bridge in great excitement while the landing boats proceeded toward the Cuban shore. He was trying to keep his spyglass trained on the tiny shapes the infantrymen had become in the distance. Although there was no sign of the enemy, he feared for the soldiers while they were in the small unprotected boats and when at last they reached the open beach. Suddenly Roosevelt shouted, "Why, they're forming by companies." All was well. If there had been any sign of Spaniards, the men would have been in battle lines, rather than getting ready to march.[34]

The First Hero

Weeks before the transports sailed from Tampa Bay, Navy Secretary Long had advised the War Department that no assistance would be given to the army for disembarkation in Cuba. Naval launches and seamen could not be diverted from the blockade of Cervera's Spanish fleet in Santiago harbor, even though the army would be in Cuba at the navy's urgent request. That was why the army had included landing barges and tugs in the plans for the expedition.[35]

At the June 20 meeting of the army, navy, and insurgent officers, however, the navy's decision had to be reversed. The army was woefully short of barges and tugs and had no experience with small boats. Aid from the navy was essential. Otherwise, Shafter's V Army Corps would have been unable to land in an organized manner.[36]

In addition, the navy had pointed out to Shafter before the voyage that every transport needed a naval officer on board and in command. This was not done, so at this vital moment in the landing, the uncontrolled civilian captains of the transports were refusing to move close enough to the coast to make disembarkation more convenient for the soldiers. The captains cited the possibility of accidental damage to the transports in the unknown cove and the danger from nonexistent Spanish guns as excuses for remaining five miles offshore.[37]

The penny-wise War Department had denied reimbursement to the shipowners for supplemental marine insurance to provide for dangers inherent in an invasion. Consequently, the captains would not assume any risk beyond acts that constituted standard coverage. When Shafter's *Seguranca* accidentally scraped the side of another transport at anchor, the captain took the flagship to sea to avoid further collisions. In doing so, he put the general out of touch with the invading army.

Roosevelt later complained that the landing was "higgledy-piggledy"—as chaotic as the embarkation. Like every Rough Rider, however, he wanted his regiment to be the first cavalrymen to reach shore and he intended to be the first in the regiment to land. He was ready to use his influence to push his troopers ahead regardless of orders, thereby contributing to the chaos.[38]

The handling of the *Yucatan* was an exception to the excessive caution shown by the captains of every other transport. The *Yucatan*'s handling was guided by a navy veteran impressed by Roosevelt's geniality as well as by his reputation in the service. When Roosevelt's former aide at the Navy Department, Lt. Alexander Sharp, Jr., drew alongside the transport in a converted yacht, the captain allowed Sharp's black Cuban pilot to board at Roosevelt's request. The pilot guided the *Yucatan* a mile and a half closer to the shore than any other ship ventured.[39]

Although the Rough Riders were not scheduled to land until the next day, the *Yucatan* was now near the wooden dock at Daiquiri.

Wood could see that the Spaniards must have been in a panic when they set fire to the wooden cribbing earlier in the morning, because the company's loyal native employees were able to douse the flames and save the structure. Wood gave the order to disembark at once. Roosevelt admitted that the Rough Riders jumped the gun, but it was "because we did not intend to be left out of the fighting if we could help it."[40]

The navy cutters were busy with scheduled assignments, so Wood employed the *Yucatan*'s few lifeboats to make the long-drawn-out landing. Burdened with blanket rolls, packs, and carbines, the troopers crawled down the companionway to the lower deck. There they eased into the small boats and the *Yucatan*'s seamen rowed them toward the wooden wharf. Roosevelt disembarked in the first boat, taking with him only the mackintosh he wore, the toothbrush in the cords of his hat, and the small amount of food he could tuck in his pockets.[41]

The heavy ocean swell made rowing difficult and the landing hazardous as waves smashed against the wharf. At the crest of a wave, the head of a man standing erect in a lifeboat just cleared the top of the dock. In the trough, his head was six feet below. Under Roosevelt's direction, each man threw his gun, roll, and pack onto the wharf. As the little boat rose on the waves, the man took a flying vertical leap for the decking. Troopers already on the dock grabbed him by the arms and pulled him up the rest of the way. There were close calls, but no Rough Rider missed his jump.[42]

The regular 10th Cavalry was disembarking at the same dock while Captain O'Neill was assembling his troop and collecting equipment. The black cavalrymen of the 10th also leaped from their cutters to the dock, but they were encumbered by the blanket rolls across their chests. When two of the enlisted men missed the top of the dock and were not caught, they fell into the sea and sank immediately, pulled down by the undertow. The men's officers and mates watched in horror.

Without hesitation, O'Neill dove into the powerful waves between the boat and the dock to try to save the two regulars, but they were gone. His "gallant but ineffectual attempt" reflected his resolve to strive for fame and was featured in the press. He was the first hero of the invasion.[43]

The horses belonging to Wood, Roosevelt, and Maj. Alexander Brodie of the Arizona contingent had been cared for by Roosevelt's servant Marshall on a different transport. Afterward, Roosevelt repeated what Marshall told him: "Our horses were being landed, together with the mules [in the pack train], by the simple process of throwing them overboard [because of the shortage of barges] and letting them swim ashore, if they could. Both of Wood's got safely through. One of mine was drowned. The other, little Texas, got ashore all right." The drowned animal had headed for the open sea. The troopers said that Texas "had more horse sense."[44]

The loss of the one mount took place away from the action and out of Roosevelt's presence. It was not important enough to be reported then. As the legend of the military Teddy grew over the years, however, the incident lent itself to enhancement.

Albert Smith was one of the Vitagraph cameramen Roosevelt had allowed onto the *Yucatan* in Tampa Bay. As Smith recalled the episode, Roosevelt's horses "were the only two" on the *Yucatan*. They "were brought up to be put ashore. The Colonel himself stood by, watching the operation. As the first animal was lowered, a huge breaker smashed against [the horse] and he was drowned. Roosevelt, snorting like a bull, split the air with one blasphemy after another, to the indescribable terror of the young crewmen."

"The disaster inspired a caution bordering on paralysis," Smith continued. "With the greatest care, they banded the second horse. Before each pull of the hoist, opinions were exchanged, until it seemed that if the animal did not collapse from the strain it would surely die of starvation. Even when Roosevelt bellowed, 'Stop that goddamned animal torture!' the crew did not quicken their movements. At last, lowered into receding water, the horse splashed safely ashore."

The Smith story, quotations and all, was accepted as true, preparing the way for the mythical military exploits to follow. The tall tale fit Roosevelt's eventual image better than the truth.

The Second Hero

The commanding officer of the Cavalry Division was Gen. "Fightin' Joe" Wheeler, a small man with a white beard. Roosevelt called him a "gamecock" who was eager for battle.

General Lawton of the regular infantry, who led the disembarkation, was soldierly and conservative while the volunteer Wheeler had a flair for the dramatic. He landed in Daiquiri on the heels of the first Rough Riders and at once noticed the empty flagstaff still standing alongside the Spanish blockhouse on Mount Losiltires. He instructed Wood, as the first cavalry colonel ashore, to have the Rough Riders' regimental flag flown from the pole.[45]

The Rough Riders had not been in one place long enough to possess an official standard. The Arizona troops, though, had a silk American flag that had been hand sewn by the women of Phoenix. Wood ordered Color Bearer Sgt. Albert Wright and Chief Trumpeter Clay Platt to climb the hill and raise the silken banner ceremoniously. The Rough Riders' chief surgeon, Maj. Henry LaMotte, went along as a lark.[46]

When the Stars and Stripes were run up the Spanish flagpole, everyone in the cove and on the shore could see the national colors and hear the trumpet. The American soldiers and sailors and the Cubans cheered. Ships joined in with blasts from their steam whistles.[47]

Inside the deserted blockhouse, the three Rough Riders found an abandoned bag of rice flour and a partly consumed bottle of Spanish wine. Wright and Platt were about to drink the wine when LaMotte grabbed the bottle from their hands. To their disgust, he smashed it against a rock. He maintained that the wine had been poisoned, although there was no way to know if he was correct.[48]

The flag-raising incident was featured in the press along with O'Neill's exploit. Surgeon LaMotte received credit as the second celebrity of the day. The episode annoyed Roosevelt and illogically embittered him against LaMotte. To Roosevelt, the regiment was his. Wood should have asked him to lead the ceremonial party. Raising the flag over the beachhead was exactly the type of ritual he would have relished. Instead, LaMotte had seized the glorious moment, adding prestige to the Rough Riders but usurping the role Roosevelt desired.[49]

The Help of the Cubans

During the voyage from Tampa Bay, Shafter had studied the details of a disastrous seventeenth-century English expedition against Santiago. The English soldiers had been decimated, not by Spanish arms but by sickness from a rainy-season march that was too long for the tropics. The American army still moved on foot, just as the Englishmen had hundreds of years earlier, so the same risk of disease was present.[50]

In the planning, Shafter rejected safe Guantanamo as the point of disembarkation. Guantanamo was too far from Santiago. He turned down a landing at Santiago itself as excessively dangerous. Santiago was too well defended. Shafter understood that the American public would not tolerate a Cuban assault entailing the number of deaths that had been common in his own Civil War experience. Daiquiri was the compromise he agreed to with the navy and the Cubans.[51]

The Spanish army in the province was commanded by Gen. Arsenio Linares. His defensive battalions were spread over thirty miles of Cuban coast, but at Daiquiri alone there had been four light field guns supported by three hundred Spanish soldiers in formidable blockhouses and trenches. The artillery and infantry unit had been strong enough to repel any attack from the sea.[52]

In the June 20 conference, however, Shafter had arranged to exploit the thin Spanish lines by having the navy feint at making various other landings early on June 22. By disguising the actual point of attack, he pinned the defenders down east and west of Santiago, so that the unit at Daiquiri could not be reinforced. At the same meeting he had asked for a thousand insurgents under Cuban Gen. D. Castillo to flush the Spanish soldiers out of Daiquiri on the evening of June 21.[53]

Documents found in the first blockhouse indicated that General Linares had ordered his officers to "annihilate" the Americans as they disembarked anywhere along the coast. All of the Spanish defenses faced the sea, ready for the American fleet. None protected against the insurgents on land. An insurgent attack from the unguarded rear forced the detachment of three Spanish companies out of their Daiquiri blockhouses and entrenchments before dawn on June 22. The ousted Spaniards retreated along the inland route to Santiago. Linares reported to his superiors that, "without the help of the Cubans" who captured Daiquiri, "the Yankees never could have disembarked."[54]

After the landing, Shafter's staff officers found that the Cuban success had rendered the stupendous naval bombardment unnecessary. The Spaniards had already retreated. The seven men killed or wounded by the warships' shells were all insurgents—Castillo's Cuban rebels, not Linares's Spaniards.[55]

In retrospect, it seems clear that Shafter had fooled Linares into believing that an American disembarkation farther west might flank Daiquiri. Linares had fooled himself, too. He had assumed that an overwhelming number of men were with Shafter, not just an audacious 16,887.[56]

A New Word

The last Rough Rider was lifted to the dock about 6 P.M. on June 22. He was one of six thousand American soldiers who landed at Daiquiri that day. Lawton had already organized his infantry division. He took the advance, marching his soldiers five miles westward toward Santiago before bivouacking along the trail for the night.[57]

As Roosevelt described the scene above Daiquiri, the Rough Riders "camped on a brush-covered flat, with jungle on one side, a fetid shallow pool on the other." He was a little put out. He had not had a chance to distinguish himself on this first day in Cuba. Two of his subordinates had made news, while he had little food, no extra clothing, and no tent or blanket to cover him. He had been told that one of his horses had drowned, and his servant was missing with the other.[58]

In comparison, the young troopers saw themselves "in a beautiful valley of grass between two ranges of hills bordering the Daiquiri river." The men built fires and rested. In the field they grouped with buddies rather than in squads. The first evening they heated and ate canned meat and beans with hardtack, coconuts, and chilies they gathered in the vicinity, and they drank coffee made with fresh river water. "We can hardly realize," they enthused, "that this delightful place is the dreaded tropical region of which we have heard so much."[59]

Shafter had ordered regimental cooking utensils to be left on board to speed the debarkation, so there was no easy way to boil the river water before drinking. They immediately came into conflict with President McKinley's primary rule on sanitation. The men also bathed in the river, their first opportunity in eight days really to cleanse themselves. The purity of the river water suffered downstream where other regiments drank and washed.[60]

There were scores of Cubans around Daiquiri. The Rough Riders viewed them as unattractive, slovenly, half-dressed, illiterate, and disconcertingly unworthy of compassion. The troopers kept to themselves. There was little for them to do but wait. For amusement, magazine photographer Burr McIntosh arranged tarantula races until one of the big venomous spiders bit him. He sterilized the puncture inside and out with raw rum and sweet Spanish wine found near the beach. The liquor was not poisoned and the tarantula's sting did not make McIntosh dance.[61]

Foreign attachés praised Shafter for his strategy. The disembarkation had been accomplished at little cost. The puzzling Spaniards had thrown away another chance to stop the expedition.[62]

American journalists were more censorious, not because of Shafter's planning but in reaction to his open distrust of all newspaper reporters. They emphasized the twenty small boats that had been smashed at the dock or upon rocks that studded the beach, the two drowned cavalrymen, and the horses and mules lost at sea.[63]

The successful landing at Daiquiri generated an addition to the American language—the "daiquiri," a cocktail composed of Cuban rum, lime juice, and sugar. Admiral Dewey had a mixed drink named after him to celebrate the victory at Manila Bay, but the popularity of his beverage was short-lived. The daiquiri was destined to endure.[64]

Chapter 11

Looking Back at Roosevelt's Navy

The naval officers on the warships escorting the transports that ferried Shafter's army to Daiquiri were lavish in their expressions of admiration for Roosevelt. As assistant secretary of the navy, he had been the principal civilian ally of the officers in readying the service for the Spanish-American War.

I Do Like a Fight

Lodge and Roosevelt had taken to "the stump" for McKinley during the presidential campaign in the fall of 1896. After McKinley's election, Roosevelt assumed that his successful efforts would get him off the New York City Police Commission and into a federal job. He settled his aspirations on the relatively modest position of assistant secretary of the navy, and he lobbied through everyone influential he could reach to induce the president to grant the appointment. He was afraid that McKinley neither liked nor trusted him, so he depended upon his mentor Lodge for the most effective support.[1]

While McKinley hesitated, pressure mounted on Roosevelt to resign as police commissioner. In consequence, his health suffered. After vigorous play with the children in one weekend at Sagamore Hill, his asthma returned. He bruised an arm chopping wood, banged his head on the mantelpiece, sprained a finger skiing, and strained a shoulder while carrying the skis home.

Then the stress was relieved. The only candidate for secretary of the navy was easy-going John Long, a former Massachusetts governor who was a Unitarian opposed to war. Lodge persuaded Long to name Roosevelt as his assistant secretary despite fears that "the job would not be enough for such a brilliant man." Long's hands-off managerial style avoided involvement in routine and technical matters. He needed an enterprising, hard-working administrator, and that description fit Roosevelt to a "T."[2]

Roosevelt's society friends told him that he would have a more congenial life in the capital than he had experienced in New York, but he shook his head doubtfully: "I don't know about that. I like a fight. I do like a fight." In truth, though, the other police commissioners had given him more fight than he could handle.[3]

In Washington, Roosevelt was reborn as a credible national figure during the deteriorating Caribbean situation in 1897. The "young Turks" among the naval officers welcomed him as he strode through the department "with quick, decisive footsteps, and eyes and teeth combining in a beam of friendly greeting. His forceful double grip imprisoned both hands. He never conveyed the remotest suggestion of self-importance."[4]

Without consulting Long, the brash Roosevelt promptly advised the Naval War College faculty that "no triumph of peace is quite so great as the supreme triumphs of war. The diplomat is the servant, not the master of the soldier." He added, "I divide the human race in two great classes, white men and dagoes, and under the term dagoes I include the entire diplomatic corps."[5]

He prodded Secretary Long for authority to develop strategies for the war he expected the navy to fight against Spain. Long made fun of Roosevelt's persistent bellicosity, but he did not forbid the planning. By the summer of 1897, the *New York Sun* was reporting that "Acting Secretary Roosevelt, in the absence of Governor Long, has the whole Navy bordering on a war footing." Roosevelt rushed to relieve the vacationing Long's apprehensions, saying that "statements that I am trying to arrogate to myself your functions render me uncomfortable." Having convinced at least himself of his rectitude, he went back to raising the war readiness of the navy in ways the relaxed secretary had never contemplated.[6]

One reason Roosevelt wanted a war was that it "would result at once in getting a proper Navy" for expansionist purposes. His idea was to have the country practice for a big war by going voluntarily into a little war in Cuba. America's past glory, he insisted, was the conquest of Indians and Latins in the West. Now, the future of the United States involved playing power politics on the world scene. He scorned McKinley's policies of compromise. He never criticized Long, though.[7]

With Mrs. McKinley and the cabinet still away from Washington in September, McKinley invited social contacts with Roosevelt, who described one conversation to Lodge: "I told him when war began, I would go. He asked me what Mrs. Roosevelt would think of it, and I replied that both you [Lodge] and she would regret it, but this was one case where I would consult neither. He laughed, and said he thought he could guarantee I should have the opportunity I sought if war by any chance arose."[8]

Roosevelt also wrote a second time to Colonel Greene of the New York State Militia: "We may have trouble with Spain. If so, let me know if I can go as one of your majors. I am going somehow. P.S. I have recommended a dry dock board; one member will be George C. Greene."[9]

George was the colonel's brother. Roosevelt was willing to bribe Greene to get in the state militia, but there was no appointment for him. The assurance from McKinley was his only hope for a commission.[10]

The Maine Exploded

The battleship *Maine* exploded in Havana harbor during the evening of February 15, 1898. Roosevelt announced the next morning, "I would give anything if President McKinley would order the fleet to Havana to-morrow. The *Maine* was sunk by an act of dirty treachery on the part of the Spaniards."[11]

In his off-hours, Roosevelt was deeply engaged in secret scheming with Lodge and Capt. Alfred Mahan, the leading advocate of a big American navy. The three believed that McKinley and Long were not allowing Roosevelt enough authority to prepare the navy for the Spanish war. Their clandestine plan was to get Roosevelt set for any opportunity he might have to upgrade the navy's readiness when McKinley and Long were out of the way.[12]

On the morning of Friday, February 25, Long was at his desk when he felt ill. At 1 P.M. he instructed Roosevelt not to take "any step affecting the policy of the administration without consulting the

President or me." He then designated Roosevelt as acting secretary and went home for a restorative nap.[13]

Roosevelt required only the four hours left in the afternoon to put the already formulated plan into effect. When Lodge arrived at Roosevelt's office at the end of the day, he found the acting secretary sending a last cable in code. Dewey and the Asiatic squadron were ordered to sail "to Hong Kong. Keep full of coal. In the event of declaration of war with Spain, your duty will be to see the Spanish squadron does not leave the Asiatic coast, and then offensive operations in the Philippine Islands." The cable was the key to the capture of the Philippines.[14]

Long's next diary entry was inscribed the following evening: "I had a splendid night and return to the office. I find that Roosevelt, in his precipitate way, has come near causing more of an explosion than happened to the *Maine*. He seems loyal, but the devil seemed to possess him yesterday afternoon. It shows how the best fellow—and with splendid capacities—is no use if he lack a cool head." McKinley and Long rescinded more than half of what Roosevelt had done. They never countermanded Roosevelt's cable to Dewey, though.[15]

To avoid the need for a rebuke, the softhearted Long said that Roosevelt was temporarily out of control emotionally because his wife and a child were ill. He did not suspect that there had been a conspiracy with Mahan and Lodge to speed war preparations, but he took no more afternoon naps.[16]

Nevertheless, Roosevelt was now popularly regarded as "the round peg in the round hole for once." *Life* magazine asked readers to "imagine Secretary Roosevelt seated at a table, sampling gunpowder by the taste, buying new ships, calling home vessels, buying coal, enlisting new men, sorting out the right men and getting them in the right place. We may be sorry for the President, or for Secretary Long, but we are not a bit sorry for Assistant Secretary Roosevelt. He must be having the time of his life." No man in Washington, according to *Life,* was "half as busy as Mr. Roosevelt. The proof is that we hear hardly anything of Mr. Roosevelt nowadays. He is too busy."[17]

Life did not mention the deep split in the Navy Department over policy. Roosevelt claimed that he was "suspected by the administration because of my dissent from their views about what our honor and dignity demand in the settlement of the Cuban question." He was in his familiar stance, feeling that he was at odds with his superiors and believing that his job was in jeopardy.[18]

My Notch on the Stick

While he was publicly "tasting gunpowder," Roosevelt was privately defending his decision to volunteer for army service. He wrote to the *New York Sun*'s Paul Dana, explaining himself:

> *If I go with the Army, my family and friends are against it, and the Secretary and the President express great reluctance at my going. But I disregard their advice. My work here has been mainly preparation. In time of war it is too late to build up.*
>
> *Secondly, I go because I wouldn't be true to the ideal I set if I didn't go. For two years I have been urging that we put Spain out of Cuba, and if there ever was a righteous war it will be this. But I don't expect military glory other than in the honorable performance of duty. Moreover, though I have a wife and six children, inasmuch as I have never been in a money-making pursuit, my loss would not materially affect their income.*

He took a similar tack while confiding in a friend:

> *If I am able to go to Cuba I certainly shall. I shall not go for pleasure. On the contrary, I like thought, and action, and it will be bitter to leave my wife and children; and while I could face death with dignity, I have no desire to go out into the everlasting darkness.*
>
> *I appreciate that diseases rather than the enemy's rifles will be what we face, but a man's usefulness depends upon his living up to his ideals. One of the commonest taunts directed at men like myself is that we are armchair jingoes. My power for good would be gone if I didn't live up to doctrines I preach.*[19]

Later, he admitted that "I would have turned from my wife's deathbed to have answered that call. It was my chance to cut my little notch on the stick that stands as a measuring rod in every family." He confessed that "he did not wish to have to give excuses to his children for not having fought in the war," the way his father had apologized for himself.[20]

He was thirty-nine years old, no longer the young phenomenon. He was living in a small house on N Street with his ailing wife and four children. The two older children had been sent to their aunt in New York City to protect them from the effects of his nervousness. He had been touted for the presidency for more than a decade. He considered himself to be fit for the office, but he thought that chance was passing him by.

Then Congress enacted the legislation authorizing the cowboy cavalry. Through McKinley and Alger, he was offered the command of the first volunteer cavalry regiment. At last his heritage and experience were merging with his ambition. The combination would lead him to behave as he did at San Juan Hill.

Chapter 12
March to Siboney

There was no commercial stevedore at the Daiquiri beachhead on June 22. After the last Rough Rider had leaped acrobatically onto the wooden dock and gradually recovered his land legs, Wood began organizing the troopers into teams to unload arms, supplies, and rations from the *Yucatan*.

Through the evening and into the early part of the night, the Rough Riders used the ship's lights to illuminate the deck area while they cheerfully lifted cargo from the holds, handed boxes and bags down into the small swaying lifeboats, and ferried the matériel to the beach. From there the loads were carried on the men's backs an eighth of a mile to the camp. Horses and mules did not become available until the following day.[1]

When the hoisting and lugging were finally suspended for the night, the troopers did not have the energy to seek high ground or to erect shelters. They stretched out on tent halves in the open, fully dressed under blankets with carbines ready at their sides. The earth was softer than the wooden bunks or the decks of the transport had been, but the air was cold and damp. A heavy dew slowly penetrated the canvas beneath them.

The officers had been sleeping on mattresses, so the transition was more difficult for them. Wood used his slicker as a ground cover. He had no blanket because his bedding was among the hundreds of bundles still on the beach. The former Fifth Avenue Boy, Hamilton Fish, noticed Wood's discomfort and gave up his own rest to search in the dark along the shore for Wood's pack. His notoriety as a carouser had been superseded by his wholehearted acceptance of responsibility as a sergeant.

By sleeping on the ground, the men unwittingly exposed themselves to nocturnal fauna. One trooper was awakened by a hard body sidling rapidly across his chest. He held his breath until the movement ended and then sprang to his feet, yelling in such terror that he awakened the camp. Lighted matches disclosed a huge land crab that had crawled over him while it was foraging for food. Throughout the first night, sentries frequently mistook the oversized crustaceans for creeping Spanish guerrillas and fired at rustling sounds. No one was wounded.[2]

When reveille was blown at 4 A.M., the invasion took on the air of a picnic. Some men still were trying to shake off the swaying motion of the sea, induced by more than two weeks on the transport. Others found and drank Spanish wine. Wobbly or not, they cooked breakfast and joyfully greeted their first full day on the lush mysterious island where each of them fully intended to win military fame.[3]

The hardier men gathered ripe coconuts to drink the milk and eat the meat. A few troopers went down to the river for a second bath, diverting the water through an improvised sand sluice in a primitive attempt to filter the dreaded yellow-fever germs. Soap was scarce.[4]

After breakfast the weather became warmer. The troopers looked forward to staying in the camp for at least a few days, so they constructed elaborately thatched huts using palm leaves to block out the sun while letting in the breeze. Soon, however, they were directed to resume their unloading chores. Speed was thought to be essential if the Rough Riders were to be ready to fight in the first battle. They had to remove the Colt rapid-fire guns quickly from the *Yucatan*, despite the painstaking handling required to balance large heavy objects in small boats.[5]

Soldiers from other regiments continued to land at the dock or to splash happily through the surf to the beach. Ten thousand men were still waiting to disembark. The Cuban troops marching westward on the trail were to support General Lawton's Infantry Division at the front near Siboney, the next village of size along the coast. The Rough Riders laughed indulgently at the rebels' appearance. The insurgents

Gun-Detail of Colt Automatic Rapid-Fire Gun, Troop K. Marcus Wright, *Leslie's Official History of the Spanish-American War* (Washington, D.C.: 1899), p. 323. No. 1. Trooper William Tiffany; no. 2. Bugler Emilio Cassi; no. 3. Provo Sergeant Cash; no. 4. Second Lieutenant Horace K. Devereaux; no. 5. Trooper George L. Smith; No. 6. Sgt. R. Ronalds; No. 7. Trooper Errig; no. 8. Sgt. S. G. Devore; no. 9. Cpl. Joe Stephens; no. 10. Trooper Allen M. Coville; no. 11. Corporal Maxwell Norman; no. 12. Corporal Henry W. Bull; no. 13. Trooper B. F. Daniels; no. 14. Trooper W. J. Clay; no. 15. Surgeon Henry H. Thorp; and no. 16. Trooper Lie.

had appropriated pieces of the discarded American uniforms. One black Cuban proudly wore the heavy overcoat of an artilleryman. Sweat poured down his otherwise naked body.

Giving a Glorious Death

Gen. Joseph Wheeler was a deceptively mild-looking little old man. After completing his military education at West Point, he had been a feared leader of the Confederate cavalry for two years, despite his appearance. Later he represented Alabama in Congress for seven terms. He was a rarity among American generals in Cuba. Most had earned commissions fighting for the North on Civil War battlefields, without having attended military school.[6]

At first the Rough Riders thought that Wheeler was suited only to advise Shafter in a staff capacity, not to command the division. They should have recognized right away that he was a kindred spirit. His enduring dream for himself was not of legislative debate or of staff meetings, but rather of leading a cavalry charge once more. The Spanish-American War would be his last chance.

Despite Wheeler's antique credentials, McKinley had made him a two-star major general of volunteers, both as a sop to the Democratic South and because of his influence in Congress. On the expedition, he ranked second only to Shafter. Immediately after his appointment, he confessed to newspapermen gathered at his home that "it would be worth 15 years of my life to die on a battlefield." He was determined to have the Cavalry Division in the van at the opening fight, draw first blood, and if necessary, spill its own. He sounded like a tinier and more aged Roosevelt with a southern drawl.[7]

Roosevelt agreed that Wheeler was elderly for active leadership, but he approved of the general's motivation. Journalists who knew Wheeler well were more critical. "That's the trouble," they warned, "with appointing a man like Joe Wheeler to such an important command. He will have 20,000 young men under him who may not want to lose 15 years of their lives to give Wheeler a glorious death."[8]

In contrast to a volunteer like Wheeler, Brig. Gen. Samuel Young who headed one of Wheeler's two brigades was part of the regular army. He was, though, of the same reckless stamp as his commander. Young claimed that his predestined role in the war was to kill Spaniards, be killed, or both. He had told Roosevelt in May, while the two were in Washington, that if the Rough Riders were able to get into the expeditionary force, he would guarantee them a place at the front and in the earliest action. The time for fulfillment of his promise was at hand.[9]

Wheeler and Young knew that Shafter's intent was to allow the men two or three days' rest after the debilitating experiences of the voyage, the landing, and the ongoing stevedoring. Shafter had given the advance to Lawton, his most responsible career general. He sent Lawton's infantry division to secure the waterfront at Siboney, instead of ordering the immediate attack on Santiago that the American newspapers had forecast.[10]

After Lawton avoided a halfhearted Spanish attempt at an ambuscade by deploying scouts generously and by firing a few random shots, he occupied undefended Siboney early in the morning on June 23. He had been instructed by Shafter to remain in Siboney until the rest of the soldiers, supplies, wagons, and pack trains were unloaded in Siboney harbor, rather than at the more distant Daiquiri.[11]

The portion of General Kent's infantry division that had not been engaged in the naval feint westward was ordered to support Lawton by camping behind him. Wheeler's dismounted cavalry division was retained near Daiquiri to patrol the roads on foot to prevent unexpected attacks from the rear by Spanish guerrillas. The patrol was a standard cavalry function, assigned as if the Rough Riders were still mounted.[12]

Wheeler knew that if the cavalry division continued in the rear, he would be the last to see action, not the first. Lawton's infantry in the advance would have the opportunity for the initial military glory. Accordingly, Wheeler left the cavalry's Daiquiri headquarters in the morning, taking the trail to Siboney with a squad of scouts. On the way, the general observed strong defensive locations where the Spaniards might have successfully resisted Lawton's advance. The enemy had fallen back without a fight, however, just as they had done before. Wheeler was not surprised.[13]

In Siboney he learned that a detachment of Cuban rebels had been repulsed at daybreak by a strong force of Spanish infantry well entrenched at a fork on a trail about four miles inland from Siboney. Lawton told Wheeler that the Spanish resistance inland was not significant. When he was ready, he planned to march his men on the alternate trail along the seacoast and flank the Spaniards. The defenders would then have to retreat into Santiago or risk being cut off.[14]

Wheeler saw the situation differently. He wanted a fight, not strategy. Spaniards standing firm in a vulnerable location sounded like a dare aimed directly at him. They were waiting for him, he thought, in exactly the kind of defensive position he wanted them in. For him, the only question was how he could avoid open disobedience of Shafter's instructions to merely patrol Daiquiri and at the same time get his cavalrymen past Lawton's sentries to engage the Spaniards at the inland fortification before they could escape. The Spanish defeat of a few Cubans at the fork did not influence his arrangements. Rebels were brush fighters, not trained soldiers. They never would attack a fortification from the front the way Americans under his leadership would.

Besides, Wheeler did not consider Spaniards to be good soldiers. He believed that they were cowards by reason of race. His bias had been confirmed. Their navy had been afraid to attack a straggling convoy and their army had run at Daiquiri and Siboney. He was certain that they also would flee from the fortified fork. Hopefully they would not retreat until after the cavalry hit them with the first major battlefield attack of the Santiago campaign.

Moreover, Wheeler considered Shafter to be weak. If Wheeler succeeded in the charge at the fork, he anticipated that Shafter would automatically cover him for the lack of instructions to take the advance from Lawton. After all, if he dislodged the Spaniards he would be a national hero and beyond censure. If he failed, he might forfeit the fifteen years of his life that he had offered and be gloriously dead. For him, the chance was worth taking.[15]

At that point, neither Shafter nor Lawton had any idea of Wheeler's wayward schemes. Shafter was still on the flagship outside the Daiquiri cove. Grossly overweight, he had an attack of gout and suffered from the heat even on shipboard. He did not intend to have himself moved to a hotter and less comfortable tent on the tropic island until the men had the transports completely unloaded so that the attack against Santiago could commence. In the interim, he trusted the veteran Lawton to retain control. He did not realize that spunky little Wheeler, who outranked Lawton, desperately wanted to recreate his exciting past.

Wheeler's break came when he received an instruction from Shafter that allowed at least part of the cavalry division to move in the right direction to implement his plan. "Send Colonel Wood's regiment to near Juragua," Shafter ordered on June 23, "to have three companies patrol the road to that place." Juragua was on the coast halfway between Daiquiri and Siboney.[16]

In Wheeler's elastic view of the map, however, Juragua was not a tiny village but a way westward. He interpreted the order loosely as allowing him to probe anywhere there might be Spaniards between

Daiquiri and Santiago. Later on the same day, a more alert Shafter reconsidered the opening he had given Wheeler. He wisely revised the instructions by ordering the cavalry division to return to Daiquiri. Wheeler claimed that he received the command too late to comply with it.[17]

Meanwhile, at the improvised Rough Rider camp near Daiquiri, the men ate their midday meal of the bacon and beans they had brought from the *Yucatan*. Troopers who had abandoned their haversacks received rations from the regimental quartermaster. Generals Wheeler and Young invited Wood to eat with them. Their menu featured canned salmon flavored with lime juice and fresh cauliflower. Cuban General Castillo whose part in the landing had been vital was also present, but the other regular officers in the cavalry division were not told about the meeting.[18]

The conference was held in the division's new field headquarters, the abandoned hut of the Spanish officer who had been in command at Daiquiri. Wheeler's failure to have the hut burned as possibly disease-infested ignored another health rule.

Young played the dissembling game along with his commander. He falsely reported to Wheeler that there was no campsite near Daiquiri with palatable water. Wheeler then authorized Young to march his brigade four or five miles toward Siboney to find a suitable camp. Wheeler also told Wood to move the Rough Riders westward with Young, in nominal compliance with Shafter's order. The rest of the matériel on the *Yucatan* would be abandoned.[19]

Wheeler's choice of cavalry regiments for the attack on the inland fortifications was governed by his twin needs, speed and secrecy. His 2nd Brigade commander, Gen. S. S. Sumner, had not yet disembarked from the transport that had steamed to the far side of Santiago as a primary ruse. Sumner would not be available in time. Some of his troopers never did get to the front.

That left Wheeler with just the three regiments in Young's brigade. Two of these units were composed of regulars and the lieutenant colonels in command of them were professionals. Wheeler had to proceed cautiously, because no career officer could be trusted to follow a volunteer unhesitatingly if the action might be in disregard of Shafter's orders.

In addition to Young, only Wood could be counted on as a risk-taking regimental commander who shared Wheeler's entrepreneurial vision of the war. Wheeler thought that Wood was a remarkable executive who had performed miracles in organizing the Rough Riders and getting them to the Cuban shore ahead of Wheeler himself.

Roosevelt had no role in the planning. He was prominent in the press, but so far he was merely Wood's subordinate. He was not privy to Wheeler's plans. When Wood returned from the conference with the three generals, he told Roosevelt only that the Rough Riders were to commence marching toward Siboney. Everyone was tense, though. The troopers sensed that a fight might be imminent.

The March Started

Before the Rough Riders left camp, the regimental quartermaster issued them an extra day's rations. He also handed out picks and shovels carried to Cuba on the flagship for digging trenches. The men received the implements willingly as another indication that they were close to battle.[20]

Roosevelt had his little stallion Texas back, but he had no saddle and his servant Marshall was absent. The prospect of military action brought on his old stomach upset. He was edgy and he showed it. He announced that he had no intention of either walking to Siboney like a trooper or riding bareback like an Indian. His testiness transformed finding a saddle into a crisis and his anguish was loud enough to unsettle everyone near him.[21]

New York Journal correspondent Edward Marshall was reminded of Roosevelt's turbulent days at the end of his tenure as police commissioner when "his wrath was boiling and his grief was heart-breaking." Marshall had a saddle but no horse, so he lent his saddle to relieve Roosevelt's distress.[22]

Wood had regained his two horses. He loaded the extra animal with personal baggage that Fish had located. Then he discovered that the regimental pack train was down to 16 mules from the 189 that had left San Antonio. They were all that had managed to swim ashore from the transport on their own and then had avoided conscription by other regiments or by the Cubans. Moreover, in the absence of O'Hara, there was no one in the regiment who would chance missing the fighting by admitting to being an experienced mule skinner. The assigned drivers were having difficulty with even the standard knots used to tie down the animals' packs.[23]

Because Wood was rushing to meet his exhilarating commitment to Wheeler and Young, he abandoned the mule train with its supplies, extra ammunition, and medical chests. To compensate, he had popular Assistant Surgeon Bob Church, the former Princeton athlete, take along some extra first-aid pouches. Surgeon LaMotte had injured his foot in the descent from the flag raising on Mount Losiltires. He was told to remain in Daiquiri with the medical chests and the mules. The Rough Riders' march toward Siboney then started at 1:30 in the afternoon on June 23.[24]

As a retired naval officer, LaMotte had applied for sea duty when war was declared. Secretary Long denied the request because of LaMotte's age. Instead, Long wrote LaMotte a recommendation to Roosevelt for a medical opening in the Rough Riders. When Roosevelt arrived in San Antonio, dissension existed among the doctors. Relying upon Long and well predisposed toward navy personnel, Roosevelt resolved the dispute by offering LaMotte the post of surgeon of the Rough Riders, sight unseen. LaMotte replied that he "believed it was his duty" to accept the offer, but the troubles were worse with him than they had been without him. He was too old for a regiment that made a fetish of youth, too set in formal naval ways, and too contentious. He was generally disliked.[25]

LaMotte was better with mules than with people. Once the regiment marched off, he took charge of the pack train as a matter of conscience. If there was to be a battle, he did not see how he could permit the Rough Riders to be without medical and surgical supplies. Otherwise, wounded men would die needlessly. Besides, he was chief surgeon. He had to go forward, against orders and whether or not he was welcome. This was a compulsion that should have won the doctor appreciation from Roosevelt for his sense of duty and courage, if not his manners.[26]

While LaMotte was retying the knots in the ropes on each mule, he found that despite the shortage of animals, one of the mules was carrying the cooking utensils of the officers' mess and some supplementary edibles. He dropped them on the ground and replaced them with medical and surgical chests.

Five more of the sixteen mules had officers' baggage, bedding, and tents on their backs. To favor his sprained foot, he dumped one load at random so he could ride bareback with a rope halter. Then he led the pack train toward Siboney. He was far behind Wood and the regiment.

The cavalry's march was strung out more than the transports had been on the voyage from Tampa Bay. The troopers were vulnerable to Spanish harassment, but attacks never came. Militant General Wheeler and his staff were far ahead. They rode rapidly through Juragua. Avoiding Lawton in Siboney, they turned inland to scout the position of the Spanish infantry entrenched at the fork. When Wheeler was satisfied that he had the terrain in mind, he returned to Siboney so as to be able to confer secretly again with Young, Wood, and Castillo in the evening.[27]

Next in the procession toward Siboney was Wood with the two squadrons of Rough Riders. Despite Shafter's original orders, Wood passed through Juragua, riding his horse steadily at the head of the plodding troopers. Roosevelt rode at the tail of the regiment, accompanied on foot by the reporters who gravitated toward him. Although Roosevelt professed an aversion for the yellow press, Marshall of the *Journal* and Crane of the *World* were with him, as well as McCready of the *Herald* and the photographer McIntosh. They were not quite as famous a group as Roosevelt would have liked. Richard Harding Davis, for one, was missing.[28]

The Rough Riders were followed by General Young in his sham search for an acceptable campground. With Young were two squadrons of regulars from the other regiments in his brigade, the white 1st and the black 10th. The two regular lieutenant colonels were still in Daiquiri.[29]

Following Young came the Fifth Avenue Boy Pvt. Hallett Alsop Borrowe and the Rough Riders' dynamite air gun. With infinite pains, Borrowe had supervised the unloading of the big gun from the *Yucatan* onto an array of little lifeboats, so as to have it available for the coming battle. Unfortunately, Private Borrowe, his small squad, and the gun were halted by a staff officer who could not understand why such a heavy armament with dynamite shells was needed for the routine patrol he knew Shafter had ordered for the Juragua roads. He turned the gun back to Daiquiri, despite Borrowe's pleas.[30]

At the end of the advancing column was LaMotte's pack train.

El Camino Real

The Rough Riders were in full marching order. Every man shouldered his blanket roll, a hundred rounds of ammunition, and his carbine. Rations were stuffed into the remaining haversacks. One man in two also carried the entrenching pick or shovel that threw his whole load out of balance.

The trail the troopers took was marked *El Camino Real,* the King's Road. It was shown on the map as a double line designating a broad passage suitable for vehicles. The troopers thought the name must have been given in jest. They were stepping out on a "road" that in places was scarcely wide enough for two men to walk abreast. The narrow trail was no better than a wagon track in the American Southwest. The men could see cracks in the hard dirt, indicating that the sunken portions were rivers of mud after heavy rains.[31]

Worse, the tropical air this afternoon was close and oppressive. The heat was intense as the debilitated troopers struggled up and down steep slopes in their first exposure to walking in the jungle. The lack of training on foot left them unfit for long marches. Rolls and packs shifted and slipped around aching backs as if alive. The burdens caught in branches of overhanging brush and caused men to stumble into neighbors or fall to the ground. In occasional open areas the sun was brilliant and the weight men carried seemed to grow from the regulation forty-five pounds to tons. The only boon was the army shoes that looked clumsy but proved to be easy on the feet.[32]

The troopers were in no physical condition to march at the stiff pace Wood set. Yet, during a ten-minute rest period for the Rough Riders midway in the hike, General Young kept his two squadrons of regulars moving right through the volunteers' lines. He still claimed to have found no site suitable for a camp and he was rushing the regulars along before he could be stopped.[33]

When the Rough Riders resumed their march, they waded across a wide, shin-deep stream. Wood sent word back to the troopers that if they did not foul the water by stirring up mud on the bottom, they could fill their canteens and drink. After replacing the little water they had with fresh water, they started on the trail again. Around the first bend they heard shouting and then they saw a great splashing coming from a troop of the 10th Cavalry crossing the same stream upriver. Some were urinating in the water. The Rough Riders poured the contents of their canteens on the ground, leaving themselves dry despite the heat.[34]

Wood was as anxious to keep up with Young's squadrons as Young was to get to Siboney undetected. Both columns had to halt more often in the second half of the march, though, to minimize heat prostration. Soon the mounted Wood and Capron who walked behind him as the senior captain began passing regulars who had fallen exhausted by the side of the trail. Compared to what Wood saw as Young's callousness, he claimed to have taken "the extreme and great care" of his troopers "necessary to get the men into camp in good condition."[35]

The Rough Riders told a different tale. Seeing regulars incapacitated by the heat and exertion was disheartening. Some of the troopers began to discard pieces of their equipment. First went the apparently useless picks and shovels. That was not enough, however, to relieve the excruciating pain they felt in their legs and backs as they stumbled along the winding hilly trail in the growing dusk, through seemingly endless forests, across more streams without bridges, and past deserted estates with magnificent but untended flowers.[36]

Soon Roosevelt at the end of the column was riding through a litter of blanket rolls and tunics being discarded by the panting Rough Riders. After that came haversacks, cans of meat and tomatoes, and extra suits of underwear. A few troopers kept only the clothes they wore, their carbines, and their ammunition. Those were the essentials for fighters, they said.[37]

Next, man after man dropped out of the ranks, overcome by the heat just as the regulars were. Four or five were on the ground in convulsions, unconscious or delirious. Nearly half the men were abandoned along the trail and had to fend for themselves as Wood pressed on. He continued to ride at a constant speed, regardless of the physical cost to his stumbling troopers.[38]

Roosevelt did not protest the pace of the march or the effect on the weakened Rough Riders he rode past after they had fallen out of formation. Instead he praised Wood for "his energy" that made him "bound to get ahead of other regiments." Roosevelt confessed that the afternoon's intense exertion "was easy for me. I was on my horse, but it was a hard march for the men."[39]

By the 1970s, the mythology surrounding Roosevelt required him to have been as compassionate as a priest and as brave as a lion. According to the revised story, "At the rear, leading his horse, came Roosevelt. All efforts to get the Lieutenant Colonel to mount failed. 'I don't want to ride while my men are walking,' he repeated stead-fastly."[40] This was another improvement on Roosevelt's own reports at the time.

The Advance of the Army

Young rode ahead of his regulars and met Wheeler in Siboney at 7:30 P.M. He told Wheeler the continuing tall tale that he wanted a more elevated site for pitching the men's tents than any location he had observed so far.[41]

Wheeler replied disingenuously that there really was such a high place. He had seen it. The location was unique, situated at a fork in an inland road, but presently it was occupied by Spanish soldiers who had fortified the position. "General Wheeler," Young responded, "give me permission to go out there." In addition to gaining the re-markable encampment, he suggested that marching to the fork would provide a reconnaissance in force to learn the position of the main Spanish army and its movements.[42]

According to Young, Wheeler had no objection. The little south-erner brought Cuban General Castillo into the discussion and then decided that he would do more than merely gather information about the Spaniards. He would attack the Spanish fortifications at the fork with the troops he had at hand as early as possible the next morning, June 24. The decision was no surprise to Young.[43]

Lawton had been warned by his subordinates that Wheeler "was scheming to leave him in the lurch and have a fight," but he refused to believe that Wheeler would behave so unprofessionally. When Young's cavalry squadrons marched through Siboney and camped to take the advance beyond the farthest tents of the infantry, however, Lawton became suspicious. He had expected Young to remain in Daiquiri. When Wood's regiment arrived at 9 P.M. and also marched past Siboney in the dark, Lawton became enraged. He knew that Wood had been ordered to patrol at Juragua.[44]

Lawton did not confront Wheeler, his superior. He tried to get a message to Shafter about the cavalry's disobedience of orders, but he failed. Shafter was still resting on the transport *Seguranca* which was anchored three miles from the Daiquiri shore. A high sea was running. It was night, and Lawton's courier could not get a lifeboat to put out from the beach.[45]

The Rough Riders realized why they had been racing toward the front as soon as they arrived in Siboney where they crossed a low platform bridge in the dark and pitched camp on a bluff overlooking the sea. Their feet were blistered. They were insect-bitten, sweaty in the growing chill, and thoroughly exhausted. Yet no other American regiment was closer to Santiago than they were. They were the advance of the army, in line to get the first crack at the enemy. That was the reason they were in Cuba.[46]

Most of the troopers were in high spirits as they started fires to cook bacon to eat with hardtack and coffee. Stragglers dragged themselves in slowly and flopped down to regain their strength. Some men gave their buddies massages. Others descended to the nearby bay and bathed in the cool sea. A few drank sweet Spanish wine with regulars from the 10th. During the night, the navy landed more soldiers from transports at Siboney. The warships' searchlights made the beach bright as a ballfield, illuminating the men around the red campfires on the shore. Back of the warships was the moonlit ocean.

Then a tropical cloudburst struck for an hour, drenching men who had no cover and dousing fires. Meals that were cooking floated away. Men who retained their blanket rolls lay down on tent halves in the cold mud. Damp went through the canvas immediately. They curled up in blankets and tried to sleep in their wet clothes.[47]

The more robust relit the fires and attempted to dry their uniforms by hanging them on branches close to the flames before settling into a brief, shivering sleep.

Premonitions

Wood had eaten his supper with Capron whose company he preferred to that of the unpredictable Roosevelt at this uncertain moment. Wood had known Capron since the captain was a boy in the West and he had watched him win promotion from the ranks.[48]

After supper General Young sent for Wood. Young said that the combined force was to move out early the next morning to attack the Spanish fortifications guarding the pass called Las Guasimas at the fork in the trail four miles inland. The rebels repulsed there the same morning had been General Castillo's soldiers who reported fifteen hundred Spanish infantrymen in place. Rumors mentioned reinforcements arriving during the day, so the rebels believed that the current force probably exceeded twenty-five hundred.[49]

Young and Wood discussed Wheeler's plans for an hour. Young decided to take his two squadrons and three Hotchkiss field guns on the main trail. The Rough Riders with 30 officers and 550 troopers in shape to walk were the largest unit present. Wood was to lead his men up a shorter, much steeper mountain path. The goal was to strike the enemy in a classical pincers movement from two directions at the same time. The total American force would be only about 1,000 troopers. Nevertheless, Young thought that this number would be enough to dislodge cowardly Spaniards without difficulty.[50]

Roosevelt was excluded from the planning, but everyone was aware that a conflict was impending. He invited journalists to eat with him, and the discussion around the fire was about the Spanish position on "the second ridge back from the coast" which the Cubans had not been able to penetrate. Roosevelt then sought out Capron to make the rounds of the guard posts with him in Wood's absence. Hamilton Fish told Roosevelt, "It would be my luck to be put out now."[51]

After leaving Young, Wood saw Capron standing alone in the firelight. In confidence he disclosed the battle plans. At once, Capron asked to act as leader of the advance squad and Wood promised him the honor. Like Fish, however, Capron had premonitions. As Wood walked away, he heard Capron murmur, "Well, by to-morrow at this time the long sleep will be on many of us."[52]

Finally Wood turned to Roosevelt who evidenced no gloomy foreboding or uneasiness. The two friends put together the bedding they had available and stretched out side by side on the wet ground well after midnight. They talked over the battle plans for another hour before Wood woke his orderly and asked for reveille at 4 A.M. Both Wood and Roosevelt knew that the next day might be significant for the rest of their lives. As Wood remembered the scene, though, "overtired bodies soon compelled sleep."[53]

At 3 A.M., Major LaMotte arrived with the sixteen-mule pack train and roused Wood to make his report. Wood was civil despite the disobedience of orders, the time, and the interruption of his rest. He advised LaMotte that there would be an engagement against the Spaniards in a few hours only a short distance from Siboney. He was taking Dr. Church and the mules with him. There was no mule available for the chests or the surgeon, so LaMotte was to remain behind in Siboney with the medical and surgical supplies needed to establish a base hospital. According to Wood, the Colt rapid-fire guns would have to be disassembled and roped to mules to manage the steep ascent. The guns were needed more than medicine or another medico.[54]

Roosevelt was awakened by LaMotte, too. He had been lying uncomfortably on his mackintosh with a piece of canvas borrowed from Wood as a cover. When he saw the mules, he got up to find his bedding. LaMotte claimed that he did not know it in Daiquiri but one of the bundles he had dumped on the ground was Roosevelt's.

LaMotte declared that Roosevelt "was not very angry at me but he seemed to think it was hard lines that I should have selected his bedding to leave behind, but as I had not brought a stitch of bedding or clothing myself, I didn't think he had any right to complain."

Roosevelt remained silent thereafter, although LaMotte's reasoning was too much for him to accept. He had the whole campaign to reflect upon this incident and upon other abrasive contacts with the surgeon. When the regiment was mustered out in the fall, he had to be dissuaded from court-martialing LaMotte.

Chapter 13
March to Las Guasimas

The two remaining squadrons of the 1st and 10th regulars, the units whose commanding officers had not been taken into Wheeler's confidence, reached Siboney at midnight. Wheeler had not told them where to camp, so they pitched their tents near the landing stage on the beach. They were inside the perimeter of Lawton's main picket lines and subject to his control.

Wheeler had separated these two squadrons from their mates even though he would be leaving behind half of the regular cavalrymen who could have marched against the Spaniards at the fortified gap.[1] He thought the split in the regiments would make his subterfuge less obvious to Lawton.

Part of the reason for Wheeler's stratagems was the traditional rivalry between cavalry and infantry. Simply because they had been the mounted riflemen, Wheeler and Young believed that they and not foot soldiers were historically entitled to make the first attack on the enemy.[2]

Striking a victorious blow in the opening engagement would also further the advancement of regular officers such as Young. There had not been an equivalent military opportunity for more than thirty years and there might never be another. Getting ahead in his profession was Young's personal justification for joining Wheeler in the unauthorized attack.[3]

Moreover, all of the officers in Cuba were afraid that the Spaniards might prove to be so weak and disorganized that there would be only this one battle in the whole war. Volunteers such as Wheeler and Roosevelt had civilian aspirations that depended upon their assuming a fearless stance at every confrontation.

Despite the secrecy ordered by Wheeler, both the regular and the volunteer officers sought press coverage of the coming battle. Newspapermen who would keep confidences before the fight and write favorably afterward had to be alerted. Journalists such as photographer Burr McIntosh who associated with Shafter's staff officers had to be kept from learning about the venture.[4]

The most influential correspondent was still Richard Harding Davis of the *New York Herald*. He would be essential to getting the exploit on the front pages. John Dunning was also desirable because his Associated Press had the widest circulation. Kennett Harris of the *Chicago Record* had been with the Rough Riders since the regiment was formed. His loyalty was unquestioned. Edward Marshall of the *Journal* ate at Roosevelt's mess. He could not be left out. Also, Wheeler approved of the literary style of Stephen Crane of the *World*, while Young appreciated the professionalism of *Harper's* Caspar Whitney.[5]

These were the chosen six of the dozens of correspondents already in Siboney. They were notified privately through Roosevelt to be ready at reveille on June 24. Except for McIntosh, the newspapermen who were excluded bore no grudge when they found out what they had missed. They understood that their mistake had been to look to regulation-bound Lawton for news rather than to the more rambunctious cavalry. Famous correspondents such as Frederic Remington and John Fox, Jr., vowed to stay closer to the advance during the rest of the campaign. They decided to focus on Roosevelt. They thought he surely would be wherever the front was.

Wood wanted to promote himself in the army through his actions in the war, but he was less enterprising than Roosevelt in catering to journalists. Although he was the decision maker for the Rough Riders, he knew that he was less likely to attract favorable publicity than the effervescent Roosevelt. He believed that the reporters thought of him as cold and supercilious and he did not expect the press to praise him. He was correct.[6]

Instead, Wood tried to make himself competitive militarily with Young who held the job he wanted next. He intended to push his regiment hard enough to be at the rendezvous ahead of Young. His men would fire the first bullets and make the first charge. The volunteer regiment he had trained in less than two months would be as steady under fire as soldiers who had been in service for years under regular officers such as Young. Wood was ready to steal the glory from his co-conspirators.

In contrast to Wood, Young thought of himself as what he was—a general in the regular cavalry—and consequently far above rivalry with Wood who was merely an army doctor. He expected Wood to follow his orders, even though he himself ignored Shafter.

The Whirl, the Unknown

El Camino Real veered inland from the Cuban coast at Siboney to parallel a mountain ridge on a mostly level course through a sparkling green valley. The road ran northward as the direct route to Santiago which was at the inner end of its long harbor. After proceeding three miles through jungle, this main trail climbed a gentle four-hundred-foot elevation to the gap in the ridge where there was a stand of West Indian elms.[7]

Immediately north of Siboney, a separate and rarely used footpath wound its way up a sharp, six-hundred-foot cliff. The rise was a dizzying 45 degrees in places. At the top of the cliff, the path continued easily through dense vegetation along the same mountain ridge that bordered El Camino Real.[8]

The main trail and the mountain path converged at Las Guasimas. The place was named for the elms whose low, widespread branches bore fruit gathered by natives to feed their pigs in happier days. The upper boughs had long ago been used by vigilantes to hang thieves. There was no habitation in the vicinity of the fork that commanded both the trail and the path. The Spaniards had defeated Cuban rebels at the gap in an earlier war, just as they had repulsed Castillo's insurgents in the clash the previous morning.[9]

During the night Young was warned that the Spanish infantry entrenched at the gap had at least two Krupp rapid-fire guns. They might also have been reinforced by Spanish guerrillas. Nevertheless, Young retained the same strategy. The advance was to start at daybreak.[10]

First call in the Rough Rider camp was at 3:30 A.M. Reveille was at four o'clock. As the troopers slowly pushed back their wet covers

The Rough Riders at La Quasima (Las Guasimas). LeRoy Armstrong,
Pictorial Atlas Illustrating The Spanish-American War (Chicago: Souvenir
Publishing Co., 1898), pp. 46–47.

in the dark, they were sleepy and sore from the hard march the previous day. When they stood up, water dripped from their sour-smelling
uniforms.[11]

Mess call was at 4:15. The men relit campfires to dry themselves
and cook their bacon. Some fried hardtack in the bacon grease. Others opened cans with knives and dished out cold tomatoes. To make
coffee, troopers heated whole beans in pans to resemble roasting,
then smashed the beans with a rock or pistol butt to simulate grind-
ing. The resulting boiled brew was not like coffee at home, but it was
brown and hot.[12]

A troop of regulars near the Rough Riders' camp did not bother
to make coffee. They were drinking from a hogshead of white Cuban
rum they had found among the plentiful supply of Spanish liquor
abandoned in Siboney. They also filled their canteens with rum.[13]

Wood and Roosevelt had slept scarcely at all. Wood looked worn
and haggard. Roosevelt was his normal chipper self. He resolved half
a dozen problems brought to him while he was putting on a long

yellow slicker he had borrowed to replace his soaked mackintosh.[14]

Henry Sylvester Ward was the headquarters cook Roosevelt had hired in Tampa. He was not suited to rigorous tropical hikes. He slept through reveille and breakfast was late. Upset by the anger of anxious officers, he gashed his thumb opening a can of tomatoes and dropped a chunk of bacon into the campfire. When the meal was over, he stuffed the unwashed dishes into a gunnysack. He had lost interest in the job.[15]

Self-reliant Captain O'Neill did not join the officers' mess. He made his own breakfast and washed the dishes in a pail before re-packing them in his baggage. Stephen Crane caught the spark of the Rough Riders in O'Neill. "He was going to take his men into any sort of holocaust," Crane wrote, "because—he loved it for itself—the thing itself—the whirl, the unknown." An equivalent if less po-etic analysis could have described Roosevelt.[16]

While makeshift muster rolls were called to form the troops for the morning march, Wood approached a disheveled Harris of the *Record*. In an attempt to be ingratiating, Wood asked Harris how far he thought the regiment had walked the previous afternoon. The foot-sore correspondent estimated a grandiose fifty miles. He was visibly annoyed when Wood, "in a maddeningly superior sort of way," as-serted that the distance had been only seven miles. Harris wrote that the march actually had been nine miles, "but then Wood rode all the way." Harris's reporting was typical of the journalists' unsympathetic attitude toward the unglamorous colonel.[17]

Wood had been instructed to synchronize his movements with Young's regulars by beginning the march at five o'clock. The final plan was for Young to hit the Spanish position first with his 465 men on the valley trail. That would force the enemy to retreat toward the ridge. When the 550 Rough Riders reached a predetermined point on the mountain path, they were to file to the right to strike the Span-iards on the other flank. That would drive the enemy back toward Young and into the classic crushing pincers.[18]

Wood had not disclosed his intent to get to the fork first. He expected to be the sword, not the stone. Again, however, the exasper-ating pack train was delaying the Rough Riders. The hitches would not hold. Wood announced angrily that if the pack train was not ready in ten minutes, he would abandon the sixteen mules once more.

It was, however, an empty threat. Three of the mules carried the disassembled Colt machine guns. If there was to be a fight, the Colts would be needed.[19]

Again Surgeon LaMotte undertook to supervise the pack train. The impatient Wood had been stamping around without a solution, so he gladly handed control of the mules to the doctor. Once Wood turned away, LaMotte again dumped enough officers' bundles to free two more mules. He put his most important medical and surgical chests on the back of one mule, checked the tightness of all packing ropes, and mounted the second mule. LaMotte was doing his duty as he saw it.

The Long Brown Column

The Rough Riders' shoulders hurt and their backs and legs were stiff. Some men who had blankets cut them in half to save weight and they discarded everything superfluous. Few troopers carried rations. They trusted to luck for something to eat at the next meal. Even so, the blanket rolls seemed heavier. The contents had been drenched during the night.[20]

Then Wood was overheard telling Roosevelt that they would all "smell powder" before the morning ended. Despite the aches, spirits rose when the Rough Riders were ready to march at 6 A.M., an hour behind schedule. The battle was getting closer.[21]

Young and Wood held a last conference at the side of the road. The Rough Riders were standing next to the troopers of the 10th who mocked them by attributing their lateness to nervousness before the battle. In response, the Rough Riders boasted that if the 10th waited in Siboney, severed Spanish heads would be brought back to them as trophies.[22]

The attitude of the individual Rough Rider was carefree. The feeling was: "We ain't frettin' about no Spaniards. What did they do when the Navy banged away at them? Nuthin'! What did they do when we landed? Nuthin'! An' you ain't goin' to make us believe they're goin' to stop us in the back country where they got nuthin'. It don't stand to reason."[23]

The Rough Riders and the regulars began the march together. They forded a small stream and crossed a railroad track where they separated. Young's troopers continued on the level main trail. Wood had two of Young's aides with him as observers. The three rode at the front of the long brown column heading to the path starting at the base of the cliff half a mile to the left. The volunteers and regulars would not meet again until after they reached the Spaniards at the gap.[24]

The Rough Riders were growing more hopeful about seeing Spaniards soon. They picked their way happily up the grade, "babbling joyously, arguing, recounting, laughing, making more noise than a train going through a tunnel."[25]

After the novelty of the climb wore off, the rising temperature and the abruptness of the ascent tired the men. Happy feelings began to dissipate. They were just two days off the transport. Most had never in their lives walked this far. Soon the strain blurred into the stress of the previous afternoon's march. The men confused the details of one march with the other when they wrote home days later.

Dawn had come with tropical immediacy. The sun was beating on the side of the exposed cliff and not enough air stirred to make a leaf flutter. The eager Wood pressed the troopers on and then was forced to call a halt because men who carried blanket rolls dropped them on the slope. Others fell out from exhaustion, as they had on the first march.[26]

Sometimes the rise over sheer limestone blocks was so precipitous that men had to pull themselves up by handholds on rocks and plants. Officers led their struggling and sliding horses. Troopers drank deeply from their canteens. Those who had accepted rum from men of the 10th were in bad shape. Swallowing the rum made them hotter and thirstier.[27]

Alongside the footpath was a blockhouse capable of preventing the Rough Riders' advance if the Spaniards had remained to man the loopholes. Roosevelt stopped to examine the abandoned wooden structure. The one room was twelve feet square and twelve feet high, with a distinctive pyramidal roof. Inside, gravel was banked against the front wall to a height of four feet. Slits in the wall faced the valley for Spanish riflemen firing from a prone position. There were higher loopholes for standing riflemen.[28]

Leafy green branches were piled in a rear corner to serve as a bed. In the opposite corner was a five-gallon tin of the ubiquitous rice flour for baking flat bread. The flour was the only food in the blockhouse. The customary wine was gone. On the whitewashed rear wall was a crude drawing of a gigantic American soldier shown as Goliath fleeing from a small Spanish David, but there was no live Spaniard anywhere in sight.

Two companies of Lawton's 22nd Infantry stood near the blockhouse. They had climbed the cliff ahead of Wood's column to relieve their pickets who had been on guard against Spanish incursions since late the previous afternoon. The officers of the 22nd were junior to Wood and they assumed that the Rough Riders' advance was an authorized reconnaissance. They told Wood that during the evening and early morning their pickets had heard the Spaniards felling trees to entrench themselves further. Although the infantrymen had never been beyond the top of the cliff, the distance to the gap was said to be three miles along the footpath, roughly the same as for Young.[29]

The men of the 22nd completed the change of pickets and were descending the cliff when they encountered LaMotte's pack train coming along the same narrow footpath. Faced with an elderly surgeon riding a mule bareback up an incline, the infantry major was not cooperative. He ordered the pack train off the path and took his companies past in single file. Halting the mules sidewise on the slope loosened the ropes again. The bundles, including the disassembled rapid-fire guns, were sliding on the mules' backs.

Finally a messenger from Wood reached the patient LaMotte with an urgent command to hurry along at least the three mules carrying gun parts. That sounded like an emergency. The infantry major let the three mules through his lines, but he continued to detain LaMotte and the remaining thirteen animals. LaMotte could only hope that the men Wood had assigned to lead the mules with the guns would get to the regiment in time.[30]

The Cuckoo Calls

Once the Rough Riders reached the crest of the slope, conditions improved. A delightfully cool sea breeze blew and overhead was a cloudless sky. As men turned to look behind them, the scenery was postcard fresh. On their right, the sun's rays penetrated into deep ravines alongside the mountain peaks as the mists lifted.

Behind them they saw the coast where they had camped. Warships and transports showed signs of life on the little deep-blue bay. The village of Siboney was partly in deep shadow, masking the blackened ruins of structures shelled by American warships two days earlier. Open areas were cluttered with army encampments that looked like a smaller, more exotic Tampa. Bugle calls floated softly upward as the daily routine commenced for Lawton's infantry division.[31]

Looking back to their left, the men saw the valley road where Young was leading his column of regulars on a companion course. The regulars could not be seen because the wooded ridge the Rough Riders were on was wide enough to block the side view. Wood was frustrated in assessing how he stood in his personal race to get to the gap ahead of Young.[32]

When the Rough Riders turned their attention to the footpath again, they stepped out for the first time upon terrain favorable for marching. The ground was moist and cushioned underfoot. The marchers were shaded by heavy forest growth on a big undulating plateau.[33]

Although the troopers could not believe they were approaching the enemy, Wood called a halt to arrange the column in a more guarded posture. His disposition of the troopers was a model of caution. At the point he had Tom Isbell, a Cherokee Indian from L Troop sharing the lead with two experienced Cuban scouts furnished by General Castillo. Two hundred and fifty yards behind the point came the advance guard of five Rough Riders who also were skilled as scouts. The advance was led by Sgt. Hamilton Fish who claimed to be an expert on ambushes because he had learned Apache tricks in classes aboard the transport.[34]

Walking alone in the middle of the path fifty yards behind the advance guard was tall, reassuring Captain Capron of L Troop. Fifty yards behind him were his sixty troopers in single file. They were in extended order with ten-yard intervals between each man.

Wood and the two aides headed the main body of troopers. In the drawn-out column, Wood was one hundred yards behind the rear of L Troop and more than half a mile behind Isbell at the point. Wood was riding as slowly as he could bear while juggling the conflicting pressures of scouting protectively, racing Young, and preserving the strength of the men.[35]

In back of Wood were correspondents Davis on a mule he had acquired and Marshall on foot. Then came a mounted Cuban interpreter and Capt. Henry McClintock of B Troop. Chaplain James Brown from Prescott, Arizona, was astride a mule as big as a camel. In San Antonio, the men had read the chaplain's smoothly rounded face as well controlled. Now he flourished a drawn pistol while maintaining that he "could settle a Spaniard at 50 paces and did not mean to be taken by surprise." When Wood advised him that the Articles of War forbade chaplains to carry arms, he did not give up the weapon. He was chagrined but not influenced.[36]

Wood placed Roosevelt in the middle of the first squadron, far from the point. Roosevelt did not complain. Instead, he soon picked

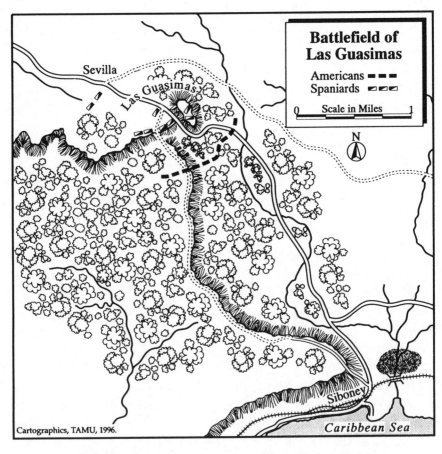

Battlefield of Las Guasimas. Map adapted from Herbert H. Sargent, *The Campaign of Santiago de Cuba* (Chicago: A. C. McClurg and Co., 1907), facing p. 2:60. Adapted by Cartographics Service Unit of the Department of Geography, Texas A&M University.

his way forward to ride nearer his favorite reporter, Davis. He was not particularly anxious about this fight and merely wanted to share his thoughts with friends. With no role in the planning and no part in the leadership, he was a model of studied nonchalance.[37]

Maj. Alexander Brodie followed the first squadron with his troopers. Three more journalists, Crane, Harris, and Dunning, were hiking at the rear of the column. Five of the six correspondents on the march had elected to accompany the Rough Riders. Only the conservative Whitney was with Young.[38]

From the moment the spread alignment was formed, however, the column began contracting. Wood's desire to hurry won over safety. The half-mile between the point and the colonel decreased steadily.

Despite the push from the rear, the scouts were proceeding deliberately as they approached enemy territory. Isbell, Fish, and Capron knew that Wood depended upon them for the security of the regiment, particularly since Wood did not put out flankers along the sides of the path. Flankers cutting through dense underbrush at half a mile an hour would have been too slow to suit the regiment's mood. Besides, Wood surely would have lost his race with the unimpeded Young.[39]

Few of the men were grumbling about the speed of this part of the march. The movement was too slow for them, not too fast. They were looking ahead to the fight, claiming that they wanted "to get into the real war business." They shoved forward against Wood just as Wood was pressing against L Troop and the advance.[40]

To a stranger, the outlook would have seemed peaceful and charming. The amateur naturalist Roosevelt had never been in Western Hemisphere tropics before. Davis and McClintock were identifying plants, birds, and insects for him. At the edge of the forest were guinea grass, guava bushes, and varieties of cactus. Towering over all was the trembling crown of the royal palm.[41]

Crawling alongside the path were large spiders, lizards, and land crabs with purple claws held high over yellow-polka-dotted black backs and orange legs. In the air was the *bijirita,* the bird the Spaniards called "the Cuban" because its claws were raised viciously against every other bird. There was also the sparrow *gorrión* which the Cubans referred to as "the Spaniard" because it was an unwelcome import contributing nothing to the country. The most insistent bird call was the plaintive voice of the unseen wood cuckoo which became audible when the Rough Riders reached the woods at the top of the cliff. Ornithologist Roosevelt heard the call frequently during the rest of the march.[42]

As the officers rode at a leisurely pace between two abandoned estates, the mood was like a casual day in the country. There were wire fences on both sides of the path. Roosevelt noticed that Spaniards used twice as many strands of wire as Americans in the West did. For once, he did not speculate as to why. He also commented that the countryside appeared to be good for deer hunting, as indeed it had been before the deer were stripped by hungry Cubans during previous insurrections.[43]

McClintock said that he was reminded of southern California. Davis thought of the trail across Honduras. While they were passing a deserted mansion on the right, Roosevelt dismounted to pick up two shovels discarded by troopers. He hung the implements tidily on his borrowed saddle.

After an hour of this pleasant rural procession, Wood halted the regiment at a sunken spot in the footpath to get his bearings. He judged the location to be less than half a mile from where he expected to initiate the pincers. The troopers were sitting on the raised margins of the trail, convivially closing their formation even tighter. Some were chatting about trivial matters and making jokes as they chewed long blades of rough grass or fanned themselves with their campaign hats. Others rolled and lit cigarettes. The Rough Riders gave the appearance of total disregard for the undiscovered enemy.

Capron walked back along the path to talk to Wood who rode ahead to meet him. A field of high grass was waving in the slight breeze to the left. Almost impenetrable bushes grew to a height of fifteen feet on the right and arched over the trail. The unseen cuckoos were calling continually from both sides. Roosevelt was laughing loudly with Marshall about a luncheon they had shared with Hearst, Marshall's publisher, at the Astor House in New York City.[44]

A frowning Wood returned after ten minutes. He was the only man in the regiment who looked worried. He did not tell Roosevelt, but while he conferred with his point, the Cuban scouts had suggested the possibility of an ambush on the path. They also mentioned that the Spaniards might make a determined stand at the gap. Anything that came from Cuban soldiers was deprecated, yet Wood was perturbed.

Completely the stiff commanding officer now, he openly disapproved of Roosevelt's frivolity. He told Roosevelt, "Pass the word back to keep silence in the ranks." Everyone except Roosevelt knew that the instruction was meant for Roosevelt himself. The order was transmitted to the troopers by Sergeant Higgins, the former New York policeman, who bawled at the top of his voice, "Stop that talkin', can't ye, damn it!"[45]

At the same time, LaMotte was hurrying the pack train along the path. However, the three mules with the gun parts had resisted being led by heavy-handed soldiers impatient to get back to Wood. When LaMotte reached the struggling drivers, he placed the balky mules in the pack train again. After catching up to the regiment just after the halted Rough Riders were silenced by Sergeant Higgins, he rode his flagging mule through the ranks and shouted to Roosevelt that he had counted fifty-two exhausted men who had fallen out of the column. This was almost 10 percent of the force. He thought that Wood did not realize how hard he had been marching the troopers.[46]

Concerned at last, Roosevelt rode up to Wood and repeated LaMotte's admonition. Wood whirled on him in anger, aroused for the second time in minutes. He snapped out the reproof, "I have no time for that now! We are in sight of the enemy, sir!"[47]

Roosevelt had seen no Spaniard. He was not impressed with Wood's reprimand until he went back to Marshall at the wire fence and casually picked up one end of a loose strand. "My God," he exclaimed. "This wire has been cut to-day. The end is bright, and there has been enough dew since sunrise to have put a little rust on it, had it not been more lately cut." He realized that the wire could have been snipped within the hour to allow Spanish pickets into the jungle. The enemy could be waiting there under cover. The cuckoo calls he had been hearing might not have been birds at all, but rather pickets' signals reporting the size and progress of the American regiment.[48]

With his own observation to support Wood's caution, Roosevelt began getting the troopers in his squadron ready for the fight. He and other nearby officers dismounted and fastened the reins of their horses to the fence. Belatedly, they took time to have the troopers' loose gear tied down to prevent noises like the rattle of cups and mess kits. Carbines were loaded.

Capron had reported to Wood that the scouts had reached the place where the move into the jungle was to be made. The rebel General Castillo had told Wood to watch for a dead Spanish guerrilla lying on the path and Isbell at the point had just come upon the corpse. The guerrilla had been picked over generously by vultures, land crabs, and insects, though enough of him remained to mark the spot.[49]

The Skirmish Begins

Meanwhile, Young had been advancing his two squadrons of regulars up the valley trail without pause. The troopers were marching easily with the long step and lagging foot characteristic of veteran dismounted cavalrymen. The trail was relatively flat and dry, so Young was able to bring the three Hotchkiss one-pound artillery pieces with him as he had planned.[50]

Wheeler's reconnoitering and the reports from Castillo were perfect. Young's scouts saw the Spaniards just where he had expected them to be. They were half a mile ahead in a solid-rock fortification on a steep and deeply-entrenched hill. The trenches were barricaded with felled tree trunks. Young sent a Cuban scout to chop through the jungle to notify Wood about the location of the Spanish defenses. Then he settled his regulars alongside the trail to give Wood time to get to the fork.

Wheeler rode up to join Young and at eight o'clock took over the command. He ordered deployment of the regulars into the jungle on the left, to be followed by an opening round of artillery fire. He was too impatient to wait for Wood.[51]

On the mountain path high above, Wood did not hear from Young's Cuban scout because Spanish pickets were concealed between the two American forces. Although none of the other Rough Riders had seen a Spaniard, the wary Wood instructed Roosevelt to deploy three troops to the right of the path to act as skirmishers in the luxuriant growth. Brodie was to take three troops into the high grass to explore the situation to the left.[52]

Before the deployment could begin, however, the Spaniards in the woods on the right suddenly commenced volley-firing their Mausers at the Rough Riders. The enemy riflemen were shooting in unison on command, yet they remained hidden from the troopers who were disoriented by the unexpectedness of the fierce attack and by the tangled brush. The Rough Riders with Roosevelt were being fired upon and hit by Spanish bullets in their first experience in battle, yet they could not see twenty feet into the thicket in front of them.[53]

Wood's recognition of the danger had come just minutes too late. The skirmish at Las Guasimas began as an ambuscade.

Chapter 14
Gallant Blunder

According to Stephen Crane, the small but bitter fight at Las Guasimas began with "simply a gallant blunder" by Wood. "This silly brave force wandered placidly into trouble" on the morning of June 24, "but their conduct was magnificent."

Because the onset of the skirmish was so sudden, the battlefield so wide and tangled, and the enemy so seldom seen, events in the grueling two-hour engagement were only a blur to Crane. Although he was a trained observer, he confessed that "the details escape me. To tell you the truth, there was too much going on."[1]

After the engagement was over, the Rough Riders were equally uncertain about exactly what had happened. Even the number of Spaniards was in dispute. Roosevelt referred to "the nearly 1,500 Spaniards in front and to the sides of us." To the self-serving Wood, "it was evident from the volume of fire that the 1,500 reported by Castillo as holding the pass had been largely increased." He objected to Roosevelt's shorter count as thoughtlessly deprecatory of the regiment. To Wood, this was a full-scale battle, not just a skirmish.[2]

The army viewed Wood as merely a middle-aged doctor who had been nominated by Roosevelt to serve as a line officer of volunteers for the duration of the war. In contrast, Wood liked being in command of a regiment and wanted to continue as a high-ranking officer after the war. To achieve that, he had to be seen as a successful leader. Although the clash at Las Guasimas started under the handicap of his marching the troopers too fast too far, he had to make himself appear to have been superior to the regular officers who were involved.

When the concealed Spanish sharpshooters began firing in unison at the surprised Rough Riders, Wood responded coolly to each unanticipated adversity. As the fighting spread into the jungle, however, he was out of contact with his men for the rest of the morning. They advanced while he established his headquarters in an open area near the path. He was rarely called upon for orders while the skirmish enlarged and then ended. The particulars of the conflict were hidden from his view. Nevertheless, he knew that the results had to be recorded favorably to him, so he claimed to be able to report on the entire episode.

He did not apologize to his men for the lives lost in the ambush. From the start of the campaign, he had known that many of his men would die in Cuba. He saw rank-and-file troopers as faceless pawns who would gladly yield their lives in the pursuit of what both he and they called patriotism. As he put it, the men would be sacrificed on "the happiest day of their lives." They would die smiling.[3]

In turn, the Rough Riders correctly believed that Wood would be as willing to die as they were, if fate required it. Officers were the primary Spanish targets.

Scatter to the Right There

In anticipation of the American advance, the Spaniards had placed the main body of their infantrymen across the junction of the valley and mountain paths. The primary fortification was a reinforced brick sugar house on a hill on the far side of the valley. The Spanish soldiers were well protected behind stone walls, wire entanglements, and the felled trees that shielded irregular entrenchments.

The Spaniards had taken the advantage by positioning themselves on the hillside above the approaching regulars. They also stretched the arms of an inverted U around the Rough Riders. Most of their sharpshooters were on the left flank of the U in the high grass. There were fewer marksmen on the right where there was less room. The ridge sloped abruptly down into the valley.[4]

The first volley from ambush was in response to a warning shot from Tom Isbell at the point. He thought he saw a Spaniard in the woods, fired his carbine in the air, and was struck seven times by Mauser bullets. He survived.[5]

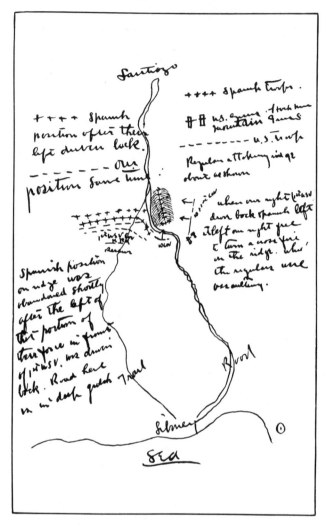

Map of the Fight at Las Guasimas, Drawn by Gen. Leonard Wood.
R. A. Alger, *The Spanish-American War* (New York:
Harper and Brothers, 1901), facing p. 106.

Wood later contended that he had been expecting the first Spanish volley for ten minutes, yet he did nothing about the contracting formation of the marchers and he was slow in deploying the men. When the ambush was sprung, Capron's L Troop was less than twenty-five yards behind Isbell. Three in L Troop were killed and seven were wounded in the opening gunfire, yet the troopers did not falter. They dove into a small patch of tall grass in front of the woods on the right, formed a line, and held their ground.[6]

Wood ordered men near him to lie down in the fire-swept path while he considered what to do. Flights of Mauser bullets whizzed by. Several Rough Riders rolled over, dead or wounded. When men began to curse their luck, Wood shouted, "Don't swear! Shoot!" There was, though, no enemy to aim at.[7]

Wood then continued the deployment ordered just before the Spanish trap was sprung. As he reconstructed the scene, amid "the singing of the first hostile bullets the troops moved up and I halted each captain and made them repeat their instructions. Repeating it steadied them and tended to prevent their rushing in without regard to the rest of the command. I tried by every means, example, and instruction to send them ahead cool and slow, and succeeded."[8]

Roosevelt had a more credible recollection. He had no command decision to defend. He said that Wood merely told him to take G, A, and K troops to the right to get behind the Spanish sharpshooters in support of beleaguered L Troop. In his exuberance, Roosevelt yelled, "It's up to us, boys!" He directed the men to leave their column of twos and "scatter out to the right there, quick, you! Scatter to the right! Look alive! Look alive!"[9]

Roosevelt admitted later that his order to "scatter out" was improper when judged by official regulations on how to form a skirmish line. He pointed out, however, that he was not on a parade ground. He was in a hurry to get off the bullet-pocked path himself and he counted on the troopers to be self-reliant. He thought that Wood's claim to have called up each of his captains in the middle of the ambush in order to feed them the "cool and slow" instruction was patently unlikely.

The Most Magnificent Soldier

Roosevelt was surprisingly modest in his writings about his activities at Las Guasimas. As he ordered his troops into the woods,

> *a sharp crash to the front told us the fight was on. We were under a brisk fire. It being my first experience, it took me a little time to make out exactly what was up.*
>
> *I took the men forward. I could not see where the rest of my regi-*

*ment was and I could not see the Spaniards. I did not know what to
do. Fortunately, I knew that if you were in doubt, go toward the guns.
I was uncertain, but I knew it could not be wrong to go forward. It
was bewildering to fight an enemy I so rarely saw.*[10]

As usual, Roosevelt had his coterie of correspondents. Marshall
and Davis viewed him in a more glamorous light than he professed to
look at himself. They made him out to be bold, not bewildered.

Marshall wrote that while Wood "gave orders with utmost calm-
ness, Roosevelt literally jumped up and down" at the start of the skirmish, "with emotions evidently divided between joy and a tendency
to run." The hopping was Roosevelt's *cholera morbus* flaring up,
however, not incipient flight. He had a touch of diarrhea in the crisis.

"Then he stepped across the wire fence," Marshall added, "and
from that instant he became the most magnificent soldier I have ever
seen. It was as if that barbed-wire strand formed a dividing line in his
life, and he left behind those unadmirable traits which have caused
him to be justly criticized in civilian life, and found on the other side,
in that Cuban thicket, the coolness, calm judgment, towering heroism, which made him the most admired and best beloved of Americans in Cuba."[11]

The flaw in Marshall's eye-witness encomium, though, was that
he stayed close to Wood near the path. After Roosevelt walked into
the woods, Marshall never saw him again at Las Guasimas. The journalist had no opportunity to observe the traits he described. For that,
he relied on Richard Harding Davis and others who moved forward
with Roosevelt.

Davis was the principal American correspondent in Cuba, but he
was confused about his role in the war. When he went into the woods
after Roosevelt, he had no notebook in his hand. Instead, he carried
a loaded carbine that a dead soldier had dropped. At that point he
would have loved the role of captain of a troop in action. Part of the
appeal Roosevelt had for Davis was his understanding of Davis's
martial dreams.[12]

When Roosevelt "stepped across the strand," the line of Spanish
sharpshooters on the right was near the edge of the ravine, only fifty
yards away. The troopers with him progressed steadily, beating their
way through bushes and vines with the butts of their carbines.

Captain O'Neill ordered A Troop to advance by crawling. Because he remained erect like Roosevelt, however, his men insisted on imitating him by walking forward in a crouch. They claimed that the sharp leaves of the plant appropriately called Spanish bayonet inflicted more pain than bullets. Apart from this one breach, the western troopers accepted the restrained pace of the advance without question. Some correspondents were surprised. Easterners in K Troop also acted with aplomb. No Fifth Avenue Boy hesitated.[13]

Wood commented later that Roosevelt's fight at close quarters and with no visibility through the vegetation was the fiercest of the entire war. Actually, the Spanish sharpshooters were retreating to avoid being cut off by Young's regulars deploying in the valley. The fight in the woods tapered off before Roosevelt had a chance to move his men far forward. He never did see the sharpshooters.

Roosevelt's troopers were now in control of their part of the ridge. As they reached the forward edge, men in front fired at the fortifications across the valley. Roosevelt, however, was at a personal disadvantage. Even with his spectacles, he was too nearsighted to spot Spaniards at that distance. With his keener vision, Davis was able to cry out, "There they are, Colonel! Look over there! See their hats!" Roosevelt could then guide his marksmen.[14]

The only gunfire directed at Roosevelt's three troops came from the Spaniards on the hill where the enemy infantrymen were discharging their rifles in rapid volleys. Hundreds of Spaniards stood behind the low stone walls as if for inspection. On command they shot in unison, holding their Mausers at the hip and pumping bullets with a quick fanning of the right hand on the lever. Then they ducked behind the walls to take cover while reloading for the next volley. The simultaneous Mauser discharges sounded intimidating and would have been equally devastating if the tendency of the Spaniards had not been to shoot high. Only O'Neill's A troopers who were standing had been hit hard. This time the A troopers did drop to a crawl. O'Neill himself remained upright.[15]

As *aficionados* of war, Roosevelt and Davis were euphorically experiencing events they had been imagining for years. Roosevelt considered the Spaniards' precision shooting to be more punishing than it was. He tried to organize the Rough Riders into his own volley-firing formation, but he could only get a few groups of five to comply. Imitating a machine gun was contrary to the troopers' sense of individuality.[16]

Z-Z-Z-Z-Z-eu

In a crisis, Roosevelt felt apprehensive at first, showed nervousness briefly, as Marshall had observed, and then overcame his fears. He had trained himself in the West to be unafraid.

From Tampa Bay he had promised his brother-in-law that "I haven't the slightest idea of taking any risk I don't feel I absolutely must take." Once in combat, however, his old-fashioned notions about the obligations of leadership obliterated caution. Unlike Wood, he ignored instructions for him to establish headquarters at the rear. Instead, he headed directly toward the action. The troopers' "business" was to fight. His "business," he maintained, "was to keep command" through inspiring his men by example.[17]

He stepped into the flight of Spanish bullets as a hazard he elected to assume. His rule was not to seek cover and not to wince. He observed that when the Spaniards fired in volleys, troopers involuntarily bobbed their heads slightly as the sound of the Mausers reached them, even though they knew that any bullet they heard had already passed them by. That was flinching and was regarded by Roosevelt as a weakness.[18]

The same valor was exhibited by other inspirational leaders. One was O'Neill whose heroics were touted by his own men but whose deeds in combat were not reported in the press. Davis concentrated on Roosevelt. When a Mauser bullet struck a tree trunk where Roosevelt was standing, a shower of wood splinters hit the side of his face and his ear, but he did not draw back. Davis wrote about this as proof of Roosevelt's nerve. O'Neill could have dispatched a Spanish guerrilla in hand-to-hand combat without getting equivalent attention.[19]

The Rough Riders engaged in a good deal of introspection concerning this first exposure to battlefield conditions. Officers, troopers, and correspondents became deeply preoccupied with how it felt to shoot at a human quarry and how it felt to be shot at. Being endangered by their own comrades caused the most violent reactions. At first, troopers could aim only in the general direction of the concealed enemy. G troopers in the woods believed that they were being fired at by the remains of L Troop and they shouted bitter admonitions.[20]

Most men were calm under the Spanish guns. Pleased at controlling their emotions, they tramped or crawled in the growing heat, throwing off all their equipment other than cartridge belts and canteens. They heard the *z-z-z-z-z-eu* of Mauser bullets and saw the dirt fly when the ground was struck, although they never found the shooters. Westerners compared firing at Spaniards with hunting elusive quail at home, except that the quail could not shoot back.[21]

Whether triggered by Spaniards or by comrades, bullets that went by sang the *zeu-zeu* sound. Bullets that struck a body could not be heard until they hit. Then the noise was a *chug*, audible a startlingly long distance away. The seriously wounded did not throw up their hands and fall backward like amateur Shakespearean actors. Rather, the muscles of most went limp all at once, as if they were puppets with their strings cut. Men fell in heaps, like dirt from a shovel. Going down, they made a compound sound: a metallic jangle of canteens, cups, and guns, mingled with the thud of bodies hitting the ground. There was no cry of distress, just an almost casual "Well, I got it that time," as the men crumpled.[22]

Troopers were not allowed to drop out of line to aid the wounded. The injured waited patiently for a medical corpsman, or for the end of the battle when a buddy might bring help, or they died. Many of the ambulatory wounded continued to fight. When Roosevelt sent three A troopers on a reconnaissance, one was killed, the second returned unharmed, and the third made it back with blood streaming from a deep gash in his hip. He remained at the front, telling Roosevelt that he could not find a doctor.

Similarly, it was common for a trooper in the field hospital to remark, "Say, doctor, this ain't much of a wound. I reckon I can go back to my troop now." The Rough Riders were resolved to maintain their reputation for toughness.[23]

Down in the Valley

After an hour of steady but slow advances on the ridge, Roosevelt saw 10th Cavalry troopers approaching through the wooded valley. He was afraid the regulars might fire at his men, so he had the first sergeant climb a tree to wave a troop guidon.[24]

At that juncture, Roosevelt thought he had fulfilled his mission on the right flank. He had eased the plight of bloodied L Troop. He had driven the Spanish sharpshooters off the ridge and had established contact with the regulars. There had, though, been no word from Wood. Roosevelt had no idea how the battle was going on the left. As second in command, he considered it his duty to find out whether he was needed there. Instead of sending a courier, he took G Troop with him and moved back toward the path where the ambush had occurred. O'Neill was left in charge of A and K troops. Davis remained on the right-hand side. He did not know that Roosevelt had gone.

In the valley, Wheeler's chief of staff was asking the general to request reinforcements. The regulars' casualties were mounting to a level that Shafter would find unacceptable in the event of a defeat, especially since there had been no need for the unauthorized engagement. Spanish resistance on the fortified hill was unexpectedly staunch. The Spaniards were not retreating into the planned pincers. Although there was no end in sight, Wheeler stubbornly resisted any change in tactics. He did not want to admit that he needed help from Lawton. Only after the regulars were completely bogged down in the jungle did Wheeler finally agree to order Lawton to send support from Siboney.[25]

Lawton was not surprised to receive the message. He had heard the guns. First he assumed there was another clash between Spaniards and Cuban rebels. Then he realized that Wheeler really had exceeded his instructions by launching an attack.

Lawton had no way of judging the size of the Spanish force. To satisfy the rule of thumb that attackers must greatly outnumber defenders, he alerted Wheeler's 9th Cavalry Regiment as well as his own infantry division. When Wheeler's message arrived, the support was ready to go to the rescue.

On the mountain path, Wood knew nothing of the interplay between Wheeler and Lawton. He was having his own troubles. Despite LaMotte's success in nursing the pack train up the steep hill past Siboney and through the 22nd Infantry, the Colt rapid-fire guns financed by Fifth Avenue Boy Kane could not be activated. The soldiers leading the mules were subjected to the same terrifying volleys as the rest of the regiment. One of them panicked. Instead of unloading the gun parts carefully from the wildly bucking mule, he let them fall to the ground. The shock disabled the Colts' mechanism beyond quick repair.[26]

Conditions to the left of the path were more desperate than on the right. The Spanish sharpshooters who formed the left flank of the ambuscade were volley-firing like clockwork. The line of Spanish soldiers rested on their knees in the high grass to pour in Mauser bullets at close range. Their aim was high, just as the volleys from the hill were, but the volume was heavy. Even the prosaic Wood described how bullets cut leaves from the trees as if they were flakes of green snow.[27]

Wood had ordered D, E, and F troops under Major Brodie to form a defensive line facing the Spaniards on the left. D Troop went into the grass first through a break in the fence. The men were compelled to lie down at once to avoid the deadly Spanish volleys. There also was a crossfire, apparently from F Troop in the rear. An officer of D Troop ran back toward F Troop, shouting, "For God's sake, stop! You are killing your own men!"[28]

Then Wood received the most personally disheartening news. Captain Capron had been mortally wounded in the initial Spanish volleys fired at L Troop. After he was hit, his last words were, "Don't mind me, boys. Go on with the fight!" Wood had been responsible for putting Capron in the advance. He exclaimed, "I shall never forget the shock."[29]

The first Rough Rider to die had been Sgt. Hamilton Fish who was killed a few yards in front of Capron. Before Davis went into the woods, he found Fish's body lying across the path. Despite a disfiguring wound, Fish was identified by an engraved silver watch and a bundle of letters in his pocket.[30]

Wood lived up to his nickname "Old Icebox" as calamities continued. Three officers were struck while standing with him in a grassy patch down a slope to the left of the path where he was holding the reins of his beloved horse Charles Augustus. Wood expected to be shot, too. He was inwardly lamenting that he had not taken out a life insurance policy for $100,000 coverage, as Roosevelt was reputed to have done.[31]

One of the officers hit was Major Brodie who was at Wood's side when a bullet smashed his forearm. Clinically, Wood watched Brodie's opposite foot go high in the air as an odd reflex action from the blow to the bone. In contrast, Wood observed that men shot in the flesh by Mauser bullets showed little effect. Wounds were small and bleeding

Body of Sgt. Hamilton Fish, Near Rough Riders' Battlefield at
Las Guasimas, Shortly after Battle. *Neely's Panorama of Our New
Possessions* (New York: F. Tennyson, 1898).

was slight. The men rubbed themselves where the bullet entered or
exited and went on fighting.[32]

Skeptical journalists searched for exceptions to the valorous. They
found few. Marshall thought that he had discovered a coward limp-
ing to the rear. In fact, the man had lost the sole of his shoe. He
hunted until he found a dead comrade with a comparable foot size,
replaced the shoe, and got back into the fight.

An enlisted man covered with blood from a chest wound pulled
himself erect with bravado. He asked Wood, "Colonel, I have only a
minute. Can you shake my hand and say good-bye?" Wood shook
the man's hand and, instead of saying good-bye, had him taken for
medical attention. Another trooper who was crawling twenty yards
behind his mates excused his slow pace by telling Wood, "I am a little
stiff, sir, and can't go very fast." As the man crept by, Wood saw a
wound bleeding freely in the man's side.[33]

Marshall had been standing close to Wood, listening to the Mauser
bullets. He described the sound as "a nasty, malicious little noise, its

beginning and ending pitched a little lower than its middle." He observed that "no one seemed frightened. These men waded in with an excited delight that amounted to ecstacy."[34]

Then Marshall himself was hit by a bullet he never heard. He was at once in agony with a shattered spine. Wood remarked that "one of the pluckiest things of the day" was Marshall "putting in what time he had left, dictating a story to the *Journal*" that was "taken down by another wounded man. All were cheerful. Not a whimper was heard." In the company of the disabled, it was unmanly to complain.

Marshall listened to "the quivering, quavering chorus" of similarly injured men in the field hospital singing "My Country, 'Tis of Thee." He was critically wounded but exalted by what he viewed as the sacrifice he had made for love of his homeland.[35]

On the Left

When Roosevelt reached Wood, he was immediately dispatched with G Troop to take Brodie's command on the left where bullets from the Mausers cut the grass beside the troopers, lopped small branches from trees, and filled the air with whistling. The effect was daunting. Men received multiple wounds strung in a row.[36]

When F Troop advanced to where D Troop was lying, two men who had become friends moved forward together. "He was a little in front of me and to the side," one of them remembered, "both of us running. There were a number of our dead around and several of our wounded, and the sight of them stirred me greatly, but as I looked at the man in front of me, the breath left my body as the whole top of his head flew up in the air, his skull blown to atoms by an explosive bullet. He fell with a thud, and I ran on, past his body."[37]

No one paid more attention than that when the man next to him was shot. The casualty was taken as a matter of course, arousing no more concern than a sprain in a football game at home. A trooper in the midst of battle could not both grieve and survive. He had to look out for himself and his regiment before taking care of comrades who were hit and out of the fight.

The wounded were treated first by the socialite Assistant Surgeon Bob Church. His medical resources were limited to what he had carried under his arm from Siboney. He had three first-aid packets rolled in rubber sheeting, each containing two gauze compresses, one triangular bandage, one sling, two safety pins, and one bottle of aromatic spirits of ammonia. With these few supplies, Church saw to more than thirty seriously injured troopers. He also attended to dozens of men with lesser complaints.[38]

Church often went into the line of fire to reach casualties. He dressed men's wounds on the spot when necessary. Otherwise, he carried the wounded to the rear on his shoulders and ministered to them before they went to the field hospital. Wood remarked that Church looked like a hog butcher. He was covered with blood.[39]

Roosevelt found his way to the head of the troops on the left. He obviously was enjoying himself. Journalist Harris heard him shout a joking remark to F Troop's Captain Luna. Both officers laughed as the men around them moved forward in brief headlong sprints. Roosevelt had no canteen. When he could not borrow a drink, his throat became so dry he was reduced to whispering orders.[40]

The Rough Riders moved steadily forward, firing only aimed shots. In the rushes, the easterners jumped up at the command to advance and ran for the next objective. To Davis, the easterners looked like men trying to get out of the rain. He said that westerners slipped silently through the undergrowth like the Indians a few of them were. Despite the half-mile remaining to reach the Spaniards' lines, the ground gained in each lunge was not much more than a ballplayer's slide to a base. The troopers were aided, though, by the decreasing effectiveness of the Spaniards' volleys. The Rough Riders were learning to time the bursts of gunfire to determine when to take cover.[41]

Like other officers, Roosevelt started out wearing a ceremonial sword that dangled from his belt. The sword got between his legs and tripped him when he ran, so he took it off and handed it to a trooper to carry for him. After the engagement he tied the sword to what was left of his baggage. He never wore it again during the campaign.[42]

He frequently verified that the dozen pairs of extra steel-rimmed spectacles he had with him were safe. The glasses were tucked away in his uniform pockets and lightly sewn into his hat. Two pairs were in his saddlebags. At the beginning of the skirmish he had been concerned when a Mauser bullet whistled close to his horse Texas. An orderly assured him that the animal was unharmed. "I know that,"

Roosevelt replied, "but what about my spectacles?" He could get along without the horse if he had to. Without glasses, he would have had to give up his command.[43]

To relieve his own emotions, heightening during the advance, Roosevelt borrowed a carbine from a wounded trooper and took one shot at the enemy. Then he heard cheering on the right and dropped the gun. He surmised that the men under O'Neill were preparing to charge. Sharp-eyed Davis had observed the Spaniards' rear guard retreating. He told O'Neill's lieutenant that it was time to launch the last assault.[44]

Without waiting to ascertain the reason for the cheers, Roosevelt ordered his own charge. Shrieking jubilantly with the men, he led the way on foot across the open field beyond the jungle where the Spanish resistance had ended.

The Spaniards had discovered Lawton's support regiments moving into flanking positions on the far right. In addition, the 9th Cavalry had progressed along the right side of the fortified hill and was opening an enfilading fire. The two Rough Rider troops under O'Neill were attacking the front of the Spaniards' line and Roosevelt was leading the charge on the left.[45]

After two hours of determined opposition, the Spaniards' position had become untenable. They were about to be overrun, so they made an orderly withdrawal. As they crossed in front of the Rough Riders while marching toward Santiago, they were not fired upon. The troopers said they assumed that the Spaniards were Castillo's Cubans who had arrived at last, despite the Spaniards' conspicuously white uniforms and big hats. Actually, the men had their eyes exclusively on the fortified hill that was their objective.[46]

From the main road, General Wheeler had a clear view of the Spanish retreat. He shouted, "We've got the Yankees on the run!" The old Confederate general was rattled, but not to the extent of fulfilling his promise to join the charge.[47]

American regulars and volunteers met at the brick walls of the abandoned sugar house on the hill. They found two dead Spaniards, heaps of empty cartridge cases, and a small amount of beans. The troopers promptly cooked and shared the beans for the midday meal.[48]

Roosevelt was beginning to station pickets in outposts on the left flank when a trooper told him that Wood had been killed in the final charge. That would put Roosevelt in command of the regiment, so he started back alone to find out what had happened to his friend. Picking his way through the thick vegetation was as difficult returning as it had been advancing. Finally he located Wood on a sunken path. Wood was uninjured and was trying to establish contact with his victorious troopers.[49]

Roosevelt was delighted to see Wood safe. He asked what the Spaniards were doing. Wood resented Roosevelt's elation at a time when he as the commanding officer had to face possible censure for unnecessary loss of life. He replied curtly that the enemy had run away. Next he reprimanded Roosevelt in front of the staff officers for leaving his post and for failing to complete the positioning of the pickets guarding the Rough Riders' left wing.[50]

The Odd Ambush

No one noticed then or later that there might have been something odd about the ambush.

The Spaniards appear to have known on the night of June 23 what Shafter and Lawton did not know, that Wheeler would attack inland the next morning rather than waiting to march when and where Shafter determined. The indicator of Spanish awareness of Wheeler's intent is the thorough preparation of defenses at Las Guasimas. The Spaniards had barricaded the trenches there on an emergency basis at night, even though the route of the American invaders might well have been along the coast as Shafter had planned and Lawton would have preferred.

Moreover, the Spaniards resolutely defended the trail that Young and the veteran regulars followed, but they set up an ambush along the route of the inexperienced volunteers. They had time to hide pickets along the flanks of the footpath, starting at the top of the cliff. As Roosevelt belatedly surmised, the pickets reported the regiment's progress by simulating the cuckoo's guttural *cu-cu-cu* call.

The Spaniards also concealed sharpshooters on both sides of the path for half a mile before the fortified fork. The ambuscade in a cul-de-sac was intended to decimate the Rough Riders, knock them out of the war, and perhaps delay the American army long enough for the rainy season to start. Las Guasimas was the Spaniards' first stand, part of Linares's strategy. The only thing that saved the Rough Riders was the Spaniards' poor aim.

The officers who were privy to Wheeler's intentions were Young, Wood, and the rebel General Castillo. Eight hundred Cubans under Castillo were scheduled to accompany the American cavalrymen on the Las Guasimas attack. However, the rebel general overslept. His men refused to wake him or to go on the march without him, and Young did not insist.

In addition, the two Cuban scouts who were at the point of the Rough Riders' long column disappeared before the ambush was sprung. Tom Isbell of L Troop was left alone in front.

Roosevelt's assessment of Cuban courage was so low that he did not suspect the rebels of venality. No other American officer did, either, yet treachery in the Cuban ranks was possible. Someone in General Castillo's confidence may have been a Spanish spy.

Chapter 15
Body Count
at Las Guasimas

Two hard marches in two days, two hours of exposure to heavy Spanish gunfire, and an all-out charge had exhausted both the Rough Riders on the path and the regulars in the valley. They were in no condition to chase the Spaniards who were retreating in good order. To catch their breath, they settled on the abandoned hill.

Thirty minutes later, three troops of the 9th Cavalry strode up, just ahead of mounted Gen. Adna Chaffee who was commanding Lawton's infantry. Last came the cautious Cubans who allegedly had slept through the engagement.

Instead of relaying Lawton's bitter denunciations, Chaffee complimented Wood and Roosevelt on standing up to such "a disastrous attack" on their men. He preferred the polite approach. He thought, though, that the Rough Riders had blundered into the ambush. In his opinion, they had been saved only by the approach of his supporting forces.[1]

In contrast, the Rough Riders were quite satisfied with their performance under pressure. Wood wrote to his wife, "I don't want to boast but we had a brilliant fight. The Spaniards said they fought the entire American Army for four hours. My men had the bulk of the enemy in front of them and the Regulars one-third."[2]

Some of the Rough Riders wandered around the fortifications, bragging about their regiment's casualties to prove how brave they had been. The deaths of L Troop's Capron and Fish would rate headlines back home in the United States, they said. The first Spanish volley from ambush also killed Tilden Dawson, a brickmaker from Nevada, Missouri, who became number three in the Rough Rider body count. Officially, however, the tally of the dead and wounded proved to be a standoff between the volunteers and the unsung regulars. This surprised the Rough Riders who had lived through the unnerving ambush while the regulars were in the supposedly quieter valley. They did not, however, question the count.

Troopers who went back to the ridge out of curiosity were able to trace the ambuscade and the counterattack by the trail of empty cartridge shells ejected onto the ground. Where the Rough Riders had been caught unawares on the path, there was only a scattering of whitish nickel casings from their Krag-Jorgensens. The Americans had fired their carbines hesitantly as long as the Spaniards were concealed. Where Spanish sharpshooters had knelt on the flanks of the path, there were hundreds of brass Mauser shells.[3]

Nickel casings also were scattered where the Rough Riders entered the jungle and advanced on the right. Next there were a few nickel shells in clusters where Roosevelt had tried to organize answering volleys. In the area where the Rough Riders began their charge, the nickel casings were spread out even farther. Finally, there were countless brass Mauser shells on the fortified hill.

Hero of the Day

Although only Harris among the correspondents had seen Roosevelt lead the final assault, newsmen were unanimous in declaring the lieutenant colonel the hero of the day. Neither Wood nor O'Neill was mentioned.

Marshall, who was injured before the charge, wrote that "the troopers about me" in the hospital "were full of tales of Roosevelt's bravery." He concluded, "Roosevelt's Rough Riders were in the forefront of the onslaught, and no more giant figure appeared than Roosevelt—millionaire, reformer, politician, a testy, troublesome, violently prejudiced and disturbing person in peace, but a true soldier, cool and daring, setting an example and pointing the way to the death-dealing enemy."[4]

Caspar Whitney was in the valley with the regulars, completely out of touch with the Rough Riders. Nevertheless, he described "the extreme left of the Rough Riders—under the command of Colonel

Roosevelt, himself leading the charge, rifle in hand—driving the Spaniards from their last stand."[5]

Davis also was on the right side of the footpath. He reported even more enthusiastically that "the final charge was led by Colonel Roosevelt, some 20 feet in advance" of his men. W. Nephew King, who was not in Cuba at all, maintained that "how Lieutenant Colonel Roosevelt escaped without being killed or wounded is almost miraculous. He was at all times in the thick of the fight."[6]

The descriptions were not wholly accurate. Roosevelt realized that "the fight was a capital thing for me," and he personally gave the particulars to Davis. Davis then added the hyperbole—such as Roosevelt carrying the rifle in front of his men—and informally disseminated the embroidered details to correspondents who had not been on the scene.[7]

The effusive Marshall was confined to the Siboney hospital, critically wounded and out of the war. Complimenting him on his fortitude the way Wood had done would have been pointless for Roosevelt. He had his eye on the future. Instead of praising Marshall, the lieutenant colonel expressed official thanks to the uninjured Davis "for services rendered to the troops." After all, Davis had located the enemy on the hill for Roosevelt. He discovered that the Spaniards were retreating, participated in the final charge, and would be continuing with the regiment. Praise would not be wasted on him.[8]

Roosevelt also insisted upon "a word for our own men. Not a man flinched. Every officer and man did his duty up to the handle." Wood's post-skirmish assessment agreed with Roosevelt by applauding his officers "one and all. It would be impossible to mention one without mentioning all." Wood refrained from making any further reference to the officer he saw as his rival. Roosevelt was the troopers' and correspondents' clear choice as the embodiment of courage. Wood gave him only mixed reviews.[9]

There were two Rough Riders who were not commended. One was the nameless soldier who dropped the parts of the rapid-fire guns. The other was Adjutant Hall, who saw Marshall wounded in the initial Spanish volleys. Frightened by the Spanish gunfire and mistaking Marshall for nearby Wood, who was of a comparable size and wore a similar shirt, Hall panicked. He scurried back to Siboney by himself and breathlessly disclosed to the press that the regiment had been wiped out in an ambush and that Wood was dead. The false story was published in early newspaper editions in the United States and was not corrected by the Siboney journalists until a disabled but vocal Marshall arrived there on a stretcher.[10]

Excluding the one civilian injury that was Marshall's, the official tally of Rough Rider losses was eight killed and thirty-four wounded. Despite the thousands of bullets fired by hundreds of Spanish infantrymen, the listed Rough Rider casualties were less than 8 percent. After the opening salvo, there were only five deaths in the regiment in two hours of fighting. The engagement that had seemed to be a major battle had been, after all, just a skirmish in the regular army's view. The war so far was a little one.[11]

Davis had reported that every third Rough Rider was killed or wounded at Las Guasimas. That would have included at least a hundred fifty men—a disaster! In substantiation of Davis's findings, Assistant Surgeon Church said he attended to more than thirty seriously injured troopers by himself. He also saw dozens of men with lesser injuries. His total of just the wounded was about a hundred, while LaMotte treated an additional forty men at the base hospital. Davis's report was correct.[12]

Yet, the official count was merely thirty-four wounded. That was because standard army practice counted only those troopers who required sustained hospitalization. Men treated in the hospital for bullet wounds and released were not classified as wounded. Neither were men who were attended to in the field but who refused to go to the hospital. Keeping the casualties light was in Wood's interest.

Conversely, at first the Spanish army listed as casualties only the two Spaniards found dead on the fortified hill. The official Spanish count proved to be nine dead and twenty-seven wounded. That was less than a quarter of the actual American losses reported in the press, but it was a reasonable number because soldiers attacking fortifications do incur more losses than defenders. Young raised the total a little, from thirty-six to forty-two Spanish casualties, using what he called information from private sources.[13]

Wood, however, wanted to enhance American gains from the engagement by creating many more Spanish casualties than there actually had been. His estimates ran the total to hundreds of Spaniards killed or wounded at Las Guasimas. Spanish casualties were increasing in Wood's mind as the number of wounded Rough Riders held steady.

The View from the Spanish Side

There were 36,500 Spanish soldiers in Santiago province. Of these, 10,000 infantrymen were positioned in and around the city. Also in the city were 2,000 sailors from the Spanish fleet blockaded in the harbor.[14]

The Spanish soldiers lived almost exclusively on a diet of white rice and what they could forage. They received only weak coffee in the morning. Midday and evening meals were rice boiled in water and served with rice bread but without meat, fat, or salt. When meat was available, it went to the officers. Feeding the sailors from army stores exacerbated the shortage of food for soldiers. Only wine and rum were plentiful.[15]

In addition, there were five hundred thousand Mauser cartridges in the Santiago arsenal. Half a million seems a large number, yet it amounted to forty cartridges for each soldier and sailor in the city. The quantity was barely enough for one battle and there could be no resupply from land or sea. Fortunately for the Spaniards, another large but uncounted quantity of cartridges already had been distributed to soldiers who would face the Americans in the field.[16]

Moreover, the Spanish treasury in Madrid no longer honored invoices from Cuban vendors to the army and navy. The soldiers had not been paid in thirteen months. Morale was as low as the food supply.[17]

General Linares had witnessed the arrival of the American invasion fleet off Santiago on June 20. His primary objective was to guard the mouth of Santiago harbor against the American army. Despite warnings from his governor general, Linares assumed that the Americans would try to disembark at Santiago, not at a remote spot like Daiquiri. There was no harbor at Daiquiri, no decent road to Santiago, the drinking water was questionable, and the distance to Santiago seemed too great to permit hostilities before the start of the rainy season.[18]

According to advice Linares received from his superiors in Havana, the New York City newspapers that Spain relied upon for information indicated there were at least fifty thousand American soldiers in the expedition. Also, the squadron of American warships in the blockade had been supplemented by the warships guarding the convoy. Such a strong force could eventually compel Linares to retreat from any place Shafter chose for the landing. A tiger can jump wherever it wants, Linares said. He envied Shafter.[19]

At this point, both Linares and Admiral Cervera already knew the sad end. Linares's strategy was to remain on the defensive, avoid decisive battles for as long as possible, withdraw slowly into the well-entrenched city of Santiago, and hope that his one Cuban ally, disease, would defeat the Americans.[20]

During the evening of June 21, Linares's spies told him that the Americans would be landing at Daiquiri. It was too late to reinforce the three hundred Spaniards there. When they were ousted by the rebels the next morning, they marched straight to Santiago.

The entire rear guard, then, was the 620 men under General Rubin who had been stationed at Siboney. They proceeded inland to Las Guasimas and took positions on the fortified hill. The only Spaniards at the fork were these 620 infantrymen. They were not reinforced. The 1,500 soldiers Roosevelt mentioned and the 2,500 Wood claimed as a minimum were a tribute to the fighting ability of the much maligned Spanish infantry.[21]

Earlier, Rubin's six companies at Las Guasimas had checked what they thought was an American advance. In fact, it was the Cuban probe on June 23. Linares considered the rear guard's assignment to be completed and he revised his plan that had made Las Guasimas a major roadblock. Instead, he ordered Rubin to retire to Santiago after breakfast on June 24, "with the precaution and deliberation necessary effectually to repel any attack."[22]

Like Wheeler, Rubin interpreted instructions to favor fighting. He knew the Rough Riders would be advancing along the mountain path at an early hour on the twenty-fourth. He obeyed his new orders by setting the ambush, ostensibly to restrain the Rough Riders until the retreat could be initiated in a prudent manner. Actually, he was looking for at least the skirmish he found.

After two hours of fighting, when Lawton's supporting regiments threatened to flank the fortifications, Rubin started the planned retreat toward the next defensive position, the entrenchments at San Juan in front of Santiago. He announced that he had defeated the entire American Army.

The Americans took several Spanish prisoners at Las Guasimas. One was a courier carrying Linares's latest order to General Rubin, instructing him to retreat at once. The Spanish strategy had changed again, but not in time to reach Rubin. No ambush would have taken place if Young and Wood had not raced their columns faster than the Spanish courier's deliberate pace.[23]

American cavalry officers continued to insist that the Spaniards had been routed. Wood boasted, "A superior force of the enemy was driven from a strong position of their own choosing and thrown into a disorderly flight in which he could readily have become destroyed." He sometimes misused pronouns as if English was a second language.[24]

Because the Americans persisted in seeing Las Guasimas as an easy win in a hard place, they learned no lesson about the cost of charging a fortified hill where the defenders stood firm.[25]

Chapter 16

Preparing to Fight Again

After a brief rest, the Rough Riders formed into troops and marched half a mile back along the mountain footpath in the direction of Siboney. They were sadly aware of the gaps in their ranks that were caused by the casualties. As they said, it "queered" them to have talked early in the morning with an absent buddy who might now be dead or seriously wounded.[1]

On the way, they filed quietly past the body of a Spaniard who had unsuccessfully tried to staunch the bleeding from a chest wound by stuffing the opening with cigarette papers. His uniform that once was white gaily pin-striped with blue was now dark red and brown. The enemy had suffered losses, too.

Camp was pitched among hundreds of empty brass Mauser shells in the tall grass and quickly named for Wheeler. The first task was to send squads of troopers to locate missing men who were presumed to be casualties because Wood said no Rough Rider would have deserted. He told the searchers that a grim way to find bodies was to watch for vultures which fly in circles over places where men bled on the earth.[2]

Other troopers marched off with borrowed shovels to dig a common grave for the Rough Rider dead. A third detail carried the critically wounded from LaMotte's field hospital to the better equipped medical station in Siboney. Litters were improvised from poles and blankets because Wood had rejected LaMotte's requisition for stretchers while they were in Tampa.

Rough Riders reacted to the dead in dissimilar ways. Most of the troopers who found corpses in the jungle or the grass laid them reverently on blankets next to bodies already placed alongside the path. Others behaved with bluster. "Here's Fish," one man remarked after identifying the corpse. "He said they couldn't catch him, and they got him the first one." The trooper's companions laughed. The man then removed a harmonica from Fish's bloodstained pocket, saying "here's his music box," and they laughed again.[3]

A little later, regimental officers were lounging only fifteen feet from Fish's body while they chuckled with Roosevelt about an incident in the fight. No matter how intimate the dead had been before the skirmish, they were best forgotten in the aftermath. The uninjured considered themselves to have been lucky. They joked because they were relieved to have come through the fight without harm.

A fourth group of troopers hunted for abandoned blanket rolls and haversacks. There was extra gear to be recovered due to the casualties but Cuban rebels had already ransacked the packs for meat and hardtack.

Canvas awnings were swung for Wood, Roosevelt, and the correspondents at five o'clock in the afternoon. In the evening a pack train from Siboney brought enough rations for a night meal and for the next morning. In the flush of victory, Roosevelt announced enthusiastically that henceforth the regiment would be called the Rough Riders on its own records. The nickname would be official for the first time.

The men turned in early, sleeping on what Wood described as the initial battlefield of the war. That night the last members of the original expeditionary force finally landed at Siboney, two long hectic days after the Rough Riders had disembarked. Meanwhile, the rest of the Fifth Army Corps was moving forward rapidly to occupy the rolling, wooded country around Sevilla, the inland village beyond the fork at Las Guasimas. Fresh infantry and cavalry units were hurrying past the Rough Riders' camp. Relinquishing the advance was a letdown for the troopers.

As characterized by military historians who were recording action in the war, the next six days were uneventful. From the soldiers' standpoint, however, the days were notable because of the shortage of food. After breakfast on the morning following the skirmish,

June 25, the Rough Riders had few rations left in the regimental stores. Men who could not forage for themselves might literally starve.

Yet, Shafter did not order a wharf to be built to expedite unloading. Instead, he made an emergency request for ten more landing barges to be sent from Florida. Nine of these barges were either lost in rough weather on the crossing or were soon wrecked on the Siboney beach by inexperienced crews. There was no further assistance from the Navy.

Roosevelt's personal problems were as vexing to him as the scarcity of food. "I have been sleeping on the ground in the mackintosh," he grumbled, "and so drenched with sweat that I haven't been dry a minute, day or night. I haven't seen my servant Marshall. My bag has never turned up, and I have nothing with me, no soap, toothbrush, razor, brandy, medicine chest, socks or underclothes." Losing the soap and the toothbrush was a blow, but those close to him knew he loved these little privations that really emphasized how well he was enduring the campaign.[4]

At eleven o'clock the next morning the Rough Riders were formed into troops again and marched forward to the hillside at Las Guasimas where the Spaniards had begun their retreat. Ahead was a vista of tropical jungle in a tranquil valley running toward Sevilla and Santiago.

Dug deep into the grassy soil amid wild flowers was a narrow fifty-foot-long trench heavily lined with palm leaves. The remains of the seven enlisted men had been wrapped in blankets and laid end to end in the grave. Wooden coffins could not be taken from the burial materials on the transports because of the pressure to unload rations. Instead, more palm leaves were heaped profusely on the sheathed corpses. Then the trench was filled with dirt.[5]

Troopers who had laughed in camp were silent now as they stood around the grave. They bared their heads while Chaplain Brown read the Episcopalian funeral service intended to encompass all religions. When Brown knelt in prayer, the troopers got down on their knees, too. He announced the hymn as "Nearer, My God, to Thee" and the deep voices of the men followed his lead. Some men sobbed. No volley was fired over the grave for fear of alarming other regiments moving toward the new front. The bugler blew taps. Troopers heard the notes as "Go to sleep. Go to sleep," and in conclusion, "Day is done."[6]

Chaplain Brown had noted the location of each body in the common grave. After the committal service he had individual markers carved in wood for each of the dead, showing the day, name, and birth date if available in the sparse regimental records. The markers would be impermanent in the tropics but the arrangement was the best that the conscientious Brown could make. Many soldiers' graves would go unmarked in Cuba.[7]

Captain Capron was the eighth Rough Rider victim at Las Guasimas. Because he had been such a strong influence, L Troop was renamed in his honor. A former cavalryman in the West, the experienced Capron had served as Roosevelt's informal tutor on military tactics.[8]

Chaplain Brown of the "Rough Riders" Preaching to the Regiment (in Cuba). Stereopticon view. (New York: Underwood and Underwood, 1898).

⟶ 174 ⟵

Capron and Roosevelt had held similar beliefs about combat. When Capron criticized Army regulations for paying too much attention to the niceties of retreating, Roosevelt agreed: "There should be no retreat. It is possible the exigencies of a situation may demand that we fall back, but our men must understand we are falling back, not retreating, and falling back was part of our original intention." The choice of bland words to represent unpleasant realities was important to men who would not retreat lightly and would not admit it if they had. They had an example of falling back in the orderly retreat of the Spanish infantry that ended the fight at Las Guasimas.[9]

Capron's funeral was held at Siboney after the mass burial of the enlisted men near Las Guasimas. His wife and mother would have preferred interment in the United States, but his father, a captain of artillery, was on hand. He recognized that the absence of embalmers, metal coffins, and refrigeration made transportation of a corpse impractical.

Capron's grave was dug into a solitary hillside overlooking the bay, rather than with other dead cavalry officers. Half of the Rough Riders were too weary to walk the hilly miles to Siboney. Sturdier troopers made the hike and stood casually along one side of the grave.[10]

At four o'clock, a 2nd Infantry company marched up the hill as a courtesy to Capron's father and formed a straight line on the far side of the grave. The chaplains of the two regiments then led the procession between the ranks. Six Rough Riders from L Troop carried the plain wooden coffin that had been secured for Capron because he had been a captain. Wood, Roosevelt, and other senior officers of the two regiments followed. The funeral service was read, a single volley was fired, and two bugles sounded taps.[11]

On the march back to Camp Wheeler, Wood had the troopers shoulder boxes of ammunition from the Siboney base to replace cartridges fired in the skirmish. In hostile country, bullets came before food.[12]

The Ambush Revisited

Publisher William Randolph Hearst of the *Journal* interviewed General Shafter on board the *Seguranca* the evening after the fight. He described Shafter as "in bad humor because of losses in the skirmish." Later, however, Shafter officially characterized the engagement as "the brush at Guasimas." The general played down the action as less than a skirmish in order to avoid charging Wheeler and Young with defying instructions and Wood with being ambushed. Wheeler had been right about Shafter's unwillingness to discipline him.[13]

In contrast, Lawton openly rebuked Wheeler for stealing the advance from the infantry and pushing the Spaniards into meaningless combat. Wheeler was not disconcerted. Angry words from a subordinate could not diminish the accomplishment of getting in the first licks.[14]

Lawton and his staff officers also denounced "the criminal recklessness" of the Rough Riders' leadership for being ambushed. When Wood and Roosevelt arrived in Siboney for Capron's funeral, though, infantry officers overwhelmed them with congratulations. The typical reaction to Wheeler's initiative, Wood's poise, and Roosevelt's press coverage was jealousy. The Rough Riders no longer were mocked by the regulars as pretentiously amateurish "horse show guards." They had proved their courage in the hardest test, enduring an ambush.[15]

It was accepted that the Rough Riders had been surprised at Las Guasimas. Davis wrote to his family, "We were caught in a clear case of ambush." Dunning reported to the Associated Press, "As perfect an ambuscade as was ever formed in the brain of an Apache Indian was prepared, and Roosevelt and his men walked squarely into it." Both correspondents had been present on the ridge.[16]

The Rough Riders bragged in letters home that the Spaniards had been waiting in ambush. During their first trips to Siboney, they proudly told other soldiers that they had fought their way out of a cul-de-sac. Surviving the "gallant blunder" was a measure of their personal valor.[17]

Photographer McIntosh was more sophisticated. He declared that "there was no question in the mind of anybody that day that they had been ambushed, although many a man is liable to make a statement on the spur of the moment which he will regret after he looks at the diplomatic side."[18]

Young and Wood soon understood what McIntosh meant. Walking into an ambush implied carelessness, an unacceptable stigma for an officer. To compensate, Wood was still inflating the number of enemy casualties. He insisted that the Rough Riders had buried 71 Spaniards on the battlefield, bringing the total of Spanish casualties to 306. That was an obvious fiction. Only 620 Spanish infantrymen had been on the hill, and substantially all of them had marched away in good order.[19]

Wood added that "our flag was the first up where we landed and we got the first fight of the war. The Infantry are jealous of us. The only surprise connected with Guasimas is that envy at our success should have been able to produce such a falsehood as the ambush." Young blamed "the account of the ambuscade" on "the demoralized reporters and the demoralized adjutant of the Rough Riders who left the service shortly afterward." Accusing the press has a modern feel.[20]

Secretary of War Alger concluded, "The engagement was no ambuscade. Colonel Wood, after learning of the presence of the enemy where he had been informed they would be, deployed five of his troops before a shot was fired." In fact, Wood knew only that the enemy was on the fortified hill. He suspected Spaniards were along the path but he reacted too slowly to avoid the ambush. He himself had admitted "the first hostile bullets" were already "singing" when "the troops moved up" to be deployed.[21]

Davis was induced to fudge his original view. He later wrote, "It is true that the fight was against an enemy in ambush, but there is a difference between blundering into an ambush and setting out with knowledge you will find the enemy in ambush." In fact, Wood did not know the enemy was in ambush when he set out. The Rough Riders were surprised. Besides, in trying to draw a line between being ambushed and knowingly being ambushed, Davis was implying that Wood had deliberately sprung the trap. If correct, this would have made the Rough Riders' casualties the result of Wood's intentional act, not mere negligence.[22]

The tarnish also touched Roosevelt briefly before turning back into praise. A congressman who knew only what he read in the Associated Press dispatch about Roosevelt's "walking squarely" into the ambuscade demanded that the lieutenant colonel be court-martialed for endangering his troopers. The War Department responded with the irrelevant explanation that the order to attack came from Wheeler, not from Wood or Roosevelt. The department also initiated a rumor that "Wood and Roosevelt may be raised to Brigadier General in recognition of recent daring exploits." The mention of promotion meant military approval and ended civilian criticism.[23]

As Wheeler expected, the army closed ranks behind him. By covering up the lack of authority for Wheeler's escapade, Shafter sent a silent message to other aggressive officers. Any command could be disobeyed at whatever cost, if the result could be publicized as successful.[24]

When the war was over, however, Major General Miles testified that Wheeler's unplanned diversion of the expeditionary force to Las Guasimas caused most of the hardships the soldiers suffered later in the campaign. Wheeler had drawn the troops five miles into the interior, away from the transports the men should have been unloading in Siboney Bay and away from the invasion route along the coast to the seaside forts at Santiago harbor. Miles was engaged in disputes with Shafter, however, and his testimony may have been biased.

Shafter's fear that a storm might drive the transports out to sea and put rations beyond reach proved groundless, but the army never did get all the stores off the transports. Some soldiers in the field were not adequately fed until the campaign had concluded.[25]

Guasimas and Gettysburg

After Las Guasimas, Richard Harding Davis's peers remarked that Davis's luck had placed him at the highlight of the skirmish and had given him the details of Roosevelt's charge. In fact, though, Davis had earned the scoop. He had allied himself with Roosevelt from the start. He went to the front with Roosevelt, and established the rapport that led Roosevelt to tell him the insider's story of the charge. The Rough Riders and their lieutenant colonel were Davis's kind of soldier, part erudite and part rough, but ready to advance with or without orders. Davis was sure that they would lead him on a direct route to the main body of the Spaniards.[26]

For his part, Roosevelt catered to Davis to secure his inflated news coverage. He had thought of Davis as a wordsmith, not as a soldier, and had believed that Davis would flinch under fire. When Davis surprised him by acting bravely in battle, Roosevelt won the correspondent's personal as well as his professional allegiance by mentioning Davis favorably in an official army dispatch. He also touted Davis's courage to General Wheeler.

Davis told his family, "If the men had been Regulars, I would have sat in the rear as others did, but I know every other one of the Rough Riders, played football and that sort of thing with them, so I thought as an American I ought to help. After it was over, Roosevelt made me a long speech before the men and offered me a captaincy any time I wanted it. He told the AP man there was no officer who had 'been of more help or shown more courage' than your humble servant. After this, I keep quiet."[27]

By praising Davis so elaborately, Roosevelt indirectly disparaged his own officers. They understood his purpose, though, and did not complain. There were more American reporters in Cuba than had covered any previous war, but divisional and regimental headquarters had to compete for the most famous. Davis commented, "The position of the real correspondent is the very best. Generals fight to have us." He had to be flattered to induce him to remain with the Rough Riders.[28]

John Fox and Caspar Whitney also joined the Rough Riders. Davis wrote, "We are welcome and Roosevelt has us at headquarters. You get more news with other regiments but the officers, even the Generals, are such narrow minded slipshod men that we only visit them to pick up information. Being with the Rough Riders in a tight place has made us friends and I guess I'll stick to the regiment. We are dirty and hungry and sleep on the ground and have grand talks on every subject. I was never more happy and never so well."[29]

One element of Roosevelt's appeal was his practiced charm. In the evening around the campfire, he fed Davis stories about his Dakota experiences to justify his role as a westerner in the Rough Riders. He described the Marquis de Mores as "a cotton-mouthed adder, exciting but not pleasant." Davis was expected to remember Roosevelt's widely circulated claim that he had faced down the Marquis when challenged to a duel. Similarly, Roosevelt characterized a Bad Lands "neighbor" as "a man of large and liberal views. He had no foolish and puerile prejudice in favor of virtue." Davis was supposed to recognize the neighbor as the notorious gunman Roosevelt had ousted from a squatter's shack.

Soon Davis had "a cot raised off the ground in [Roosevelt's] tent and am very well off." When Davis broke his chair in the officers' mess, troopers were ordered to make a new one. The men had already put in six hours with picks and shovels broadening the trail and removing stones big enough to block wagons, but Davis was a priority.[30]

Through Davis, the military legend of Teddy was spreading. There was still the predictably negative reaction from regular officers, however, because a promotion that was slated for Roosevelt would mean no advancement for them until after Roosevelt was accommodated. They grumbled that there were more newspaper articles about Roosevelt and his regiment in the insignificant scuffle at Las Guasimas than had been penned about both sides in the Civil War battle of Gettysburg.[31]

In addition, the regulars who were ignored by the press challenged Roosevelt's qualifications as an officer. Right after the skirmish, they alleged, an excited Roosevelt had "talked vociferously" to General Wheeler, "elated over what he said were heavy losses" in his regiment and giving Wheeler "a weird impression of his military ideas and capacity." Roosevelt was seeking to benefit from deaths he caused, they insisted, to improve the recognition of his own performance.

The regular cavalry officers told the journalists they were able to buttonhole that the most colorful account of the war thus far was being ignored. The true story was not Roosevelt's courage but his survival. They maintained that "the vaunted socialite soldier and his white millionaire friends" in the Rough Riders had been on the verge of being wiped out in the ambush at Las Guasimas. They were saved by black regular troopers in the valley who threatened to cut off the Spanish sharpshooters on the ridge. The unsung blacks had won the day at the cost of many casualties, rather than the headline-hunting civilian soldier Roosevelt.[32]

The reporters paid no attention. Even if the regulars' assertions had been wholly true, printing them would not have sold newspapers.

We Lined Up with Teddy

Admiring correspondents observed that the Rough Riders were like a whole newspaper. They were composed of a society page, financial column, sports section, and advertisements for Wild West shows. At Las Guasimas, they also made the front page as prime news. The obituaries were in the back of the paper.[33]

Davis added to the social notes: "This is the best crowd—they are well educated and interesting. The Regular Army men are dull and narrow and bore one to death. Here, it is funny to see Larned, the tennis champ, whose every movement at Newport was applauded by hundreds of women, marching in wet grass. Whitney and I guy him. Today a sentry on post was reading 'As You Like It' and half the men want to know who won the boat race."[34]

As a snob, Davis appreciated the Fifth Avenue Boys the most, despite the lack of discipline shown by flagrant reading on guard duty. After the skirmish, he applauded a song that expressed their soldierly pride

> They scoffed when we lined up with Teddy.
> They said we were dudes and all that.
> They imagined that 'Cholly' and 'Fweddie'
> Would faint at the drop of a hat.
> But let them look there in the ditches,
> Blood-stained by the swells in the van,
> And know that a chap may have riches,
> And still be a hell of a man.[35]

The campaign hat that was dropped in the song was a new Roosevelt hallmark on the sartorial side. Hats were styled distinctively by the different services, and the more battered they were, the more they were valued as proof of experience on the battlefield. After a splash of water, regular infantrymen creased the crown, dented the sides, and left the brim straight. Regular cavalrymen pulled the crown out to a point like *gauchos*. To be different, Rough Riders creased the crown, turned the back up, and pulled down the front. Roosevelt achieved his special look by punching the crown into shapelessness and fastening the left side of the brim to the crown with the cavalry insignia.[36]

Famous authors doubling as war correspondents searched for Roosevelt's camp to interview him in his military garb. He did not look at all like the dapper Story Teller they had listened to at the Fellowcraft Club in New York City. They described him now as dressed like his soldiers, in brown trousers, a blue flannel shirt open at the throat, and leggings. His headquarters were no better than the troopers' tents. The correspondents claimed, however, that his personality had become so much more striking that he could appear at future club festivities dressed anonymously the way he was in Cuba and still be recognized by everyone.[37]

Even in the field, Roosevelt let nothing interfere with his contacts with Washington. Aware that his political future might depend upon President McKinley, he addressed a series of letters to the White House extolling the regiment and the performance of Wood who "is the

best Colonel in the Army." He praised Wood to get the colonel promoted out of the Rough Riders. In turn, Wood slighted Roosevelt to
keep his lieutenant colonel from receiving the promotion that would
force Wood upward into the unknown.[38]

At the same time, Senator Lodge was telling Roosevelt that "the
newspapers are nominating you for Governor of New York and I
have no doubt that you can go to Congress if you want to, and if you
keep on as you have been and succeed in living through the war you
can hope for much better things than a seat in Congress."[39]

As Lodge noted, editorials in Republican newspapers supported
"Theodore Roosevelt for Governor" in 1898 as "an ingenious idea."
This was a Good Government "movement to nominate Roosevelt
the soldier, the leader of the desperate charge in the Cuban chaparral,
against the [political] machine's heelers." Nominations for governor
would be deferred until the end of the war, but the editorials gave
support to the earlier recognition of Roosevelt by "easy boss" Senator Platt.[40]

Meanwhile, Roosevelt was relishing his exciting role in the war
so far, not in politics. He "said he would not have missed the fight at
Las Guasimas for the best year of his life." Even his souvenirs were
soldierly. He "kept for the [male] children three of the empty cartridges we got from a dead Spaniard."[41]

His wife understood his priorities. When she read Davis's account
of Roosevelt's role in the final charge, she thought, "How like
Theodore, and how he must have loved it!" She believed him capable
of the exaggerations Davis added.[42]

Such Rain You Never Guessed

At eight o'clock on the morning of Sunday, June 26, the Rough Riders were ordered to break camp and advance three miles toward
Santiago. The march was an example of the army's disarray. The
regiment would move forward a couple of hundred yards as part of a
long column, then wait half an hour for no apparent reason. Dense
foliage along the trail blocked any breeze. Staff officers rode rapidly
through the ranks, raising clouds of choking dust.

Once established in the new location, discouraged troopers questioned whether the move had been worth the effort: "Our camp
ground was disappointing. The brush made it quite a job to get to

headquarters. The heat and wretched conditions have begun to tell on everyone." In contrast, the optimists and the fit remarked that "a finer country we never saw. There are mountains all around us covered with coconut and mango trees, with a few pineapples and limes." They would not go hungry.[43]

The city of Santiago was just three miles away, clearly visible from elevations around the camp. In the city, General Linares was telling the Spanish infantrymen, "Soldiers, we left the coal region" on the coast "because I did not wish to sacrifice your lives in unequal battle, under cover of armored ships. The encounter is at hand, and it will take place under equal conditions."[44]

Linares was better at explanations than he was at strategy. He had retreated from Daiquiri, Siboney, and Las Guasimas to take a stand at Santiago. Now he was trapped. Seven thousand Americans and three thousand Cubans were already camped at Sevilla and more Americans were on the way. European attachés advised their governments that "the position of the Spanish naval and military forces at Santiago is absolutely without hope."[45]

Las Guasimas had given the Rough Riders confidence in their ability to handle the coming hostilities. The next morning, June 27, they insisted that they had slept "like rocks" after the hike. The schedule for the day required them to be up at 4:30. They were prepared to eat breakfast at five, dinner at noon, and supper at five. The listing of times was only the scheduling of the meals, however, and not the reality of when they ate. Some soldiers were handed only one slice of bacon for the day, along with three hardtacks and a cup of sugarless black coffee.[46]

This was the third day of deprivation. Many men were unable to think of Spaniards at all, despite the proximity. Their ears were attuned to the bells on pack trains bringing rations, even though the next sound might be gunfire instead.[47]

When Shafter had seven pack trains organized, he still allowed only ammunition, medical supplies, hardtack, salt pork, and coffee to go forward. The ration issued to each man was increased to twelve hardtacks a day, ten slices of salt pork, and a generous three tablespoons of Arbuckle's unground coffee. The salt pork was more suited to the frigid Klondike than to Cuba, but the fat meat was welcomed by most men. The army ignored climate in diet as well as in dress.

The quantity of food, however, remained below the subsistence level. The Rough Riders believed that the privation was imposed unnecessarily by the unpopular Shafter. Thousands of rations with fresh fruit and vegetables were on the transports in the bay. The vegetables were rotting while the ships were off-limits to soldiers who otherwise would have helped themselves.

A few of the gastronomically adventurous troopers traded part of their rations for sugar and pepper. They supplemented their meals with fruit and vegetables picked in the jungle. "We are faring finely," they wrote. "We have become experienced cooks—mangoes boiled in sugar which is like applesauce; fried in sugar is like sweet potatoes. We have hardtack fried in bacon grease which is as good as anything toasted. We also soak four hardtack in water until it is dough, add salt, then mix in some coffee, fry in bacon grease, put a little sugar on top and enjoy it." Soldiers who could not add jungle pickings to salt pork went hungry.[48]

Smokers were in trouble, too. There was no government issue of tobacco and the supplies men had ran out. An eight-cent plug brought two dollars. Enlisted men with the habit but without money smoked dried horse manure mixed with grass. Troopers begged tobacco from Cuban soldiers who had plenty. The Cubans just waved in good-natured acknowledgment and continued to smoke.[49]

Another problem was how to keep clean. A clear stream ran beside the camp, but the water was reserved for drinking. Sentries were posted along the banks to prevent bathing or washing clothes. Men ladled water from the stream into containers to bring back to camp.[50]

All at once, however, tropical rains took over the afternoons, just as the Spaniards had anticipated. Almost simultaneously, there would be a zigzag flash of lightning often hitting the ground nearby, a deafening clap of thunder, and a cataract of icy water. Davis wrote, "It rains every day and such rain you never guessed. It is three inches high for an hour. Then we all go out naked and dig trenches to get it out of the way."[51]

The heavy rains allowed the men to take real baths. As many as forty soldiers at a time lathered themselves with soap and cavorted in the cold downpour. Some troopers had retained both of the fleece-lined cotton union suits supplied by the government. Once the spare suit was washed in rain water caught in a canvas, men were able to feel cleaner.

Storms ended as abruptly as they began each day, but the rain water receded less. Stagnant pools formed. The sun emerged hotter than ever and the ground steamed. Repulsive hordes of crawling and flying insects emerged into the muggy air. As annoying as these insects were, though, they were feared less than the vultures and the scavenging land crabs said to eat flesh in this season. Men were not yet aware that mosquito-borne diseases followed the rains.[52]

To add to the discomfort, food rotted. The hardtack ration was packed in wooden cases. Even under cover, the boxes became caked with mud which penetrated to the flat bread. Cheesecloth wrappings for salt pork sides and bellies turned slimy as the meat molded.[53]

The Rough Riders were camped alongside a trail three feet below ground level in some places. After the rains stopped, the trail was a huge gutter running liquid mud a foot deep. The earth became soft down deep. At night, officers' hammocks were swung from posts driven far into the swamped ground. The hammocks were five feet high and the officers were dry. By morning the posts were loose and the officers' backs rested on saturated soil.[54]

The troopers' uniforms became more bedraggled and torn every day they spent in the Cuban jungle. The men received the greatest sartorial shock when sailors from Sampson's flagship rode the ten miles from Siboney in a borrowed wagon to take a look at famous Roosevelt and his Rough Riders. The contrast between the sailors' immaculate whites and the troopers' ragged and muddy stable clothes disconcerted both groups. The Rough Riders looked more like tramps than chivalric knights.

A Feast We Had

On June 27, Roosevelt wrote, "To my great relief, my bundle came. Also poor Marshall turned up, too sick to be of any use to me. I am personally in excellent health."[55]

The next day General Shafter and his staff rode by to scout the front. Roosevelt was amused to see that the obese general looked as if he almost outweighed the huge horse he straddled.

Off the record, Roosevelt learned that General Young was to be sent back to the United States because of a high fever. Wood was expected to be breveted to brigadier general in Young's place and the command of the Rough Riders would fall to Roosevelt, right on schedule. He had told Secretary Alger that he would be ready to serve as colonel after six weeks in the field and this was just six weeks after he had arrived in San Antonio. He was filled with pride at the prospect of promotion and determined to do something special as a celebration for his men who were depressed because of their privations.

The Rough Riders were camped in brush and long grass beaten into diagonal tracks like those the forest animals make. Roosevelt was standing at the end of a track, under the canvas tent fly that served as regimental headquarters. Captain O'Neill was there, describing the consortium of mining, ranching, and agricultural enterprises he planned to start in postwar Cuba. Suddenly, Roosevelt thought of an appropriate reward for the men.

The next morning he asked for five volunteers from each of the eight troops and marched them over the mountains to Siboney. The Rough Riders' mule train had long since been commandeered by Shafter, but Roosevelt took along the officers' horses and a few Cuban mules he borrowed. At the port he led the group to the commissary to secure extra rations for the regiment.

Rebuffed because food was available for sale to officers only for their own consumption and not for distribution to enlisted men, he "bought all the beans an elastic stretch of my conscience would allow me to say could be used for the officers." The eight hundred pounds of beans in hundred-pound sacks from the commissary cost him three hundred dollars, a hugely inflated price. He had only two hundred dollars with him, so he borrowed the rest from the Fifth Avenue Boys.[56]

Afterward "I got a boat," he added, "and went out to the transport and brought in about 500 more pounds of beans, and I got all the canned tomatoes I wished and put them on the horses and the backs of men and marched back to camp." Then, Roosevelt gloated, "Oh, what a feast we had!"[57]

The unexpected treat solidified Roosevelt's hold on the Rough Riders. A few officers in other regiments attempted to secure extra rations for their men, but they failed. No other regiment had a commander who was in a position to spend his own money. No other commander would have plundered a transport.

The episode of "the boughten beans" was reported widely in the press, adding tremendously to the tender side of the composite image that was the military legend of Teddy.

Stephen Crane was excluded from the Roosevelt inner circle because of questionable morality. Nevertheless, he remarked that Roosevelt "worked for his troopers like a cider press. He tried to feed them. He helped build latrines. He got quinine. Let him be a politician if he likes. He was a gentleman down there in Cuba."[58]

Chapter 17

March to El Poso

On June 28, Stanhope Sams of the *New York Times* conjured up a fanciful view of the lieutenant colonel leading a desperate charge in the Las Guasimas chaparral while firing western-style revolvers with both hands. Actually, Roosevelt did have one revolver, the one salvaged from the sunken battleship *Maine* and given to him by his brother-in-law, Lt. Comdr. William S. Cowles. That memento had remained tucked in his waistband while he fired a borrowed carbine.

In Roosevelt's opinion, Las Guasimas had provided him with only a preliminary opening to fame and eventually to political office. The key still would be his role in the one more battle he expected before Spain capitulated. If he could position himself at the front again, he would need merely to avoid death, disability, and official censure. Then, on that field where courage would be common, Richard Harding Davis would make sure that Roosevelt's efforts were praised the most.

Roosevelt counted on Davis. They had known each other long before the war. Both were elitists, although Davis was not quite as Ivy League as he pretended to be. Both gained by the puffing of Roosevelt's deeds. Roosevelt secured the inflated reputation he needed, while Davis made himself controller of the Rough Riders' press contacts.

Roosevelt was certain that he was entirely qualified to command the Rough Riders. He could see no aspect of military management that was beyond him. Wood had been a splendid organizer, but he had blundered into the ambush. Young had planned the attack, but his pincers scheme had failed to nip the Spaniards at the fort. Wheeler had chosen his terrain carefully, yet he had to ask Lawton for assistance. Roosevelt knew that he could cope better than they had.

The men in the regiment would make it easy for him. Despite Wood's rash sacrifice of lives, the survivors were not resentful. Rather, they were thrilled to have had the chance to prove their manhood in a tough fire fight. On that basis, they would welcome Roosevelt as the new commander. Whatever he ordered, they would do. He would put them at more risk than Wood had, and they would thank him for it.

It bothered him, though, that other Rough Riders who fought at Las Guasimas now were lying about the ambush. Immediately after the skirmish, the troopers had boasted about surviving the Spanish volleys while Roosevelt headed the impromptu charge. Within days, though, the significance of his bravura performance was being diminished in the army, if not in the press. The troopers were following Wood's lead in denying that an ambush had occurred. They insisted that they had flushed the Spanish quail from the Cuban thicket as Wood had planned. Roosevelt merely had executed his part of the plan.[1]

Despite being seriously ill with fever, Young continued to claim that the purpose of marching the cavalry to Las Guasimas had been to secure the better watered camp on higher ground. He would not have made the attack at the fork if he had known how badly he was outnumbered, he maintained, but of course—heh, heh, heh—he did not at all mind having had the little brush with the Spanish army.[2]

Wheeler's official report specified that Shafter had ordered his advance to Las Guasimas. Shafter confirmed the misstatement and rewarded Wheeler by channeling communications to other generals through him rather than through the strait-laced Lawton. "Keep your front picketed but do not try any forward movement until further orders" was the only constraint Shafter placed upon the little southerner.[3]

Like Wheeler, Roosevelt saw that rules set by Shafter could be broken. As Wheeler had succeeded in flaunting authority in order to precipitate a fight, so would he if it became appropriate. Shafter would never discipline him. He had too strong a connection with the press. If he could maintain the Las Guasimas pace, he knew he would vault into the high political post that was waiting for him. Senator Platt had opened the door, Lodge had told him what was inside, and liberal Republicans would carry him over the threshold.

He also would lay to rest, once and for all, the ghost of his father's

Civil War draft evasion. In the modern vernacular, he would prove he had clean genes.

Plans for the Attack

Like a practiced ward-heeler in grassroots politics, Roosevelt knew every Rough Rider by name or moniker. Yet he was Colonel Roosevelt to all, never Teddy to his face. He was not one of the boys. No man spoke against him, though. His loyal troopers agreed that he was the best man in the regiment.[4]

To promote this image of spurious egalitarianism, he accepted the same privations as the enlisted men after the disgruntled head-quarters cook Henry Sylvester Ward absconded with the officers' provisions, dirty dishes, and one mule. Until the accomplished "rus-tler," Chaplain Brown, replenished the officers' larder, Roosevelt had no food of his own. He had to eat wherever he was invited. So did the correspondents who had attached themselves to the Rough Riders.

The fastidious Davis soon became depressed by the scrounging for meals and the hardships the tropical rains caused in the primitive Rough Rider camp. When Shafter brought his headquarters unit ashore on June 29 to finalize plans for the attack on Santiago, Davis shifted his base from the Rough Riders to the more comfortable quarters of the general staff. He was better fed and housed there, as well as closer to the source of strategic news on the eve of what he too expected would be the final advance.[5]

Davis was not popular with headquarters personnel. Photographer McIntosh observed that Davis looked through the same pair of field glasses to evaluate Shafter and Roosevelt, but he got opposite results. He used the glasses in the normal position to enlarge Roosevelt. Although he was Shafter's guest, he reversed the glasses before examining the general. He saw the obese sixty-one-year-old professional soldier as a fat, gray midget.[6]

In turn, Shafter resented all newspapermen. He particularly disliked the pretentious Davis. The general complained that journalists like Davis tried to instruct him on how to conduct the Cuban campaign. He did not "encourage" them, as he put it euphemistically.[7]

To prepare for the attack on San Juan, Shafter concentrated on road improvement, reconnaissance, and rations. He assigned the repair of the supply route from Siboney to Sevilla to General Duffield who had just arrived in Cuba with a fresh brigade. For fear of Spanish guns, however, nothing could be done about improving the route the invasion would follow from Sevilla to San Juan.[8]

Wheeler supervised espionage. From the start, his spies were ineffectual. Lt. Harry Smith of the topographical service found a sketch of neighboring Spanish army posts chalked on the wall of an abandoned hacienda, but the data were stale. Spanish maps of Cuba were outdated.[9]

Chief of Engineers Col. George Derby and six aides were responsible for reconnaissance. Their exploration of the countryside was narrow and superficial. The one Spanish fort on the hill defending the main trail was in plain sight from neighboring elevations, yet Derby provided no detail concerning side paths and streams. He gave Shafter no more information than would be contained on a modern highway map showing just the interstates.[10]

Because the rainy season was at hand and the particulars of the terrain were sketchy, Shafter's campaign had to be bold, quick, and simple. He "estimated the troops would have immunity" from Cuban diseases "for two or three weeks, and to be successful with my force it was to be a dash into Santiago or nothing." In his opinion, he had to capture Santiago before July 4. After then, his soldiers would be "confronted with all the diseases incidental to the Cuban climate" and he would have to postpone the advance until fall. President McKinley would never accept the delay, regardless of the reason. The American navy needed help at once.[11]

The pressure Shafter felt to act quickly also reflected his awareness that the soldiers' vigor and aggressiveness soon would be sapped by their unbalanced and inadequate diet, the broiling sun, torrential rains, and insect bites. Neglect of sanitary precautions also invited sickness. Water was drawn from streams and pools and drunk without having been boiled, because the camp kettles had been left on the beaches at Daiquiri and Siboney. Roosevelt ordered latrines dug for the Rough Riders, but few other regiments bothered. Biblical scholars among the correspondents insisted that the army was not meeting even the minimum sanitary standards set in Deuteronomy.[12]

In addition, the Cuban insurgents told Shafter that there were eight thousand Spanish regulars marching the seventy-five miles from Manzanillo to relieve Santiago. If the relief column arrived before Shafter acted, defenders would outnumber the attackers, a bad prospect.[13]

General Linares did not count on the column arriving in time to save Santiago. The march was inland through rebel territory, and Manzanillo was too far away for easy walking in the tropics. Even if the column reached Santiago, the marchers would be in poor condition, and there would be neither rations nor ammunition for them.

Instead, Linares continued to look to disease and debility as his protectors, just as they were threats to Shafter. Invading armies never stayed healthy in Cuban summers. Judging by Linares's own soldiers, the principal problem would be malaria. He anticipated that a quarter of the American army would be disabled in two or three weeks. One after another, men would be forced out of action for many days by chills, fever, and anemia. Substantially all of the American soldiers on the island would become too ill to fight. After they recovered, they would be feeble for another month.[14]

Malaria was crippling, but yellow fever was a killer. The infectious disease, which had been widespread on the island for a hundred years, was sudden, extensive, and deadly, like germ warfare. Linares simply did not believe that Americans would deliberately expose the best of their young men to malaria and yellow fever during the height of susceptibility from July through September. He knew that the Yankees would eventually win the war, but he thought they would be quiet until fall while acclimatizing themselves in Cuba. Just as his country's diplomats had stalled in prewar negotiations, his ace in the hole was delay. By September, anything might happen.[15]

Moreover, Linares was convinced that Shafter would pull the American forces at Sevilla back to the coast. He still assumed that Shafter would assault the vulnerable old forts at the entrance to the harbor, rather than the relatively well-protected interior city of Santiago. He acted as if he had been informed of the original Shafter-Sampson arrangement targeting the harbor mouth to give Sampson access to the Spanish fleet. If Linares had decided on a plan of action with his opposite number in the Spanish navy, Admiral Cervera, he would have pursued the plan to the end. He expected that Shafter would, too.[16]

Of twelve thousand Spanish infantrymen and sailors now in and around the city, fifteen hundred had a recurrence of malaria and were unfit for duty. Most of the rest of the force was deployed to protect the harbor, where Linares thought the Americans would advance.

Secondarily, to forestall any back-door attack like the rebel assault at Daiquiri, he defended the far western side against the unpredictable insurgents. In fact, though, there was no significant rebel presence close to the city on the west. The insurgents were harassing the column marching from Manzanillo.[17]

Linares anticipated no great threat from the direction of Sevilla, so he stinted on men facing east. He stationed only 520 infantrymen at El Caney, the small outlying fort to the northeast. Then he divided his eastern detachment into three lines of defense. He placed 1,500 men on his strongest line nearest the city. This was his fallback position. Another 324 men were held in reserve in an intermediate line between the city and San Juan Heights. A mere 137 soldiers were in the third line on San Juan Hill and the heights to garrison the fortifications there. This was just a tentative front, an outpost that could be abandoned readily after blunting the American assault.[18]

That made less than five hundred Spanish soldiers on the front line and in the intermediate reserve east of San Juan. More entrenchments and rifle pits were dug to strengthen the position. Earthworks were also thrown up, but they were directed toward protecting the harbor. In addition, Linares had small shiny metal squares placed on trees at measured distances south and east of the heights to give accurate ranges for artillery to be stationed at San Juan.[19]

After completing these defensive dispositions, the Spaniards rested while they waited for Shafter to attack the harbor forts and the rebels to strike from the west. They felt secure, although ultimately almost fifteen thousand American soldiers could menace them from the direction of Sevilla when Shafter finished the inland concentration of his forces.[20]

Shafter was blind to all of Linares's preparations that were not in plain sight. He lacked sufficiently detailed espionage and reconnaissance. He had to believe, however, that most of Linares's infantrymen would be posted effectively against him.[21]

By June 29, American soldiers who were still laboring as stevedores on the transports finally had unloaded three days' rations beyond the daily requirements of the men. At last Shafter's army corps had enough food on shore to survive a storm that might drive the transports out to sea. Eager to participate in the next engagement, only one trooper in fifty reported sick. This was the time when Shafter and his staff rode through Las Guasimas and Sevilla to establish corps headquarters in a deserted hacienda a mile before the hill named El Poso, the well.[22]

Early the next morning, June 30, Shafter rode to the top of El Poso with his staff. The Cuban rebels had established their camp on the west side of the hill near an old sugar factory. They greeted him enthusiastically.[23]

Santiago was three miles away, but Shafter could see the city clearly. The trail from El Poso ran through a gap in the San Juan Heights, the range of protective hills making a natural bulwark half-way between El Poso and Santiago. San Juan Hill to the left of the trail commanded the direct route to Santiago. The hill was only about 125 feet above the floor of the valley, but it was prominent because the crest was higher than other nearby elevations. There was a block-house on the crest, behind entrenchments the Spaniards had been digging for three days. To the right of the trail and in front of the heights were a few hillocks. Shafter saw no strategic importance to them and did not mark them on his map of the area. No defender was visible there.[24]

Davis was with Shafter's staff. He looked at the dense, unexplored, and apparently trackless jungle stretching a mile and a half across the valley on both sides of the trail. The San Juan Heights were quiet and sunny, now reminding the imaginative Davis of a New England land-scape. The blockhouse on San Juan Hill resembled a Chinese pa-goda. On a hillock to the right there was a deserted Mediterranean blue bungalow. The colorful landscape exuded the serenity that was a false sign of peace.[25]

El Caney was three miles north of El Poso. Generals Lawton and Chaffee personally had explored the jungle as far as the outskirts of the little village. They reported to Shafter that a small number of Spanish infantrymen, perhaps only five hundred, were garrisoned at El Caney. They were sure the fort could be captured in passing, in an hour or two. With this information and what Shafter himself had seen, the battle plan was completed.[26]

Shortly after noon on June 30, Shafter called a meeting of the ranking line officers at his headquarters. In attendance were General Lawton and Gen. Jacob Kent who were in command of the two in-fantry divisions, and Gen. Samuel Sumner who was acting commander of the cavalry division. Shafter explained that Sumner of the 1st Cavalry Brigade was replacing Wheeler who had not been advised of the meeting because he was incapacitated by fever. The staff surgeon had recommended rest.

In addition, there were infantry brigade commanders Adna Chaffee, Hamilton Hawkins, William Ludlow, and Henry Duffield, as well as Castillo, the Cuban general with questionable connections. Young was too ill to be present. Wood and Carroll, who would be Sumner's acting brigade commanders, also were missing. They had not yet been notified of their promotions.[27]

Shafter told his generals that he had discarded the original plan of coastal attack because most of the army was now located inland at Sevilla. Backtracking through Siboney would take too long. Also, he felt he might surprise Linares by a direct assault on the city. That made San Juan Hill the key to capturing Santiago. El Caney was a secondary objective, to be seized because of the road to Santiago that ran through it and because its garrison might fire on the Americans from the rear if bypassed.

To accomplish his goals, Shafter divided his forces. As a feint, Duffield was ordered to lead his independent brigade of 2,500 men along the shore toward the harbor entrance where Linares expected the assault. Sampson's fleet would bombard the coastal forts to play up the Duffield threat.[28]

Lawton was to start his infantry division of 6,900 men marching toward El Caney at once. He would bivouac along the trail for the night and attack the few Spaniards at El Caney at daybreak on July 1. Kent and Sumner were to march their divisions from Sevilla to El Poso Hill and camp there for the night. When Lawton became engaged at El Caney, Kent with 5,200 infantrymen and Sumner with 2,700 troopers were to march westward from El Poso toward San Juan. They were to get into position to attack as soon as Lawton captured El Caney and filled out the right flank in front of San Juan Heights.[29]

Shafter assigned one field battery of four light guns to the action against El Caney and a second battery to El Poso. Two other batteries were held in reserve, along with a thousand men under General Bates.[30]

The heavy artillery consisting of eight siege guns remained on the transports in Siboney harbor. They had been supplied by General Miles, but Shafter did not believe in the efficacy of big guns to ease the infantry's path in assaults, especially here where he was contemptuous of the Spanish soldiers despite their performance at Las Guasimas. Besides, the heavy guns would have been difficult to unload from the transports without lighters. After they were unloaded, horses might not be able to pull them along the muddy trail to the front.[31]

The schedule for the push against San Juan had to be flexible. Lawton thought of El Caney as a lark and of San Juan as the real test. He insisted that by rank he was entitled to get into the bigger battle. He told Shafter's adjutant general, Col. E. J. McClernand, "Do not order the other divisions to attack until I get up there!"[32]

The timing was contingent upon Lawton's speed in wiping out El Caney. The conjecture was that after Lawton's guns opened fire at 6:30 in the morning on July 1, the artillery would need an hour to breach the walls of the fort. The infantry would capture the village easily by 8:30 A.M., clean up the area, and deal with the few dead and wounded on both sides by 10:30 A.M. The soldiers would eat a cold early lunch, form again into companies, and start marching the two miles to the heights well before midday in order to arrive no later than one o'clock in the afternoon. Such was the worst-case scenario.[33]

Any unexpected delay, though, might keep Lawton's division from getting to San Juan for an assault that day. In that case, the three divisions would have to bivouac in the woods near San Juan for the night and the action would be pushed back until July 2. The loss of one day was not considered to be consequential. Shafter believed that he could take care of any contingencies as they came up. Of the 18,300 men under his command, he was committing 14,800 to the San Juan battlefield. That would be a remarkable concentration of his strength.[34]

To counter Shafter, Linares made few changes in the disposition of the Spanish forces. He realized that his thin garrison on San Juan Hill had become more important, so he moved up two companies from the intermediate reserve. He also added 60 volunteers from the Home Guard and, early on July 1, two Krupp field guns. In spite of the token reinforcement, the total number of Spaniards on both San Juan Hill and San Juan Heights was only 461 men, fewer than had served as the rear guard at Las Guasimas. The Spanish artillery included seventeen antique bronze cannons on the main defensive line nearest Santiago.[35]

In Fact as Well

When the conference of generals was over, Capt. Albert Mills of Shafter's staff was dispatched to carry orders to the brigades and regiments. He rode up to the Rough Riders' headquarters tent at 2:30 P.M. to advise that Wood was succeeding Young as head of the 2nd Cavalry Brigade which consisted of the 1st and 10th regulars and the Rough Riders. Roosevelt would take over Wood's regiment. He would be subordinate to Wood in the brigade but at last officially in command of the Rough Riders.[36]

As the only full colonel in the 2nd Brigade, Wood was entitled to the promotion by rank. The other two regimental commanders in the brigade were lieutenant colonels like Roosevelt. Nevertheless, the regular officers were disgruntled. Young had left them out of the action at Las Guasimas and now they attributed Wood's preferment to political shenanigans necessary to elevate the civilian soldier Roosevelt with his close ties to Washington. Their grievance was not with Wood whose permanent status was still captain in the medical corps, but with Roosevelt and with civilian politicians in general.

Captain Mills was too pressed for time to tell Roosevelt about the promotions. When Wood relayed the message, Roosevelt did not seem excited. His modest reaction was that he "was very much pleased. I wouldn't have wanted it until I had had experience, but having been through the skirmish I thought I could handle it." Events in Cuba were maturing him. He passed up the opportunity to do one of his dances. The correspondents were equally calm. They wrote only that now "Roosevelt's Rough Riders go as Roosevelt's in fact as well as name."[37]

Captain Mills had also instructed Wood to have the 2nd Brigade "break camp and move forward at 4 o'clock." Similar orders were given to the other brigades in the two divisions left at Sevilla. All were anxious to be first to start on El Camino Real, the one narrow trail shown on their maps.[38]

Roosevelt had watched the Rough Riders spend the morning like previous Sevilla mornings. They had been working on their canvas and palm-leaf shelters in efforts to cope with the climate and the insects. The troopers had been confined to the same spot for too long and they were restless.[39]

Despite a heavy rain falling straight down, the men were glad to receive instructions to make ready to march. They struck camp, discarding everything they could not carry easily on their backs. Except for his precious toilet articles, Roosevelt's personal baggage was left behind again. The surplus equipment, soggy campfire ashes, and deserted shelters remained at Sevilla as mementos.[40]

At four o'clock, the Rough Riders were handed three days' rations. The rain stopped as they began the march by drawing up in columns of two behind the halted 1st Cavalry. Then they sat on the wet ground and waited. The trail that belied its grandiose name was already choked with marching infantry regiments, pack trains, and artillery.

Thousands of men would move slowly along the one trail. Before twenty-four hours passed, every sixth man would be a casualty—killed, wounded, prostrated by heat, or missing.

Having a Bully Time

When the Rough Riders finally stepped onto the trail, a jubilant Lieutenant Colonel Roosevelt rode the little stallion Texas in front of the regiment. Ahead were the 10th Cavalry under Lt. Col. John Baldwin and the 1st under Lt. Col. Charles Viele.

Roosevelt's ebullient leadership during the march contrasted with the demeanor of the stolid Wood. Full of enthusiasm, Roosevelt was shouting, "Oh, aren't we having a bully time!" His regulation dark blue shirt had handsewn yellow shoulder straps and the designation USV was affixed to his collar in yellow cloth letters. The original silver oak leaves that were his insignia had been lost. Replacements had been hammered from a lead spoon, and they looked it. A big blue bandanna with white polka dots was tied cowboy fashion around his neck, handy for covering his nose and mouth.[41]

At the start, there were cool streams at the sides of the relatively open trail. As the march progressed, however, the air stopped moving and the late afternoon became more sultry. Heat was a significant burden. Light from the descending sun made the horizon shimmer and stenches rose from stagnant pools in the jungle. Deep mud in the trail stuck to shoes that seemed to gain weight with every step. Yet the soldiers' mood was cheerful. Regiments jostled each other to take the lead. The men wanted to be the first to fight.[42]

Deep holes in the trail and fords over shallow unbridged creeks slowed the advance. Delays were frequent. The lines seemed to halt every few minutes, as regiments were shoved aside for pack trains, wagons, artillery, and mounted staff officers with their retinues. There were pauses while aides on horseback splashed between the files of soldiers to hurry a lagging regiment.

Impenetrable jungle hid both sides of the trail. The heat was now intense and the creeks the men waded across were too muddied to provide clean drinking water. Empty canteens could not be refilled. After an hour, some men began nibbling at pieces of hardtack while they waited or walked. Others were fatigued and threw away their rations to lighten the load.

As far ahead as Roosevelt could see, the trail was filled with soldiers carrying weapons slung over their shoulders. Colorful crimson, yellow, and white guidons accompanied mounted regimental commanders. Correspondents claimed that the thousands of men slipping and sliding in the muck had no end. They had to be the same soldiers marching around and around on a turntable to impress any Spaniard who might be watching.

Roosevelt had been told to have the Rough Riders follow close behind the two cavalry regiments leading the way, but the delays created confusion. In their efforts to move ahead, other units repeatedly cut into line ahead of soldiers who had been stopped. When an infantry regiment marched into an opening in the trail ahead of the halted Rough Riders, Roosevelt was compelled to accept a long wait. The rest of his cavalry brigade was soon out of sight. He was adrift in a river of soldiers.

Luckily, staff officers of the cavalry division noticed the mishap. They switched the Rough Riders onto a narrower path they had discovered at the side of the trail. Although the regiment marched in single file through the mud on the footpath, they made better time. By then it was night and turning cooler. Suddenly, Sgt. Royal Prentice of E Troop slipped in the mud and went down under the hooves of a horse. His mate yelled quickly, "Look out, Colonel! A man has fallen in the path!" Roosevelt answered reassuringly, "Don't worry. No horse will step on a Rough Rider."[43]

When Roosevelt reached the end of the path, he was back at the main trail, almost caught up with the rest of the brigade. Two companies of regular infantry blocked the exit. By this time, Roosevelt had learned the ropes. He called on the infantry captains to give way and he marched right onto the trail without waiting. The first squadron got through. The second squadron was split off and delayed again.[44]

Just past Shafter's headquarters, the cavalry division was shunted to the left, across a meadow to an even narrower track through the jungle. As the moon rose, the night became bright enough for men to cast long deep shadows. Cuban rebels were camped along the sides of the track, preparing their evening meal of army rations. The Cubans grinned as the weary Americans filed by. They yelled "Santiago," pointed westward, and drew their forefingers across their throats. The Russian military attaché riding with Roosevelt smiled back at them superciliously and remarked, "Save me from my friends."[45]

General Sumner had reached El Poso at dusk. Wheeler's aides were with him. After the rebels cleared the underbrush, he pitched his camp on the west side of the hill in view of the black mass that was San Juan. For the ridgepole of his tent, he symbolically used the abandoned staff of a Spanish regimental flag that had flown over the same hill days earlier.[46]

Roosevelt arrived at the regiment's designated location for the night at 9 P.M. under a paler moon. It was another hour before the second squadron appeared. With the expenditure of great effort, the regiment had advanced two miles in five hours, an excruciatingly slow pace. Like Wood earlier, Roosevelt had ridden all the way and thought the distance was less than it had been. The troopers estimated six miles. They would have walked farther than that to get at the Spaniards.[47]

They camped on the slopes of El Poso and across the main trail at the edge of the jungle. Exhausted troopers lay down with their heads on their packs and blanket rolls. The order was for ammunition belts to be worn and carbines to be ready to repel a surprise Spanish foray. In addition, a dozen troopers were detailed to stand guard in four-man posts in the flat area beyond the hill that now was crowded with soldiers, horses, mules, and packers. On the hilltop were the deserted ruins of an adobe hacienda and a barn that had housed sugar-processing equipment.[48]

Other regiments were marching a short distance beyond El Poso. A quarter of a mile past the Rough Rider camp, there was a patch of newly dug earth with a strong odor of putrefaction and a bare human arm protruding in the moonlight. A Cuban who sat smoking nearby explained, "Espagnols." He showed his brown teeth in a grin and then opened and closed his hands into fists twice, tapped the handle of his machete, and made the familiar sign of the cut throat. The Cubans had no facilities for housing prisoners. They beheaded Spaniards caught by American soldiers and turned over to them for disposition.[49]

A few captains allowed campfires for cooking the same fat bacon, hardtack, and unsugared black coffee. Most captains did not permit fires. Their men had cold suppers, chewing on raw bacon and hardtack. There was no complaint.

Rough Riders who remained awake pumped up their courage by talking about Roosevelt's promotion and the sight of an American observation balloon in a trial ascension during the early part of the march. They knew they would be going into battle, perhaps as soon as the next day. Others sat up cheering and singing with great animation, "There'll Be a Hot Time in Santiago To-morrow!" Then they wrote letters home by the light of the fires. There was no bugle call to end the day. Men slept on the ground, in the open, after reflecting happily that "there will be a lot of fun for us in the morning."

Speculating upon the Morrow

Wood had reached El Poso with Sumner. He waited there for Roosevelt to arrive so they could discuss plans for the next day. He was not yet divorced from his intimate connection with the Rough Riders.

As brigade commander, Wood was eating Young's provisions. Two aides presented Roosevelt with a big canned corned-beef sandwich which he shared with his orderly William Saunders of B Troop. The two friends Wood and Roosevelt conversed for awhile. Wood explained that the brigade had been brought forward to support an artillery battery that would open fire on San Juan in the morning. According to Wheeler's staff, there were Spaniards only a mile and a half away.[50]

Roosevelt ordered reveille without bugle for 4 A.M. Because he would be up during the night to make the rounds of the sentries, he anticipated little rest. His supercharged emotional state would compensate. Wood and he curled up on the ground, atop their saddle blankets and under their coats. Roosevelt expounded earnestly upon military philosophy, telling Wood how he was honing the fighting edge both in his men and himself. Wood had heard this before and he dozed off. They soon slept side-by-side under a moonlit Cuban sky.[51]

A little later, Stephen Crane walked back along the trail to look for his baggage. Passing El Poso Hill, he stumbled over the sleeping form of an intemperate Roosevelt who awakened for a moment to insult Crane vigorously.

Davis was standing on the crest of the hill, looking westward into the night and speculating upon the morrow. He could see street lamps in the city, across an ocean of mist in the valley. He was thinking about the columns of American soldiers, some of them his friends, who would descend into the basin. The column with Roosevelt and the Rough Riders would be under Sumner, an untested general.[52]

Davis had been briefed by the generals on the army's goal of capturing "the little villages of San Juan and El Caney. There is no intention to rush the city to-morrow, but to occupy San Juan and so threaten the city's walls." Capturing the ridge at San Juan would give American artillery the advantage. They would be shooting down at the lower Spanish defensive line protecting the sea-level city.[53]

Sumner and his staff were awake, too. The general was making pencil sketches of the terrain by candlelight to prepare for the disposition of his troops on the field. By the time he finished the drawings and retired to his cot, the lights of Santiago were out. The sleeping armies were ready for the new and crucial day.[54]

Linares could not rest. He tried to judge how many Americans were bivouacked on El Poso by counting the campfires and was misled into thinking there were fewer men than were actually present. He decided not to reinforce or withdraw the isolated garrison at El Caney and not to commit more soldiers to San Juan. He knew that his forces would be outnumbered when they faced the Americans on his eastern front, but defenders generally were in the minority. He did not know how disproportionate the numbers were.[55]

At 3 A.M., an hour before reveille for the soldiers, Shafter summoned Colonel McClernand. Shafter had been prostrated by the heat after viewing the battle site the previous morning. Gout was causing severe pain in his foot and he was running a low fever from a touch of malaria. Too uncomfortable to sleep or even move, he asked McClernand if the staff and line officers understood the plan of attack. Assured that they did, he directed McClernand to set up battle headquarters on El Poso Hill. He said he would stay where he was and keep in close contact with events by employing a relay of junior officers.[56]

Shafter's plan was flawed. He was depending too heavily upon the advice of his veteran generals concerning El Caney, underestimating the difficulty of Lawton's assignment. He also had failed to provide for the possibility that personal illness might make him unable to respond to crises. For his part, Linares had misjudged American inventiveness, fortitude, and perseverance from the beginning of the campaign.

Where Death Might Smite

The moon was low in the sky when the Rough Riders were awakened by voice and touch at 4 A.M. on July 1. There was no bugle call.

As usual, Roosevelt woke up happy. While he performed his morning ablutions in the dark, he looked forward to this new opportunity to fight. He cleaned his teeth vigorously with his retrieved brush and shaved out of a bowl of yesterday's river water from his canteen. Then he ordered his favorite, Capt. Buckey O'Neill, and Troop A to go down the hill to relieve the outposts and to scout the jungle to the unoccupied south. As Roosevelt said, "I freely sent the men for whom I cared most, to where death might smite them. My men would not have respected me had I acted otherwise."[57]

Meanwhile, troopers were gathering dew-soaked kindling to light breakfast fires in the previous night's cold ashes. Fresh water for coffee was carried in canteens from the nearby stream.

Roosevelt had something extra for his own breakfast. Despite his fever, his servant Marshall had gone to Shafter's headquarters during the night and had brought back sugar for black coffee along with handfuls of kidney beans. He soaked the beans in river water and cooked them with bacon. To repay Wood for the sandwich shared for supper, Roosevelt invited Wood and the two aides to join in this special meal.[58]

Roosevelt looked unkempt. Through necessity, he wore his hair a little longer than he had as a civilian. Curls capped his head. When he was sweaty, wet ringlets hung down his forehead. The shapeless crown of his stained campaign hat was pierced with small holes cut by his orderly to promote ventilation. Later that morning, he had the blue bandanna with the white dots sewn onto the rear brim of his hat. One yellow shoulder strap on his blue shirt had come loose. The other strap was missing. He did not have time to bother with dress conventions that would have made his rank more obvious to Spanish sharpshooters.[59]

Even in the army, Roosevelt was proud of his small feet. He shunned standard cavalry boots in favor of custom-made, mahogany-colored hiking shoes that had taken on the tan of dried tropic mud. His leggings were regulation issue at thirty-one cents the pair. They were caked with mud, too, as were his cravenetted pants. It was apparent that this customarily dapper man had been sleeping on the ground in his uniform. He was without a valet. Marshall's last appearance in the campaign was at breakfast when he became ill again.

As day broke, Roosevelt climbed to cavalry headquarters to find out from Wood whether there was any change in the plan of attack. He could see other cavalry and infantry campsites around the hill and near the trail to Santiago. The cavalry was in the advance and the 1st Infantry Division under General Kent was in the rear. Wheeler was ill for the fourth day, so Sumner remained in command of the cavalry.

At each regimental camp, dogs that were mascots ran in the grass and nosed around the bases of bushes. The morning birds sang, uninhibited by the movements of the soldiers.

The Base of the Triangle

As Roosevelt reached the hilltop, he looked west toward Santiago, away from the level rays of the blinding sun. The mist hung close to the ground in the basin. He watched while the vapors lifted into the coconut palms. The sky was reddish blue and cloudless, the air soft and balmy. The landscape seemed almost oriental in its unaccented, gently rounded, well-brushed contours that were consonant with the pagoda shape of the blockhouse roof on San Juan Hill.

He could take in the whole scene without field glasses. His vista was a triangle. The base was El Camino Real straight ahead from El Poso, down into the basin and then up to the gap in San Juan Heights. The apex of the triangle was three miles to the north at the fortified village of El Caney. After Lawton marched his infantry division up the right side of the triangle to take El Caney, he was to march down the left leg to meet the Rough Riders on the northern end of the American army's right flank facing the heights.

Roosevelt was told that no serious resistance was expected at El

Caney. The village would be evacuated by the Spaniards as soon as they realized the immense size of Lawton's division. While Lawton was mopping up El Caney during the morning, Kent's infantry and the cavalry division would execute the preliminary advances. Their movements would be protected by the American artillery firing at the San Juan blockhouse. The Rough Riders would merely support the artillery at this first stage. They would have no combat role until joined by Lawton in the early afternoon.[60]

What Shafter did not take into account was that the Spaniards now saw themselves as having retreated as far as they intended to go. San Juan was the gateway to Santiago and so would be defended energetically. The natural conformation of the countryside lent itself to defense. Even Roosevelt's unpracticed, myopic eye could see that the only practical route west from El Poso was the rough trail over deep unbridged streams. The primeval jungle lay on both sides of the trail. The earth was covered with a dense growth of prickly shrubs, thorny vines, and spiny cactus difficult to penetrate.[61]

Once the Americans were within range, the trail would be subject to unobstructed enemy fire. Worse, the jungle ended in an open meadow squarely in front of the hill and heights, offering little cover for attackers. Also, Spanish engineers had supervised the placement of blockhouses, entrenchments, and entanglements on high places around the city. Each fortification was designed to command another, so the attackers would be exposed to enfilading fire.

The pensive Roosevelt was not the planner of the assault. For him, the landscape was only a pretty backdrop. The San Juan range ran north and south across the valley, defining an amphitheater almost three miles wide. On the hill to the left of the trail, he could dimly make out the main Spanish fortification as a dark streak.[62]

A quarter-mile before the heights and well to the right was a smaller hill, freestanding and separated from the heights by a shallow pond in the meadow. The Mediterranean blue bungalow was on this knoll and a red bungalow sat on a higher elevation farther to the right. The two houses appeared to Roosevelt to be outside the arena of battle. Shafter had come to the same conclusion.

Looking beyond San Juan Heights, Roosevelt could see the rest of Santiago's defenses. They were topped by the peaceful spires of the sleeping city.[63]

Chapter 18
The Correspondents' War

The Santiago campaign took place during the "Golden Age" of American journalism. Correspondents roamed the world, sending back personalized versions of esoteric events and places. Through their by-lines—Richard Harding Davis, Stephen Crane, Frederic Remington—they were known as widely as stage or sports stars.[1]

The army listed 150 national and foreign correspondents in Cuba, including the obscure as well as the famous. Many more were uncounted. The sheer numbers of writers, photographers, and illustrators reporting from Cuba and their unrestrained movements on the battlefield caused the altercation to be dubbed "the correspondents' war."

These all-male journalists were clustered in three different locations, depending upon how close to the front they were willing to go. Some remained in Siboney in relative comfort, near the ships used to dispatch copy to publishers via a cable station in Florida. The stories they sent either were garnered at second hand from men returning from the front or were tales composed mainly from the journalists' imaginations.

More privileged newspapermen attached themselves to Shafter's field headquarters. They were less comfortable than they would have been in Siboney, but they were at the source of official news without being in danger from the Spaniards. They based their articles either on interviews with officers passing through headquarters or on the general's handouts. This group included Davis, who also was alert to the movements of Roosevelt at the front.

After his private interview with Shafter, publisher William Randolph Hearst remained in Cuba for the duration of the fighting. Like Richard Harding Davis, he wrote regularly to his mother. He told her, "I am at the front"—which was not true. Instead, he was part of the group at corps headquarters. Referring to his reporter who had been critically wounded at Las Guasimas, Hearst reassured his mother by saying that, "since poor Marshall was shot, the General has made rules limiting newspapermen to localities well within the lines so there is no opportunity for us to get hurt even if we wanted to."[2]

The most enterprising correspondents formed a third group, those already at the front. Paying no attention to Shafter's restrictions, they accepted primitive and hazardous conditions in order to gather news. Keeping them away from the danger zone would have required the diversion of hundreds of soldiers, so Shafter quietly acquiesced, implicitly granting them freedom to roam the arena. He wanted to be able to focus his attention on the Spaniards, not on policing unmanageable newspapermen he heartily disliked.

The crabby old general played favorites among the correspondents. He even disclosed his battle plans to the few who were his cronies. He had them briefed individually, starting with the Hearst reporter James Creelman who had replaced Marshall.[3]

Shafter also had the battlefield described in detail for selected correspondents, telling them more than could be observed from El Poso Hill. Given the absence of worthwhile information from the engineers who were performing reconnaissance on the ground, Shafter had unveiled the imported war balloon that the Rough Riders noticed the previous day. He considered the new apparatus to be the finest for painless spying. The French manufacturer had forty years of experience with the craft, including limited use in the Civil War. The company's representatives had promised that the balloon and the observers would not be affected by enemy gunfire, because the gas-filled bag and the basket were swaying targets above the usual trajectory of rifles fired from the ground. The observers themselves protested use of the balloon in a forward zone.[4]

Friendly correspondents were given the latest report from the officers in the balloon who described the major streams and trails. The Aguadores River approached the valley from the east, that is, from Shafter's right, near the path to El Caney. The main trail was

The War Balloon. LeRoy Armstrong, *Pictorial Atlas Illustrating The Spanish-American War* (Chicago: Souvenir Publishing Co., 1898), p. 80.

said to ford the river halfway between El Poso and San Juan. The San Juan River flowed from north to south, parallel to the hill and the heights, beyond the Aguadores. The banks of the river were covered with luxuriant chaparral, only six hundred yards from the base of the hill. The two rivers joined farther south to run to the sea.[5]

Looking west toward San Juan, past the rivers, the lush growth soon gave way to an open meadow of waist-high grass visible from El Poso. Because the grassland's entire expanse was in full view of the Spanish infantrymen on the heights, Shafter told Creelman that the meadow was where enemy pressure would commence.[6]

What Shafter did not know was that the distance between San Juan Hill and the ford of the Aguadores was less than the officers performing the balloon reconnaissance had indicated. From the ford of the Aguadores and all along the banks of the San Juan River, every bit of terrain was within range of the Spaniards' rapid-fire guns and Mauser rifles. The Spaniards would not have to wait for the Americans to reach the meadow to inflict casualties.[7]

According to Shafter, the final plan explained to his favorite correspondents had Sumner's cavalry division crossing the first stream, the Aguadores, at the ford. Then the cavalry was to turn to the right into the pathless brush and spread out to wait for Lawton. Meanwhile, Kent's infantry was to cross at the ford and move to the left of the trail to menace San Juan Hill where the blockhouse was.

Shafter pointed out that the American forces were the pick of the army. The regulars had been tested in campaigns in the West. They were commanded by veteran generals and colonels. Most had been Civil War officers. Carrying out his instructions would be routine. For some of the correspondents, however, Shafter's plan was too bold and too risky to be acceptable, regardless of the quality of the soldiers involved.[8]

The Rough Riders openly resented the press' negative evaluation of Shafter's strategy. They were the only cavalry volunteers picked for the battle and they wanted to fight under any scheme. A sergeant explained, "I am in favor of beating the faces off them dagoes, and then let the war correspondents make up the strategy, as they seem to be the only ones worrying about it."[9]

Not Seriously Engaged

No written instrument existed for Shafter's battle plan. Oral instructions covered who was to do what and when they were to do it. Later, everyone agreed that Lawton was told to go toward El Caney. The cavalry also was directed to head northward. Kent was to go southward.[10]

Recollections differed, though, on when Shafter intended the attack on San Juan to commence. The general claimed that his approach was to be flexible. He told his officers that the assault would occur on July 1, if possible. Timing would depend on Lawton.

In contrast, Shafter whispered to his friend Creelman just before midnight on June 30 that the only fight on July 1 was to be at El Caney. Kent and Sumner "would not be seriously engaged" at San Juan until July 2.[11]

Similarly, the other correspondents briefed by Shafter understood that the attack on San Juan definitely was not to take place until daybreak on July 2. Stephen Crane, for example, was advised by Shafter's aides on June 30 that there would be little fighting on July 1. The critical attack on San Juan would not start until Lawton had swept through El Caney and the three American divisions had bivouacked for the night in the chaparral along the river.[12]

Crane and Creelman shared their information on the scheduling with fellow correspondents Davis, Whitney, Fox, Stephen Bonsal of the *New York Herald,* Frank Norris of *Century* magazine, John Atkins of the *Manchester (England) Guardian,* and a dozen other writers, artists, and photographers. They prepared themselves to trudge to Lawton's sector at daybreak on July 1. Coverage of their favorites, the Rough Riders, would be postponed for a day.[13]

There was, however, a discrepancy between what Shafter and his aides advised Crane and Creelman on June 30 and what Shafter told his officers concerning the timing of the assault at San Juan.

Shoot and Shear

The dozen foreign correspondents like Atkins considered themselves to be more experienced at contemporary warfare and more proficient in military strategy than American generals trained in the Civil War. While the American correspondents poked mild fun at Shafter, the Europeans ridiculed both Shafter and the War Department in Washington.

Their biggest laugh was at the War Department's well-publicized but harebrained scheme to hand "an immense pair of shears" to every soldier in Shafter's V Corps. After the army's siege guns drove the Spaniards back from their defenses at San Juan, the soldiers would use the shears to cut the wire entanglements, pass through, and charge on to the next Spanish defenses, where the heavy bombardment, wire

Col. Theodore Roosevelt and Richard Harding Davis with Stephen Bonsal
and Major George M. Dunn. *Neely's Panorama of Our New Possessions*
(New York: F. Tennyson Neely, 1898).

clipping, and assault would be repeated, time after time, all the way
to Havana. The correspondents knew that no such shears existed
and that the siege guns were still on the transports.

To the Europeans, siege guns had a place in capturing even a
modestly fortified position such as San Juan Hill. They said that before any assault by European infantry, heavy guns would bombard a
fort, breach the walls, and intimidate the defenders, much as the big
guns on Sampson's warships had been intended to drive the Spaniards from Daiquiri a week earlier.[14]

Instead, the Europeans insisted, Shafter courted disaster by ignoring the siege guns. His only precaution in the advance, they said,
would probably be to set one scout at the point, a hundred yards
ahead of 7,900 soldiers marching toward San Juan on the narrow
jungle trail. Despite the lesson of Las Guasimas, there would be no
flanker. Shafter had not learned to beware the cuckoos.[15]

No matter what Shafter claimed as his concept of the attack, the

Europeans emphasized, in essence there was no plan at all. Shafter was merely getting ready to punch the Spaniards as hard as he could by massing his forces at the point where they would assault San Juan Hill without siege guns. There was no finesse. The European journalists believed that Shafter was blindly sending the army corps into a death trap.[16]

In contrast, Shafter viewed the risks involved as readily assumable, given the urgency for action. He disparaged the fighting ability of the Spaniards. Even though he thought that their numbers would come close to equaling those of his forces, he and his fellow officers believed that Spaniards were racially unfit to defend against an American attack. He expected to capture Santiago easily, without fancy strategy and by relying mainly on the high quality of the American army.[17]

He would not coddle the men. Although there were streams to cross, there would be no bridge. The men would be required to wade through waist-high water and keep on going. The pontoons he could have employed remained on the transports with the big guns. They could hardly have been advanced through the jungle in any event.[18]

Shafter did not indulge his officers, either. He was putting them in position to attack, yet allowing them no freedom to improvise. He was sending McClernand to El Poso Hill, a mile closer to the front, to relay his instructions to the field officers, but he provided McClernand with no discretionary authority. His young assistant, Lt. John Miley, was being dispatched to the front to coordinate operations, not to direct them. Shafter intended to be available to give every command that might be needed. He did not anticipate that his health would fail when his presence was most in demand, so that the battle would be left to fight itself. The question was whether Shafter would be able to control the attack or whether aggressive individual officers such as Roosevelt would take over in the heat of battle.[19]

Shafter distrusted Wheeler, Wood, and Roosevelt, as most regulars did. By treating Wheeler as an invalid, he eliminated the southerner from the command. He blamed Wood and Roosevelt for the ambush at Las Guasimas and promoted them only because their rank required it. Aware that Roosevelt might not respect authority, he planned to restrain the Rough Riders by keeping them in reserve at the rear of the regular cavalry.[20]

On the Spanish side, General Linares was not harassed by the apathetic Spanish press. He knew that he could not sustain a defense for long against serious pressure from the east. His artillery was typical of his military equipment. The only modern guns he had were a few cannons borrowed from the blockaded fleet. Most of his cannons were so ancient they had pet names. One old gun was called Votan for a Mayan hero-god. It bore the foundry's date of 1751.[21]

Almost as if he wanted to lose the campaign, he distributed his soldiers over seventeen far-flung points. He placed the men in four eastern stations, at El Caney, on San Juan Hill, across the trail to the north in a farm building on the heights, and in an unfortified outpost on a knoll east of the heights. When he finally comprehended that the American attack was committed to proceeding along the main trail from the east, he acknowledged the direction of the assault by taking his personal stand on the reserve line between the city and San Juan Hill. There, just a few half-starved soldiers and Home Guards separated him from the Americans.[22]

Linares benefited from one unmentioned asset. His stated reason for continued resistance was to preserve Spain's honor. Actually, however, his men were governed by a drive for self-preservation. They knew the Cubans took no prisoner.

Meanwhile, the correspondents had been primed by Shafter to watch Lawton wipe out the Spaniards at El Caney on July 1. The wily old general wanted the unruly journalists out of the way of the crucial fight that was to take place at San Juan.

Chapter 19
Starting Toward San Juan

General Lawton began the new day on July 1 by staring at the isolated Spanish fort at El Caney, fearing that the Spaniards would again retreat toward San Juan without a fight. His light artillery commenced firing on schedule at 6:30 A.M. Surprisingly, it soon became evident that he would be delayed by the 520 Spaniards who resisted the advance of his almost 6,900 crack infantrymen.[1]

Lawton was a cautious commander, unwilling to risk his soldiers' lives needlessly. The attack degenerated into a slow rifle duel from behind fixed objects. Lawton had expected to take El Caney in two hours, but he encountered a hard fight that lasted all day.

Most of the news correspondents on the scene had not been at Las Guasimas and had never witnessed war, even on a scale as small as this. They rhapsodized about

> the sensation when for the first time one finds bullets whistling around him, yet seeing nothing, only hearing them as they rush by, crashing through the leaves on their deadly errand. In some cases, the danger did not strike home until there were heavy thuds nearby, and, on looking around, they saw men on the ground, dead or wounded. Then it came home that this was war in earnest and they found themselves wondering if they should be next, and whether they should be killed or merely wounded.[2]

Neither Lawton nor the correspondents grasped the fact that once a substantial delay occurred at El Caney, the coordinated heavy hitting that Shafter had planned for San Juan would become impossible and an entirely different situation would arise. At headquarters, Shafter's physical condition continued to deteriorate. The ability to revise his battle plans gradually slipped out of his fevered grasp.

Heard at El Poso

The detonations of Lawton's artillery were heard distinctly at El Poso where the Rough Riders were camped. Half an hour after the barrage started at El Caney, twenty-four spirited horses pulling Capt. George Grimes's four light field guns were driven at a dash toward the top of El Poso Hill. The spectacular animals were straining as the artillerymen used whip, spur, and traditional curses. Once on the summit, the guns were placed in position to fire at San Juan Hill where the Spanish blockhouse stood. Then Grimes, who wore spectacles and had the demeanor of a college professor, waited with his battery.[3]

Noncombatants, including foreign attachés and a few correspondents, were in the barn, the only building on El Poso with a roof. The Rough Riders were massed in the barnyard, directly behind Grimes's battery. The 1st and 10th Cavalry regiments were placed a hundred yards in back of the Rough Riders.[4]

These three regiments, making up Wood's 2nd Brigade, had been directed to their locations by Colonel McClernand. The troopers were on the hill in support of the artillery, protecting the emplacements against Spanish guerrillas. Roosevelt's men were in high spirits. They were spectators, sitting in what the easterners said was "like the royal box at the opera on a gala night" while they gossiped about what they saw across the valley.[5]

General Sumner was talking to McClernand in front of divisional headquarters on the hill. Sumner was impatient to get on with the advance so as to divert Spanish attention from Lawton. "Well," he demanded, "When are we going to begin this thing?" McClernand pulled out his big pocket watch, peered toward El Caney, and replied, "Our orders are not to do anything until Lawton gets through over there, but he seems to be pretty busy."[6]

That was taken as a negative response. When the fidgety Sumner approached again, McClernand looked at his watch a second time. The timepiece was no help and McClernand took it on himself to answer, "Well, I guess you might as well begin." At 8 A.M. Sumner ordered Captain Grimes to commence firing.[7]

Immediately, Grimes turned to his veteran gun crew. "Aim!" he cried, although the guns had been fixed on the target for thirty minutes. "Fire!" Along with the big boom, a tremendous cloud of smoke rose from the charcoal gunpowder. The battery was hidden from the watching troopers.[8]

Grimes's guns continued to fire at San Juan Hill, releasing great bursts of smoke without noticeable effect on the enemy and without evoking any response. In fifteen minutes, Grimes discharged twenty shells. The relaxed Rough Riders enjoyed a pleasant interlude in the bright sunshine. The standardized rhythmic procedure in loading and firing was mesmerizing.

The experienced English war correspondent George Musgrave "had the temerity," as he put it, to warn Wood of the danger to the troopers if the Spanish artillery responded to the American barrage. The smoke from Grimes's guns marked their location. Despite his own apprehensions, Wood replied firmly, "We have our orders and cannot move from here." The command to support the battery had presumably come from Shafter. There was no easy appeal. The unconcerned troopers remained at hazard, although there was no way that Grimes's guns could conceivably need support on the exposed hilltop.[9]

Roosevelt took no more action in the troopers' behalf than Wood did. He was willing to defy orders to perform a courageous deed, but he would never disobey instructions to act protectively in a manner that might be regarded as cowardly. Selectivity was a real part of his valor.

Wood and Roosevelt were standing together when Wood began fretting aloud about the danger to the troopers directly in line with Grimes's battery. He was about to risk loss of face by asking Sumner for permission to move the men when the first Spanish shell was fired. The detonation was accompanied by a dull roar. The cannons probably were the two mountain guns but may have been the three-inch and five-inch guns borrowed from Spanish battleships and located behind the heights. The Spanish powder was smokeless, so the position of the emplacement was not disclosed.[10]

Suddenly a round shell appeared, sailing high above the valley in the direction of the battery at El Poso. A little thread of white smoke trailed from its timed fuse. The flight of the shell was accompanied by a high-pitched, long-drawn-out hissing that cut the air until the shell burst with a bang overhead. Then the sound became a ghostly, rattling, scuttling, and caterwauling of hundreds of pieces of shrapnel searching for human targets.

There was, however, no damage or injury. The shell had been aimed high in the Spanish manner, exploding thirty feet beyond the hill. The Rough Riders laughed and cracked jokes a little uneasily, but the Spanish artillery had the range.

Another dull roar was heard from San Juan. The second shell steamed along like a railroad train, again too high to injure the American gunners, but the burst was right over the troopers. The air was filled with flying balls of shrapnel. One Rough Rider was killed and three were wounded, along with a larger number of Cuban casualties. One of Wood's two horses was killed. Men were groaning in agony as Roosevelt received his first injury of the war. A piece of shrapnel struck a glancing blow on the back of his left wrist, raising a bump as big as a hickory nut without breaking the skin or immobilizing his hand. He was proud of the pain and the visible trauma.[11]

When the shrapnel cut their comrades down, the Rough Riders stampeded. They said bullets from Mauser rifles could be faced without flinching, as they had proved at Las Guasimas. Mauser bullets went zip by their ears before they had time to think, but the wobbling and hissing and whistling of the artillery shells lasted for what seemed a long time. The troopers could see and hear the shells coming, and they thought they might have a chance to get out of the way if they ran in the right direction. The option was what made the men nervous. Indecision caused panic.

The exchange of artillery fire was beyond the Rough Riders' control. The enemy was shooting at them, but they could not return the fire. They hated the feeling of impotence. As they explained it, if the enemy had been a man in the street at home who took a swing at them, they would have swung right back. Now they wanted to shoot back, but the Spanish artillerymen were out of sight and too far away for carbines. The order was to hold their fire.

In minutes, the Spanish artillery was silenced, perhaps by a shortage of shells. Despite being underfed, unpaid, poorly equipped, ill, and commanded by officers who had no hope of winning the war, the outnumbered Spanish soldiers put up a defense characterized in every instance by courage and discipline.[12]

That's the First One

In the stampede, many Rough Riders had tumbled down the unprotected west side of El Poso in front of Grimes's guns while Wood and Roosevelt scrambled down the east side. Roosevelt had his pocket handkerchief bound tightly around the swelling on his wrist. He remarked confidently, "Well, that's the first one. They'll have to do better next time."[13]

Told to prepare to move forward, he led the troopers who had not panicked to where he had gone to ground on the hillside and instructed them to lie there. Then he mounted Texas and rounded up the men who had fled. With difficulty he formed the regiment on the plateau behind the hill.[14]

While the American wounded, including one trooper with his leg blown off, were being treated by the regimental surgeons, Roosevelt castigated the rest of the men for flinching. "What's the matter with you fellows?" Roosevelt demanded. "What are you, a bunch of sheep? Clerk, call the roll!"

Although the men anticipated further Spanish shelling as they lined up, they responded to the clerk by yelling "here" as their names were called. "Dress on Sergeant Higgins," Roosevelt told them, but the men said afterward that the sergeant was stooped over just like the rest of them. "Now," Roosevelt commanded, "get ready to march down the road."

The Rough Riders brought their wounded to the headquarters hospital, buried the dead without taking time to leave an identification marker, and pulled in pickets and scouts. They stacked their remaining equipment in neat piles, keeping only their carbines, ammunition, and canteens. Tents, blanket rolls, haversacks, and most rations were left behind as they assembled in formation and closed to the right toward the trail. It was still only 9 A.M. when the Rough Riders with mounted Roosevelt in the lead were ready to march out at the head of the 2nd Cavalry Brigade.

In the absence of communication between El Caney and El Poso, McClernand could not know that Lawton was totally bogged down.

Lawton would be completely unable to effect a timely rendezvous with the impatient Rough Riders on July 1. Unwittingly McClernand was committing Kent and Sumner prematurely to the Battle of San Juan. That commitment would present a contingency not provided for in the Shafter plan.

Chapter 20
The Best of a Bad Situation

Shortly after 8:45 A.M., Colonel McClernand initiated Shafter's plan by telling General Sumner to march the cavalry division forward from El Poso.[1]

Once McClernand gave the order, he was impatient to see the men move out. Continuing gunfire from the north made him believe that he had to engage the Spaniards on San Juan Hill quickly, before General Linares learned how effective the resistance at El Caney was and rushed reinforcements there. More Spaniards around El Caney would delay Lawton further.

Sumner had selected the 1st Brigade to head the cavalry in the march, but the troopers did not respond fast enough to satisfy McClernand. He turned to Kent and asked, "Why don't those people move?" Without thinking, he gave Kent's infantry the lead so "the others would follow."[2]

They'll Pot You

Kent's infantry was led by Gen. Hamilton Hawkins, the tall, white-haired veteran whose ability and courage had been demonstrated during the Civil War. Hawkins had progressed only a quarter of a mile when he was overtaken by a courier from El Poso. Despite the resulting delay in engaging the Spaniards, he was ordered to have his men step aside to let the cavalry through. McClernand had made a mistake. He remembered belatedly that Shafter's plan called for Sumner to take and retain the advance. The troopers ultimately would face the time-consuming task of picking their way north along the trackless banks of the Aguadores and San Juan rivers to meet Lawton. The route of the infantry was expected to be easier.

When the cavalry assumed the lead in the interrupted march, Lieutenant Colonel Carroll was in the van with his own 9th Regiment and the rest of the 1st Brigade. There was no breeze as the troopers stepped briskly along the narrow trail in columns of two. The rank vegetation blocked vision into the jungle, but fortunately for the cavalry, Linares had prepared no ambush.[3]

Wood continued to identify more with the Rough Riders than with the regular cavalry, so he chose Roosevelt to head the 2nd Brigade. When it was time for the Rough Riders to enter the trail, McClernand personally ordered Roosevelt to proceed. He observed that his command patently pleased Roosevelt, even though the regiment started the march in back of the 1st Brigade.[4]

The two veteran cavalry officers who commanded the regular regiments in Wood's brigade were incensed as they rode onto the trail behind the volunteer Rough Riders. Both officers had been in the

General Hamilton S. Hawkins at San Juan. *Harper's Pictorial History of the War with Spain* (New York: Harper and Brothers, 1898), p. 335.

army since 1861. They bitterly criticized the medico Wood for again giving the limelight to Roosevelt. Sumner was riding forward to meet Wood and stopped the complaints by making excuses for his brigade commander. It was the Rough Riders' turn to lead, he explained, and not a matter of preference. Besides, the Rough Riders would be posted farthest north in front of the San Juan heights. They would have the greatest distance to go.

The morning grew hotter. In a few places, the trail that was lined with hundreds of waiting infantrymen was also blocked by decomposing bodies of horses that had foundered in the enemy's rapid retreat from Las Guasimas. Nevertheless, Roosevelt's men marched boisterously, muffling the sound of Lawton's artillery fire at El Caney.[5]

The march soon slowed drastically. The cavalrymen had the advance to themselves, but they paused occasionally to throw off what little was left of their personal possessions. Crossing small streams that ran deceptively fast forced longer delays. Some of the fords were deep. Men who slipped were carried away by the current. A few who could not swim had to be rescued from drowning.[6]

Kent was dissatisfied with McClernand's indecisiveness and with the cavalry's slow pace. Worried about the safety of his infantrymen who now were at the end of the long procession, he and Hawkins galloped to the head of Wood's brigade where they found Sumner and Wood. Shafter's young aide Lieutenant Miley rode by just then to take his designated position with Carroll in the front of the cavalry column. Later, Miley remembered the officers he saw conferring, but he did not recall seeing Roosevelt. The Rough Rider was not prominent enough in the decision making for Miley to have noticed him.[7]

Kent and Sumner looked around in a futile attempt to determine precisely where they were in the dense jungle. They shared what little instruction they had received from Shafter and McClernand. Sumner knew that he was to proceed to the Aguadores River, halt there, and wait for confirmation of orders. Kent had been told that his first target was an unoccupied, unnamed, and apparently unimportant rise to the left of San Juan Hill. He had seen the rise only on Shafter's hand-drawn map. Both officers were apprehensive.[8]

General Wheeler also joined the group. Ignored by Shafter ostensibly because he was ill, Wheeler had been awakened by the sound of the gunfire at El Caney. He dressed and rode past the marching cavalrymen, but he did not take it upon himself to replace Sumner who had received Shafter's briefing. Instead, he stationed himself as the link between McClernand and the two divisional generals who were marching toward San Juan. As the ranking officer on the field, he saw that the few orders coming from McClernand were put into effect.[9]

Meanwhile, the cavalry's advance guard approached the ford of the Aguadores River after an hour of marching over the muddy and obstructed trail. There they paused. The track behind them was choked with cavalry and infantry in tight double lines the whole mile back to El Poso.[10]

When the Rough Riders were halted hundreds of yards before the ford, Roosevelt dismounted to find out what was going on. The Spaniards had cleared most of the brush and trees from the river banks at the ford to provide an open target for Mauser volleys. Lieutenant Miley was there, reclining comfortably beneath a rare sheltering bush, although the Spaniards were not yet firing in the direction of the ford. He called to Roosevelt, "Colonel, better get down, or they'll pot you." Roosevelt was pacing around the clearing, his eyes dancing, as he replied with his usual bravado, "I'm not going to lie down for any confounded Spaniard!"[11]

Although maneuvering was difficult on the trail wedged with impatient soldiers, Major Derby took the observation balloon up for another scout. Held by ropes in the hands of the unlucky infantrymen assigned to the hazardous and awkward job, the craft was raised behind Roosevelt's regiment.

From the elevated basket, Derby sent word to Kent of a previously unknown footpath ahead, leading off the trail to the left. The path was a valuable alternate route toward San Juan Hill. Derby also observed that surprisingly few Spaniards were visible. He assumed that the rest of them were behind the crest.[12]

Sumner had continued to ride ahead through the tail end of the 1st Cavalry Brigade and was standing impatiently near the deforested ford, waiting for the command to cross into the less exposed jungle. The only member of Shafter's staff present was Miley who walked over to meet him. Sumner began pleading with Miley to approve the further advance in Shafter's name when Sumner's adjutant, Capt. Robert Howze, rode up to report. One regiment of the 1st Cavalry Brigade was already across the ford, he said. The men were positioned as skirmishers on the far bank, "waitin' to go at 'em!"[13]

In recognition of the accomplished fact, Miley gave in to Sumner's request to be allowed to follow with the rest of the 1st Brigade and with the 2nd Cavalry Brigade led by Roosevelt. Miley acknowledged, "Well, you gentlemen are older than I am."

Shortly afterward, Sumner also received a confirming order from McClernand's courier to have his division wade across the Aguadores in accordance with the second step in Shafter's plan. He was advised to deploy his men into the jungle where the 1st Brigade already was and to wait there for Lawton's arrival. Although it was almost 10 A.M., McClernand continued to assume that Lawton would capture El Caney in time to start the assault on San Juan by early afternoon.[14]

Roosevelt and his Rough Riders crossed the river as soon as they had Wood's approval. Afterward, Roosevelt maintained that he hurried the troopers because he was afraid the war balloon would endanger their position by hovering behind them over the ford. He predicted that later crossings might be "hot work."[15]

To that point, the cavalry had sustained no casualty on the march. The Spaniards were holding their fire until the American army was wholly committed to crossing the river. When the enemy saw the big balloon coming toward them, however, they realized that the Americans had reached the ford. They were not sure what the lighter-than-air craft did, but it was another costly American advantage in the war, emphasizing the magnitude of the invaders' combat equipment compared with the Spaniards' universal shortages.

The balloon was an easy outlet for the Spaniards' resentment. They opened fire from San Juan with a fusillade of shells and bullets that quickly shredded the air bag, causing the balloon to sink slowly into a treetop at the side of the trail. Major Derby descended from the basket without injury.[16]

Tragically for the American soldiers, gunfire aimed at the balloon also raked the crowded trail below. Roosevelt and most of his men were across the ford and out of immediate danger, thanks to his placement at the head of the 2nd Brigade and to Sumner's persistence with Miley. The remaining two regiments of Wood's brigade and Kent's entire infantry division were behind the balloon and caught in a box, unable to move forward quickly or backward or to either side. They suffered eighty casualties, although the Spaniards fired only while the balloon hung provocatively above the trees. The Battle of San Juan opened disastrously for the Americans because of the original reconnaissance report that had overestimated the distance between San Juan Hill and the ford across the Aguadores.

The ford came to be called "Hell's Crossing." The trail just beyond the ford was "The Bloody Angle." In Wood's brigade, both the 1st and 10th regulars lost heavily at Hell's Crossing. One of the officers remarked that "what the balloon didn't get hit us." Nevertheless, the gallant black cavalrymen of the 10th, waiting at the ford for the last of the Rough Riders to cross, elected to stand at attention as a sign of indifference under stress. They saluted in mock deference when Spanish shells with their peculiar little shrieks passed overhead at balloon height. The shells then burst directly over the massed infantry.[17]

Wood and correspondent Davis blamed Shafter, although the general was incapacitated at the time. Wood described the balloon episode as "one of the most ill-judged and idiotic acts I have ever witnessed." Davis reported that the same mules used to bring the balloon from Siboney had been denied to the Rough Riders for transporting their repaired Colt machine guns to the front. He claimed that the balloon cost American lives, while the rapid-fire guns might have saved them.[18]

Spanish gunfire directed at the balloon caused many of the losses suffered during the American advance toward San Juan. The episode of the observation balloon at Hell's Crossing is studied in military schools, but not as a model to be followed.[19]

Don't Forget You Are a Rough Rider

After Roosevelt and his troopers marched fifty yards beyond the ford at the head of the depleted 2nd Cavalry Brigade, they began to deploy into the jungle by the right flank to get into position to meet Lawton at the undetermined location. Wet to the hips once again, they were unaware of the nature of the terrain in front of them. They did not know the strength of the Spanish defenses they would come upon or where the deadly encounter would occur.[20]

In honor of dead Captain Capron, Roosevelt had given L Troop the advance to move into the dense brush. When Sumner's courier rode up, the order he brought was twofold. The first was for Roosevelt to put out flankers to avoid another ambush. That was a little deprecatory. Flankers were an obvious impossibility in the dense, trackless brush. Sumner himself had not been able to use flankers in the march from El Poso. The best Roosevelt could do was to deploy a narrow skirmish line with himself on foot at the point.[21]

The second order was for the Rough Riders to refrain from firing their carbines because troopers of the 1st Brigade were between them and the Spaniards on the heights. The implication was that the Rough Riders already had been relegated to the rear, nominally because they were the volunteers in the division but also because of the stigma remaining from the ambush and Shafter's fear of Roosevelt's impetuosity.[22]

While the Rough Riders were stepping cautiously on their way north, parallel to the San Juan Heights, they unexpectedly came upon six Latins in ragged uniforms who claimed to be Cuban rebels. There was no facility to hold prisoners and no authentic Cuban rebel to identify the six men, so Roosevelt could not determine whether they really were allies or Spanish guerrillas. He let them go and they quickly vanished back into the brush.

At that point, the Rough Riders began to attract occasional Mauser fire from the Spaniards on the heights and on the hillock that was in line with any assault they might make. Both the elevations were barely visible from the jungle. Wood later named the knoll East Hill because of its direction from San Juan. That was also the Spanish name. Wheeler called it San Juan House after the deserted Mediterranean blue farmhouse on its knobby top, but the slight elevation was not truly connected to the San Juan range. The designation that stuck was Kettle Hill, in recognition of two large sugar kettles near the farmhouse.[23]

As Roosevelt edged the Rough Riders toward full deployment, other American military movements were going on all over the entire arena. The 3rd Cavalry regiment of the 1st Brigade had safely crossed the Aguadores ahead of the Rough Riders and had formed to the left of the trail alongside the infantry, instead of on the right with the rest of the cavalry division. The 3rd gradually came under fire from San Juan Hill, while its position on the left was confirmed by the brigade commander, Carroll.[24]

Carroll was inspecting his other two regiments when Captain Howze shifted the 3rd to the right of the trail, to place the troopers properly according to his interpretation of Shafter's oral instructions.

When Carroll returned, he angrily transferred the 3rd to the left of the road once again. Next, Lieutenant Miley appeared. He had the regiment return to the right. The casualties in the regiment mounted each time the troopers crossed the trail. Carroll appealed to General Sumner who ended the confusion by upholding Howze and Miley.[25]

Carroll's costly mix-up was understandable. He was the replacement for Sumner as brigade commander. He had not been at Shafter's planning session, there was no written procedure for him to study, and his briefing by Sumner and McClernand had been sketchy. Wood had the same difficulty. He avoided controversy by issuing few orders.

Kent's division experienced trouble, too. Placed in the rear of the cavalry on the march and subjected to numerous delays, his infantrymen were under heavy fire before they reached the ford. Yet they could not respond, because the jungle blocked their view of the Spanish fortifications. Kent also suspected that there were Spanish sharpshooters in back of him. He believed that his men were in a circle of bullets, but he could not see the guerrillas any better than he could see the Spaniards on the hill.[26]

Hawkins's regiments helped the Bloody Angle earn its name as they followed the trail between the Aguadores and San Juan rivers. The 6th Infantry lost many of its men in an assault on a blockhouse. The veteran regulars fell back in momentary confusion before continuing toward the hill.[27]

After Hawkins passed the ford, Kent ordered the 71st New York Volunteers to take the advance into the footpath to the left that Major Derby had discovered from the doomed observation balloon. Spanish rifle fire from the hill was so intense at this point that the untested 71st was officially recorded as having "recoiled in disorder." The regulars who marched through the panicked 71st to take over the advance had four commanding officers shot, one after the other, in half an hour.[28]

Moreover, the situation at El Caney had not improved. Lawton's artillery battery remained ineffective at its extreme range. The rifle duel persisted, while the unsupported infantrymen suffered casualties as they crept ahead to try to surround the small Spanish garrison. There was no indication of whether—let alone when—the fort would be captured. Lawton would not be joining Kent and Sumner soon. The Rough Riders would wait under fire in vain.[29]

Roosevelt might well have been the first human to penetrate this primeval jungle. He knew nothing of the misadventures of Lawton, Kent, and Carroll. He was out of touch with Sumner and Wood. Under an increasing barrage of Mauser bullets, he headed his isolated regiment through the bush in a blind advance against an invisible but deadly enemy. With his orderly leading Texas where he could not ride, he again disregarded army protocol by staying with the scouts.[30]

The steaming humidity was debilitating. Some troopers cut off their pants at the knees, but then their legs were severely bitten by insects and scratched by thorny shrubs. Troopers who wore red wool bands next to their stomachs as a folk remedy to avoid malaria developed discomforting prickly heat. They threw the homemade bands away.[31]

The Rough Riders struggled half a mile through the chaparral along the river bank with the Spanish volleys getting hotter. Then the Aguadores curved back toward the east, away from the line of march northward to meet Lawton. Soon Roosevelt reached the east bank of the San Juan River. According to Arizonans in the regiment, Roosevelt called the hill and river "the San Jew-an" until troopers "who talked Mexican told him the name was pronounced 'San Hwan.'"[32]

Rough Riders soaked from the Aguadores crossing also were running sweat, but they acted like veterans picking their way through the jungle. Under fire now, they considered themselves to be "seasoned soldiers, and we now smiled in contempt at the man who ducked his head when a bullet popped near him. When we came to a dead man, we simply glanced at him to see if he was an acquaintance, then passed on." "Passed on" was an unfortunate choice of words.[33]

When the Rough Riders were fully deployed at 10:30 A.M., they halted among the trees by the river to wait for further orders from Wood. They had worked their way three-quarters of a mile northward from the main trail. The troopers were being harassed by converging fire from the three principal Spanish positions they faced—San Juan Hill, the heights, and Kettle Hill which was still not seen clearly.[34]

The six regiments of the cavalry division were in two wavy lines parallel to the heights. Carroll's three regiments of the 1st Brigade were the front line, across the San Juan River toward the meadow. The 3rd Regiment of the 1st Brigade was on the left with its flank at last set firmly against the main trail. The 6th was in the center. The black troopers and white officers of the 9th were on the far right, in front of the Rough Riders, facing Kettle Hill.[35]

Wood's brigade was the second line, spread over both banks of the San Juan River. The 1st and 10th regiments were across the river in reserve of the 1st Brigade. They were ready to march forward if directed to, but otherwise they were not permitted to shoot or advance. The 1st Regiment was on the left and the 10th, also with black troopers and white officers, was in the center. The Rough Riders were in support of the 1st and 10th on the right of this wandering second line. They were also slightly more to the right than the 9th while they waited defenseless in the brush for the missing Lawton.[36]

Roosevelt realized that his regiment was the rearmost of the six and likely to be kept out of action. While considering his options, he positioned himself and some of his men in the river, wet to their waists once more but partially protected from gunfire by the earthen bank. He instructed the rest of the troopers to lie down in a sunken lane running at an angle from the river to little round Kettle Hill and beyond to San Juan Heights and Santiago. The Spaniards were volley firing more accurately than they had at Las Guasimas. Trooper after trooper was hit. The wounded were carried to the shelter of the river bank where they were treated by the surgeons.[37]

The Rough Riders had escaped losses at Hell's Crossing, but now they were suffering heavily. The steady depletion of his force made Roosevelt uneasy. He was getting restless. In addition to the Spanish volley firing, there were enemy guerrillas hidden in the trees overhanging the river. They spared no one, not even medical corpsmen. The bullets came from places the sharpshooters among the Rough Riders could not locate. The regiment was under severe fire from front and rear that could not be answered and did not diminish.

As Roosevelt established regimental headquarters near the river in the sunken lane under sheltering trees, the Rough Riders found themselves caught in a ring of fire. Anxious about the lethal trap he had been ordered into, he exclaimed to the troopers near him, "Boys, this is the day we have trained for. You know we are being watched by the regulars. Don't forget you are a Rough Rider. Don't forget, boys, that we must get through this battle so your reward can come in the future."[38] He was speaking as if to each man personally. As the leader, he planted in each man some of the determination and courage he possessed in abundance. The reward he was offering would follow ultimate victory.

Roosevelt ordered more troopers to move into the lane, taking all the cover they could. Others he sent to the edge of the open field where waist-high grass was growing. They dove into the meadow and lay flat. There was not a single yard of ground that was not inside the zone of Spanish fire. Every trooper in the regiment was within range of the Spanish guns. Yet the Rough Riders were not permitted to respond with their guns.[39]

The end of the morning was approaching. It was intolerably hot. Sweat poured off the men clinging to the earth. The battle noise was becoming fearful. The little stallion Texas was tethered among trees to the right, a prime target for the Spaniards. The horse could not be wholly concealed, yet it remained unharmed.[40]

For a long and bitter hour, the Rough Riders endured their casualties, still without a chance to return the fire. Mauser bullets volleyed at them in sheets. They could hear bullets go *z-z-z-eu, z-z-z-eu,* through leaves and grass. When a bullet found its mark, the stricken trooper would bounce up to deny the injury. Then he would sink again into the meadow or lane, wounded or dead.

Two novelists who were in Cuba as correspondents had refrained from following their peers to El Caney. Instead, they had headed toward San Juan. One was Stephen Crane who had changed his mind about going to El Caney despite the briefing emphasizing Lawton's role for the day. Crane could not see the front, but he reported that the whole field at San Juan was bursting with a roar like a raging brushfire on the prairie. The sound was swelling and swelling. Frank Norris remembered the battle only as a hideous blur.[41]

A Very Uncomfortable Time

The terrain at San Juan was extremely unfavorable for the cavalry division. Carroll's 1st Brigade was only half a mile from the heights, and the meadow concealing them was swept by the enemy's artillery as well as by Mauser fire. Wood's 2nd Brigade had moved forward to where it also was exposed to the same Spanish firepower. Even worse, there were guerrilla sharpshooters hidden among the American soldiers.[42]

Through it all, Roosevelt sought to show composure. While under severe pressure, he wrote what he considered to be a reasoned note to veteran Lt. Col. John Baldwin of the 10th who was positioned ahead of him and to the left. He advised the experienced regular officer that "there is too much firing" by the 10th. Roosevelt quoted absent Colonel Wood in directing that "there be no more shooting unless there is an advance or unless you are certain you locate a sharpshooter and can get him." All he accomplished was to endanger the messenger and infuriate Baldwin.[43]

Roosevelt was stretched out on the west bank of the river near his headquarters, trying to talk quietly to young Lt. Ernest Haskell who was on leave from West Point. The subject was cavalry tactics as taught in the school. When Haskell did not respond to a question, Roosevelt turned to look at him inquiringly and found that the lieutenant had been shot in the stomach without crying out or jerking his body around. "Don't bother about me," Haskell replied, adding the requisite bold note to the dramatic situation: "I'm going to get well." He did.[44]

The most distress that Roosevelt would confess to was having a very uncomfortable time, although he hated lying inactive while the enemy's bullets were wounding and killing troopers around him. His two military orderlies were incapacitated, one temporarily by the heat and the other permanently with a bullet through the carotid artery in his neck. When Roosevelt gave an order to a trooper who was replacing the second orderly, the man stood up enthusiastically, saluted, and fell back over the startled Roosevelt's knees with a bullet through his brain. Conditions were more serious for the Rough Riders than they had been in the ambush at Las Guasimas.

Then Roosevelt's favorite, Capt. Buckey O'Neill, was shot. Like Roosevelt, O'Neill had been looking for martial fame to attain civilian goals. While training in Texas he had written, "I am ready to take all the chances." On the transport to Cuba, he had joined Roosevelt in the toast to the officers, stating that the war must last until each was killed, wounded, or promoted.[45]

Though relatively untutored, O'Neill had quoted poetry to surprise Roosevelt and at Daiquiri and Las Guasimas had shown himself to be equally combative and courageous. After the first Rough Rider casualties, O'Neill had asked, "Colonel, isn't it Whitman who says of the vultures that 'they pluck the eyes of princes and tear the flesh of kings'?" Roosevelt had been surprised because he was not familiar with the poet Walt Whitman. Now the regimental toast had been fulfilled. O'Neill was dead and food for the vultures, while Roosevelt had been promoted.

Roosevelt had ordered O'Neill to take A Troop to the front of the Rough Riders' position. There the captain had placed his men under what little protection there was while he stood erect, twenty yards past the river, smoking a hand-rolled cigarette.

In contrast to Roosevelt's cautious example at the river, O'Neill retained the romantic idea that an American officer should always stand, even in the open, and had been repeating to his remonstrating troopers that the Spanish bullet capable of hitting him had not yet been made. As he turned forward on his heel, he was struck in the mouth by a Mauser bullet that came out the back of his head. He was killed instantly, offering an extravagant example of the persistence of the Civil War view of life as cheap. The death was so shocking that no one in A Troop knew what to do until a regular cavalry officer passing by instructed one of the troopers to report the casualty to Roosevelt.

The shooting of O'Neill affected Roosevelt visibly. Coming after Capron's death a week earlier, the loss personified tragedy for the whole regiment. Despite their killed and wounded comrades, Roosevelt and the Rough Riders had accomplished nothing at San Juan but to obey orders to await further orders. He sent repeatedly to Wood and then to Sumner for authority to attack the hills in front. There was no response.[46]

It was apparent to Roosevelt that the Rough Riders were suffering from Spanish gunfire as much while lying in reserve as they would be if they charged ahead. In another hour or two of inaction, they might be reduced to impotence as a regiment and perhaps wiped out. He told the messenger from A Troop to return there and to advise any officer he found to prepare to deploy the troopers as skirmishers.

In addition to the gunfire casualties, Roosevelt was concerned because he could hear the men's breathing become labored in the heavy, moist air. He could see that their strength was diminishing although the hotter part of the day was still ahead. By afternoon they might not be physically able to mount a charge.

Another factor Roosevelt considered was the deleterious emotional impact on men forced to watch buddies being killed or wounded. Q.M. Sgt. Stephen Pate was stout. His mates in B Troop laughed as he hugged the earth in desperation while telling a thinner man, "If I could lie as close to the ground as you do, I would pay a thousand dollars." When Pate received a flesh wound from a Mauser bullet, however, he endured the discomfort silently.[47]

Other wounded men responded with astonishment rather than anguish when they were struck. They simply could not believe that Mauser bullets had singled them out of all the troopers in the regiment. "I'm hit," they remarked casually, or "I'm done," or "They've got me." They raised themselves and then fell back.

Wounded troopers were carried to the field station by overworked medical corpsmen. A few of the wounded were hit again by the murderous Spanish sharpshooters in the trees. After the pain set in, some men screamed in agony when they were unintentionally bumped or rolled on the improvised litters. Then they were gone from the front and forgotten by the survivors for as long as the battle lasted.

The uninjured Rough Riders were old campaigners now. They grumbled, "It is hard enough to face bullets with your own carbine smoking in your hand, but it becomes doubly hard when you lay under a hell of fire and can't fire in reply." The troopers complained that they were "banked up behind the regulars. We wanted to open fire but the Ninth and Tenth Cavalry were between us and the Spaniards. The bullets kept raining thick. It was like being shot in the dark and yet seeing men fall like tenpins."[48]

The only consolation the troopers had was that the Spaniards who paused to aim their Mausers focused on American officers rather than on enlisted men. A disproportionate number of officers became casualties. The enemy sharpshooters concentrated first on officers who stood out, like Roosevelt when he was on horseback. Second, they aimed at those who wore swords, and third, on anyone who had a stripe down his trousers.

You Won't, I Will

After the popular O'Neill was shot, the Rough Riders "got their mad up," as they put it. At Las Guasimas they had fired at Spaniards methodically in the course of responding to the ambush. Now they began to hate the Spaniards they blamed for their continuing discomfort, for guerrillas sharpshooting them in the back, and for killing O'Neill. They were after Spanish blood. Their anger solidified them behind Roosevelt, who symbolized valor, resolution, and achievement. They made the determined Roosevelt into an even more charismatic figure than he already was. Rudderless members of A Troop attached themselves to him for the rest of their lives. He was their militant father image.[49]

This was Roosevelt's first full day in command of the regiment he prized. He loved the heady feeling of sole responsibility and had responded to O'Neill's death by implicitly assuring A Troop that the regiment would soon be advancing on the Spanish lines. The need to move forward was obvious to him. He was committed to vengeful aggression, despite the lack of authorization from his superiors.

He had finally made up his mind to lead the Rough Riders in an all-out charge. The advance would be with the rest of the cavalry division if he could get approval from Sumner in one last try, but on his own if he could not. His civilian history had featured a frequent flaunting of authority. The difference here was that lives and not politics were at stake.

Roosevelt realized that the Rough Riders and the other regiments in the cavalry and in Kent's infantry division already were inextricably engaged in the battle. They could not pull back. The main trail from El Poso was wedged with infantrymen still heading toward San Juan. They could not be turned around. On the other hand, the Rough Riders could not remain where they were. They were being shot to pieces. There was only one way to save lives. That way was to go forward into the Spanish guns.[50]

He assumed that he would be charging forts manned by trained defenders, protected by entrenchments and entanglements, and elevated on commanding hills. According to the European experts, a successful assault on these fortified defenses would be a military impossibility without the siege guns they did not have. Nevertheless, the charge had to be made.

Generals Sumner and Kent also knew that the attack was necessary. When Roosevelt insisted upon affirmative instructions, however, Sumner did not sanction an advance because he did not have the authority. He did not expressly forbid Roosevelt to act because he expected new orders soon. Roosevelt was now making his final request, though, saying to himself, "If you won't move forward against the enemy, I will!"[51]

While lying on the river bank, Roosevelt was thinking about his role in the assault, acting out the part in his mind. Despite his long-time dreams of a mounted charge, he originally planned to lead on foot. On the other hand, the heat was so oppressive that he would be limited in range and capability if he chose to walk. The enhanced risk of being shot on horseback never occurred to him. So, at the last minute, he decided to ride Texas.[52]

He knew that the men could see him better if he went ahead riding Texas. The sight would be inspirational for everyone. Additional encouragement would come from the colors carried beside him. After O'Neill was killed, six-feet-and-one-inch Color Bearer Albert Wright of A Troop had attached himself to Roosevelt with the flag from Phoenix that had flown at Daiquiri. Pvt. Henry Bardshar had volunteered to serve as a replacement for Roosevelt's orderlies. The two Arizonans remained with him for the rest of the campaign.

Placed to Return the Fire

Meanwhile, Wood was not communicating with the brigade from his isolated command post in the rear. He was bemused, walking back and forth in a clearing, oblivious to the danger from Spanish bullets while he considered what to do. His orderly was petrified with fright because he was obliged to stand near Wood, holding the reins of the big gray horse Charles Augustus.

Wood's pessimistic estimate was that the brigade had already lost 20 percent of its strength. He was muttering to himself, "If this keeps up, I don't see anything but to order an advance." He was unaware that at the same moment Roosevelt was positioning the Rough Riders for a charge or that on the left of the main trail, Kent's infantry division was forming an assault line without orders from McClernand. General Hawkins was ready to take the lead on foot.[53]

At El Poso, McClernand still had no word for Sumner or Kent, although his instructions had sent the two divisions into the raking San Juan fire. He had not yet heard from Shafter who remained ill. Sumner was exasperated because he could not pry a response from McClernand. His irritation surfaced when he demanded a decision from Wheeler, the ranking officer present. The cagey little southerner bucked the question back to McClernand.

The only response McClernand gave Wheeler was double-talk.

He told Wheeler that division commanders like Sumner "were expected to fight all their men when they could do so to advantage. Our men were now being shot down in the road without an opportunity to fight. They should be placed in form to return the enemy's fire." McClernand criticized Sumner for causing "considerable delay" merely by raising the issue.[54]

What Sumner wanted to know, though, was not generalities but specifically whether he was authorized to attack the Spanish fortifications in a charge. What Wheeler relayed to him from McClernand was no help. He would have to look elsewhere or make up his own mind.

While Sumner was deliberating, the regular cavalry officers were assuming that an assault would be ordered soon. They were busy surveying initial obstacles such as the barbed wire entanglements that they would have to surmount. Lt. Col. Charles Viele of the 1st Regiment took his two squadron leaders through the trees to point out the blue farmhouse on Kettle Hill as their objective. Lieutenant Colonel Baldwin of the 10th placed one of his squadrons in front and the other behind as its support, pushing the Rough Riders another stage to the rear.[55]

At last Sumner decided on a modest course of action. He interpreted McClernand's permission "to place the men to return the enemy's fire" as allowing him to position his division in readiness to charge the San Juan Heights but not yet to make the actual assault. He issued orders to cover what his regimental commanders were already doing.[56]

For the next step, Sumner found his way to Lieutenant Miley who was Shafter's sole representative at the front. Sumner hoped that Miley could be persuaded to authorize the charge, since the lieutenant could see for himself the rapidly deteriorating situation.

Miley's only instruction from his superior McClernand had been the same message Wheeler received. That was a carefully cryptic bit of advice to be given to a powerless young lieutenant confronted by an angry general. Miley found it in himself, however, to approve the charge of the cavalry in Shafter's name but on his own authority. He earned a second unrecognized but deserved credit for helping to save Shafter's command at San Juan.[57]

Chapter 21
Making Ready to Charge

By 11:30 A.M., well-directed Spanish gunfire had been punishing the Rough Riders for an hour. As far as Roosevelt knew, Colonel McClernand was still silent and it was obvious that there would be no timely help from General Lawton. In the absence of new orders, the Battle of San Juan would be in the hands of the colonels of the line.

Despite the humiliation of being stationed farthest to the rear, Roosevelt said later that he was the first commander to decide to start the assault on his own, without authorization from the generals and without the other regiments joining in. In his opinion, Kettle Hill had to be taken first. Otherwise, Spanish rifles on the slight elevation would rake the whole battlefield, endangering Kent's infantry division as well as both cavalry brigades in a charge.[1]

Happy to be acting decisively at last, Roosevelt formed the regiment into a column of troops, with each trooper deployed as a skirmisher. When the first line of troopers was ready for the advance, he shouted, "Well, come on!" According to the adjutant who observed Roosevelt's consternation, no one moved. "What, are you cowards?" he shrieked. "Come on!" Still no one moved. A tall trooper in the front of the first skirmish line grinned and replied, "We're waiting for you to give the correct military command." "Oh," replied the colonel, calmed but not abashed. "Forward, march!"[2]

Just as the soldiers of the 9th had saluted shells at Hell's Crossing, the Rough Riders demonstrated their coolness under fire by withholding their response to Roosevelt's direction. Now they went forward in good order, although the command was still not correct for skirmishers.

Roosevelt mounted Texas and rode forward, accompanied by Wright, Bardshar, and the rest of the Rough Riders on foot. While reining his horse from side to side along the line to herd the troopers into a rough formation, he discovered one man lying under a bush. He asked sarcastically, "Are you afraid to stand up when I am on horseback?" The trooper tried to rise, but bloodstains showed that a bullet had gone into him lengthwise from the shoulder. After a few words of encouragement, Roosevelt urged his horse ahead. His rules precluded attention to the wounded until the action was over.

His face was streaming with sweat and streaked with dirt. His blue shirt was soaked and the brown khaki trousers were caked with mud. The polka-dotted blue bandanna flapping from the back of his campaign hat became the symbol of the day for the Rough Riders, for other cavalrymen, and for journalists.

Although no Spaniard was now in sight on the round hillock, Roosevelt believed there were hundreds of Spanish soldiers behind the crest or concealed in trenches at the top. Nevertheless, he advanced the regiment boldly between wire fences on both sides of the sunken lane and proceeded to the edge of the meadow.[3]

The going was slow as they started to pass around the northern flank of the 10th Cavalry. The Rough Riders took cover, then jumped up, bent low, and ran ahead for a few paces. As soon as the troopers' heads popped up, the enemy let loose with rifles and the men dropped down to the protection of the grass. Each time the routine was repeated, a little ground was gained.[4]

Because he was riding in front of the Rough Riders, Roosevelt was the constant though charmed target of the Spanish riflemen. The advance began what he regarded as the high point of the greatest day of his life. He called the charge his "crowded hour," after the popular couplet by Sir Walter Scott: "One crowded hour of glorious life is worth an age without a name."[5]

Let My Men Through

After Roosevelt commanded the Rough Riders to commence their movement forward, Sumner's courier handed him an order to support the 10th Regiment from behind in the charge that was being

readied. Sumner was basing the instruction upon McClernand's ambiguous advice to Wheeler.

Roosevelt said he interpreted this order to hold back as "the welcome order to advance." By going around the 10th, he had already
proceeded farther than Sumner could have imagined. "I received instructions to move forward and support the regular cavalry in the
assault on the hills in front," Roosevelt explained later, without specifying how far toward the front he was authorized to go, "and we
moved forward. I advanced the regiment in column of companies,"
as he had in fact been doing for fifteen minutes.[6]

Roosevelt believed that relegating the Rough Riders to a supporting role was a clear expression of the regulars' desire to subordinate him. He felt that he had not come this far, however, only to be
suppressed by Shafter or the general's agents, McClernand and Sumner.
They were involved in policy determinations formulated at headquarters in the rear. He was the one on the line, under fire, with his life
and the lives of his men at stake.

The Rough Riders kept moving behind their mounted leader at
skirmish intervals of six feet. Sometimes they ran a few steps. Occasionally they had to crawl. After the last of them left the San Juan
River, the water had the viscosity of churned mud. Men stopped to
drink anyway and to refill their canteens. Drinking the dirty water
was against a direct order from the scorned Adjutant Hall who had
run away at Las Guasimas. There was, however, no other source of
cooling liquid this hot day. Men could only hope that the mud would
settle on the canteen bottoms.[7]

Roosevelt remained the sole mounted man in the front of the
arena and the one most exposed to the enemy. He was getting more
and more excited while pressing the Rough Riders toward the front
line. The feeling was contagious. To move the troopers along at a
steady pace and incidentally to compose himself, he turned back and
again rode between the uneven ranks, joking with some men, en-
couraging others, and swearing at a few. He knew them all as individuals. He gave them the personalized stimuli he felt that they needed
in order to carry on.[8]

When the Rough Riders penetrated the end of the thicket on the
western bank of the river, they could see clearly the round knob of
Kettle Hill rising before them. Rifle volleys from the unseen Span-

iards were constant, but the troopers thought they would at least be leaving the sharpshooters in the trees behind them. As long as the men remained within Mauser range, however, the guerrillas sniped at them from the rear and the right flank.

Bullets seemed to be coming from all around. The troopers believed that some of the shooting was from a careless American volunteer regiment in back of them, although they could not stop to find out. In fact, there was no regiment behind them. The suspected 71st New York Infantry was on the other side of the main trail, recovering from panic.

Crawling and taking cover were disdained now, despite the added risk of being shot. The Rough Riders stepped out joyfully as skirmishers in the meadow's high grass. On their left they passed the forward squadron of the 10th Cavalry which they were supposed to support. They were going far beyond the point of the advance authorized for any regiment.[9]

Positioned ahead of the 10th, the black troopers of the 9th Regular Cavalry were lying flat in the grassy field. They were under great tension because their proximity to the enemy brought them the severest fire. They too were steadily being killed or wounded, while not being allowed to respond to Spanish bullets and shrapnel. All their attention was fixed on the Spaniards in front of them when the line of Roosevelt's skirmishers unexpectedly appeared behind them. The Rough Riders were approaching from the right and shouting colorful but unintelligible oaths as they drew near. Their brown outfits made them hard to distinguish from muddy regulars and from enemy guerrillas.[10]

Looking back from their prone positions, the besieged black cavalrymen were relieved to identify the skirmishers as the high-spirited Rough Riders. In the van they recognized the mounted Roosevelt and they quickly warned him not to shoot at them. Roosevelt pushed past the rear rank of the 9th and started forcing his way through the rows.[11]

Colonel Carroll, whose 1st Cavalry Brigade included the 9th regiment, was standing in the rear near the river. He was waiting for a response to his latest unanswered plea for new instructions from General Sumner when he was surprised to see Roosevelt riding toward the 9th's front line, followed by more than five hundred shouting Rough Riders who were splitting the formation of black cavalry-men. Carroll sent the squadron commander, Capt. Eugene Dimmick, to find out what Roosevelt was doing. When Dimmick reached the impatient Roosevelt, he said that the 1st Brigade remained without orders to charge the Spanish positions. He asked if the Rough Riders had received a contrary directive.

Meanwhile, the Rough Riders were starting to take their places at the front of the 9th Cavalry's lines. Before responding, Roosevelt told the men to lie down in the grass. They were not to fire, although the Mausers were shooting bullets at them in sheets.

Then he turned to Dimmick. His response was evasive as to au-thorization but positive on the action he was going to take. He as-serted that orders from Sumner could be damned. The murderous situation they were in was not good enough for Rough Riders. He insisted that the only chance left for everyone's survival was to rush the fortifications on the round hillock, despite the incessant gunfire.

His regiment had been ordered to support the regular cavalry, he explained. He was going to give that support by exercising his best judgment. That would call for rushes up the hill. His argument sounded like General Young ostensibly searching for the high ground that turned out to be Las Guasimas. The captain of the 9th hurried back to relay this rebellious reply to his colonel.

The Rough Riders who heard Roosevelt's animated discourse with Dimmick nodded their heads. They passed their leader's words to their mates alongside them. Even in the fire-swept meadow, the Rough Riders found Roosevelt's unmilitary and one-sided dialogue with Dimmick amusing.

By the time Dimmick reported to Carroll and discussed the alter-natives, it was past noon. That was too long for Roosevelt to wait under fire. According to his recollection, he stood up straight in his stirrups and announced firmly to the 9th's junior officers around him, "I am the ranking officer right here and I will give the order to charge. If you don't wish to go forward now, please let my men through."[12]

The 9th's officers looked incredulous at this breach of discipline, but one young captain obviously was about to join the Rough Riders in their charge. Other captains certainly would follow. They said, "We must go in with our troops! We must support them!"[13]

As Roosevelt bragged later, he felt he had put it all over on the slower-witted regular army officers. When the leaders of the 9th delayed, he recalled with a proud smile, he took his troopers clean through them while small groups of their junior officers edged forward to join him rather than to stay with Carroll and Dimmick.

Roosevelt was unaware that Sumner already had obtained Miley's approval for the assault. The absence of affirmative orders from Sumner and Wood no longer concerned him. He was embarked on his own quest. He had directed his men into a position to lead the assault against the Spaniards on the round knoll, successfully inducing part of the 9th to join him without their having any more authorization than he had.[14]

In a separate assessment of the cavalry's situation, Wheeler noted later that "the enemy had our range very accurately established" for its artillery "and it would not increase our casualties to charge, but would shorten the time spent by our troops subject to galling fire." He was in the rear, however, and did not give the order for the troops to charge.

Because of the irregular terrain and the advance of the Rough Riders, the regiments on the field were not where the division commanders had intended. All, however, were ready to attack. The cowboy whoops and military hurrahs from the regiments of the cavalry division surged into an uproar that rolled out over the meadow. In addition, a cheer commenced on the left of the road where the infantry was, six hundred yards from San Juan Hill.

Everything was ready except for the command "Go!"[15]

The One Who Gave the Order

Many of the senior officers on the battlefield and on Shafter's staff claimed to have been the one who expressly or implicitly gave the order "Forward to the Charge!" in the San Juan arena. The group included Shafter himself, Wheeler, Sumner, Kent, McClernand, Wood, Carroll, Dimmick, Miley, and Roosevelt. There were lesser lights, too, such as Captain Taylor and the intrepid Rough Rider, Henry Clay Green, a tall mining engineer from Santa Fe, New Mexico. Others of the regimental officers swore that no order to charge ever was issued. The assault at San Juan really was spontaneous, they said, or at least was accomplished through an unspoken consensus.[16]

Typically, even professional observers' reports of compound incidents like battles differ widely, as they had on the smaller stage of the Las Guasimas skirmish. Few events are as difficult to describe as a massive battle that involves thousands of men moving at the same time as parts of different units spread over a jungle theater a mile and a half wide. In terms of American involvement, the scope of the battle at San Juan was more than ten times the size of Las Guasimas.[17]

Participants comprehend less than observers. They witness only what is in their immediate angle of vision and then they do not register all that they observe. They can be supremely exhilarated and swept up into a high pitch of excitation, leading them to skip over details. Men who play active roles in a life-threatening conflict undergo profound experiences. One hour of heightened sensations may feel like ten long hours to some and ten quick minutes to others. As a result, few participants at San Juan could describe accurately what happened there. Later they discussed the events with their peers, arriving at compromises concerning informally negotiated "facts" acceptable to their group. The "facts" were not necessarily correct.

The need for compromise to arrive at truth does not apply, however, to commanding generals like Shafter. Generals—usually without fear of contradiction by lower-ranking officers—can recreate history after a battle is over and can wipe their slates clean.

During the decisive segment of the fighting on July 1, Shafter was in his bed at Corps headquarters three miles in the rear, prostrated by fever, gout, and the heat. He did not direct the American forces in the conflict. McClernand and Wheeler, his links in the chain of command, did not consult him.[18]

In the book Shafter wrote about the campaign, however, he claimed that he was on El Poso Hill before 9 A.M., in time to decide that Lawton was in trouble at El Caney. He claimed that he then ordered Kent and Sumner to move forward into position to charge the Spanish fortifications. The two generals, he said, understood that they were to make the assault as soon as they were ready, without further word from him. His account was false.[19]

McClernand also wrote a book. He made no mention of an appearance by Shafter until after the charge was completed, indirectly putting the lie to his superior officer. McClernand insisted that he ordered Kent and Sumner into readiness to charge. They should have known enough, he maintained, to launch the assault without further instruction from him. What he thought they should have done, though, was not the same as ordering them to do it.[20]

A third book was by Wheeler. He recalled that "at my suggestion McClernand authorized me to move forward my division, and also to give orders to Kent to move forward. This I did in person." Despite his claim to have initiated the assault, however, he was describing only the premature advance to get the men into the bullet-swept arena in front of San Juan. He did not authorize the charge.[21]

In his semiofficial book, Secretary of War Alger whitewashed the ailing Shafter. He maintained that Kent received orders directly from the commanding general "to make the assault at once, and Wheeler notified Sumner" who instructed Carroll's 1st Brigade to charge Kettle Hill. Wood's brigade was held in support. Alger was in Washington on July 1, though, not in Cuba. His second-hand account did not tally with any other tale.[22]

Miley penned his version, too. In the absence of timely instruction from Shafter, Wheeler, or McClernand, he said, he issued the oral authorization that Sumner followed in initiating the cavalry charge. Miley was only a lieutenant, though. He was not supposed to make critical decisions and he received little credit from his superiors for having made them.[23]

Wood was a diarist, not an author. He recorded that he secured Miley's permission early in the morning to allow the 2nd Cavalry Brigade to advance against Kettle Hill. When Wood looked for Roosevelt in order to launch the assault, though, he was told that Roosevelt was making an impromptu personal reconnaissance to locate Lawton at El Caney. Wood claimed that he sent a staff officer to bring Roosevelt back. Meanwhile, Wood said he explained the details of the advance to Viele of the 1st and Baldwin of the 10th. As soon as Roosevelt returned, everything was ready. According to Wood, the time was almost 1 P.M. when he announced that "we might as well go ahead."[24]

Wood did not publish his diary, for good reason. His unlikely account was wholly uncorroborated. Sumner's order to Wood had been clear. Wood's brigade was to remain in support of Carroll's brigade. Wood never would have violated Sumner's instructions. He wanted to stay in the army as a line officer after the war.

The Rough Riders' E Troop had the most unique explanation for the charge. The troop had trailed Roosevelt to the front line, stepping over regular cavalrymen who were in the way or shoving them to the side. One of the displaced units of the 9th was its own E Troop which had been pushed toward the rear. To bring the regulars back into line, Captain Dimmick yelled, "E Troop to the front!" His southern accent sounded like the voice of the Rough Riders' Maj. Micah Jenkins from South Carolina who had been an officer in the regulars.[25]

Capt. Frederick Muller of the Rough Riders' E Troop was a short man, a tax collector from Santa Fe. He understood the command to be for him and he jumped up, shouting the same order, "E Troop to the front!" He said that he already was on the firing line. The only place farther to the front was the Spaniards' positions. The only way he could comply with the order was to advance. "Forward, men!" he roared. "We're going to get 'em! Come on, everybody!"

Muller's objective was the red-roofed blue farmhouse on Kettle Hill. That was where he claimed he pointed E Troop. Lt. Sherrard Coleman remembered that they broke into a run. Trooper Henry Clay Green took the lead. He was whooping and hollering the cowboy yell, without any idea of what he was doing other than "to get there!"[26]

E Troopers said that the 9th's soldiers sat up and asked them in the stereotypical southern dialect, "Wha you-alls gwine, white folks?" Green said, "We're goin' to get the damned greasers!" "Wal," replied the regulars, "ah reckon we-all is gwine wid you, if dat's wha you-alls is gwine." The men of the 9th rose and joined the Rough Riders in the charge that ignited the whole front into the action where Green was killed. At least that was what the diminutive Muller claimed.[27]

Where Is Your Colonel

In the moments just before the charge, the lineup of the 1st Brigade remained the 9th on the right, the 6th in the center, and the 3rd on the left. When a squadron of Viele's 1st Cavalry saw a gap between the 9th and 6th regiments, the men marched right into the opening and up to the front line. Like the Rough Riders, they no longer were in reserve.

Roosevelt did not bother himself with niceties like filling a gap. He already had forced five of his eight troops onto the firing line, splitting the 9th Cavalry in two. Sodden Fifth Avenue Boys were indistinguishable from soaked New Mexican cowboys in the midst of equally muddy regulars.[28]

The whole front line of the cavalry now was shooting at the Spaniards who were on the three defensive elevations. A few troopers fired in volleys in imitation of the Spaniards. Others held their fire until they found a target. Experienced riflemen searched for small trees with crotches close to the ground that could be used as gun rests. The more excitable troopers just pointed their carbines in the air and pulled the triggers. The small number of men who were still in the rear had to be restrained from firing at figures ahead of them, because the figures were their own mates.[29]

Despite the disorder and the lack of artillery, the rifle fire from the thousands of American soldiers was heavy. Spanish General Linares realized that his sparse first line of defense on San Juan Hill, the heights, and Kettle Hill would not be able to resist the full-scale American onslaught that was coming. It was too late for substantial reinforcements, so he dispatched an aide to pull the few soldiers on Kettle Hill back to the heights. That would tighten his line.[30]

In addition, Linares ordered the 140 mounted guerrillas who formed his next defense to ride forward to cover a withdrawal of the Spanish infantrymen from San Juan Hill when the American threat grew into a real danger. He was preparing the retreat from San Juan even before the battle began. To replace the mounted guerrillas in the reserve, he took 100 convalescent soldiers from the Santiago hospital and armed them. That was all he elected to do. His infantrymen at El Caney were surrounded and had to be sacrificed.

Roosevelt wrote about the beginning of the battle many times. Each expression was a little different, but the essence was always the same. He was the one who began the charge, thus breathing life into the martial dreams that had possessed him for years. His trademarks on the field were white suspenders over his blue shirt and the blue polka-dotted bandanna hanging from his hat. This costume and his seat on Texas easily distinguished him from all of the other officers.[31]

In one of his versions of the charge, he said that he rode up to the 9th's officers, dismounted, and told them, "I understand you are to take that hill by rushes and we are to support you. Where is your Colonel?" He then discovered that the 9th was under orders not to advance. Colonel Hamilton was far away at the south end of the firing line, reestablishing linkage with the 3rd and 6th regiments after Viele's 1st had filtered through.[32]

In this account, Roosevelt claimed that he took advantage of Hamilton's absence. As the senior officer present, he leaped back on Texas, swept off his hat with the attached bandanna, waved furiously, and was first to give the command "Forward to the charge!" Along with the Rough Riders, the junior officers of the 9th caught his enthusiasm and audacity. He said they jumped up and guided their cavalrymen into the charge he had initiated.[33]

He swore that he alone had launched the whole forward movement both of the cavalry division and ultimately of Kent's infantry. Although he had neither an order nor an ally to sustain him, he insisted that he personally began the offensive that would engulf the entire Army Corps. His crowded hour was in full force as he headed the cavalry's advance into the volleys of Mauser bullets that were sweeping the field.

The officers of the 9th did not question Roosevelt's courage or his fervor, but they did challenge his veracity. They maintained that they and not Roosevelt began the assault. They pointed to the semi-official *Army and Navy Journal,* which agreed with their claim. The *Journal* reported that "about 30 minutes after noon, the 9th Cavalry moved forward. The 6th Cavalry also moved forward, by rushes of about 15 yards. Colonel Roosevelt immediately joined the line with his command." The regiments were getting into position.

"Shortly after," the *Journal* continued,

> Captain Taylor of Troop C Ninth Cavalry initiated the charge in the open field. Troop D Ninth Cavalry followed immediately on the right. The charge conformed to the movement of Colonel Roosevelt's regiment, as that brave officer was mounted and could be plainly seen by the troopers in the long grass and undergrowth. "We ought to take that hill," shouted Colonel Roosevelt, for he had tired of seeing his men slaughtered while lying near the San Juan River for over an hour. The whole Cavalry Division moved in a gallant rush up the hill rising from the bank of the river.

That was Kettle Hill, transported a little closer to the river.[34]

The article was a bow of soldierly respect for Roosevelt for his undoubted valor and leadership, but according to this authoritative source, Taylor and not he "initiated the charge." Taylor was wounded in the battle.

Three officers of the 9th substantiated the *Army and Navy Journal*'s view of the sequence of events. As Roosevelt rode up to their section of the front, they maintained, Colonel Carroll was present. Colonel Hamilton was nearby. While Roosevelt dismounted and was holding forth with the junior officers, Capt. Charles Taylor of the 9th's C Troop called out. He said the regiment had new orders from General Sumner to charge the hill at once. Taylor was about to start the attack.[35]

Captain Dimmick decided that "we must support Taylor." Dimmick insisted that he was the man who gave the actual order to assault Kettle Hill. Lieutenant Hartwick, the adjutant of the 9th, claimed that he then told Roosevelt that the command "Forward to the Charge!" had been given by Dimmick. The right side of the 9th's line already had started ahead under Taylor when Roosevelt leaped on Texas to lead five troops of the Rough Riders in joining the 9th. The forward squadrons of the 1st and 10th were drawn into the charge without any command from their officers. Dimmick also signaled to the three Rough Rider troops left behind by Roosevelt. They went ahead with the 2nd squadron of the 9th.[36]

Some of the key officers who would have been witnesses did not survive the day, but the official reports of the 9th verified that Dimmick had originated the assault. Later there also were private letters from the 9th's officers to Roosevelt vehemently denying his well-publicized claims. That was all the 9th's officers said for the record.[37]

Unofficially, the regular officers joked that after Dimmick gave the command to charge, "a volunteer field officer, who all morning had been rather heard than seen outside of his own regiment, called out with a theatrical wave of the hand: 'This hill must be taken! If there are three men who will go with me, we will take it!' Already, parts of the line were in motion, however, and shortly the entire column surged forward, carrying this excited volunteer with it."[38]

Regardless of who started the charge, though, it was clear that Roosevelt soon took the lead in his sector. The vision that all who saw the assault remembered was Roosevelt riding ahead of the entire line of dismounted cavalrymen.[39]

The battle as a whole admittedly was too complex for easy comprehension. Yet the sight of this one man performing his valiant but apparently foolhardy feat became the symbol of the whole campaign.

No one who witnessed the ride would ever forget it. No one thought Roosevelt would live through the afternoon. He appeared to be offering his body to the Spanish guns. In his own mind, however, he was denying that Mauser bullets would be able to penetrate the aura surrounding his person and so put him out of the action.

Troops who claimed to have started ahead of him were now aligned behind him on the left and right. In the meadow all were open targets, at the mercy of the Spanish defenders. Mauser bullets came zipping down the slopes. The ordinary man got cold all over. His teeth chattered and he felt the hair move on his scalp. He couldn't pray or think nostalgically of home and wife or mother. He was simply afraid, until the yelling began and the thrill of the moment made his adrenaline flow.

Not Roosevelt. From the outset he realized that the men thought of him as totally unafraid, cloaked in a rage. To them he was the embodiment of an invincible folkloric warrior. He understood, however, that the trick to appearing to be brave was to avoid a display of emotion. At that point, he quit speculating about risks and futures.[40]

He had no idea of textbook tactics appropriate to the situation. There was no support for the charging men and there was no reserve. There was no advancing by squads or troops or regiments. Roosevelt led a mad, mixed rush of troopers anxious to get to the source of the Spanish bullets. In the absence of artillery, the men were sustained by their own loud cheers.

Private Borrowe's detachment had dragged the dynamite gun and its ammunition all the way from Daiquiri to provide the Rough Riders with artillery in the big fight. When the gun jammed in front of San Juan, though, it was abandoned in the men's haste to carry on with the assault. Everything was forgotten but getting there. This was the once-in-a-lifetime adventure everyone had been waiting for. Mauser bullets continued to rain down from entrenched elevations, but most American faces, black and white, sported wide grins. The cavalrymen were like gleeful schoolboys on a holiday escapade while they followed Roosevelt.[41]

Many more of the troopers would have become casualties if the Spanish defenders had held firm at San Juan like their embattled compatriots at El Caney who fought to the end because Linares could not pull them back.

Chapter 22
Charge at San Juan

During the charge up Kettle Hill, troopers from the Rough Riders, the 9th Regiment, and parts of the 1st and 10th regiments continued to form the right flank of the two cavalry brigades. They attacked Kettle Hill. The 3rd, 6th, and the rest of the 1st and 10th regiments were the left flank. The troopers on the left passed Kettle Hill to head directly toward the more strongly defended San Juan Heights. None of the cavalrymen faced San Juan Hill.[1]

Riding abreast of the skirmishers, Roosevelt was fully exposed to enemy fire while cheering, bantering, and bullying the troopers and appealing to their pride as members of his regiment. Then he turned Texas toward Kettle Hill to catch up to the men who were leading the assault on foot.[2]

The Spanish volleys continued. Rough Riders complained that the enemy fire in front of the knoll was more devastating than they had experienced earlier. Medical corpsmen bent over fallen troopers, pinning white tags on the slightly wounded, blue and white tags on more serious cases, and blood red markers on those requiring urgent care. The dead were ignored. A corpsman exclaimed, "We thought we had a soft snap" with a demoralized enemy, "and we got a tough proposition here."[3]

Fortunately for the Rough Riders, the few Spaniards on Kettle Hill began the retreat toward the heights in compliance with Linares's order. They had to avoid being cut off by the cavalry's left wing. Broadsides from distant San Juan Hill and from the heights behind the knoll became less effective against the troopers on the right flank.[4]

The cavalrymen on the slope of Kettle Hill were delayed by the first of the Spanish entanglements. Enemy engineers had used green palmetto poles set in the ground twenty-five feet apart and strung with thick strands of barbed wire. The advance was halted while two men of the 9th forced enough of the wire down to let Roosevelt get his horse across and into the lane leading up the knoll. Looking over his shoulder, Roosevelt saw troopers moving in back of him and in the field to the right. Some were screaming epithets as loud as they could, while Roosevelt again waved his hat to rally them.[5]

Next the men faced a dense hedge where openings had to be cut with machetes. Troopers poured through the narrow passages they made, further blending the 9th and the Rough Riders. The men also had to vault over an old brush fence. One Rough Rider recalled landing on top of a black trooper from the 9th. Despite the urgency, he turned to ask the man's pardon and saw that the trooper was dead. Without moving the body out of the way, the Rough Rider hastily rejoined the flow of volunteers and regulars in the short rushes that had been ordered.[6]

As the Mauser volleys slowed, the pace of the charge quickened. Roosevelt said later that the whole cavalry division was "tired of waiting and eager to close with the enemy." Once more, the assault was a mob going all-out. Roosevelt was racing against both his own men and the other troopers to reach the crest of Kettle Hill. He was determined to get there first.

A Little Black Ant

Most of the war correspondents covering the battle of San Juan heeded Shafter's advice and went to El Caney during the morning of July 1. Only six journalists and two photographers remained on the hill at El Poso. They could see the entire field of battle at San Juan in the bright tropical sunlight.[7]

The correspondents noticed a lone Spanish sentinel standing quietly on a rise far to their left, holding the reins of his motionless horse. On San Juan Hill, there was a Spanish officer who looked to be half as tall as a pin. Wearing a dapper Panama hat while strolling along the Spanish defenses, he signaled by gesturing with a stylish walking stick. From the trenches at his feet came volleys of Mauser bullets. From his side the artillery seemed to roar. The correspondents did not

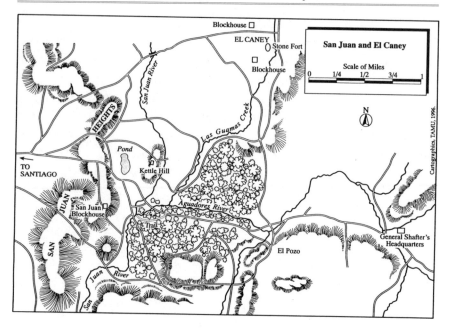

San Juan and El Caney. Map adapted from Herbert H. Sargent,
The Campaign of Santiago de Cuba (Chicago: A. C. McClurg and Co., 1907),
facing p. 2:94; R. A. Alger, *The Spanish-American War* (New York: Harper
and Brothers, 1901), facing p. 152; and Caspar Whitney, "The Santiago Campaign," *Harper's Monthly,* October 1898, p. 802. Adapted by Cartographics
Service Unit of the Department of Geography, Texas A&M University.

think the American cavalry would survive the murderous Spanish
gunfire.[8]

Finally, when it looked from El Poso as if the American forces
would have to retreat, the pessimistic correspondents were aston-
ished to see what looked like a little black ant crawl into the yellow-
ish green of the open meadow in the valley. The shape that from far
away seemed tiny was Roosevelt, hurrying Texas toward the lead of
the assaulting troopers: "An inch or two behind him was the ragged
line of other littler ants, and then another line of ants at a different
place, and then another, until it seemed as if somebody had dug a
stick into a great big ants' nest down in the valley, and all the disturbed
ants were on their way to scramble up the slope." More convivial
newsmen compared the flow of the distant American troopers to the

efflux of bubbles from opening a magnum of extra-dry champagne.[9]

With field glasses, the correspondents could distinguish clearly that Roosevelt was riding at the head of the cavalrymen running toward the round hillock. To the veteran journalists, Roosevelt represented the finest in American manhood. He made the correspondents want to applaud his audacity. To history buffs, the blue polka-dot bandanna floating behind his head like a pennant was reminiscent of the scarf of British Gen. Henry Havelock at the Sepoy Mutiny in India. Roosevelt's white suspenders were crossed over his blue shirt. Journalists knew that a heavy revolver was tucked inside his belt. This was the weapon that had been recovered by divers at the wreck of the battleship *Maine* in Havana harbor.[10]

Roosevelt had the casual air of the amateur of war. He was a gentleman volunteer rather than a methodical professional soldier who got the job done effortlessly and selflessly. No one who saw Roosevelt take that dangerous ride believed he would finish it. His part in the assault looked like utter recklessness, but unquestionably he set the pace of the Rough Riders' charge up Kettle Hill. He motivated his men to win the day.[11]

Rimmed Eyeglasses and a Beaming Smile

Roosevelt took a calculated view of the risks he ran. He was having what he considered to be a bully fight. To him, the charge was great fun. He saw no man ahead of him to detract from his achievement.

He never thought, he insisted later, that he would last through the day without getting hit. He was a student of war and he had a theory about his role in this campaign. Even if struck by the Spanish bullet he anticipated, he figured that the odds would be at least three to one in favor of his being merely wounded rather than killed. He did not believe that a single bullet wound could stop him from being first on the crest of the hill.[12]

A Fifth Avenue Boy watched as the elated Roosevelt galloped by, yelling "like a Sioux." The trooper turned to his Arizonan mate while they were prone during a pause between rushes. He confessed that he had learned to respect Roosevelt as a soldier, although "a couple of years ago we people in New York didn't think Teddy knew enough about the military to review a parade of cops." The westerner saw controlled violence erupting from an unexpected source. He admitted, "I don't never again trust no man with rimmed eyeglasses and a beaming smile."[13]

Yet Roosevelt also took time to be compassionate, by his lights. While riding along the line, he noticed a trooper bleeding heavily from a facial wound and ordered the man to the rear for medical attention. The trooper knew his commander well. "You go to hell," he snarled. "I'm not going back!" Roosevelt turned his horse away without responding.[14]

After Roosevelt and his men advanced on the slope of the little round hill without significant hindrance, they came to a more difficult entanglement, another six-foot-high barbed-wire fence set zigzag by Spanish engineers. Roosevelt could not get Texas over or around the wire. He was at a standstill, fired on while he looked for men with nippers.

"We can do better than nippers," the Arizonan Bardshar shouted. Despite Mauser bullets *zeu-zeu-zeu*-ing around them, he put four men at wooden posts in the fence and lifted each of them out of the ground. After laying the fence flat, he covered enough barbs to let Roosevelt walk his horse carefully across. The men also advanced over the wire and started running up the slope again.[15]

A short distance past the downed fence, Roosevelt's eyeglasses were shot off by a bullet from the rear. This loss he had prepared for. Uninjured, he fumbled in his pocket for another pair of eyeglasses, found them, and put them on while still riding ahead. He made no mention of the incident at the time because he was afraid the regulars would accuse him of having turned to the rear like a coward. He too erroneously thought the weak 71st Volunteers from New York had been behind him. He could not accept that the bullet came from a wild-firing Rough Rider.[16]

Only four troopers kept pace with Roosevelt as they hustled on foot up the lower part of the hillock. In addition to Bardshar and Color Bearer Wright, the man from K Troop who had the most ear-splitting voice in the regiment was alongside Roosevelt. Known to his comrades as "the human megaphone," he remained near the colonel to repeat orders in the hubbub of the battle. The men bragged that his voice was audible even where bugle notes would not carry.[17] The human megaphone was so loud that English-speaking Spanish officers on the heights claimed they heard him. After the battle, they asked what he had shouted. They said the command had sounded like "Johnson's breeches," but they couldn't find anything close in their dictionary. Roosevelt replied that he had ordered "charge by rushes," a puzzling explanation for the Spaniards.[18]

The fourth trooper who sprinted next to Texas' saddlebags was a private worried about his own safety. He told himself, "If Teddy was not on that horse, the bullets would not be coming so close. It is not good for the Colonel to be on horseback. He might get hit." After debating with himself while he ran, he implored Roosevelt to dismount. His pleas were ignored.[19]

Following Roosevelt were the Rough Riders' troop guidons streaming yellow in the sun. Some of the troopers behind the guidons fell out under Spanish fire. The rest closed ranks and pressed on, some ignoring head and chest wounds to stay with the troops. The cavalrymen shot rapidly as they ran up what they described as a forty-degree incline. Like Roosevelt, they appeared to be enjoying the charge. One trooper from Oklahoma had his campaign hat knocked off by a bullet that went through the crown without hitting him. He stopped to pick up the hat, saying, "I'll have to patch that up with a bit of sticking plaster, or I'll get my hair sunburned." His companions laughed. The trooper's hair was the reddest in the regiment.[20]

Because of their split alignment at the start, most of the 1st and 9th regiments were advancing up the sides of the hillock at 180 degrees to each other. The Rough Riders were in between.

Blue and Brown Traces

The experienced British attaché who was with the correspondents on El Poso declared that he was distressed to see Roosevelt at the head of the gallant attack. He believed the exposure would inevitably lead to tragedy for the colonel and the Rough Riders. Nevertheless, the attaché claimed that the fight for Santiago would rank as one of the glorious battles in the world's military history. The Englishman compared the assault by the Rough Riders to the charge of his own country's legendary Light Brigade.[21]

The attaché had observed the Mauser fire coming from San Juan Hill as the Rough Riders struggled to ascend the knoll. He watched men dropping from injury or exhaustion as the troops surged upward. To him, the crest of San Juan Hill was sputtering like a smoking volcano erupting into bits of metal that penetrated and stung, but there was no sign of Americans faltering. Even when Spanish gunfire was at its height, he could tell from the Americans' resolute stance that they intended to reach the top, just as members of the doomed Light Brigade might have thought they would gain their goal.

The advance up Kettle Hill was slow, as the attaché saw it. In paintings and drawings of the charge, the troopers are shown running up the grade in long regular rows behind mounted Roosevelt. No photographer recorded the true picture, but only the four troopers ran at Roosevelt's side. The rest of the men were spread out in back of them, not in rows but as individuals. During pauses, men placed themselves behind widely scattered bushes despite the lack of protection from bullets. As the soldiers tired, they climbed slower, knowing that personal disaster could come at any step, but not drawing back. From El Poso they were seen as thin brown traces creeping higher on the hillock.[22]

Many of the men going up the slope had hand-rolled cigarettes stuck in their mouths, the result of an unexpected issue of tobacco that morning. They were running, shooting, and smoking at the same time. Others held plugs of tobacco inside their mouths, against their gums. They wanted to savor the moist flavor of the oily nicotine before drying out the leaves to use another day.[23]

A few troopers were humming, not noisily but quietly to themselves. Their favorite tune was "There'll Be a Hot Time in the Old Town To-Night." No one sang, not even hymns. Most were just hollering, letting air out of their lungs to relieve tension.[24]

The men were in the open, but their basic emotion was anger, not fear. They said the Spaniards hitting them hard were hiding behind fortified walls. In addition, the Dons' flag flew from a staff stuck in the earthworks on the heights. It was the first time most of the Rough Riders had seen the Spanish ensign that close. The flag hung there like a red rag waving in the face of a bull already mad. It gave the men a destination.

On the slope, the troopers of the other regiments could not see Roosevelt. In turn, the Rough Riders did not know where the troopers of the 9th or the 1st were. Roosevelt had struck Kettle Hill on the southeast, in full view from El Poso Hill. His ascent was a series of rushes and turns in a course along the eastern gradient where the Spanish fire from San Juan Hill did not quite reach.[25]

The other regiments were running along their own routes. The 1st Cavalry was still to the left of the Rough Riders. The men were being shot at as they went along the exposed southern flank. C and D troops of the 9th were on the far right, on the northern side of the knoll, hidden from the correspondents at El Poso and from the enemy.[26]

The troopers were so exhausted that they were resting more than they ran. The ground was spotted now with shrubbery and small trees providing minimal concealment. Men were ascending in brief dashes, crouching, before flopping on their chests to fire a few rounds. Bullets ricocheted off the kettles on top of the knoll, adding an incongruous ringing to the battle's din.[27]

The assault had been going on for twenty minutes. Colonel Carroll was wounded and Colonel Hamilton was dead. The cavalry attack was seen by the press on El Poso as an aggregate of acts of high heroism. Courage was a common commodity.[28]

No one was aware that from the start of the battle, Kettle Hill had been defended by only a handful of Spanish infantrymen and not the thousands available to Linares. No one knew that these few Spaniards had already abandoned Kettle Hill to fight again from the San Juan Heights.

He Grabbed a Red-Hot Rifle

At that point Roosevelt was nicked in the elbow by a Mauser bullet. The wound bled freely. As he bound the gash, his calm little stallion was scraped by a couple of bullets.[29]

Roosevelt was ahead of the main body of cheering Rough Riders. Forty yards from the top of the knoll, he came to the final wire entanglement. Texas could not get through and there were not enough men around to lift out the poles or cut the wire. With the agility that remained from his ranchman days, Roosevelt twisted out of the saddle without hesitation, jumped free, and landed on his feet. He handed the reins to a trooper who had caught up with him, scrambled over the wire, and ran toward the crest. He was the freshest man on the field.

This was the apocryphal episode popularized after the battle in the "Ballad of Teddy's Terrors": "He grabbed a red-hot rifle where a guy had let it fall, and fixin' of his spectacles more firmly on his face, he started to assassinate the Dons, all around the place!"[30]

Chapter 23

First to the Top

When the right flank of the cavalry began the assault on Kettle Hill at
1 P.M. on July 1, the blue guidons of General Kent's infantry division
were still restrained from attacking the San Juan Hill blockhouse.
Less than ten minutes later, approval to advance was received and
the informal shout "Let's Go!" set the foot soldiers off across the
nearly six hundred yards of green meadow.[1]

The 6th and 16th Infantry regiments took the advance as skirmishers behind tall and imposing General Hawkins, with his distinctive white hair, mustache, and goatee. He was a brigade commander
like Carroll and Wood, but he did not establish his headquarters in
the rear. Instead, he stepped out in front of his men. As an infantryman, he chose to be on foot.[2]

On Top of the Round Hillock

Half a mile north of the infantrymen advancing toward San Juan
Hill, General Sumner's dismounted cavalrymen were closing in on
their twin objectives, the heights and the knoll that was Kettle Hill.

Roosevelt had played exacting civilian roles in his thirty-nine years,
but this dramatic part as commander of a world-famous cavalry regiment in combat was the most satisfying. As he neared the crest, he
was sprinting as hard as he could to stay in front of his troopers. The
Rough Riders who trotted after him were younger and many had
longer legs. Some had been intercollegiate athletes and could easily
have outstripped him. All of them were content, however, to stay a

respectful distance in the rear. Although they saw that running fast was not one of his skills, they deferred to his rank.[3]

Roosevelt never looked behind him as he struggled up the last stretch of the incline. His regiment was the most disorganized on the field, but it was enough for him that he could hear the men's high-pitched yips and war whoops. The cries spurred him on. To him they represented approbation. Some of the shouts sounded like Rebel yells, intended to frighten the enemy who supposedly occupied the loop-holed farmhouse.

Half an hour after the charge began, Roosevelt burst onto the top of the knoll and eased forward a few yards. The hard-earned crest had been won at last. The farmhouse was taken. A disoriented Spanish bugler boy ran into Roosevelt's arms and was captured.

Roosevelt confessed subsequently that he would not have gone back down Kettle Hill for any reason, not even if one of his own sons had been wounded and needed medical attention. "No man was ahead of me when we charged," he asserted, "and now I think my men would follow me literally anywhere."[4]

The troopers told each other that the battle had been fierce. Hundreds of them had been sprinting, dodging, shooting, smoking, and shrieking. They said that every hairy-chested man in the country would have relished the fight. Bugles had been blowing and the Spaniards' Mausers had been firing at them in steady volleys. The run under pressure had been the finest thing ever, particularly when they bounded on top of Kettle Hill and gave the loudest war whoop. They bragged to each other that it had been "the whole cheese."[5]

Battle fever still raged in the troopers. Just breathing smoke from the gunpowder discharged in that terrific assault made men feel like giants. They had no time to spare for casualties. They did not think about their dead or wounded or heat-struck buddies who had dropped out of the race.

Instead, the main topic among these exhilarated men was the bravura performance of their fantastic colonel. He was the only officer in the Corps who was referred to by his first name when the men were talking among themselves. There was only one Teddy in Cuba.

"Whew! Wasn't Teddy a wild Indian in that charge!" shouted the Rough Rider known as the Gambler. "I wouldn't have taken 20 to one on his chances of getting to the top alive! He was 'way ahead of the line all the time!"

"Tell you what broke me up," confessed the Spider. "In the middle of the hill, the boys faltered for a minute behind him, and Teddy turned around and said in that surprised, reproachful sort of way, 'Why boys, you aren't going back on me, are you?' I felt as if my mother had accused me of striking her."

"An' that's the feller we Western cowpunchers was dubious about," grinned an Arizona trooper. "I'd like to find the man now that would call him a four-eyed college-bred dude!"[6]

Roosevelt basked in the appreciation and the pride shown by the admiring troopers. He was convinced that he had been first on the crest of the captured hillock, followed closely by the four troopers who were with him. He personally had taken the first Spanish fortification at San Juan. Moreover, he claimed that the first guidons planted on the crest were the yellow banners of his Rough Riders' E and G troops.[7]

As if he wore blinders, he looked only at the terrain straight ahead of him, across the valley where the last of the Spaniards from Kettle Hill were hastening toward the entrenched heights. Afterward, he could not remember all the detail of the charge, except that to have been first on the crest of this glorious hill was what he had been living for. In his mind, the top of Kettle Hill had been his alone for one wholly satisfying moment. That was before the rest of the Rough Riders and the other cavalrymen raced up to join him and the summit became crowded with soldiers.[8]

As Roosevelt had said, he did not enjoy Las Guasimas, but "the San Juan fight was entirely different." He was jubilant as he watched Bardshar shoot in the back and kill two Spaniards who had lagged behind in the retreat. He hopped around with overflowing joy as his men "planted good shots in the rear ends of fleeing Spaniards," potting them like partridges.[9]

He reported officially that he "had the honor" to have captured "in gallant shape the first entrenchment carried by any of our troops, the first break in the Spanish line. I," he boasted, "was the first man in!" He valued the capture of the deserted red-roofed farmhouse as if it really had been what he made it out to be, "a strong blockhouse with rifle pits."[10]

In his formal report to Wood, he described his achievement a little more circumspectly: "The guidons of my Troops E and G were the first planted on the summit, though the first men up were some of the A and B troopers who were with me and got in ahead of my troops E and G." He was asserting that the first men onto Kettle Hill were the four troopers who in fact were immediately in back of him, as everyone knew. In his eyes, this convoluted concept in false modesty made him the king of Kettle Hill.[11]

Later statements by others, however, began to cast doubt on Roosevelt's version of the order of arrival on the knoll. Lieutenant Coleman of the Rough Riders' E Troop "saw Colonel Roosevelt ahead, but only for a few minutes." If he was not "ahead" at the end, obviously he could not have been first.[12]

New Mexican Nova Johnson, color bearer of the Rough Riders' H Troop, was among the earliest on the hillock. Known as Long John because he was thin and six feet, two inches tall, he claimed that "you should have seen the amazement Colonel Teddy's face took on when he reached the top of that first ridge, only to find that the colored troopers had beat us up there." Roosevelt had restrained Texas to the pace of the four Rough Riders running alongside his saddle. He could not have seen the black regulars because they were to the north. They must have climbed faster.[13]

These "colored troopers" Long John referred to were the blacks of the 9th Cavalry. When they reached the top of the knoll, they were to the right of the farmhouse. Roosevelt insisted that he never saw them or their white officers when he sprinted onto the crest. Conceivably, they were outside his tunnel-vision gaze, which was fixed straight ahead at his next objective. His battle would not end at the knoll. Storming the farmhouse was only the first stage. His eyes were already focused on the heights in front of him.

In turn, the 9th's officers contended sarcastically that Roosevelt must have been swallowed in the mass of mixed regiments at the foot of the southern slope of Kettle Hill, not to be heard from again until after the 9th had stuck its standard into the ground at the top. They were willing to admit that Roosevelt had been "among the first to reach the top," but they insisted that he arrived after they got there. The official report of the secretary of war backed the 9th's claims. The report stated positively that two troops of the 9th gained the crest first. Roosevelt and the Rough Riders were ignored.[14]

According to the army brass, the 9th's officers not only had given the first command "Forward to the Charge!" but also their troopers had carried out the order by being first on the crest. The officers of the 9th were hitting Roosevelt with their best one-two punch by denying his claim to priority in both events. The vehemence of their response to Roosevelt and his volunteers had nothing to do with politics or money. They just resented Roosevelt and wanted recognition for doing their jobs as regulars.[15]

In addition, the black troopers of the 10th Cavalry had gone up the knoll to Roosevelt's left. They too claimed to have unfurled their colors at the red-roofed farmhouse before Roosevelt's men did. They received no acknowledgment from anyone.[16]

If the runners for the crest of the knoll had been race horses galloping for win, place, and show at a track, Roosevelt's entry would only have placed, according to the official judge, the secretary of war. The secretary was unwilling to let Roosevelt grasp the glory for the charge, even though they both were Republican politicians and he had appointed Roosevelt to the Rough Riders. Neither he nor the regulars had control over the press, however, and the newspapers gave all the plaudits to Roosevelt and none to the black cavalrymen.

Later the military authorities democratized the charge on Kettle Hill. They judged the assault to have been made in unison by every cavalry regiment in the sector that day and not by any one unit. Everybody was first, the army bureaucrats decided. Neither the 9th nor the Rough Riders nor the 10th was ahead.

Intrepid Hawkins

As the Rough Riders started to recover from their emotional highs, they could see that they still were subject to the same Mauser fusillades from the San Juan Hill blockhouse and from the entrenchments on the heights. In addition, they were more exposed and concentrated on top of the captured knoll than they had been in the meadow or on the slope.[17]

Roosevelt had a birds'-eye view of the whole battlefield from the southwest corner of the crest. He focused first on the paramount struggle, the one being waged by Kent's infantry against the Spaniards on San Juan Hill. The enemy forces on the hill had been strengthened by a battery of two mountain guns and a company of sailors from the fleet in the harbor. The reinforcements brought the total of defenders on San Juan to 520, the same number as those resisting Lawton at El Caney.[18]

Soon the mountain guns began dropping shells on Kettle Hill. In response, Roosevelt organized a squad of marksmen to silence the enemy battery. Next he again turned the marksmen onto the few Spaniards retreating across the valley. The enemy soldiers had plunged into the shallow pond instead of racing the longer way around the shore. In the water, they made such splendidly slow-moving targets that most of those who took the shortcut never reached the heights.[19]

In comparison with their countrymen who had defended Kettle Hill, the Spaniards on San Juan Hill were in an excellent defensive posture. They were protected by the blockhouse, entrenchments, rifle pits, and a triple line of barbed-wire entanglements on the hillside.[20]

Moreover, the meadow the American infantrymen had to traverse was a third of a mile wide. There was no cover for Hawkins's attackers all the way from the jungle to the hill, other than the same kinds of sparse bushes and infrequent trees that grew in front of Kettle Hill. Also, the east face of San Juan Hill was very steep. The infantrymen could see that parts of the ascent might have to be made by pulling themselves up with their hands. The prospect was much more arduous for the infantry than Kettle Hill had been for the cavalry.

Nevertheless, resolute Hawkins and his two regiments crossed the meadow and approached the hill while Roosevelt watched from the knoll. Just behind the advance were other regiments of infantry regulars. The valley to the left of the Santiago trail was filled with cheering and charging American foot soldiers. The infantrymen jammed down entanglements or climbed over them, suffering heavy losses while advancing in the face of Spanish gunfire. The soldiers halted only to raise their rifles high above their heads to shoot over the men in front. Then they ran on again until they began to mount the hill itself. Roosevelt said he prayed for the general.[21]

Fortunately for the Americans, the Spanish engineers had ordered the enemy trenches built on the geologic summit of the hill, rather than on the military crest that was yards closer to the slope. The military crest would have controlled the ascent by giving the defenders a clear view of all the attackers. Instead, there were pockets where Americans climbing the sheer incline could not be reached by the

Mausers on the true summit. Hawkins's soldiers clung there, safe for the moment but precariously situated. The Spaniards could not shoot at the infantrymen in the niches without standing and exposing themselves to retaliatory fire from the soldiers in the valley. On the other hand, the infantrymen could not continue their climb without incurring more casualties.[22]

The Spaniards were plastering the rest of the infantry and Roosevelt's force with everything they had left. The summit of Kettle Hill was lower than San Juan Hill and the fortified heights, so the troopers there were swept by a raking fire. Some used the large iron kettles as breastworks.[23]

Roosevelt recognized that the infantry was meeting stubborn resistance and that he had to act quickly to help Hawkins. If he failed to act, Hawkins might be forced to retreat. The colonels in command of the other cavalry regiments on Kettle Hill had been killed or wounded or were someplace else. Sumner and Wood were absent, too, so Roosevelt was the ranking officer on the round hillock, in command of all the troopers. He relished the responsibility.

To aid the infantry, Roosevelt kept the marksmen among his Rough Riders together to fire at the Spaniards on San Juan Hill. The regulars of the 9th and 10th also lined up to direct their carbines at the San Juan blockhouse and entrenchments. The Spaniards' heads were all that could be seen, and then only when they rose to fire on command. At that range the targets were tiny and they were fleeting.[24]

The infantry's situation was desperate, even after ten minutes of carbine fire from the cavalrymen. The pressure applied to the Spaniards was enough, however, to allow Lt. John Parker of the Gatling Gun Detachment to bring his three rapid-fire guns to the south side of Kettle Hill. Then the Gatlings began their lethal operation.[25]

As soon as Roosevelt heard the distinctive chattering, he shouted, "It's the Gatlings! It's the Gatlings!" The Rough Riders cheered as the machine guns quickly shot an overpowering number of bullets into Spanish lines on the hill. Within five minutes, the Spanish colonel commanding the defenders had been killed. The Gatlings created havoc with his soldiers, while Roosevelt continued his carbine volleys at the diminishing number of Spanish heads.[26]

General Linares's orders to his soldiers on San Juan Hill had been to retreat whenever it was necessary to avoid hand-to-hand combat with the American forces who could now be seen to outnumber the Spaniards drastically. The moment was at hand. The Spanish positions on the hill had become indefensible, like the outpost at El Caney. The hill had taken its toll on the attackers and now Linares was prepared to sacrifice it in a staged withdrawal. He expected to make his stand not on the hill but at his more strongly fortified line closer to Santiago and its resources where he had thousands of fresh soldiers in reserve. He did not believe that his line could be breached by force of arms. In fact, it never was.[27]

All at once, Roosevelt saw the Spaniards in their white and pale blue uniforms leap from the trenches and run out of the blockhouse on San Juan Hill. They fled in the face of steady hammering from the Gatlings and carbines. In a few minutes, the Gatlings and carbines ceased firing, so that Hawkins's infantrymen on the slope could rush over the crest and seize the vacated blockhouse and trenches. When the infantrymen swarmed in, only dead and seriously wounded Spaniards who could not be moved were left.[28]

Rejoicing was so widespread on Kettle Hill that Roosevelt had difficulty getting the men's attention. Exhausted troopers still were struggling up the knoll in small groups. They were screaming with elation they wanted to share with earlier arrivals. The noise was deafening, while casualties from enemy rifles on the heights continued to mount. Nevertheless, Roosevelt claimed to have chuckled when he overheard a black cavalryman of the 9th say, "This shuah am a fine place to make a fightin' reputation—but it shuah am dangerous!"[29]

After another few minutes, Roosevelt was able to assemble the Rough Riders and talk to them. Holding his right hand aloft as he punched the air with his left fist for emphasis, he shouted, "Men, our cause is just and God is with us. Let all brave men attend to my orders!" He intended to lead another advance at the first opportunity.[30]

The British attaché who had climbed the knoll on the heels of the Rough Riders congratulated Roosevelt. Somehow the Briton who was dressed in conspicuous white from head to toe, had remained immaculate despite the jungle and the rivers. Putting his monocle to his eye, he told Roosevelt, "It's a great day for us Anglo-Saxons!"[31]

First on the Heights

Roosevelt said, "The fight was all right. I could see the Spaniards"—in contrast with Las Guasimas where the enemy had been invisible. He now had completed most of what he poetically rephrased as "the crowded and glorious hour of my life, that hour for which I would not trade my whole existence." Actually, two hours had elapsed from the time when he began the advance from the river.[32]

Although the infantry had taken the San Juan Hill blockhouse at 1:50 P.M. and the soldiers there were looking out over Santiago itself, the Rough Riders were still on Kettle Hill, vulnerable to the small amount of fire from Spanish defenders left in entrenchments on San Juan Heights. When the enemy on the heights was reinforced by Spanish soldiers retreating from Kettle Hill, gunfire directed at the knoll became a little heavier. Roosevelt could hear the two large copper kettles ring more frequently as they were struck by bullets.[33]

His new orderly Bardshar had taken refuge between the kettles. He was crouching there with two friends from his E Troop when a shell exploded directly over them. The other two troopers were blown to bits by shrapnel balls. Bardshar was splattered with blood and flesh. Stunned and conscious of a sudden silence, he started to walk slowly down toward the shallow pond in the valley, thinking only of the water he needed to wash off the terrifying smears. He was unaware that he was approaching the enemy.[34]

Roosevelt saw him move away, sensed his danger but not his disability, and yelled at him to return. There was no reply, so Roosevelt ran after him, clapped him on the shoulder, and shouted, "Didn't you hear me call you?" Bardshar turned around. For the first time he realized he was deaf. He pointed to his ears with his index fingers to indicate he could not hear anything. His hearing improved gradually, but he kept Roosevelt in sight for the rest of the day.

When Roosevelt started to survey the strength of his forces on the knoll, he found the surviving Rough Rider captains and lieutenants sorting the troopers back into manageable units. "What is going on here? What are you trying to do?" bellowed Roosevelt. "I am trying to restore troop formation, sir," was one response. "Well," snapped Roosevelt, "let the formation take care of itself. There is no award for neatness here. The main thing is to win the fight." He objected to the initiation of any procedure that might inhibit the regiment's readiness to attack.[35]

Helping Kent's infantry take a position ahead of the Rough Riders had made Roosevelt testy. He feared being excluded from what could be the day's final encounter, the capture of the heights that would align the Rough Riders with the infantry's advance. In a relatively protected spot under the brow of the knoll, he quickly called a meeting of what was left of his officers at 1:55 P.M. He pointed out that the portion of the cavalry division passing Kettle Hill to head directly toward the heights had been slowed by enemy fire. The troopers had not yet completed the crossing of the open valley. The Rough Riders might yet beat them.[36]

Roosevelt took for granted that his assault on the heights would take place. He emphasized that the best chance to capture the next elevation would come immediately while the Rough Riders were excited and on their feet. He advocated proceeding by rushes, as before. His captains privately believed that coming after everything the regiment had experienced since reveille, another assault would produce only an unacceptable loss of more lives. They were silent, however, in the presence of a headstrong Roosevelt who was elated at the prospect of leading the second charge.[37]

It was a brief meeting. Taking his officers' reticence for wholehearted approval, Roosevelt shouted, "I will lead the way!" He felt that "you must have in your men, and in your self, the fighting edge. On my own hook," he asserted, "I ordered another charge." He believed that the deadly fire from the heights had to be stopped. He ran to the front of the knoll and cried, "Forward to the Charge! Charge the hill ahead!" He was commanding his men to follow him.[38]

Later, the officers of the 9th who were on the knoll agreed that this time it was Roosevelt alone who initiated the charge against the heights. The only problem with crediting him was that he was delirious with excitement. When he stood in front of the Rough Riders and ordered the charge, he did not notice that only five of the hundreds of troopers came after him. He started sprinting down the more gradual descent on the far slope, leaping over a wire entanglement without looking back. Three of the five who followed him were struck immediately.[39]

The rest of the Rough Riders hesitated. They were a mob, separated from their troop commanders and buddies. They were worn out. Also, they were facing what they saw as a solid sheet of Spanish bullets and shells coming over the top of the knoll, fired from what they thought must be a combination of rifles, machine guns, and cannons. It appeared to the men that no one would live if he tried to get past the crest. The command to advance was too reckless to be obeyed, even by the officers.

When at last Roosevelt noticed from the silence around him how few troopers were with him, he realized that the others either had not heard him or had not heeded him. Telling the men with him to wait under fire where they were, he ran back alone toward the crest, leaping the fence again. On the way he met the regimental farrier who had blood streaming from a wound on his neck. Roosevelt stopped to ask, "Are you seriously wounded?" He then patted the farrier on the back and told him he was plucky to keep on fighting.[40]

Roosevelt rallied the troopers on the knoll by cursing them and demanding to know why they had not supported him. He shouted in an agitated manner, "I never thought you would refuse to follow where I lead, men! We must advance!" A look of injured pride spread slowly over the sweaty faces. The troopers responded, "We didn't hear you. We didn't see you go, Colonel. Lead on now and we'll follow you." When Roosevelt called "Rough Riders, forward!" they let out one modest whoop, submissively repeated, "Everybody charge," and prepared to run after him and the flag carried by Color Bearer Wright. A few men from other regiments joined them.[41]

At that point, General Sumner rode up the knoll to take command. Roosevelt trotted over to him at once and demanded authorization to continue the charge he had started. Sumner gave his approval, but he ordered Lieutenant Colonel Viele who had arrived with part of the 1st Cavalry to remain behind to form a belated reserve. Viele also had three troops of the 3rd Cavalry under him and a few Rough Riders from E Troop. By then, almost seven hundred troopers had crowded onto and around the crest of the knoll.[42]

E Troop cowboy John Robinson was one of the Rough Riders detained for the reserve. He begged Lieutenant Coleman, "For God's sake, let me go! This will be the only chance I will ever have to fire this gun. I came all the way from Texas for this chance. Let me go!"

When there was no response to his plea, Robinson deserted Coleman. He joined the troopers around Roosevelt, shrieking at the top of his lungs. He participated in the charge on the heights, but the next day he was killed in a meaningless exchange of gunfire with the Spaniards.[43]

Once Roosevelt had Sumner's consent, he gave the order for the third time to charge the San Juan Heights. He was waving his arms while holding the revolver from the battleship *Maine* in his right hand as he commanded, "Let all brave men follow me!" This time, the response from the Rough Riders was a firm "We'll follow you." Despite the continuing Spanish fire, the troopers ran happily after him and Color Bearer Wright. Everyone was grinning.[44]

Captain Dimmick headed the 9th Cavalry after the death of Colonel Hamilton. He did not see the Rough Riders leave Kettle Hill. As soon as he was told what Roosevelt had started, he ordered a movement forward in support of the Rough Riders. After fifty yards, the white troopers were mixed with the black.[45]

Crossing the valley was hot, strenuous work on foot and under fire. The charge began like a flying wedge in the football games of the day. Roosevelt was the point, with the revolver stuck in his belt. When a westerner started the cowboy yell, the whole regiment took it up and the sound boomed into a roar. Roosevelt again interpreted the roar as the backing he expected. He too gave a shout of exultation. With sweat streaming down his face, he impulsively turned to the deafened Bardshar trotting at his heels and screamed, "Holy Godfrey, what fun!"[46]

Critics said later that while Roosevelt was leading the second charge, "the wolf rose again in his heart," and he was simply "reveling in victory and gore." The need to prove he was not a coward still prodded him. He was rejoicing at the unbelievable extent of his success. In addition to his personal motivation, he was demonstrating to the regiment once more that "God is with us."[47]

Among the first to be hit during the charge was Theodore Miller of D Troop. In violation of Roosevelt's orders to leave casualties to the medical corpsmen, Miller's friend stopped to hear him whisper, "I'm going, Harry, but it's in a good cause, isn't it." Like many others, he died believing Roosevelt's preaching.[48]

To the surviving Rough Riders, wounds had become marks of valor, especially if they bled profusely. Death, however, was a subject forbidden for discussion. The illustrator Frederic Remington noted that well-educated, youthful troopers like Miller expected to be killed in the campaign. "Terror," Remington remarked, "was old talk" to them. In what was meant as admiration of toughness and not censure, Remington had claimed from the beginning that "Wood and Roosevelt were bad men and would certainly get the young men killed."[49]

In this context, bad meant "good at their job."

I've Got It

When Roosevelt and Bardshar came to the final wire entanglement, they crawled under and went on. A trooper in back of them smashed the staples out of two of the wood posts with the butt of his carbine. He freed the barbed wire and the rest of the men crossed easily. Parker's Gatling guns were advancing, too, in the midst of the mixture of K and L troops.[50]

From then on, the charge degenerated into complete disorder as the Rough Riders sprinted onward. They fired as they ran, hitting nothing and not caring. Carbine barrels became so hot that men were afraid to throw in another cartridge. Thousands of bullets were dropped in the grass. The self-generated din of their own detonations was loud enough to persuade the troopers that the Spaniards were shooting at them as heavily as before.[51]

Roosevelt tired while plodding through marshy ground at the north end of the pond. Soon younger and stronger runners caught up to him. In their euphoria, they swept by him and the disintegrating wedge. They were still screaming their cowboy yell, as if noise alone could frighten the Spaniards.[52]

When Roosevelt passed the pond, a spent bullet struck him on the back of his left hand. This was his third minor wound. Without breaking his trot, he waved the hand in the air so the troopers near him could see the blood slowly seeping. He shouted, "I've got it again, boys! I've got it again!" Then he turned to a more seriously wounded trooper who was keeping pace with him and exclaimed laughingly, "You needn't be so damned proud!" At that moment he considered himself the happiest man in Cuba.[53]

To the left and well ahead of him, most of the 1st Cavalry Brigade that had been Carroll's was proceeding straight for the sector of the heights nearest the main Santiago trail. As soon as these troopers reached the edge of the rise, enemy fire from the heights tapered off. The Spaniards were faced with a thousand cavalrymen charging from left of the pond, another thousand approaching from the front, and five thousand infantrymen flanking the heights from the south. Reduced in number by this time, the Spaniards abandoned the San Juan Heights in good order and fell back to their defensive line closer to Santiago. The heights was the last of the Spanish fortifications to be abandoned at San Juan.[54]

After the enemy retreated, the only casualties the cavalrymen suffered that day were stray shots from the inner Spanish line and from the few remaining sharpshooters in the trees. The noise generated by the troopers, however, continued. The Rough Riders could not yet know that resistance to the charge was over. Roosevelt was still ecstatic.[55]

By the time the Rough Riders, the 9th Cavalry, and panting Roosevelt reached the heights, regulars of the 6th and 3rd Cavalry already had taken possession. In the relative quiet, 10th Cavalry troopers came up on the right. The surviving Spaniards were gone, including their wounded. Few prisoners were taken. Those who remained to fill the trenches were dead. Most of the corpses had little bullet holes in their temples with their brains oozing out.[56]

Roosevelt and Bardshar were hurrying along the top of the ridge when two Spaniards unexpectedly "leaped from the trenches" of the dead. The enemy soldiers stood erect, leveled their Mausers, "and fired at us, not ten yards away." Despite the slight distance, the harried Spaniards failed to hit their mark. "As they turned to run," Roosevelt reported, "I closed in and fired twice" with the revolver salvaged from the *Maine,* "missing the first and killing the second." Bardshar had stepped aside to let Roosevelt have the honor. Now he finished off the man Roosevelt missed.[57]

Rough Rider Cliff Scott of D Troop explained, "The Colonel jerked his gun and made a hip shot that was good, and he told a number of us boys he would rather we didn't say anything about it." To make the "good shot," Roosevelt had yanked the pistol from his belt in true western style, but he asked for secrecy because he was not sure that shooting a man in the back would enhance his image at home.[58]

For a few days, the men did not mention the killing of the Spaniard who had "turned to run" in a vain attempt to get away. They talked about it only to each other, boasting about their colonel. Then they found that Roosevelt himself had been retailing the episode to correspondents and in letters recounting the battle's highlights for politicians and his civilian friends.

Roosevelt finally decided that slaying the enemy soldier was a coup. He could not discover any other regimental or staff officer who had fired a weapon and hit his human mark at almost point-blank range. His kill proved he had been in the van.

"Did I tell you," he wrote to Cabot Lodge, "I killed a Spaniard with my own hand when I led the storm of the first redoubt?" The enjoyment was enriched because he accomplished the Spaniard's end "with the pistol Will gave me which was raked up from the *Maine*." By firing his brother-in-law's souvenir, he felt he had done his bit to "remember" the battleship whose destruction he had long charged to the Spaniards.[59]

When his friends questioned Roosevelt about how shooting another human being at less than ten yards made him feel, he insisted that he was "not in the least sensitive about killing any number of men if there is an adequate reason." The motive he cited was that this was war, but there also were unmentioned personal emotions. His friend 2d Lt. Bob Ferguson who had enlisted in the Rough Riders solely to be near Roosevelt observed that "no hunting trip so far has ever equaled this in Theodore's eyes. When I caught up with him he had just 'doubled up a Spanish officer like a jack-rabbit' and all the way down to the next line of entrenchments he encouraged us to 'look at these damned Spanish dead.'"[60]

To a big-game hunter like Roosevelt, a running man was the ultimate prey, especially after he transformed the slain soldier into a Spanish officer.

Chapter 24
Ending the Charge

After the capture of San Juan Heights, the troopers gathered around the loopholed hacienda. They were more concerned about their empty stomachs than they were about the Spanish dead they would have to bury in the trenches. The men had not eaten since the early breakfast that seemed to have been consumed days ago, but their rations were in the packs they had been ordered to leave near the hill at El Poso.

Fighting made men hungry. One Rough Rider asked plaintively, "What in hell has become of the dinner bell? I can see where I'm going to miss my eats." His sergeant told him to quit grumbling. No one really expected to be fed that afternoon or night.[1]

Unknowingly, however, Roosevelt had emulated Civil War Col. Lew Wallace of the Union army who captured the Confederate soldiers' breakfast at Romney, Virginia. Here on the San Juan Heights, the Spaniards' dinner was still cooking on a big wood stove in the officers' mess. There was a large pot full of the Castilian equivalent of mulligan stew, made from meat the Rough Riders hoped was beef. There were a couple of smaller pots of rice and peas and a dozen rice-flour loaves of flat bread. In addition, the Spanish larder included salted flying fish, bottles of wine, and a demijohn of rum that Roosevelt referred to as "fiery spirits." A few men got into the wine and the rum before Roosevelt had the jugs broken.[2]

Surgeon LaMotte gave the predictable warning that the stew might have been poisoned as a culinary booby trap. Roosevelt paid no attention. Typically, he fed enlisted men first. The food intended for twenty-five Spanish officers was divided into small feasts for the first one hundred troopers to line up. There were some cups to receive the stew, but only a few plates or utensils.[3]

Spanish seasonings proved to be much like the Rough Riders' own southwestern fare. Those who ate the scant meal declared the Spaniards to be good cooks as well as much stronger fighters than had been expected.

The Charge to the Overlook

The hacienda on the heights had no offensive value to the cavalry. Its location menaced only approaches from the east. The line of sight to Santiago was not at the hacienda but on an overlook another three hundred yards farther west that was aligned with Kent's advance on San Juan Hill. The overlook was not occupied by the Spaniards. They had retreated to defensive lines not yet visible.

Because the taking of the heights was not yet complete, Captain Howze was welcomed when he rode up to the farmhouse with an order from General Sumner to the 6th Cavalry's Captain West who had been the first officer to reach the heights. The instruction was for West to seize possession of the overlook. West started his regiment marching right away.[4]

Casualties among the Rough Riders still were uncounted, but there were many. Nevertheless, Roosevelt rallied the troopers in support of the 6th. By this time he had caught his breath, and the men had gained a needed respite. Without authorization from Sumner who might have preferred to keep the Rough Riders away from the front, Roosevelt raced his men across the ridge on the double in the only picture-book charge of the day. The terrain was open, the distance was short, and there was no Spanish resistance. The troopers were able to hold a straight course. They stopped only to kneel and fire their carbines eagerly at enemy lines they could not see.[5]

At 2:30 P.M., the Rough Riders joined West on the final ridge. Roosevelt found himself directly opposite Santiago, staring down into city streets that were deserted except for soldiers' movements. The heavily manned Spanish trenches between the overlook and the city were on a significantly lower elevation merely three hundred yards away.

Roosevelt was the ranking officer at this section of the front. He took the command from Captain West at once. Men from all six cavalry regiments were present, but they amounted to only four hundred troopers. Most of the other cavalrymen were milling around at the farmhouse the Rough Riders had just vacated, were placed unhappily in reserve with Viele at Kettle Hill, or were located somewhere in between. There was also an infrequent infantryman on the overlook, although the main body of infantry was digging in on San Juan Hill.

Roosevelt had not calmed down. He was aggressively considering the feasibility of organizing the four hundred troopers on the ridge into an assault on Santiago itself when Captain Howze arrived and told him not to advance farther. He was to hold the overlook at all costs, Howze explained, because the heights had become the key to an attempt to draw a horseshoe of containment around the approaches to the city.[6]

Howze also advised Roosevelt to retreat fifty yards to gain a more protected position on the ridge. He was surprised to hear Roosevelt respond truculently, "Retreat! There go my men! Stop them if you can! I can't!" Fifty Rough Riders and a dozen black regulars under daring Captain Jones of the 10th had continued one hundred yards past the overlook to a point where they were exposed, subjected to strong enemy fire, and unsupported. Roosevelt was tempted to join them with the rest of the troopers, but he reconsidered. On command, Jones reluctantly returned to the overlook, while Roosevelt grudgingly agreed to fall back a couple of strategic paces from the edge to mollify Howze.[7]

According to the novelist Stephen Crane who arrived a little later, the cavalry on the ridge "was dusty, disheveled, its hair matted to its forehead with sweat, its shirts glued to its backs with the same sweat, and indescribably dirty, thirsty, hungry, and aweary from its bundles and its marches and its fights. It sat down on the conquered crest and felt satisfied. 'Well, hell! Here we are.'"[8]

Roosevelt was not satisfied. He stood recklessly in the open and gazed at the city through borrowed field glasses. Then he sauntered up and down past clusters of prone troopers, considering whether to obey Howze's order not to advance. Just as dead Buckey O'Neill had thumbed his nose at danger, Roosevelt behaved without regard for bullets cutting the grass at his feet. The men lying on the ground said nothing to him, but they remembered O'Neill vividly. They were wondering how long it would be before Roosevelt was hit.[9]

With the field glasses, Roosevelt also peered into the crowns of a grove of royal palm trees where enemy sharpshooters were hidden near the Spanish trenches. The guerrillas in the treetops soon were dispatched by a detachment of thirty picked Rough Rider marksmen. There was nothing scientific about the procedure. When they saw a Spanish sharpshooter, they killed him. When he was invisible in his perch, the Rough Riders simply flooded the branches with random bullets until the Spaniard was hit and fell out of the tree.[10]

Roosevelt observed that the main Spanish defensive line in front of the city below him was laid out in formidable triple entrenchments and triple entanglements. From the trenches, enemy artillery and rifles were thundering their fire up at the unseen American soldiers. Roosevelt reacted by reforming the exhausted men into a firing line on the overlook. He had them lie flat just behind the edge of the ridge where they were relatively safe but could respond if needed. Although it was mid-afternoon and sultry, he distributed captured Spanish blankets. There were enough for only one Rough Rider in ten. The rest of the men went without, as he himself did when he stretched out on the ground to take a brief respite.[11]

With the danger from enemy fire lessened, the tension on the overlook eased. According to Roosevelt, however, he remained on the alert. There were black cavalrymen without their wounded or killed white officers. He believed that white troopers who lost their commissioned officers would carry on with sergeants in command but that even veteran black troopers would be unreliable in the absence of whites in control. Why else, he thought, would the War Department have provided white officers for black regiments?

As Roosevelt had anticipated, some of the black soldiers "began to drift to the rear, either helping the wounded or to find their own regiments." Claiming that this retrograde movement had to be halted before it turned into a stampede endangering everyone on the overlook, he said that he "jumped up, drew my revolver, and called out that I would shoot the first man who went to the rear. The 'smoked Yankees' flashed their white teeth and broke into broad grins."[12]

Roosevelt emphasized that apart from this one incident, the courage shown by blacks in combat had been exemplary. Even Rough Riders who were prejudiced southwesterners, he maintained, henceforth would be willing "to drink out of the same canteen."[13]

Howze remarked that the blacks were impressed with both the colonel's determination and the proven killing power of the big revolver from the *Maine*. They stayed on the overlook, as they would have if Roosevelt had simply ordered them to remain instead of indulging in histrionics.

Next Roosevelt acted to strengthen his defenses. Because his troopers were so few compared to the thousands of Spaniards they faced, he feared a counterattack and set the men to digging trenches. A few used captured Spanish shovels. The rest employed any implement they could find. They wielded cooking utensils, cups, dishes from the few mess kits, cans, machetes, sticks, pointed rocks, and as a last resort, fingers.[14]

The Rough Riders dug without complaint. Willingness to obey orders despite fatigue was typical of them, although the entrenching promised to last into the night and could not accomplish much with the primitive tools at hand. Meanwhile, foreign attachés declared that the American advance up the San Juan hills was something no other army in the world could have improved on. Correspondents were describing the battle as having been like a string of exploding dynamite sticks three miles long.[15]

In the Air

Shortly after 2 P.M., couriers from Lieutenant Miley advised General Shafter a little prematurely that "undoubtedly we have the heights." Shafter got out of bed, dressed, and rode to the top of the hill at El Poso.

The afternoon was getting hotter, adding to Shafter's malaise. By 2:30 he could see from the hilltop that the heights were unoccupied by American forces for a half-mile north of the Rough Riders. It was critical that the gap be filled. This was the position Lawton was supposed to have taken, but he was still bogged down at El Caney. Sumner had dispatched urgent messages to Kent requesting support but had received only one regiment, the 13th Infantry. Kent's forces were at least as mixed and as spent as the cavalry, and they had to cover the expanse east and south of San Juan Hill.[16]

Under the circumstances, Sumner described the whole cavalry position as "in the air"—that is, unsettled. The northern flank might be turned by the strong Spanish force Roosevelt feared, routing the cavalry and forfeiting the entire advance. Another American division was needed quickly. That could only be Lawton's. At two o'clock, however, Lawton had just ordered his artillery moved up for the first time, and then only to a thousand yards from the village. At 2:30 he finally was calling for an organized advance against the fort.[17]

By this time, Shafter was ruefully aware that he had erred in splitting his forces between El Caney and San Juan. Fearful of the outcome in both arenas, he sent an aide to Lawton with the demand that the infantry division disengage at El Caney at once. "You must proceed with the remainder of your force and join immediately upon Sumner's right," Shafter ordered.[18]

Lawton had no confidence in Shafter's ability to judge the extent of the danger at San Juan. Moreover, he was afraid that abandoning El Caney would be an admission of defeat jeopardizing his career. He did not obey the order. In fact, he did not acknowledge receiving it as part of the day's official record. To him, El Caney was a quarry he would chase to the end, regardless of consequences. On the strength of this intractable behavior, his subordinates exclaimed that "Lawton is a lion." He joined Wheeler, Young, Wood, and Roosevelt in violating Shafter's specific instructions without incurring a penalty.[19]

The Spaniards soon tried to take advantage of Lawton's recalcitrance. At 4 P.M. the Rough Riders' entrenching was interrupted by a company of four hundred Spaniards advancing in spread formation. The intention was to turn Roosevelt's right flank where Lawton was to have been.[20]

Roosevelt thought the Spanish infantry "showed nerve" in their only offensive of the campaign. After the Spaniards had advanced a hundred yards, however, Parker let one Gatling gun loose on the exposed enemy. Roosevelt maintained that they simply "disappeared." The Spaniards fled and the Rough Riders put down the carbines they had not fired. Then they went back to their digging and scraping.[21]

Typically, Spanish General Linares had dispatched too few soldiers in the counterattack. With the drubbing, the San Juan fight concluded satisfactorily for the Americans. At the same time, Lawton's division took El Caney. The 520 Spaniards at El Caney had resisted Lawton's 6,900 men for ten hours. As the village and then the fort became untenable, the survivors retreated toward Santiago through an American crossfire.[22]

There were 300 Spanish casualties at El Caney. Almost 60 percent of the enemy infantrymen were killed or wounded. A hundred soldiers escaped to Santiago and 120 were captured. In contrast, Lawton lost 450 men, about 7 percent of his force. He had fought cautiously, despite both the urgency that developed for him to win quickly and his characterization as a lion. By five o'clock, the valley and the San Juan range were quiet, except for occasional rifle shots fired by skittish sentries.[23]

After the Spanish counterattack was stopped by the Gatling, Sumner sent two hundred men from the reserve on Kettle Hill to support Roosevelt. The entire cavalry division at the front had been reduced to the equivalent of four full regiments out of the six that started the day. One trooper in three had become a casualty or was away from the front aiding the wounded, on burial detail, or not yet accounted for.[24]

From his headquarters near El Poso, Shafter put Wheeler back in command of the cavalry division. He returned Sumner to the 1st Brigade where there was an opening because Colonel Carroll had been shot. Wood retained the 2nd Brigade during the continuing disability of General Young. Roosevelt remained joyously in command of the Rough Riders.

Nearly Plunked

Roosevelt had held the overlook against the Spaniards in compliance with Howze's order. Now Wheeler rode up to tell him that Shafter's staff wanted the Rough Riders ready to fall far back to a more defensible line.

Elated by his glorious day, Roosevelt demurred at discussing a negative like a retreat that brought back memories of talks with dead Captain Capron. "Well, General," Roosevelt replied, contemplatively, "I really don't know at this point whether we would or would not accept an order to fall back. If we move out of here at all, I should be inclined to make a rush in the right direction, to take the city."

"Is it compulsory in the Army," he asked the general in mock ingenuousness, "to obey orders that are oral?" He insisted that he wanted his instructions in writing if they went against his grain. The Rough Riders would go forward on any pretext to take Santiago, he asserted, but they would not retreat toward El Poso without at least an official document he could retain.[25]

After Wheeler left, Roosevelt told his officers that the old general had eventually agreed with him in refusing to fall back. Roosevelt believed that if there had been someone more decisive than Shafter in command that afternoon, they would already have taken Santiago. Instead, they were standing around on the ridge, discussing a retreat he was not going to make. As darkness began to fall, he mounted a borrowed horse to inspect his part of the battlefield while thinking about Wheeler's visit.

Ninth Cavalry marksmen had been placed on guard at the adjacent sector. They were told to keep their eyes fixed on the chaparral between the Spanish and American lines. The first head they saw was to be shot.

The marksmen had settled down to watching the brush when they heard the threatening sound of a breaking twig. Next there was

Hill Charged and Taken by the "Rough Riders," San Juan, Cuba. Stereopticon view. (New York: Underwood and Underwood, 1898).

the muffled tread of a horse. The marksmen were alert as sharpshooter Johnson whispered, "I've got him." At that instant, the brush parted. A horse and rider stepped out. Johnson took aim with his carbine.

Just then, the horseman bent in his saddle and his eyeglasses flashed in the dim light. Johnson turned away in shock. He exclaimed, "My God, it's Roosevelt! I nearly plunked him!" He threw his gun to the ground.[26]

Roosevelt rode straight to the guards and greeted them informally. When they told him about the order to shoot intruders on sight, he was surprised, saying, "This is the first I've heard about it." He did not seem overly concerned. He rode back to his own sector, not realizing how close to death he had been.

The men of the 9th Cavalry maintained that the more they thought about the near miss on Roosevelt, the more "in the dumps" they got. The black troopers admired the Rough Riders' colonel. They wanted him alive. Not only was he was a brave man, but he was considerate of his troopers and he appreciated the efforts of black soldiers.

Counting the Cost

Roosevelt proudly proclaimed that the Rough Riders suffered the greatest losses of any American regiment in the campaign: "We went into the fight about 490 strong; 86 were killed or wounded, and there are half a dozen missing. The great heat prostrated nearly 40 men." That was the preliminary count. This time Wood agreed with Roosevelt's numbers. Wood had reverted to his role as medic. He personally had dressed the wounds of 30 troopers at the field hospital while putting brigade business aside.[27]

Only two of the eight Rough Rider troops were led by the captains who had begun the fight. The rest were casualties. Three troops were now headed by first lieutenants, two by second lieutenants after the first lieutenants were also hit, and one by a noncommissioned sergeant, after all the officers in the troop were out of action. Roosevelt calculated that almost half of the Rough Riders who landed at Daiquiri had been rendered unfit for duty in the one week.[28]

The official determination of Rough Rider casualties in the battle for Santiago was 15 percent, a little less than Roosevelt figured. The blacks in the 10th Cavalry suffered a 17 percent loss, the most in the cavalry division.[29]

The severest losses were in Kent's infantry regiments. The San Juan Hill attack was the most damaging by far. The 6th Infantry under Hawkins lost 26 percent of its men. The 13th which later backed the cavalry on the overlook lost 23 percent. The 16th lost 19 percent. As a historical comparison, however, there were much bloodier Civil War battles. Army losses there exceeded 40 percent.[30]

Enemy casualties at San Juan were initially put conservatively at 35 percent, in addition to the losses at El Caney. By 3:30 P.M., however, three hundred wounded Spaniards had been taken from the hill and the heights to the military hospital in Santiago. That was more than 50 percent. Additional casualties were being brought in steadily. Stray American bullets were falling on the hospital—without, however, causing injuries.[31]

The Spanish soldiers were demoralized. They did not think that retaining Cuba as a colony was worth their lives. In addition, they resented the luxuries officers still enjoyed in meat, vegetables, and ice. They also complained to each other that Americans fought in a manner contrary to what they had been trained to think of as appropriate in war. European soldiers fired their rifles in unison and fell back to reload. That was what the Spanish infantrymen usually did. Americans generally kept advancing while firing at individual targets. They used their rifles accurately as marksmen.[32]

General Linares had not adequately supplemented his sparse defenses at El Caney, San Juan Hill, or Kettle Hill. He brought to these outer defense lines only an eighth of the soldiers and sailors available to him in and near the city. This was less than a sixteenth of the soldiers he commanded in the district and less than a hundredth of the Spanish soldiers in Cuba. Despite the axiom that one trained soldier behind elevated defenses is equal in fighting power to seven attackers, he had allowed his forces at San Juan to be outnumbered fourteen to one.[33]

Yet Linares blamed his loss on the Cuban rebels once again. He claimed that they had caused his reserve column from Manzanillo to fail to arrive in time. He did not acknowledge that his own disposition of soldiers had been faulty or that the effectiveness of the Spanish infantry had been reduced by the formal style of volley firing. The Spanish soldiers' marksmanship was poor in volleys. They consistently fired high. If there had been more defenders on the hill, however, and if there had been better support by Spanish artillery, they might have held off the Americans despite volley firing. Then malaria and yellow fever would have become the decisive factors for the short term.[34]

The battle for Santiago was one of the few times an American army routed an enemy of potentially superior strength positioned on a fortified hill. Although the Americans did not realize it, they already had won the battle for Santiago. The Spaniards discovered that the end had come when El Caney was lost to Lawton. Linares had not known that Santiago's entire supply of fresh water was piped in from El Caney. When that was cut off, only the water in cisterns was left.[35]

The conclusion of foreign military experts was that "Shafter's conduct of the campaign was incompetent and culpable, and his ultimate success was undeserved good fortune. No precautions were taken against reverses. The daring of American troops was exceeded only by their extreme rashness." Roosevelt and the Rough Riders were the prize examples of audacity laced with imprudence.[36]

Finally Darkness Fell

When evening came, the situation of the American soldiers at San Juan was dangerous and uncomfortable. Their lines were thin. They were merely three hundred yards from hundreds of rested Spaniards. Except for the lucky few who had shared the meager portions of the Spanish dinner, the troopers had not eaten since early morning. There was no water. The men were soaked with sweat. The night was growing cold. Coats and blankets were scarce.[37]

Despite the hardships, the soldiers expressed no discontent. There was only a determination to hang on to what they had earned. Roosevelt said he told Wheeler, "We could not have taken the hill if the Spaniards had held out, but after we got to the top, all the Spaniards in Spain could not have moved us."[38]

Other officers were not as optimistic. Wheeler reported to Shafter at 8:20 P.M. that "a number of officers have applied to me to have the line withdrawn and take up a strong position further back, and I expect they will appeal to you. I have positively discountenanced that, as it would cost us much prestige."[39]

Finally it was dark. The night's respite was welcomed by the Rough Riders. Roosevelt shared one captured Spanish blanket with two troopers. He quickly fell asleep.

Chapter 25
The Legend of Teddy

Before the Battle at San Juan, Senators Platt and Lodge had dangled the bait of high political rewards in front of Roosevelt. Success would depend on how the electorate appraised his performance in Cuba.

The press coverage of the charge at San Juan qualified Roosevelt for these postwar opportunities. No one who read a newspaper article about Roosevelt's role in the war could fail to be thrilled by the description of this brave volunteer soldier galloping boldly at the head of the most picturesque regiment in the annals of the army.

The Roosevelt Vision

Roosevelt saw San Juan as his personal triumph over lesser mortals. "Many other men," he insisted, "had the same experience in the West and could have raised a regiment as I did, but they did not." He forgot that Wood had organized the regiment in Texas while he was shuffling paper in Washington.

Once the Rough Riders were trained, Roosevelt felt "it was a necessity to get this regiment into action; otherwise it would have been laughed at. We came near being left behind, but I admit that I pulled every wire in sight to get the regiment to Cuba, and we got there. If we had not, I should never have been President." Actually, the Rough Riders were in Cuba in large part because Wood had shaped the volunteers into timely readiness and not simply because of Roosevelt's influence in Washington.[1]

After the action started, Roosevelt claimed that his goal was to keep other regiments from getting closer to the Spaniards than the Rough Riders did. To him, the high points of the campaign were the three cavalry charges that he said he led in quick succession at San Juan. He boasted that he "spent the blood" of the Rough Riders "like water when there seemed to be an objective and had flung them straight against entrenchments and kept them hour after hour, dropping under rifle and shrapnel fire." The danger truly had been there, but the duration and the extent of the exposure were exaggerated.[2]

Roosevelt also boasted that the part played by the Rough Riders in the war was so outstanding that American regulars informally christened his volunteer regiment "the Eleventh U.S. Horse Cavalry." Eleven was the next number after the ten regular regiments. He claimed that the encomium was a mark of professional acceptance of the Rough Riders, although he did not identify the regulars who supposedly supported him. Substantially all of the regular officers openly deprecated his contribution.[3]

Roosevelt never acknowledged these deprecations. He had achieved his lifelong dream. "I would not have missed this for anything," he exclaimed, "even were I to die tomorrow." He already had admitted that he would have abandoned a dying wife and a wounded son to lead the charge.[4]

Disseminating the Roosevelt Vision

Before the battle for Santiago, Roosevelt had been discounted as "Terrible Teddy, liable to do anything." He had been seen by his superiors as an unpredictable eccentric. Now, however, the public called him reliable and fearless.[5]

The transformation from irresponsible bureaucrat to martial hero was not just a stroke of good fortune. Rather, the new image was achieved through newspaper contacts Roosevelt had been nurturing for more than fifteen years. Throughout his civilian career, Roosevelt had concentrated on relationships with big city reporters. He comprehended that journalists had to have fresh copy every day and he regularly fed them items calculated to attain his ends. No one else in the military in Cuba was able to captivate the correspondents and, through them, the public to the same extent. No other combatant had prepared himself as thoroughly for fame.[6]

His manner with newsmen was always confiding. He trusted them and respected them. He knew the value of a news article about him, especially when he controlled the content and tone. He had influenced the reporters in every way he could before the war, even by giving them framed and inscribed photographs of himself in western garb.[7]

At home in Washington, he had frequently played host to the authors of the day in his literary role as a published historian. The most productive association was with war correspondent Richard Harding Davis, who also wrote adventure novels and so was experienced in creating romantic characters.

From Tampa on, Dick Davis was regarded by his peers as the correspondent singularly "accredited" to Roosevelt and the Rough Riders, even though other lesser correspondents had attached themselves to the Rough Riders while the regiment was still in Texas. Reporters there had already preselected Roosevelt as the hero-to-be. The rationale for the concentration on Roosevelt was recognition that "it was a big promotional gamble we were all taking" in projecting Roosevelt as the most likely protagonist of the war, "but we journalists hold the cards and we don't often lose."[8]

Davis expected the colonel to be a winner at war because he was a gut fighter who would fear nothing, not even his senior officers if they got in the way. Davis and Roosevelt were alike in thinking that battles were merely a kind of football game to be won by physically penetrating an opponent's line. Roosevelt was to carry the ball. Davis would be the partisan scorekeeper.[9]

The correspondent knew that the public would quickly tire of articles about old generals. Instead, vibrant younger men would make "good copy," and he made Roosevelt his personal connection. He arranged it so other correspondents would have to come to him for details about Roosevelt after the colonel actually accomplished the deeds required to make him a national celebrity.[10]

Davis had pressed Roosevelt for intimate biographical data and for opinions on war and peace. He had Roosevelt photographed and drawn in soldierly poses and he learned how to obtain family photographs that could be captioned "Hero Roosevelt as an Infant," "Hero Roosevelt as a Cowboy," and "Hero Roosevelt as a Father," all popular subjects. Davis believed in preparedness, if he was to sell Roosevelt as a military phenomenon.

The Reporters' Role

The work of the correspondents who walked to the battles was dirty and dangerous. Featured reporters Marshall and Creelman of the *Journal* were seriously wounded. Nevertheless, publishers of newspapers insisted on "journalism that acts." For them, good reportage was measured by a newsman's enterprise both in finding facts and in embroidering on or even inventing "facts" where necessary.[11]

Correspondents in Cuba also gave their personal opinions on the planning and execution of the campaign. Their views were presented as part of the news, permitting newspapermen to act as if they and not General Shafter were directing the army. "Years ago," an editor might have explained, "we took the news as it came. That was all that was expected of us, but if we tried that now, we'd have to shut up shop in a week. We would have no readers. To-day, when we have to, we create the events and the personalities that make the news."

An editor willing to level with Roosevelt from the start also might have said:

> We understand you are a promising military man and you intend to distinguish yourself in the Cuban war. You expect to come home as the conquering hero, confound your political enemies, and sweep into public office as the popular war idol.[12]
>
> Suppose you do distinguish yourself in the war. What good will it do if nobody hears of it? There are lots of ways of our telling your story in the newspaper. We might put it in at the bottom of an inside page and give only a stick to it, or we might let it have the whole front page with your portrait at the top and headlines in letters six inches high.

Despite the editors' claims about their options, Roosevelt knew that their business was to push the sale of papers. The biggest headlines, not squibs, captured the greatest circulation. Conquering heroes had to be created for the benefit of the publishers, and a soldier's cooperation with journalists was the price of his fame. Roosevelt was a ready ally of the press.

The highest-paid correspondents were the ones like Davis who could romanticize a prosaic situation. They were expected to find soldiers in Cuba who had earned headlines or else they were supposed to inflate lesser accomplishments into unmatched valor. In his performance at San Juan, Roosevelt fell into the crack between the earned and the enhanced. It was Davis's job to meet his employer's requirements by giving Roosevelt a boost.

That is just what Davis did when he used Roosevelt's version to formulate the events.

Creating the Legend

The story Davis reported in the *New York Herald*, in magazine articles, and in books was transcribed from his field notes. The substance was what Roosevelt told him. The only additions were bits of hyperbole too strong even for the colonel to have provided.

The headline in the *Herald* was "COLONEL ROOSEVELT LED HIS MEN THROUGH THE LINES OF THE REGULARS AT SAN JUAN AND THEIR MAGNIFICENT CHARGE INSPIRED THE ARMY." The article continued:

> *Since Lieutenant Colonel Roosevelt has had control over the Rough Riders, the devotion of his men to him is fine to see. Roosevelt in the last 15 years has played many parts—cowboy, big game hunter, Civil Service Commissioner, Police Commissioner, Assistant Secretary of the Navy and writer of American history. He is now making American history, and making it very well.*
>
> *On Friday, when he was ordered to take his regiment into the open, he found regulars lying in the grass under heavy fire. They were being shot without being allowed to make any return.*
>
> ROOSEVELT'S GALLANT CHARGE. *This did not seem good enough, and Roosevelt led his regiment through their lines and rode ahead of his men toward the blockhouse on the hill. Younger officers and the colored soldiers of the regulars followed instantly. No one who saw Roosevelt take that ride expected he would finish it alive. As the only mounted man, he was the most conspicuous object in range of the rifle pits, then only 200 yards ahead. Mounted high on horseback and charging the rifle pits at a gallop and quite alone, he made you feel you would like to cheer.*
>
> *It looked like foolhardiness, but he set the pace with his horse and inspired the men to follow. He reached the blockhouse with four troopers before all the Spaniards had abandoned it, and killed one of them who was still firing, with his own revolver. The charge was followed almost immediately by another to the hill on the right, which he occupied with 300 men, the fragments of six dismounted cavalry regiments.*

TRUE AMERICAN GRIT. The grit of the cowpuncher has never been doubted, but when we wished to illustrate the fact that the swell will fight, we have had to refer to the bravery of the English. Now we can refer instead to the courage of the young men of the university and of the Knickerbocker Club when they forced the pass at Guasimas and charged up the hill of San Juan. It is a more up to date example, and the men are Americans.

Colonel Roosevelt has been nominated for the Medal of Honor for gallant conduct in action during the charge of San Juan.

Richard Harding Davis[13]

Davis the snob relished writing about the "swell" rather than the more plebeian regulars. Some of the unusual wording in Davis's article, such as "fragments" of cavalry regiments, was identical with the phrasing in Roosevelt's official reports to Wood, indicating that the wording came from Roosevelt. Davis located Roosevelt's charge as "up the hill of San Juan," a placement Roosevelt was later forced to defend. San Juan Hill was the elevation that Kent's infantry charged, not the Rough Riders.

Passing the Version On

The other correspondents in Cuba accepted Davis as their beau ideal, the perfect journalist. He agreed with them. He looked and dressed the part, acted braver than they did, said so in print, and wrote for the highest pay.

Leslie's photographer Burr McIntosh acknowledged that "no man who accompanied this expedition as correspondent was more successful than Richard Harding Davis. His entire conduct was such as any man should be proud to imitate. Richard Harding Davis treats people as people treat him."[14]

Inexperienced correspondents like novelist Frank Norris remembered the whole war as ugliness seen darkly, "and when you try to recall the campaign, it's only the horrors and hardships and nothing of the finer side." Norris depended on senior writers like Davis to identify "the finer side." From Davis he heard mainly about the glory that was Roosevelt's.[15]

Davis worked industriously at his job. The night before the July 1 attack, most of the journalists were gathered in groups to share bacon, beans, hardtack, coffee, and gossip. In contrast, energetic Davis made a solo visit to the general staff to discuss the schedule for the next day. Despite contrary advice from Inspector General Breckenridge on behalf of General Shafter, Davis suspected that the El Caney advance might become a drawn-out, secondary affair.

Davis deserted El Caney during the morning of July 1. At midday he was making his way toward Wheeler at the bloody ford. Less dedicated journalists were lunching. Crane, Whigham of the *Chicago Tribune,* and Scovel of the *World* were eating together until "a mule, which had been shot through the nose, wandered up and looked at Whigham. We ran away." They then met Hemment of the *Journal* who had a Japanese servant holding an open umbrella as a sunshade in one hand and a lunch basket in the other. Hemment offered them fried chicken and cloth napkins. After they accepted, the servant brewed real coffee over an open fire.[16]

Davis avoided such distractions. When Roosevelt waved his campaign hat to spur the Rough Riders into the charge on Kettle Hill at 1 P.M., Davis was three-quarters of a mile south. Standing with General Wheeler, he was the reporter closest to the charge, but he could not see Roosevelt's actions. The jungle was in the way. It was hearing the cowboy yells and the rise in intensity of gunfire that alerted him.[17]

To observe the assault, Davis hurried northward along the bank of the river until he came to the open meadow and the knoll. He followed the path of Roosevelt and the Rough Riders across the meadow. By then, however, Roosevelt and his troopers were off on their second charge, headed for the San Juan Heights. Davis changed direction to follow them. He was in no great danger. The fire from Spanish guns had slackened in his vicinity. When Davis caught up to Roosevelt, the third charge was over. The troopers were resting on the final overlook above Santiago. Davis was the only correspondent there. He made the most of the opportunity.[18]

Roosevelt was even more exuberant than he had been at Las Guasimas. He spouted forth the whole story of what he believed he had done in each of the three charges and in taking command at the overlook. It was the first charge, the one to the crest of the first elevation, that was the high spot. According to the excited colonel, he was the one who had shoved the black regulars of the 9th Cavalry out of his path. He had ordered the first assault. He was the first American on top of the first hill, in the first breach of a Spanish entrenchment in the Battle of San Juan.

Go back and "look at those damned Spanish dead" in the trenches on the heights, Roosevelt told Davis. He was gloating over the casualties once again. "I do not want to be vain, but I do not think anyone else could have handled this regiment quite as I have. I rose over those regular army officers like a balloon." The simile was ill-chosen, evoking memories of the bloody crossing.[19]

After listening to Roosevelt and making voluminous notes, Davis returned to the hacienda on the heights to verify Roosevelt's version of the battle. The Rough Riders there substantiated and even augmented Roosevelt's extravagant description of the three magnificent charges he said he had headed. The troopers were accustomed to Davis. They were aware of his favorable bent toward the colonel and themselves. They never would contradict Roosevelt or disappoint Davis who saw no need to question the officers of other cavalry regiments.[20]

Next, Colonel Wood came striding up the slope. He too was impressed by the tale that the persuasive Davis repeated. Wood announced on the spot that he would nominate Roosevelt for the Medal of Honor for conspicuous gallantry.[21]

Almost an hour after Davis began his interview of the bubbling Roosevelt on the overlook, a few of the other correspondents managed to reach the heights. They found Davis already there, completing his talks with Wood and the Rough Riders. When Crane, Harris, and Fox appeared, they found Davis in possession of the day's lead story. Before they talked to the regular cavalrymen, they asked Davis to tell them what had happened. Davis repeated Roosevelt's tale as gospel.[22]

During the rest of the afternoon, Davis related Roosevelt's version to a dozen other newspapermen. Even those who had watched from El Poso had to find out from Davis who had ordered the assault and who was first on the crest. Gradually, Roosevelt became surrounded by newspaper correspondents and foreign observers who were questioning him. He confirmed what Davis had told them. Roosevelt had successfully conveyed his personal vision of the action to Davis. What Roosevelt said he had done was now set in concrete for the newspaper public.

Davis's elaborate preparations had paid off. To Davis's eye as an experienced newspaperman, the stereotypical image of one man's heart-stirring ride under heavy Spanish fire was worth more in the telling than the grand panorama of an entire campaign fought by the faceless multitude who were the remainder of the American army in Cuba.

By evening, Davis was suffering severe pains in his hip that he diagnosed as a recurrence of his sciatica. Crane and Harris helped him limp slowly back along the trail to El Poso. There Scovel was arranging supper for *World* correspondents and their associates in a deserted sugar-drying yard.[23]

The table was a big wooden box. Scovel, other *World* employees, Musgrave the Englishman, Rea of *Harper's Weekly,* Hare of *Collier's,* and photographer McIntosh were seated around the box on the ground. The first portions of fried pork had been served when the hobbling Davis appeared, supported by Crane and Harris and looking for food and rest. Fifteen of the leading journalists in Cuba came to Scovel's table before all the food was consumed.

McIntosh who idolized Davis recalled, "It was an interesting party and the recounting of scenes and incidents of the day would have made one of the most readable books of the war." As usual, the principal raconteur was Dick Davis. His lively narrative about mounted Roosevelt heading the courageous charge up "the hill of San Juan" was a blessing to the others. Most of them had been no closer to San Juan than El Caney. Now they too had a story about one man's pluck that would sell papers.[24]

At nine o'clock the supper party broke up. The tired correspondents went their various ways, seeking places to sleep. In their turn they spread the legend of Teddy farther. They shared both Davis's story and a few discarded cavalry blankets with more journalists, as they bivouacked in the dew-soaked grass.[25]

The Legend Full-Blown

For the eager readers of the *Herald,* Davis continued to depict the bespectacled thirty-nine-year-old bureaucrat-turned-volunteer-cavalry-officer as leading his elite regiment hell-bent at a gallop against a succession of fortifications high on steep hills swept by volleys from thousands of trained Spanish riflemen. The blue polka-dotted bandanna floated like a pennant from the back of his sombrero. This was the stuff of American myths.[26]

Most journalists copied Davis, adding their own elaborate details. Roosevelt did not halt until the evening of this fabulous day, they wrote, and then only after he had victoriously attained the final crest, the one before Santiago itself.

Yellow-press correspondents were obliged to go Davis one better. To make their newspapers more salable than Davis's *Herald,* they exaggerated his account on the false basis that they had witnessed the charge. They handed Roosevelt a sword to brandish and they shot his fiery stallion from under him.[27]

The *Journal* reported Roosevelt's ride most feverishly:

ROOSEVELT: THE AMERICAN SOLDIER. *No finer picture of young American manhood in war has ever been presented than that of Theodore Roosevelt at the head of his Rough Riders and the colored Cavalry storming the blockhouse at San Juan.*

The Spaniards were entrenched at the crest of a hill up which, under the pitiless storm of Mauser bullets, the assailants were forced to advance. Men fell fast, but the ranks closed up mechanically and pressed on, firing rapidly. Roosevelt rode a hundred feet ahead of the line, waving his sword and "yelling like a Sioux," says the Journal correspondent who watched the charge. His horse stopped, staggered and fell dead, but, with the agility of a practiced cowboy, Roosevelt twisted out of the saddle and, sword in hand, rushed over the crest of the hill and into the trenches of the enemy.

We think that Mr. Roosevelt's military career affords a fine illustration of the possibilities inherent in American character. Born to the walks of peace, equipped with every facility for living a purposeless and idle existence, Roosevelt, after creditable essays in political life, manifests the very highest qualities which go to make up the successful soldier.[28]

Life magazine added:

Without doubt the military man who has made the biggest renown is Mr. Theodore Roosevelt. He stormed the heights of glory with the eagerness of a milk-fed puppy rushing to his first piece of meat. To think of him is like thinking of a comet with a tail all exclamation points.

With his customary unconventionality, he avoided military style, went
in with a whoop to knock down and drag out the Dagoes. He got his
men into the worst fights and charged at the head of them uphill on
horseback, had his horse shot under him, lost about a third of his men,
and lived to see the Spanish soldiers driven back and to have the story
told by Richard Harding Davis. He became a favorite son of New York,
and New Yorkers said he was It.[29]

Even in fiction of the day, Roosevelt and the Rough Riders symbolized audacious masculinity: "The colonel of the —th Regular
Cavalry summoned Captain ——— who was all-fired anxious to smell
Dago powder. 'Ought to have joined the Rough Riders' growled a
grizzled lieutenant. 'They'll be in the fight tomorrow.'" Implicitly, the
veteran regulars might not be.[30]

As the author of *Hero Tales in American History,* Roosevelt had
earned a chapter about himself in his own book. He covered the
episode in articles and in his autobiography. Others noted that "there
was page upon page of Roosevelt's exploits, portraits of all kinds,
biographies, anecdotes, interviews, headlines. They've even got a song
about Roosevelt." In fact, these were many songs set to patriotic airs
by amateur poets.[31]

One was a primer:

R is for Roosevelt, a tireless chap,
With a chip on his shoulder, out hunting a scrap. . . .

Another was humorous:

So Teddy, he came runnin' with his glasses on his nose,
An' when the Spanish saw his teeth you may
*   believe they froze. . . .*

A third was Western:

He led his boys a-dancin' on, a-shootin' left and right,
An' not missin' many Spanish knobs that shoved 'emselves in
*   sight. . . .*

A fourth was an anthem:

When the Spanish shells and shrapnel burst,
Our losses were the worst—

The chaplain even cursed.
'Charge!' cried Colonel Roosevelt, and charged,
The first to carve our way to glory. . . .

A fifth was sardonic:

Damsels to the right of them, Beauties to the left of them,
Honors ahead of them, Dash the Rough Riders. . . .

A sixth was a saga:

Cow punchers, some of them, Blue stockings, some of them,
Born heroes, all of them, Teddy in front. . . . "

A seventh was the legend:

Just then, biff! a bullet knocked over his horse,
But Teddy jumped off him, right side up, of course.
And he brandished his sword and went up on that hill,
With a yell that the Spaniards are shaking at still. . . .

An eighth was from the grateful ranks:

Our chief has never a tremor shown,
He's grit cinched up in a belt.
Oh, they must be for their courage known
Who ride with Roosevelt. . . .

A ninth was the plaintive:

My pa's a great Rough Rider,
He was one of Teddy's men. . . . [32]

In this barrage of impassioned stretching of the truth, Roosevelt and his Rough Riders hogged most of the newspaper space about the battle for Santiago. They were praised as if they had been the only actors in a war designed just to showcase a valiant Roosevelt. He was distilled into the essence of cowboy cavalryman, the fearless rider on the "white" horse, the foremost example of real American manhood.[33]

He was described as having been a primordial force in the hostilities. He was neither calculated nor reckless, they said, but instinctively playing out the ancient gladiatorial competition to kill or be killed. His personal view of the war was reported to have been ex-tracted from Social Darwinism. The superior Anglo-Saxon race nec-essarily won over the decadent Spaniards.[34]

He was said to dominate the Rough Riders completely. He drew their devotion to himself as though no one else mattered to them. They were preoccupied with him. When he was with them, every man wondered what extraordinary thing the colonel might say or do next. When he was away, they spent their time anticipating his return and imagining what he might do when he came back.[35]

To Roosevelt, the adulation of the men and the reporting of the one day's fighting was the fulfillment of personal needs stemming from his sickly childhood, his father's draft avoidance, his political ambitions, and his aspirations for his country as a world power.[36]

When he wrote about the San Juan episode in a letter to his men-tor Henry Cabot Lodge, he characterized his accomplishment as one that would endure: "I feel I have done something which enables me to leave a name to my children of which they can rightly be proud and which will serve in some sense as a substitute for not leaving them more money." He had come to accept the exaggerations in the published story.[37]

Roosevelt had never been prouder of anything in his life than he was of what he called his charge at San Juan Hill. In turn, the Ameri-can people celebrated him as the ideal hero.

The legend of Teddy was firmly in place.

Chapter 26
Alone in Cubia

Although the press chose Roosevelt as the hero of the land battle for Santiago, the standard military texts on the campaign did not mention him. He had not been involved in the development of whatever strategy there was. From the standpoint of military historians, he accomplished nothing in the field that would not have been done without him.

He had not even been in the right sector of the battlefield to be able to act as significantly as, for example, General Hawkins. Confined as he was to relatively undefended Kettle Hill, his performance could not have equaled the importance of the storming of San Juan Hill. On the other hand, he indisputably was a courageous and inspirational leader of his regiment. He was a supremely determined man. Just to get as far as he did at Kettle Hill, he had to disobey General Shafter's specific orders and expose himself and the Rough Riders to extreme hazards.

He was at the front in the only two fights against the Spaniards in the entire Santiago campaign. He made the most out of what was available to him. As he commented, his role in Cuba was "analogous to the legendary local gambler who, reproached for his foolishness in playing poker with a team of professional cardsharps, excused himself on the ground that it was the only game in town."[1]

While the Las Guasimas skirmish and the assault on Kettle Hill were slighter encounters than the charge up San Juan Hill and the many more meaningful battles in the annals of American warfare, these two engagements were all there were for Roosevelt in Cuba. "We did not have much of a war," he admitted later, "but it was the best to be had at the time, and we did the best we could."[2]

As an inveterate risk taker, he put his life on the line to prove his valor at Santiago. He really did do all he could have done. That was demonstrated by the enduring respect he earned from the men who knew him most intimately, the Rough Riders. There was, however, no equivalent recognition from the military historians. They did not acknowledge his presence in Cuba.

The Force of Subconscious Wishes

When reporters questioned Roosevelt about details concerning San Juan, he did not contradict statements he knew to have been falsely inflated by Davis and the yellow press. He was asked how he felt when he ordered and then led the charge up San Juan Hill. Reporters inquired about apprehensions he might have had when he rode a hundred feet ahead of the troopers. Photographers wanted him to pose with the sword he waved while galloping in the van. They sympathized with him on the loss of his famous stallion.

In his euphoria, he allowed himself to believe the exaggerations and untruths. As the lion of the moment, he escaped close cross-examination. He smiled mysteriously and bobbed his head a trifle in silent acquiescence, letting the newborn legend stand, even though his sword was tied to his luggage in the rear and uninjured Texas was concealed in a restricted area behind the new divisional headquarters east of Kettle Hill. The little stallion eventually died of natural causes in Oyster Bay and was buried in the pet cemetery on Sagamore Hill.

Roosevelt was not alone in his self-aggrandizement. Every officer who recounted Spanish-American War episodes focused favorably on his own actions. After all, no participant in the battles could remember all that happened. Sequences and surroundings frequently were rearranged. As Roosevelt admitted, "It is astonishing what a limited area of vision and experience one has in the hurly-burly of a battle." His ambition required him to fill in gaps appropriate for his ends.

Other officers who wrote about the war were not asked, though, to deal with excessively laudatory fictions about themselves. Only Roosevelt had this problem. He reacted by clothing himself in the legend of Teddy as if the tale had been wholly real. His duality was the key. The aggressive man was still twinned with the romantic adolescent. The man acted. The boy enhanced.

Eminent psychiatrists diagnosed his stretching of the truth as the continued assertions of the asthmatic child who compensated for his physical incapacity by doing everything as intensely as he could. Mark Twain saw the boy in Roosevelt, too, but as a manipulative "Tom Sawyer, always hunting for a chance to show off."[3]

There were disciples of Freud in Roosevelt's time who explained why he overstated his actions. They declared that he was certain "to go down in history as one of the most illustrious psychological examples of distortion of conscious mental processes through the force of subconscious wishes." Surprisingly, they ignored the peculiar relationship with his parents. What they were saying was that he had the knack of self-hypnosis. They too found that it had to do with the child loose in the adult's subconscious. The knack was an asset for "a political Colonel."[4]

Like the psychiatrists, most of the journalists close to Roosevelt considered him to be an honest man—up to a point. They claimed that he would never affirm what he did not know to be right, but that he could in time convince himself that fiction was fact. He never could tell a lie until he made himself believe that the falsehood was true.

When Roosevelt was a New York City police commissioner, the muckraking newspaperman Lincoln Steffens had observed Roosevelt's transformation of the truth at first hand. One morning he found the commissioner in the departmental office, unable to choose between two deceptive news releases prepared for him to cover up an awkward incident concerning the police.

"Look here," Steffens suggested to the stymied Roosevelt, "why not pick the one of those statements you prefer, set it up on your desk, and read it before and after meals. In a day or two, you'll come to believe it yourself. Then give it to the press. It will be true then." In response Roosevelt muttered, "I *can* do that! I *can*!"[5]

When Steffens returned after three days and read the issued release aloud in the commissioner's office, Roosevelt exclaimed, "It's true, that statement." Self-hypnosis had done the trick. The same knack enabled Roosevelt to accept exaggerations about his role at San Juan. He wanted to believe the stories about his singular gallantry, so he did believe them.

Roosevelt's personal magnetism made it easy for correspondents to take him at his word. After the battle, middle-aged journalists in poor physical condition hiked miles in tropical heat in order to reach him on the overlook. Although they were tired and discouraged, they drew sustenance from his excess energy.

When the journalists were ready to leave, they proclaimed that Roosevelt had made them happier to be alive. They were glad this commander of tough men had survived his ordeal in combat and was already prepared to "fight like the devil," either in another charge against Santiago or against repressive superiors. The power of his personality made him persuasive as a military hero. He became a role model for the nation. The sometimes endearingly juvenile Teddy suited the emotional needs of an adolescent country.[6]

In his opinion, war was the severest individual and national test. Battle was the epitome of the strenuous ideal in American life, with values derived from sports, hunting, Social Darwinism, and "muscular" Christianity. Although he said he did only what he expected any young white man of his social class to do under pressure, if given the same chance, he was the soldier called bravest by other brave men in his regiment.[7]

The Myth Revisited

Rough Riders and regular cavalrymen on the overlook saw Roosevelt surrounded by renowned correspondents and foreign attachés who were eager to hear the battle's real story straight from the hero's mouth. The troopers had no sense of envy or complaint. They admired Roosevelt. To the cavalrymen, Roosevelt had earned his special prominence. The plaudits he received reflected well on them, too.[8]

At the same time, Kent's infantrymen were digging trenches facing Santiago on top of San Juan Hill. They were wholly occupied with staying alive in the face of heavy Spanish fusillades coming from the main defense line. They could not see Roosevelt and the cavalry half a mile north.

If the infantrymen had fewer correspondents questioning them while they scooped and scraped, they did not notice the discrepancy. They had no idea that by suffering the greatest number of casualties while assaulting the principal Spanish blockhouse on San Juan Hill, they had been contributing to the creation of the legend of Teddy for civilians.

The infantrymen were unaware of headlines at home. Mail shipped to Cuba from the mainland was being transported by the army and not the postal service. Food and ammunition still came first, so letters were delayed as much as three weeks.[9]

The Sunday *New York Herald* containing Davis's original account of the battle arrived in San Juan two weeks late. The going price was ten dollars and the few copies available quickly became tattered with use. Only then did the regulars learn that Roosevelt had received more than the lion's share of glory. Feelings against the Rough Riders' colonel suddenly were strong.[10]

When Roosevelt nominated himself as the hero of the Spanish-American War, he must have suspected that the regular officers' reactions would be negative. The virulence of the response, however, surprised him. He told a Rough Rider that if he had anticipated the heat and volume of the accusations against him, he never would have staked out his claims in print. He was not telling the truth. He would have wanted glory at almost any price.[11]

Roosevelt's fellow volunteer Gen. Joe Wheeler remarked to the ever-present Davis, "It is touching to see the regulars get American newspapers, read how redoubt after redoubt was taken by the volunteers, with scarcely any mention of the regular army. How disappointed and disgusted they are! One captain turned to me and said, 'Depend on it, the truth will be told when history is written.'" Wheeler did not name Roosevelt and the Rough Riders, but he was referring specifically to them. They were the only volunteers in his division.[12]

Regular infantry officers were not so squeamish. As Davis reported, "Regulars Are Jealous of the Honor Done to Volunteers. The credit and notoriety accorded to the volunteers, and especially to the Rough Riders, in the operations about Santiago have not been viewed with entire equanimity by the regulars who bore the brunt of the fighting." By "Rough Riders," he meant Roosevelt.[13]

Despite having directed the Roosevelt boom, cagey Davis also wrote these little sops to the regulars. He walked both sides of the street to retain the veterans as friendly sources of news. Besides, the officers' grievances amounted to good if inside-page squibs running counter to the front-page Roosevelt raves. Even minor controversies built circulation.

Some regular infantrymen had taken it for granted that if the well-known Davis had written about Roosevelt charging up San Juan Hill, the Rough Rider really must have been there. The perplexing fact was, they explained, they never saw him. Capt. John Bigelow of the 10th Cavalry maintained that he never noticed Roosevelt anywhere in the arena, though that was a conscious misrepresentation. Bigelow had been on Kettle Hill.

Other infantrymen claimed that their officers had realized from the beginning that the Rough Riders would "steal their thunder." Only Roosevelt had the ear of the correspondents. A private wrote, "I thought we would be the whole thing on account of having taken the hill but the adjutant says the Rough Riders will get all the credit because they have their press agents along. And what do you think, they were not even in the fight. They say our charge will make Roosevelt President some day. Well, I suppose I shouldn't kick, as I am looking for a laurel wreath myself." Many soldiers at San Juan were glory seekers. Roosevelt was just the most proficient.[14]

Regular infantry officers continued to be bitter. War was their best chance to move up in grade, but opportunities were diminished by the lack of public awareness of their efforts. Roosevelt had appropriated their reward. Even temperate General Hawkins "flayed" the Rough Riders—meaning Roosevelt—in the press. The attack reached its height when Commanding General Miles expressed anti-Roosevelt sentiments during a Washington speech. He stated flatly that Roosevelt "was not at San Juan Hill at all."[15]

The regulars expected Roosevelt to be either court-martialed or given the Medal of Honor for his actions at Las Guasimas and Kettle Hill. He was considered for both extremes, but his achievements and malfeasances were not that unique. Equally brave, if less insubordinate, acts were performed by unpublicized officers.

Accusations against Roosevelt appeared frequently in newspapers, periodicals, and books. There were many different grounds for the attacks, but in the press they were confined to squibs. One comment was that Roosevelt acted "very big" but had commanded less than six hundred of the eighteen thousand American soldiers engaged in the conflict. He was a small cog in a huge army wheel to be making such a disproportionately loud squeak. The remark was true, but it would have been equally accurate for any other candidate for hero. Also, acting important did not justify a court-martial.[16]

More to the point, Roosevelt admitted that he had voluntarily abandoned his support assignment in the rear of the battlefield. He bragged about putting one over on the regular officers. This deliberate violation of orders was solid grounds for a court-martial, but it was also an integral part of the heroism that followed.[17]

In addition, regulars claimed that Roosevelt commanded the Rough Riders in a most unmilitary manner. He led by example, charging at the head of his regiment like an out-of-control squad leader, not like a colonel. The complaint, though, was the basis for the proposed Medal of Honor, not an indictment.[18]

The long string of grievances continued. The regulars maintained that it took "a regiment of Negroes to save Roosevelt and his Rough Riders" at Kettle Hill. After the worst of the fighting at San Juan was over, a Rough Rider allegedly grasped the hand of a black trooper of the 10th, acknowledging, "We've got you fellows to thank for getting us out of a bad hole." The trooper who was a veteran of the Indian Wars was supposed to have replied, "Dat's all right, boss. It's all in the family. We call ourselves the Colored Rough Riders."[19]

The episode clearly was apocryphal. What the "bad hole" could have been at San Juan is not clear. The 9th and 10th Cavalry and the Rough Riders all approached undefended Kettle Hill from different sides. Neither the 9th nor the 10th aided the Rough Riders.

Further, the infantrymen said there were few Spaniards and no fortifications on Kettle Hill. Charging this relatively undefended knoll did not require the highest order of courage. They joked that taking the hillock entailed "little more danger than an attack on City Hall" in Roosevelt's native New York.[20]

Besides, the regulars insisted, the indisputable hero of San Juan was not Roosevelt but General Hawkins who did not receive the Medal of Honor even though he was the white-haired favorite of the infantry. By heading the truly desperate charge on foot against the blockhouse on San Juan Hill, Hawkins was the indispensable officer who had guided the army to victory. If his resolute advance had failed, the consequence would have been a disastrous defeat for the infantry division and probably for the entire army. In contrast, Roosevelt's charge up Kettle Hill was called a sideshow—hardly critical to the outcome of the campaign. It was not equal to Hawkins's contribution.[21]

Roosevelt already had persuaded himself, however, that he had headed the advance at San Juan Hill just as much as Hawkins had. Although San Juan Hill and Kettle Hill were separated by geography and by a difference in the quality of defenses, Roosevelt lumped together the hill, the knoll, the valley before them, and the heights as "the battlefield at San Juan Hill." He glossed over the clear physical difference between San Juan Hill in particular and the entire San Juan battlefield.

Roosevelt appeared to be sincere in his reasoning. As proof, he cited the Civil War battle of Gettysburg where Round Top had been a key to the Union position. He claimed that soldiers who fought at Round Top also participated in the Gettysburg conflict by definition. Gettysburg was the generic name of the entire battle.[22]

To Roosevelt, "the cavalry charged at 'San Juan Hill' just as much as the infantry did; to deny this is merely to quibble." He insisted that "the famous charge up San Juan Hill was made by both Cavalry and Infantry, at different points, and the contrary position is merely disingenuous." His error was that San Juan Hill was the proper equivalent of Round Top in his comparison and the battle for San Juan and ultimately Santiago was the equivalent of Gettysburg.

Two Frenchwomen who were traveling on a train from Paris to the Midi were concerned enough about the distinction to ask an American passenger whether "Mr. Roosevelt was not at San Juan Hill?" The American replied that he had been a Rough Rider. He added firmly, "Well, Teddy was *very much* there!"[23]

Nevertheless, doubt persisted. In his statements, Roosevelt had left the comparative safety of the conceivably accurate "Cavalry charge at San Juan" for the patently wrong "Cavalry charge up San Juan Hill." He had moved from the possible generic to the refutable specific.

Fifteen years after the famous charge, the *New York Sun* published the editorial "Once More the Old Fiction." The *Sun* was still asking Roosevelt to correct the record concerning the locus of his Kettle Hill charge. He ignored the request. After all, what more could he say that would be new?[24]

Another lingering indictment came from his foes in civilian life. Army officers did not mention his vivid description of shooting a

Spaniard at close range after the second charge. The officers were envious. Civilians, however, continued to carp. They asserted that Roosevelt "stands out as the solitary biographer from the days of Caesar until now to write himself down boastingly as a slayer of his fellow man. His one military deed was firing his pistol at some poor devil who was running away." Roosevelt's response to these humanitarian cries that he had admittedly "shot a man in the back" was only, "He wasn't shot in the back but in the left breast as he turned."[25]

Civilian opponents also complained that Roosevelt did not arrange for an organized interment of the dead after the battle. Surviving soldiers had dug the graves, using flimsy wooden boards as markers, while rifle fire was still being exchanged and the chaplain was helping with the wounded. Some Rough Rider burial sites could not be located later, but fellow officers did not bring this up as an indictment. Even in hospital cemeteries, they knew, only a third of the graves were identifiable. This was far fewer than in the Rough Riders' interments. Roosevelt did more about burials than most officers did, even though Shafter had said duty was due first to the living, not the dead.[26]

Finally, a hostile politician offered one thousand dollars to anyone who could disprove his derogatory allegations about Roosevelt. He stated that Roosevelt became a hero only as the result of a knowingly false report of actions supposedly taken at San Juan Hill but actually performed elsewhere. The nine accusations ranged from the charge that Roosevelt never saw a Spaniard during the battle to the claim that Roosevelt never was on horseback. No one, the politician asserted, rode a horse at San Juan Hill. The grade was too steep.[27]

Surprisingly, no one came forward to claim the thousand-dollar prize. Roosevelt's worst enemies admitted that he was a courageous man. He saw plenty of hostile Spaniards and he did ride Texas on the battlefield, if not up San Juan Hill.

Nevertheless, Roosevelt gave volunteers a bad name that endured in the eyes of the regulars. When Gen. John J. Pershing commanded the armies in World War I, he rejected all volunteers, including a proposed division to be headed by Roosevelt. As a lieutenant in the 10th, Pershing had seen Roosevelt and the Rough Rider volunteers in action at San Juan. Two decades later, he still recalled the officers—including Roosevelt—as not "thoroughly trained and disciplined."[28]

The Medal of Honor

A disconcerting rejection of Roosevelt's well-publicized role as the paramount hero of San Juan came from the War Department.

Writing on a page carefully torn from his notebook, Wood had recommended Roosevelt "for a medal of honor for distinguished gallantry in leading a charge on one of the intrenched hills to the east of the Spanish position." Wood knew what gallantry was. He had received a Medal of Honor for his own bravery. The first endorsement of the recommendation was by Wheeler, Wood's superior. The second was by Shafter, Wheeler's superior and the ranking army officer in Cuba. The recommendation and endorsements were from the highest possible sources in the V Army Corps.[29]

The award should have been automatic for Roosevelt. Appropriate military and civilian bases were touched. Davis had reported the nomination in the *Herald*. There were approvals from powerful Republican politicians, including Senator Lodge and Senator Platt. President McKinley was alerted. The word in Washington was that Roosevelt "wants the medal awful badly." He meant to get it.[30]

For four months, however, nothing happened. Skipping ceremony and the usual channels starting with Wood, Roosevelt wrote directly to the adjutant general of the army in Washington. He noted that a board had been convened to consider medals and asked where he stood. Two weeks later, the adjutant general replied that he had located the application which had been mislaid in the War Department. "It will give me great pleasure," he maintained, "to know that Wood's recommendation received favorable consideration."[31]

That sounded promising. Soon, however, Roosevelt wrote to the adjutant general again. He complained, "I was a good deal surprised and chagrined to hear that Secretary Alger had said" in public that "I was not entitled to the medal of honor. I don't want it if I am not entitled to it, but it is an honor I very keenly desire if I am entitled to it."[32]

Roosevelt's awareness of the army's resistance to awarding him the medal brought an immediate answer from the adjutant general. "I am fully persuaded the Secretary never made any such statement," he prevaricated. "What he probably did say was 'the case as presented by General Wood would not, under the rules of the office, entitle you to the consideration,' and you must agree that Wood's recommendation was lacking in the special features that warrant the issuance of medals to any one. Should he set this forth in detail, I undertake to say the Secretary will share with me the pleasure of bestowing this honor upon you." In other words, the recommendation Wood filed was not specific enough to enable the army to award the medal.[33]

Wood was now a brigadier general and Roosevelt had left the army as a full colonel. After a delay of another two weeks waiting in vain for Wood to expand his recommendation by listing the "special features," the adjutant general improperly shifted the burden to Roosevelt. He asked the Rough Rider to obtain statements from the officers who had been on Kettle Hill with him. "Medals of honor are not issued for gallantry alone, which will be met by conferring a brevet," he explained. "Medals of honor will be made only in extraordinary service, over and above gallant conduct. I want your case made particularly strong and the *evidence* to merit favorable action."[34]

Roosevelt coveted the medal badly enough to let himself be diverted into collecting his own proofs. Wood added weakly that Roosevelt "was the first to reach the trenches in his part of the line and killed one of the enemy with his own hand." A Rough Rider major swore that Roosevelt "headed, on horse back, the charge on Kettle Hill. He then headed the charge on the next hill." Captain Howze asserted that "at the base of the first hill, Roosevelt jumped through the fence and by his enthusiasm, example and courage succeeded in leading to the crest of the hill."[35]

Comments from regular officers conflicted. A captain in the 2nd Cavalry observed, "I witnessed Roosevelt leading his regiment, among the very first to reach the crest." His use of "among" was belittling.[36]

Roosevelt never seemed to realize that the depositions he collected failed to make his case. The witnesses attested only to courageous leadership of his own regiment. There was no documentation of "extraordinary service" exceeding gallantry.

The affair of Roosevelt's Medal of Honor dragged on. When he did not receive the medal immediately and was jockeyed into attempting to secure proofs on his own, it was obvious to everyone but Roosevelt that he would never get the medal. Except for his use of Texas, he had done no more than other brave officers who were not recommended for medals. Moreover, he was in the impolitic position of being an advocate for himself where personal pleading was unseemly.

The honors board considering medals had field reports from all regiments, as well as Roosevelt's depositions. The board could judge what was an exaggeration or in dispute. Regular officers who contradicted Roosevelt's claims to having been first anywhere had the last laugh. They could not control the press when it created the legend of Teddy at their expense, but they made up the board that denied the award he hungered for to validate the legend.

In the press, Roosevelt was the bravest man in Cuba, but he never did receive the Medal of Honor from the regular army.

Alone in Cubia

Roosevelt's book on the Rough Riders was published a year after the war. Some readers thought Roosevelt overdid his description of his own contribution toward winning the war. The satirist Finley Peter Dunne wrote an amusing review of the book through his fictional character Mr. Dooley:

> 'Tis "The Biography of a Hero by One who Knows." 'Tis "The Daring Exploits of a Brave Man by an Actual Eye Witness." 'Tis as it fell from the lips of Theodore Roosevelt and was taken down by his own hands.
>
> When Teddy was blown up in the harbor of Havana he concluded there must be war: "The Secretary of War had offered me the command of a regiment. I selected from among my acquaintances in the West men confronting perils almost as great as any that beset my path. In a few days I had them perfectly tamed. On the transport going to Cuba, I would stand beside one of these rough men treating him as an equal, which he was in everything but birth, education, rank, and courage.
>
> "We had no more landed in Cuba than it became necessary for me to take command of the army, which I did at once. A number of days were spent by me in reconnoitering, attended only by my brave and fluent bodyguard Richard Harding Davis. I discovered that the enemy was entrenched on top of San Juan Hill immediately in front of me.
>
> "At this time it became apparent that I was handicapped by the presence of the army. One day I ran into the entire military force of the United States lying on its stomach. 'If you won't fight,' says I, 'let me through.' 'Oh, excuse me,' says the general in command, rising to

his knees and saluting, so I sent the army home and attacked San Juan Hill.

"There has been some discussion as to who was the first man to reach the summit of San Juan Hill. Many gallant soldiers, statesmen, correspondents and Kinescope men claim the distinction, but I will say for the benefit of Posterity that I was the only man I saw, and I had a telescope."

You'll have to take a squint into the book yourself, but if I was Teddy I'd call the book Alone in Cubia.[37]

Sophisticated readers relished Mr. Dooley's widely circulated lampoon of Roosevelt's overblown treatment of his part in the Santiago campaign. The concept of the colonel with his tunnel vision fighting single-handedly on the "Cubian" front was funny. Roosevelt himself sent a note of rueful appreciation to Dunne. He wrote, "I regret to state that my family and intimate friends are delighted with your review of my book. I think you owe me one."[38]

Roosevelt also admitted to Dunne that "at a reception, I was introduced to a pretty young lady. She said, 'Oh Colonel, I've read everything you ever wrote.' 'Really! What book do you like best?' 'Why that one, you know, *Alone in Cubia.*'" Dunne said he "never knew a man who could take a joke on himself with better grace."[39]

The most telling jabs at Roosevelt's story, however, were private and casual. A year and a half after the Santiago campaign, Roosevelt's wife was in Cuba as the guest of Leonard Wood who was then in command of American occupation forces. She toured the San Juan battlefield, but she said the ascent was not nearly as steep as Roosevelt had led her to expect. Even so, she was not aware that Wood had shown her the face of San Juan Hill which had seemed so precipitous to Kent's infantry. She never noticed the much lower knoll that was Kettle Hill.[40]

Six years later, Roosevelt's older daughter Alice rode over the same trail and "felt a letdown. The mountains she had imagined him scaling were miles away."[41]

Being savaged by a professional humorist was one thing. For an ordinary man, losing face at home might have been more difficult to accept. Roosevelt never noticed. By then he was president of the United States.

Chapter 27

The Cravenette Man

When books on the Santiago campaign were written by correspondents enlarging on their original newspaper articles, Davis's version of what had happened was accepted as factual. The authors did not investigate where Roosevelt had been at San Juan or what he had done there.

Some of the books dealt sarcastically with the regular officers, particularly the generals. According to these writers, the Spanish-American War in retrospect was a comic opera played by buffoons—except for Roosevelt's role. This enraged the officers once more, but the aura that Roosevelt had fashioned was proof against their accusations and jibes.

Besides, while most officers criticized Roosevelt as a pretender to their achievements and as "a layman in command," there were a few who granted that Roosevelt had shown "all the qualities of a leader. The Colonel had the confidence and admiration of his men and that is nine-tenths of the battle." The few who praised Roosevelt received the most attention. After the war, they became part of his circle.[1]

Long after the fighting was over, the Rough Riders continued to give Roosevelt their total "confidence and admiration." When veterans sneered that he was merely a talker, Rough Riders made it plain that "if anybody thinks Colonel Roosevelt got up this outfit just to parade with, that person is a fool. We Rough Riders are the toughest men you ever met." They were willing to pick a quarrel with fellow soldiers to defend their intrepid colonel.

An F Troop easterner with an engineering background was still bragging to the press, "It's a sight to see him in a fight. You'd think his hide was double-chilled steel in three thicknesses, to watch him running around just to show you how." A New Mexican cowboy confessed to reporters, "When I seen him at San Antonio, I figured he was raised a pet. Now I wouldn't undertake to harness him with a pitchfork." Their pride was evident.[2]

Roosevelt was portrayed by the Rough Riders as being tender as well as fierce. "You ought to have seen him talk up when some of our fellows weren't treated well in the hospital," a trooper remarked. He insisted that Roosevelt "spent $5,000 of his own money at Santiago to give us better food and medicine." The amount was closer to $500, but that was a lot of money, too.[3]

Roosevelt reciprocated his troopers' feelings, asserting, "I am proud of my regiment. It set a record that will be hard to beat. We have men from about every State in the Union and it is a thoroughly American regiment. We have got about every race and religion represented. In the last five promotions from the ranks to second lieutenant, one was a Jew, one a Catholic, and two Protestants. The religion of the fifth I know nothing about."[4]

Forty-six states and territories and thirteen foreign countries were said to be represented in the regiment, but no Rough Rider was black or Asian. Only a few were red or brown. Moreover, although Roosevelt was remarkably unprejudiced for his class and era, he knew the fifth trooper was another Catholic. He was playing to the intellectual gallery by implying that he had promoted the regimental freethinker.

He claimed that when he rode to hounds on Long Island, a good hunting dog not only took hold of the quarry, he held fast. Now Roosevelt held as hard as he could to the Americans whose imagination he had seized. To counter any appearance of self-promotion, however, he gave himself an air of modesty by publicly criticizing the authors who were most flattering to him. With tongue in cheek, he complained because their books did not "tell of our disasters as well as our triumphs. Complete truthfulness must never be sacrificed to color." When a few books did "tell of disasters" he had experienced, he did not acknowledge them.[5]

His strength was that ordinary people trusted him. "What," he asked, "is the explanation for my hold on the headlines? Isn't it because correspondents know I am always sincere? Men who do not know me may doubt my sincerity, but no one who knows me does!"[6]

The American public chose him as the standard for the new century's cult of masculinity and strenuosity. Nothing could diminish the country's admiration for him. He had become the Cravenette man. He was criticism-proof, the way his khaki uniform was waterproof. His reputation was as resistant to personal attack as his treated tunic was to showers.

He wrapped his own interpretation of reality around himself as a shield shedding deprecation. His unshakable self-assurance inspired faith in his veracity. He was always credible, confident, and easy, never defensive or hesitant. People wanted to believe him. Regardless of their origins, Americans preferred to think they could become rich or good-looking or gallant—or, like Roosevelt, at least two of the three.

He was able to put across the notion that if his particular dream could come true, so could everyone else's hopes for whatever they desired. His success validated their aspirations.

On that basis, the question remains: Why did Roosevelt find it necessary to exaggerate his role at San Juan? His actual accomplishments would have made him one of the principal heroes of the campaign in any event. The answer lay in the insecurity that persisted from his childhood. He could not be sure what level of approbation would be required to elect him to high office. Only by making himself the unparalleled exemplar could he be certain that he had done all he could to achieve his postwar goals.

He Credited His "Crowded Hour"

One of his detractors was a radical priest in a Labor Church in Massachusetts who claimed that "Roosevelt is the Don Quixote of this war." He contended that Roosevelt merely charged at imaginary windmills in comedic assaults in Cuba. Don Quixote, however, was brought back to his village in ridicule. Roosevelt returned to New York City as the national hero.[7]

He traveled at a fast pace in 1898. He was assistant secretary of the navy in April, a Rough Rider in Texas in May, a leader of the attack at Las Guasimas in June, and star of the Santiago campaign in July. By August, he was trying to get out of the army as fast as he had managed to get in. He was mustered out with the rest of the Rough

Riders in September and notified of his nomination as governor of the state of New York in October. In November he was elected governor.

When he became president of the United States in 1901, he credited his elongated "crowded hour" at San Juan as the catalyst. He took his later triumphs more casually, although some were of worldwide significance. He favored the consummation of his adolescent daydream above the mature attainments of his unique political career.

Notes

Abbreviations

LC   Library of Congress
NA   National Archives
TR   Theodore Roosevelt
TRC   Theodore Roosevelt Collection, Houghton Library, Harvard University, Cambridge, Mass.
TRPP   Theodore Roosevelt Presidential Papers, Library of Congress, Washington, D.C.

Chapter 1. The Beginning

1. Dixon Wechter, *The Hero in America* (New York: Charles Scribner's Sons, 1941), 11, 13, 373.

Chapter 2. The Cowboy Cavalry

1. Otto L. Sues, *Grigsby's Cowboys: Third United States Volunteer Cavalry, Spanish-American War* (Salem, S.D.: James E. Patten, 1900), 2, 4, 5.
2. William Draper Lewis, *The Life of Theodore Roosevelt* (N.p.: United Publishers, 1919), 135.
3. Ferdinand C. Iglehart, *Theodore Roosevelt: The Man as I Knew Him* (New York: Christian Herald, 1919), 123.
4. Theodore Roosevelt, *An Autobiography* (New York: Macmillan Co., 1913), 238.
5. Hermann Hagedorn, *Leonard Wood: A Biography* (New York: Harper and Brothers, 1931), 30.
6. Ibid.
7. Ibid., 138.
8. Ibid., 141.
9. James Brough, *Princess Alice: A Biography of Alice Roosevelt Longworth* (Boston: Little, Brown, and Co., 1975), 90.
10. Hagedorn, *Leonard Wood: A Biography,* 141; Clifford P. Westermeier, *Who Rush to Glory* (Caldwell, Id.: Caxton Printers, 1958), 32.

11. *New York Herald,* Apr. 26, 1898.
12. William Draper Lewis, *Life of TR,* 135.
13. Gerald Langford, *The Richard Harding Davis Years* (New York: Holt, Rinehart and Winston, 1961), 103.
14. Charles Belmont Davis, ed., *The Adventures and Letters of Richard Harding Davis* (New York: Charles Scribner's Sons, 1917), 227.
15. Mark Sullivan, *Our Times* (New York: Charles Scribner's Sons, 1927), 2:232.
16. *Harper's Weekly,* May 7, 1898, p. 434.
17. *New York Herald,* Apr. 26, 1898.
18. *New York Times,* Apr. 28, 1898.
19. Letter from TR to W. A. Wadsworth, Apr. 25, 1898, in TRPP.
20. Arthur Wallace Dunn, *From Harrison to Harding* (New York: G. P. Putnam's Sons, 1922), 261.
21. Lawrence Shaw Mayo, ed., *America of Yesterday* (Boston: Atlantic Monthly Press, 1923), 186.
22. Henry F. Pringle, *Theodore Roosevelt: A Biography* (New York: Harcourt, Brace and Co., 1931), 181.
23. John A. Garraty, *Henry Cabot Lodge* (New York: Alfred A. Knopf, 1953), 193.
24. Clifford P. Westermeier, "Teddy's Terrors: The New Mexican Volunteers of 1898," *New Mexico Historical Review* 27 (Apr. 1952): 107–36.
25. *Albuquerque (N.M.) Morning Democrat,* Apr. 28, 1898.
26. Eric Fisher Wood, *Leonard Wood: Conservator of Americanism* (New York: George H. Doran Co., 1920), 51; Hagedorn, *Leonard Wood: A Biography,* 145.
27. Gregory Mason, *Remember the* Maine (New York: Henry Holt and Co., 1939), 149.
28. Westermeier, "Teddy's Terrors," 117.
29. John G. Holme, *The Life of Leonard Wood* (Garden City, N.Y.: Doubleday, Page and Co., 1920), 50.
30. Ibid., 45.
31. R. A. Alger, *The Spanish-American War* (New York: Harper and Brothers, 1901), 13; Holme, *Life of Leonard Wood,* 45.
32. Hagedorn, *Leonard Wood: A Biography,* 145.
33. Eric Fisher Wood, *Leonard Wood: Conservator,* 72; *New York Herald,* May 3, 1898.
34. Hagedorn, *Leonard Wood: A Biography,* 145.
35. Letter from Frederick A. Stokes to TR, May 7, 1898, TRPP.
36. Westermeier, *Who Rush to Glory,* 34.
37. Wechter, *Hero in America,* 378; *New York Times,* May 1, 1898.
38. Westermeier, "Teddy's Terrors," 117.
39. Ibid.; *New York Herald,* Apr. 1, 1898.
40. Chris Emmett, *In the Path of Events* (Waco, Tex.: Jones and Morrison, 1959), 75.
41. Charles Herner, *The Arizona Rough Riders* (Tucson: University of Arizona Press, 1970), 42.
42. Henry F. Keenan, *The Conflict with Spain* (Philadelphia: P. W. Ziegler and Co., 1898), 94.
43. *New York Herald,* May 6, 1898.

44. Emmett, *In the Path of Events,* 75.
45. Tom Hall, *The Fun and Fighting of the Rough Riders* (New York: Frederick A. Stokes Co., 1899), 13.
46. William Draper Lewis, *Life of TR,* 135.
47. *New York Herald,* May 6, 1898.
48. *New York Herald,* May 7, 1898.
49. Ibid.
50. Hagedorn, *Leonard Wood: A Biography,* 145; *New York Times,* Apr. 1, 1898; Westermeier, "Teddy's Terrors," 117.
51. Emmett, *In the Path of Events,* 75.
52. *New York Times,* Apr. 3, 1898; Elting E. Morison, ed., *The Letters of Theodore Roosevelt* (Cambridge, Mass.: Harvard University Press, 1951), 2:829.
53. Thomas Beer, *Hanna* (New York: Alfred A. Knopf, 1929), 195.
54. Mayo, *America of Yesterday,* 188.
55. Lawrence F. Abbott, *Impressions of Theodore Roosevelt* (New York: Doubleday, Page and Co., 1919), 211.
56. *New York Herald,* May 7, 1898; *New York Times,* May 11, 1898.
57. Anna Roosevelt Cowles, ed., *Letters from Theodore Roosevelt to Anna Roosevelt Cowles* (New York: Charles Scribner's Sons, 1924), 213.
58. Dunn, *From Harrison to Harding,* 265.
59. Ernest R. May, *Imperial Democracy* (New York: Harcourt, Brace and World, 1961), 220; Julius W. Pratt, *Expansionists of 1898* (Baltimore, Md.: Johns Hopkins University Press, 1936), 254; H. H. Kohlsaat, *From McKinley to Harding* (New York: Charles Scribner's Sons, 1923), 326; George Clarke Musgrave, *Under Three Flags in Cuba* (Boston: Little, Brown, and Co., 1899), 251.
60. Margaret Leech, *In the Days of McKinley* (New York: Harper and Brothers, 1959), 215.
61. TR to William Wingate Sewall, May 4, 1898, TRPP. Also E. E. Morison, *Letters of TR,* 2:823.
62. *New York Herald,* May 3, 1898.
63. Walter Millis, *The Martial Spirit* (Cambridge, Mass.: Literary Guild of America, 1931), 197.
64. Theodore Roosevelt, Diary of the Spanish-American War, May 12, 1898, TRC; *New York Times,* May 12, 1898.
65. E. E. Morison, *Letters of TR,* 2:1216.
66. Mayo, *America of Yesterday,* 198.
67. Margaret Long, ed., *The Journal of John D. Long* (Rindge, N.H.: Richard R. Smith Publishers, 1956), 225.

Chapter 3. Looking Back at "Teedie"

1. G. Edward White, *The Eastern Establishment and the Western Experience* (New Haven, Conn.: Yale University Press, 1968), 61.
2. Karl Schriftgiesser, *The Amazing Roosevelt Family* (New York: Wilfred Funk, 1942), ix.
3. Lincoln Steffens, *The Autobiography of Lincoln Steffens* (New York: Harcourt, Brace and Co., 1931), 349; Noel F. Busch, *T. R.: The Story of Roosevelt and His Influence on Our Times* (New York: Reynal and Co., 1963), 14.

4. Carleton Putnam, *Theodore Roosevelt* (New York: Charles Scribner's Sons, 1958), 1:1; James Morgan, *Theodore Roosevelt the Boy and the Man* (New York: Macmillan Co., 1907), 2; David McCullough, *Mornings on Horseback* (New York: Simon and Schuster, 1981), 39.
5. McCullough, *Mornings on Horseback*, 53.
6. Carleton Putnam, *Theodore Roosevelt*, 47.
7. Ibid., 123.
8. Ibid., 25.
9. McCullough, *Mornings on Horseback*, 35.
10. Jack Franklin Leach, *Conscription in the United States* (Rutland, Vt.: Charles E. Tuttle Publishing, 1952), 185.
11. Eugene Converse Murdock, *Patriotism Limited* (Kent, Ohio: Kent State University Press, 1967), 18.
12. McCullough, *Mornings on Horseback*, 57.

Chapter 4. The Making of a Soldier

1. Virgil Carrington Jones, *Roosevelt's Rough Riders* (Garden City, N.Y.: Doubleday and Co., 1971), 35.
2. Edmund Morris, *The Rise of Theodore Roosevelt* (New York: Coward, McCann and Geoghegan, 1979), 444.
3. E. E. Morison, *Letters of TR*, 1:501.
4. Ibid., 436.
5. *Life*, Oct. 13, 1898, p. 284.
6. Emmett, *In the Path of Events*, 78.
7. Ibid.
8. Bradley Gilman, *Roosevelt the Happy Warrior* (Boston: Little, Brown, and Co., 1921), 145.
9. Hall, *Fun and Fighting*, 26.
10. A. C. M. Azoy, *Charge! The Story of the Battle of San Juan Hill* (New York: Longmans, Green and Co., 1961), 52.
11. Hall, *Fun and Fighting*, 31.
12. Emmett, *In the Path of Events*, 102.
13. Ibid., 88.
14. Hagedorn, *Leonard Wood: A Biography*, 145.
15. Emmett, *In the Path of Events*, 94.
16. Ibid., 81.
17. Hall, *Fun and Fighting*, 39.
18. Emmett, *In the Path of Events*, 104.
19. Ibid.
20. John C. Rayburn, "The Rough Riders in San Antonio, 1898," *Arizona and the West* 3, no. 2 (Summer 1961): 119.
21. Emmett, *In the Path of Events*, 104.
22. John Bigelow, Jr., *Reminiscences of the Santiago Campaign* (New York: Harper and Brothers, 1899), 17.
23. Ibid., 16.
24. Emmett, *In the Path of Events*, 75.
25. Rayburn, "Rough Riders," 121.
26. TR to Kermit, May 26, 1898, TRC.

27. Louis J. Lang, ed., *The Autobiography of Thomas Collier* (New York: B. W. Dodge, 1910), 368.

28. Azoy, *Charge!*, 52.

29. Hagedorn, *Leonard Wood: A Biography*, 151.

30. Ibid.

31. Thomas H. Rynning, *Gun Notches* (New York: Frederick A. Stokes Co., 1931), 145.

32. Hall, *Fun and Fighting*, 39; H. B. Hening, ed., *George Curry* (Albuquerque: University of New Mexico Press, 1958), 122.

33. Hermann Hagedorn, *The Boys' Life of Theodore Roosevelt* (New York: Harper and Brothers, 1918), 152.

34. Ibid.

35. Hening, *George Curry*, 122.

36. Hagedorn, *Leonard Wood: A Biography*, 151.

37. Herner, *Arizona Rough Riders*, 45; Hall, *Fun and Fighting*, 39.

38. Hall, *Fun and Fighting*, 43.

39. Ibid., 45.

40. Keenan, *Conflict with Spain*, 95.

41. Hermann Hagedorn, *The Rough Riders* (New York: Harper and Brothers, 1927), 263.

42. Herner, *Arizona Rough Riders*, 67.

43. Emmett, *In the Path of Events*, 106; TR, Diary of War, May 19, 1898, TRC.

44. Herner, *Arizona Rough Riders*, 64. *Albuquerque (N.M.) Morning Democrat*, June 17, 1898; Emmett, *In the Path of Events*, 107.

45. *Albuquerque (N.M.) Morning Democrat*, June 17, 1898.

46. Will L. Clemens, *Theodore Roosevelt the American* (London: F. Tennyson Neely, 1899), 143.

47. Albert W. Thompson, "I Helped Raise the Rough Riders," *New Mexico Historical Review* 14, no. 3 (July 1939): 297.

48. TR, Diary of War, Apr. 20, 1898, TRC; *New York Herald*, May 16 and 25, 1898.

49. *New York Herald*, May 18, 1898.

50. Ibid., May 16, 1898.

51. Ibid., May 20, 1898.

52. Rynning, *Gun Notches*, 147.

53. G. Edward White, *Eastern Establishment*, 153.

54. Emmett, *In the Path of Events*, 83.

55. Herner, *Arizona Rough Riders*, 45.

56. *New York Herald*, May 5, 1898.

57. Emmett, *In the Path of Events*, 115; Rayburn, "Rough Riders," 127.

58. Adjutant General to Colonel Wood, memo, May 23, 1898, Military Archives, R and PO Doc. File 536595, NA.

59. *New York Herald*, May 24, 1898.

60. Ibid.

61. Henry Cabot Lodge, ed., *Selections from the Correspondence of Theodore Roosevelt and Henry Cabot Lodge* (New York: Charles Scribner's Sons, 1925), 2:300.

62. TR to McKinley, May 25, 1898, R and PO Doc. File 536595, Military Archives, NA.

63. McKinley to Secretary of War, May 30, 1898, R and PO Doc. File 536595, Military Archives, NA.
64. Secretary of War to Rough Riders, May 27, 1898, R and PO Doc. File 536595, Military Archives, NA.

Chapter 5. Looking Back at Body Building

1. William Allen White, *Masks in a Pageant* (New York: Macmillan Co., 1928), 284; Betsy James Wyeth, *The Wyeths* (Boston: Gambit, 1971), 441.
2. Jacob A. Riis, *Theodore Roosevelt the Citizen* (New York: Outlook Co., 1904), 15; George Haven Putnam, *Memories of a Publisher* (New York: G. P. Putnam's Sons, 1915), 153.
3. McCullough, *Mornings on Horseback*, 93; Carleton Putnam, *Theodore Roosevelt*, 32.
4. Henry I. Schneer, *The Asthmatic Child* (New York: Harper and Row, 1963), 93.
5. Busch, *TR: The Story*, 91.
6. Carleton Putnam, *Theodore Roosevelt*, 140; Gilman, *Roosevelt the Happy Warrior*, 25.
7. Pringle, *TR: A Biography*, 29; McCullough, *Mornings on Horseback*, 160.
8. Theodore Roosevelt, private diary, June 21, 1878, TRPP.
9. Ibid., Feb. 23, 1878; David McCullough, *Mornings on Horseback* (New York: Simon and Schuster, 1981), 204.
10. TR, private diaries, Nov. 28, 1878, and Jan. 30, 1880, TRPP; Schneer, *Asthmatic Child*, 92.
11. TR, private diary, Feb. 10, 1880, TRPP.
12. Ibid., Oct. 27, 1880.
13. Walter F. McCaleb, *Theodore Roosevelt* (New York: Albert and Charles Boni, 1931), 31.
14. Busch, *TR: The Story*, 37; J. W. Bennett, *Roosevelt and the Republic* (New York: Broadway Publishing Co., 1908), 5; William H. Berge, "The Impulse for Expansion" (Ph.D. diss., Vanderbilt University, 1969), 17.
15. Poultney Bigelow, *Seventy Summers* (New York: Longmans, Green and Co., 1925), 275.
16. Pringle, *TR: A Biography*, 65; William C. Hudson, *Random Recollections* (New York: Cupples and Leon Co., 1911), 144.
17. *New York World*, Apr. 15, 1883.
18. McCullough, *Mornings on Horseback*, 250.
19. Carleton Putnam, *Theodore Roosevelt*, 306.
20. Paul Russell Cutright, *Theodore Roosevelt the Naturalist* (New York: Harper and Brothers, 1956), 38; Carleton Putnam, *Theodore Roosevelt*, 345; Cutright, *TR the Naturalist*, 38.
21. Carleton Putnam, *Theodore Roosevelt*, 368.
22. Ibid.
23. Brough, *Princess Alice*, 30.
24. Andrew Dickson White, *Autobiography* (New York: Century Co., 1906), 201; G. Edward White, *Eastern Establishment*, 153.
25. TR, private diary, June 9, 1884, TRPP; Pringle, *TR: A Biography*, 92; Lilian Rixey, *Bamie* (New York: David McKay Co., 1963), 55.
26. McCullough, *Mornings on Horseback*, 336.

27. Pringle, *TR: A Biography*, 99.

Chapter 6. The Trip to Tampa

1. Hagedorn, *Boys' Life of TR*, 155.
2. Thompson, "I Helped Raise the Rough Riders," 290.
3. *New York Herald*, May 26, 1898.
4. Ibid.
5. Hall, *Fun and Fighting*, 28.
6. *Harper's Pictorial History of the War with Spain*, 316.
7. French Ensor Chadwick, *The Relations of the United States and Spain* (New York: Charles Scribner's Sons, 1911), 2:11.
8. Hall, *Fun and Fighting*, 65.
9. John Bigelow, Jr., *Reminiscences of the Santiago Campaign*, 27–31.
10. Hall, *Fun and Fighting*, 65.
11. Leonard Wood to Louise Wood, June 4, 1898, LC.
12. Emmett, *In the Path of Events*, 118.
13. Ibid.
14. Henry Caster, *Theodore Roosevelt and the Rough Riders* (New York: Random House, 1954), 45.
15. Jack [John] Willis, *Roosevelt in the Rough* (New York: Ives Washburn, 1931), 36, 37.
16. Keenan, *Conflict with Spain*, 96.
17. Theodore Roosevelt, *The Rough Riders* (New York: Charles Scribner's Sons, 1899), 48.
18. *New York Herald*, June 2, 1898.
19. Leonard Wood to Louise Wood, June 9, 1898, LC.
20. *Albuquerque (N.M.) Weekly News*, June 4, 1898; Royal A. Prentice, "The Rough Riders," *New Mexico Historical Review* 26, no. 4 (Oct. 1951): 266; Hall, *Fun and Fighting*, 65.
21. *New York Herald*, June 2, 1898.
22. George E. Vincent, ed., *Theodore W. Miller, Rough Rider* (Akron, Oh.: Privately printed, 1899), 82.
23. Leonard Wood, Diary, June 1, 1898, LC.
24. Hall, *Fun and Fighting*, 77.
25. TR, Diary of War, June 3, 1898, TRC; TR, *Rough Riders*, 53.
26. Westermeier, *Who Rush to Glory*, 171; Virgil Carrington Jones, *Roosevelt's Rough Riders*, 59.
27. Edmund Morris, *Rise of TR*, 628.
28. Virgil Carrington Jones, *Roosevelt's Rough Riders*, 47; Lodge, *Selections from the Correspondence*, June 6, 1898.
29. Brough, *Princess Alice*, 95.
30. Mason, *Remember the* Maine, 145.
31. TR, Diary of War, June 3, 1898, TRC; Richard Harding Davis, *The Cuban and Porto Rican Campaigns* (New York: Charles Scribner's Sons, 1898), 46.
32. Charles H. Brown, *The Correspondents' War* (New York: Charles Scribner's Sons, 1967), 207; E. E. Morison, *Letters of TR*, 2:835.
33. Joseph Bucklin Bishop, ed., *Theodore Roosevelt's Letters to His Children* (New York: Charles Scribner's Sons, 1919), 13.

34. Hall, *Fun and Fighting,* 82.
35. Bishop, *TR's Letters to His Children,* 13; John Bigelow, Jr., *Reminiscences of the Santiago Campaign,* 36.
36. George Kennan, *Campaigning in Cuba* (New York: Century Co., 1899), 35.
37. John Berryman, *Stephen Crane* (New York: William Sloane Associates, 1950), 219.
38. TR, *Rough Riders,* 54.
39. Norman Beasley, *Frank Knox, American* (Garden City, N.Y.: Doubleday, Doran and Co., 1936), 14; Burr McIntosh, *The Little I Saw of Cuba* (London: F. Tennyson Neely, 1899) 14.
40. Richard Harding Davis, *Cuban and Porto Rican,* 60.
41. Musgrave, *Under Three Flags in Cuba,* 255.
42. Sylvia Jukes Morris, *Edith Kermit Roosevelt* (New York: Coward, McCann and Geoghegan, 1980), 171.
43. Leonard Wood to Louise Wood, June 9, 1898, LC.
44. Hall, *Fun and Fighting,* 82. TR, Diary of War, June 6, 1898, TRC.
45. Emmett, *In the Path of Events,* 90.
46. Hall, *Fun and Fighting,* 92.
47. Westermeier, "Teddy's Terrors," 122; Brown, *Correspondents' War,* 212; Herner, *Arizona Rough Riders,* 79.
48. Herner, *Arizona Rough Riders,* 79.
49. Hall, *Fun and Fighting,* 55.
50. Frank Freidel, *The Splendid Little War* (New York: Bramhall House, 1958), 59.
51. Sylvia Jukes Morris, *Edith Kermit Roosevelt,* 171.

Chapter 7. Looking Back at the Westerner

1. Carleton Putnam, *Theodore Roosevelt,* 518.
2. Edmund Morris, *Rise of TR,* 331.
3. Carleton Putnam, *Theodore Roosevelt,* 518.
4. Gerald F. Roberts, "The Strenuous Life" (Department of History, Michigan State University, Lansing, 1970), 134; Carleton Putnam, *Theodore Roosevelt,* 529.
5. Carleton Putnam, *Theodore Roosevelt,* 531.
6. Wechter, *Hero in America,* 376.
7. Carleton Putnam, *Theodore Roosevelt,* 563.
8. Cowles, *Letters from TR to Anna Roosevelt Cowles,* 79.
9. Carleton Putnam, *Theodore Roosevelt,* 582.
10. Ibid.; McCaleb, *Theodore Roosevelt,* 44; Cutright, *TR the Naturalist,* 48.
11. Cutright, *TR the Naturalist,* 48.
12. Lincoln A. Lang, *Ranching with Roosevelt* (Philadelphia: J. B. Lippincott Co., 1926), 217.
13. William Roscoe Thayer, *Theodore Roosevelt: An Intimate Biography* (Boston: Houghton Mifflin Co., 1919), 69.
14. Edmund Morris, *Rise of TR,* 342; Robert Underwood Johnson, *Remembered Yesterdays* (Boston: Little, Brown, and Co., 1923), 386.
15. Carleton Putnam, *Theodore Roosevelt,* 592; Sylvia Jukes Morris, *Edith Kermit Roosevelt,* 110.
16. Edmund Morris, *Rise of TR,* 376, 377.
17. Cutright, *TR the Naturalist,* 57.

18. Willis, *Roosevelt in the Rough,* 25.
19. Ibid., 55.

Chapter 8. Starting Toward Cuba

1. Beer, *Stephen Crane,* 184.
2. Graham A. Cosmas, *An Army for Empire* (Columbus: University of Missouri Press, 1971. 2d ed., Shippensburg, Pa.: White Mane Publishing Co., 1994), 1.
3. Ibid., 36.
4. Ibid., 177.
5. Ibid., 121.
6. Arthur L. Wagner, *Report of the Santiago Campaign* (Kansas City, Mo.: Franklin Hudson Publishing Co., 1908), 21.
7. Cosmas, *Army for Empire,* 197.
8. Musgrave, *Under Three Flags in Cuba,* 255.
9. Brown, *Correspondents' War,* 230; TR, Diary of War, June 6, 1898, TRC.
10. Cosmas, *Army for Empire,* 181; Marcus F. Wright, ed., *Leslie's Official History of the Spanish-American War* (Washington, D.C.: n.p., 1899), 301.
11. Edmund Morris, *Rise of TR,* 628; Emmett, *In the Path of Events,* 122.
12. Emmett, *In the Path of Events,* 122; Hall, *Fun and Fighting,* 84.
13. Freidel, *Splendid Little War,* 59.
14. Stephen Bonsal, *The Fight for Santiago* (New York: Doubleday and McClure Co., 1899), xvi.
15. William R. Shafter, "The Capture of Santiago de Cuba," *Century Magazine* 57, nos. 80–81 (Feb. 1899): 613; Freidel, *Splendid Little War,* 59; John Black Atkins, *The War in Cuba: The Experiences of an Englishman with the United States Army* (London: Smith, Elder and Co., 1899), 63.
16. *New York Times,* June 14, 1898.
17. Freidel, *Splendid Little War,* 59.
18. David F. Trask, *The War with Spain in 1898* (New York: Macmillan Co., 1981), 185.
19. Freidel, *Splendid Little War,* 64; Frederick S. Wood, *Roosevelt as We Knew Him* (Philadelphia: John C. Winston Co., 1927), 52.
20. Hall, *Fun and Fighting,* 92.
21. Ibid.
22. TR, *Rough Riders,* 57.
23. *Leslie's Weekly,* July 7, 1898; Azoy, *Charge!,* 59.
24. Charles Johnson Post, *The Little War of Private Post* (Boston: Little, Brown, and Co., 1960), 82.
25. Hall, *Fun and Fighting,* 96.
26. Vincent, *Theodore W. Miller,* 91; Leonard Wood, Diary, June 8, 1898, LC.
27. Virgil Carrington Jones, *Roosevelt's Rough Riders,* 70.
28. TR, *Rough Riders,* 60; Azoy, *Charge!,* 60.
29. Hugh Hastings, *New York and the War with Spain* (Albany, N.Y.: Argus Co., 1903), 171.
30. Ibid., 197.
31. Leonard Wood, Diary, June 8, 1898, LC.
32. Grenville M. Dodge Commission, *Report of Commission Appointed by the President to Investigate the Conduct of the War Department in the War with*

Spain, 56th Cong., 1st Sess., Sen. Doc. no. 221 (Washington, D.C.: U.S. Government Printing Office, 1900), 8:525.

33. Hall, *Fun and Fighting,* 96; *Albuquerque (N.M.) Morning Democrat,* June 17, 1898.

34. Leonard Wood to Louise Wood, June 9, 1898, LC.

35. *New York Times,* June 15, 1898.

36. Ibid.

37. Roosevelt to Ted, June 10, 1898, TRC.

38. *New York Times,* June 15, 1898.

39. John D. Miley, *In Cuba with Shafter* (New York: Charles Scribner's Sons, 1899), 32.

40. *New York Times,* June 10, 1898.

41. Hastings, *New York and the War,* 198; E. Ranson, "British Military and Naval Observers in the Spanish-American War," *Journal of American Studies* (Great Britain) 3, no. 1 (July 1969): 33–56; A. D. Webb, "Arizonans in the Spanish-American War," *Arizona Historical Review* (Jan. 1929): 50–68.

42. *New York Herald,* June 12, 1898; Miley, *In Cuba with Shafter,* 32.

43. Allan Keller, *The Spanish-American War* (New York: Hawthorne Books, 1969), 115.

44. Hastings, *New York and the War,* 203; John Bigelow, Jr., *Reminiscences of the Santiago Campaign,* 74.

45. Hastings, *New York and the War,* 203.

46. *Albuquerque (N.M.) Morning Democrat,* July 22, 1898.

47. Hall, *Fun and Fighting,* 100.

48. Ibid., 98; *Albuquerque (N.M.) Morning Democrat,* July 22, 1898; Trask, *War with Spain,* 195.

49. F. Allen McCurdy and J. Kirk McCurdy, *Letters from Two Rough Riders* (New York: F. Tennyson Neely, 1902), 2.

50. TR, Diary of War, June 11, 1898, TRC.

51. Sylvia Jukes Morris, *Edith Kermit Roosevelt,* 171; *New York Herald,* June 19, 1898.

52. *Harper's Weekly,* June 11, 1898.

53. Azoy, *Charge!,* 62; Vincent, *Theodore W. Miller,* 103; Post, *Little War,* 84.

54. *New York Times,* June 10, 1898; Herner, *Arizona Rough Riders,* 85.

55. Caster, *TR and the Rough Riders,* 90; *Albuquerque (N.M.) Morning Democrat,* June 17, 1898.

56. Edward Marshall, *The Story of the Rough Riders* (New York: G. W. Dillingham Co., 1899), 61.

57. Vincent, *Theodore W. Miller,* 109.

58. E. E. Morison, *Letters of TR,* 2:843.

59. *Albuquerque (N.M.) Weekly News,* July 4, 1898.

60. *New York Times,* June 15, 1898.

61. Vincent, *Theodore W. Miller,* 101; McIntosh, *The Little I Saw of Cuba,* 42.

62. *New York Times,* June 15, 1898.

63. *New York Herald,* June 13, 1898; *New York Times,* June 17, 1898.

Chapter 9. Looking Back at the Uncivil Servant

1. Garraty, *Henry Cabot Lodge,* 103; Lodge, *Selections from the Correspondence,* 74.

2. Garraty, *Henry Cabot Lodge*, 103.
3. Iglehart, *Theodore Roosevelt*, 100.
4. Garraty, *Henry Cabot Lodge*, 103; Iglehart, *Theodore Roosevelt*, 100.
5. John M. Blum, *The National Experience* (New York: Harcourt, Brace, and World, 1963), 465.
6. William Draper Lewis, *Life of TR*, viii; McCaleb, *Theodore Roosevelt*, 51; Edmund Morris, *Rise of TR*, 400.
7. Gilman, *Roosevelt the Happy Warrior*, 97.
8. Cowles, *Letters from TR to Anna Roosevelt Cowles*, 104; Lodge, *Selections from the Correspondence*, 79; E. E. Morison, *Letters of TR*, 1:200.
9. Cowles, *Letters from TR to Anna Roosevelt Cowles*, 126.
10. Ibid., 299.
11. William Roscoe Thayer, *The Life and Letters of John Hay* (Boston: Houghton Mifflin Co., 1929), 333.
12. William Henry Harbaugh, *Power and Responsibility* (New York: Farrar, Straus and Cudahy, 1961), 81; Bennett, *Roosevelt and the Republic*, 51; Busch, *TR: The Story*, 95.
13. Hermann Hagedorn, *The Roosevelt Family of Sagamore Hill* (New York: Macmillan, 1954), 44.
14. Harbaugh, *Power and Responsibility*, 81; James Morgan, *Theodore Roosevelt Boy and Man*, 89.
15. Thayer, *TR: Intimate Biography*, 103; Lodge, *Selections from the Correspondence*, 148.
16. Cowles, *Letters from TR to Anna Roosevelt Cowles*, 158.
17. Lodge, *Selections from the Correspondence*, 181.
18. McCaleb, *Theodore Roosevelt*, 63; Lodge, *Selections from the Correspondence*, 179.
19. Steffens, *Autobiography*, 257, 275.
20. Matthew Josephson, *The President Makers* (New York: Harcourt, Brace and Co., 1940), 53; McCaleb, *Theodore Roosevelt*, 63; Pringle, *TR: A Biography*, 132.

Chapter 10. Landing at Daiquiri

1. Leonard Wood to Louise Wood, June 9, 1898, LC.
2. TR, *Rough Riders*, 67.
3. Vincent, *Theodore W. Miller*, 103; *New York Times*, June 16, 1898; Leonard Wood to Louise Wood, June 15, 1898, LC.
4. TR, *Rough Riders*, 64; Hall, *Fun and Fighting*, 100.
5. Hall, *Fun and Fighting* 103; Nelson A. Miles, *Annual Report of the War Department for the Fiscal Year Ending June 30, 1898: Report of the Major-General Commanding the Army*, 55th Cong., 3rd Sess. (1898), House Doc. no. 2. (Washington, D.C.: U.S. Government Printing Office, 1898), 663; Herner, *Arizona Rough Riders*, 87.
6. TR to Kermit, June 10, 1898, TRC; Freidel, *Splendid Little War*, 75.
7. Vincent, *Theodore W. Miller*, 103.
8. Hall, *Fun and Fighting*, 100; Post, *Little War*, 98.
9. Hall, *Fun and Fighting*, 103.
10. TR, Diary of War, June 16, 1898, TRC.
11. Leonard Wood to Louise Wood, June 20, 1898, LC.

12. Ranson, "British Military," 40; John Black Atkins, *War in Cuba,* 76.
13. Musgrave, *Under Three Flags in Cuba,* 263; Edward Marshall, *Story of the Rough Riders,* 61.
14. Prentice, "Rough Riders," 275.
15. Leonard Wood, Diary, June 21, 1898, LC.
16. Shafter, "Capture of Santiago de Cuba," 614.
17. Ranson, "British Military," 43.
18. Roosevelt to Ted, June 20, 1898, TRC; R. W. Stallman, *Stephen Crane* (New York: George Braziller, 1969), 361.
19. Azoy, *Charge!,* 63.
20. Roosevelt to Ted, June 20, 1898, TRC; Herner, *Arizona Rough Riders,* 90.
21. *The Chicago Record's War Stories* (Chicago: Chicago Record, 1898), 97.
22. Ibid., 98.
23. Vincent, *Theodore W. Miller,* 114; *New York Times,* June 24, 1898; "The Spanish-American War Survey," U.S. Army Military History Institute, Carlisle Barracks, Pa., Royal A. Prentice, "The Cuban Campaign," in "Scrapbook: The Rough Riders Look Back," ch. 4, p. 52.
24. *New York Times,* June 24, 1898; Caspar Whitney, "The Santiago Campaign," *Harper's Monthly* 97 (Oct. 1898): 799.
25. Elbridge S. Brooks, *The Story of Our War with Spain* (Boston: Lothrop Publishing Co., 1899), 156; Alger, *Spanish-American War,* 101.
26. Brooks, *Story of Our War,* 156; *New York Times,* June 24, 1898.
27. Edward Marshall, *Story of the Rough Riders,* 66; Whitney, "Santiago Campaign," 799.
28. *New York Times,* June 24, 1898.
29. Musgrave, *Under Three Flags in Cuba,* 271; Brooks, *Story of Our War,* 158.
30. *New York Times,* June 24, 1898.
31. Herner, *Arizona Rough Riders,* 93.
32. *Leslie's Weekly,* June 24, 1898.
33. Herner, *Arizona Rough Riders,* 93; Thomas J. Vivian, *The Fall of Santiago* (New York: R. F. Fenno and Co., 1898), 92.
34. Hall, *Fun and Fighting,* 103.
35. Dodge, *Report of Commission,* 1:224.
36. Ibid., 222.
37. Chadwick, *Relations of the U.S. and Spain,* 20.
38. Theodore Roosevelt, *An Autobiography* (New York: Macmillan, 1913), 255.
39. Dodge, *Report of Commission,* 5:2260.
40. Hall, *Fun and Fighting,* 111; TR, *Autobiography,* 255.
41. "Spanish-American War Survey," Royal A. Prentice, "Scrapbook: A Rough Rider Looks Back," ch. 4, p. 52.
42. Brooks, *Story of Our War,* 161.
43. *New York Herald,* June 25, 1898.
44. TR, *Rough Riders,* 69.
45. Millis, *Martial Spirit,* 266.
46. Hall, *Fun and Fighting,* 113.
47. *New York Herald,* June 25, 1898.
48. Stallman, *Stephen Crane,* 377.
49. *New York Herald,* June 25, 1898.

50. Freidel, *Splendid Little War,* 75.
51. E. J. McClernand, "The Santiago Campaign," *U.S. Infantry Journal* 21, no. 3 (Sept. 1922): 280.
52. Trask, *War with Spain,* 212; TR, *Rough Riders,* 75.
53. Shafter, "Capture of Santiago de Cuba," 618.
54. John Black Atkins, *War in Cuba,* 94; Philip S. Foner, *The Spanish-Cuban-American War* (New York: Monthly Review Press, 1972), 355.
55. Ranson, "British Military," 42.
56. James A. Moss, *Memories of the Campaign of Santiago* (San Francisco: Mysell-Rollins Co., 1899), 174.
57. Alger, *Spanish-American War,* 102; Millis, *Martial Spirit,* 266.
58. TR, *Rough Riders,* 75.
59. Stallman, *Stephen Crane,* 377; Caster, *TR and the Rough Riders,* 106.
60. McClernand, "Santiago Campaign," 280.
61. Hall, *Fun and Fighting,* 114.
62. Vivian, *Fall of Santiago,* 132.
63. Ibid., 92.
64. Mason, *Remember the Maine,* 161.

Chapter 11. Looking Back at Roosevelt's Navy

1. Mrs. Bellamy Storer, "How Theodore Roosevelt Was Appointed Assistant Secretary of the Navy," *Harper's Weekly,* June 1, 1912, p. 8; Lodge, *Selections from the Correspondence,* 240.
2. H. Wayne Morgan, *William McKinley and His Administration* (Syracuse, N.Y.: Syracuse University Press, 1963), 250; William Draper Lewis, *Life of TR,* xii; Lodge, *Selections from the Correspondence,* 252.
3. Thayer, *Life and Letters of John Hay,* 334.
4. Lincoln A. Lang, *Ranching with Roosevelt,* 359.
5. E. E. Morison, *Letters of TR,* 1:621; Philip Dunne, *Mr. Dooley Remembers* (Boston: Little, Brown, and Co., 1963), 192.
6. John A. S. Grenville, "American Naval Preparations for War with Spain, 1896–1898," *Journal of American Studies* 2, no. 1 (1968): 33–47; E. E. Morison, *Letters of TR,* 1:681.
7. Josephson, *President Makers,* 71.
8. Cowles, *Letters from TR to Anna Roosevelt Cowles,* 208; Lodge, *Selections from the Correspondence,* 276.
9. E. E. Morison, *Letters of TR,* 1:758.
10. Joseph Bucklin Bishop, *Theodore Roosevelt and His Time* (New York: Charles Scribner's Sons, 1920), 101.
11. Ibid., 85.
12. Howard K. Beale, *Theodore Roosevelt and the Rise of America to World Power* (Baltimore, Md.: Johns Hopkins University Press, 1956), 62.
13. Stephen Lorant, *The Life and Times of Theodore Roosevelt* (Garden City, N.Y.: Doubleday and Co., 1959), 283.
14. Mayo, *America of Yesterday,* 169; Garraty, *Henry Cabot Lodge,* 185; E. E. Morison, *Letters of TR,* 1:784.
15. Mayo, *America of Yesterday,* 169; Walter LaFeber, *The New Empire* (Ithaca, N.Y.: Cornell University Press, 1963), 328.

16. Mayo, *America of Yesterday,* 169.
17. *Life,* Mar. 24, 1898.
18. Roosevelt to William Astor Chanler, Mar. 30, 1898, TRC.
19. E. E. Morison, *Letters of TR,* 2:801.
20. Harbaugh, *Power and Responsibility,* 103.

Chapter 12. March to Siboney

1. Leonard Wood, "Las Guasimas," *Century Magazine* (June 1898): 5.
2. "Spanish-American War Survey," Royal A. Prentice, "Scrapbook: A Rough Rider Looks Back," ch. 4, p. 53.
3. Hall, *Fun and Fighting,* 124.
4. Webb, "Arizonans in the Spanish-American War," 59.
5. Hall, *Fun and Fighting,* 125.
6. Private St. Louis [pseud.], *Forty Years After* (Boston: N.p., 1939), 34; Marcus F. Wright, ed., *The Official and Pictorial Record of the War with Spain* (n.p., 1902), 207.
7. Dunn, *From Harrison to Harding,* 241; Trask, *War with Spain,* 219.
8. Dunn, *From Harrison to Harding,* 241.
9. TR, *Rough Riders,* 73.
10. Dodge, *Report of Commission,* 7:3251.
11. Bonsal, *Fight for Santiago,* 86; John P. Dyer, *"Fightin' Joe" Wheeler* (Baton Rouge: Louisiana State University Press, 1941), 347.
12. Bonsal, *Fight for Santiago,* 86.
13. Ibid.
14. Ibid., 88.
15. Dyer, *"Fightin' Joe" Wheeler,* 347.
16. Alger, *Spanish-American War,* 102.
17. Hall, *Fun and Fighting,* 131; Dodge, *Report of Commission,* 1:225.
18. Whitney, "Santiago Campaign," 581.
19. Dodge, *Report of the Commission,* 1:224.
20. Herner, *Arizona Rough Riders,* 95.
21. Edward Marshall, *Story of the Rough Riders,* 71.
22. Ibid.
23. Virgil Carrington Jones, *Roosevelt's Rough Riders,* 110.
24. Dodge, *Report of Commission,* 5:2557.
25. Ibid., 6:2565.
26. Ibid., 5:2558.
27. Joseph Wheeler, *The Santiago Campaign* (Philadelphia: Drexel Biddle, 1899), 16.
28. Matthew Forney Steele, *American Campaigns* (Washington, D.C.: United States Infantry Association, 1935), 599; Stallman, *Stephen Crane,* 379.
29. Wheeler, *Santiago Campaign,* 16.
30. Leonard Wood, "Las Guasimas," 8.
31. Vivian, *Fall of Santiago,* 95; Wagner, *Report of the Santiago Campaign,* 39.
32. Leonard Wood, "Las Guasimas," 8; Prentice, "Rough Riders," 269.
33. "Spanish-American War Survey," Royal A. Prentice, "Scrapbook: A Rough Rider Looks Back," ch. 4, p. 54.
34. Edward Marshall, *Story of the Rough Riders,* 80.

35. Leonard Wood, "Las Guasimas," 9.
36. "Spanish-American War Survey," Royal A. Prentice, "Scrapbook: A Rough Rider Looks Back," ch. 4, p. 54; Hall, *Fun and Fighting,* 125.
37. Stallman, *Stephen Crane,* 379.
38. Webb, "Arizonans in the Spanish-American War," 59.
39. Dodge, *Report of Commission,* 5:2260.
40. Virgil Carrington Jones, *Roosevelt's Rough Riders,* 110.
41. Dodge, *Report of Commission,* 1:225.
42. Ibid.
43. Wheeler, *Santiago Campaign,* 16.
44. Dodge, *Report of Commission,* 7:3251.
45. Wagner, *Report of the Santiago Campaign,* 51.
46. Caster, *TR and the Rough Riders,* 106; Leonard Wood, "Las Guasimas," 9.
47. "Spanish-American War Survey," Royal A. Prentice, "Scrapbook: A Rough Rider Looks Back," ch. 4, p. 54.
48. Leonard Wood, Diary, June 22, 1898, LC.
49. Leonard Wood, "Las Guasimas," 10.
50. Ibid.
51. Hall, *Fun and Fighting,* 128; Virgil Carrington Jones, *Roosevelt's Rough Riders,* 113.
52. Leonard Wood, "Las Guasimas," 11.
53. Ibid., 12.
54. Dodge, *Report of Commission,* 5:2558.

Chapter 13. March to Las Guasimas

1. Bonsal, *Fight for Santiago,* 88.
2. Ibid.
3. Ibid.
4. McIntosh, *The Little I Saw of Cuba,* 82.
5. Jack Cameron Dierks, *A Leap to Arms* (Philadelphia: J. B. Lippincott Co., 1970), 84.
6. *Chicago Record's War Stories,* 64.
7. Azoy, *Charge!,* 82.
8. Leonard Wood, "Las Guasimas," 15.
9. Brooks, *Story of Our War,* 169.
10. Charles Belmont Davis, *Adventures and Letters of Richard Harding Davis,* 249.
11. *Hero Tales of the American Soldier and Sailor* (N.p.: A. Holloway, 1899), 82.
12. "Spanish-American War Survey," Royal A. Prentice, "Scrapbook: A Rough Rider Looks Back," ch. 4, p. 54.
13. Ibid.
14. Edward Marshall, *Story of the Rough Riders,* 90.
15. *Chicago Record's War Stories,* 64.
16. Stallman, *Stephen Crane,* 379.
17. *Chicago Record's War Stories,* 64.
18. Dodge, *Report of Commission,* 5:2558.
19. Bonsal, *Fight for Santiago,* 88; Dodge, *Report of Commission,* 5:2559.
20. S. T. Norvell, "Las Guasimas," *Journal of the U.S. Cavalry Association* 12, no. 44 (Dec. 1899): 351; Webb, "Arizonans in the Spanish-American War," 60.

21. Leonard Wood, "Las Guasimas," 14.
22. Herschel V. Cashin, *Under Fire with the Tenth Cavalry* (New York: F. Tennyson Neely, 1899), 162.
23. Hagedorn, *Rough Riders,* 300.
24. Norvell, "Las Guasimas," 351.
25. Stallman, *Stephen Crane,* 381.
26. Edward Marshall, *Story of the Rough Riders,* 91.
27. "Spanish-American War Survey," Royal A. Prentice, "Scrapbook: A Rough Rider Looks Back," ch. 4, p. 54.
28. *Chicago Record's War Stories,* 66.
29. Ibid.
30. Dodge, *Report of Commission,* 5:2259.
31. Edward Marshall, *Story of the Rough Riders,* 92.
32. Leonard Wood, "Las Guasimas," 15.
33. *Chicago Record's War Stories,* 66.
34. Richard Harding Davis, *Cuban and Porto Rican,* 138.
35. Azoy, *Charge!,* 84.
36. Hall, *Fun and Fighting,* 131; *Harper's Weekly,* July 30, 1898, 750.
37. Edward Marshall, *Story of the Rough Riders,* 92.
38. Brown, *Correspondents' War,* 313.
39. Bonsal, *Fight for Santiago,* 91; Richard Harding Davis, *Cuban and Porto Rican,* 138.
40. Murat Halstead, *The Life of Theodore Roosevelt* (Chicago: Saalfield Publishing Co., 1902), 95.
41. Edward Marshall, *Story of the Rough Riders,* 93.
42. *Harper's Weekly,* July 30, 1898, 750; TR, *Rough Riders,* 85.
43. Hall, *Fun and Fighting,* 131.
44. Richard Harding Davis, *Cuban and Porto Rican,* 140; Edward Marshall, "The Santiago Campaign: Some Episodes: A Wounded Correspondent's Recollections of Guasimas," *Scribner's Magazine* 24 (Sept. 1898): 273–77; Edward Marshall, *Story of the Rough Riders,* 94.
45. Brown, *Correspondents' War,* 315.
46. Dodge, *Report of Commission,* 5:2559.
47. Azoy, *Charge!,* 84.
48. Edward Marshall, *Story of the Rough Riders,* 94.
49. Alger, *Spanish-American War,* 107.
50. Bonsal, *Fight for Santiago,* 88.
51. Herbert H. Sargent, *The Campaign of Santiago de Cuba* (Chicago: A. C. McClurg and Co., 1907), 2:53.
52. *Chicago Record's War Stories,* 67.
53. Ibid.; Charles Belmont Davis, *Adventures and Letters of Richard Harding Davis,* 249.

Chapter 14. Gallant Blunder

1. R. W. Stallman and E. R. Hageman, *The War Dispatches of Stephen Crane* (New York: New York University Press, 1964), 154, 159; Stallman, *Stephen Crane,* 386.
2. *The Spanish-American War: The Events of the War Described by Eye Wit-*

nesses (Chicago: Herbert S. Stone and Co., 1899), 102; Leonard Wood, "Las Guasimas," 12.

3. Leonard Wood, "Las Guasimas," 26.
4. *Spanish-American War Described by Eye Witnesses,* 102.
5. *Hero Tales of the American Soldier and Sailor,* 82.
6. Edward Marshall, *Story of the Rough Riders,* 101; Hall, *Fun and Fighting,* 131.
7. *New York Herald,* June 26, 1898.
8. Leonard Wood, "Las Guasimas," 5.
9. TR, *Autobiography,* 246.
10. Theodore Roosevelt, *Address and Papers Taken from the Proceedings of the Convention of the National Guard Association of the State of New York, Feb. 8, 1900* (Albany, N.Y.: Weed-Parsons Printing Co., 1900); TR, *Rough Riders,* 94.
11. Edward Marshall, *Story of the Rough Riders,* 101.
12. Azoy, *Charge!,* 92.
13. Webb, "Arizonans in Spanish-American War," 60.
14. Azoy, *Charge!,* 92.
15. Vivian, *Fall of Santiago,* 107; Webb, "Arizonans in Spanish-America War," 61.
16. Whitney, "Santiago Campaign," 801.
17. Corinne Roosevelt Robinson, *My Brother, Theodore Roosevelt* (New York: Charles Scribner's Sons, 1921), 169.
18. Beasley, *Frank Knox, American,* 18; Edward S. Ellis, *From the Ranch to the White House* (Chicago: Albert Whitman and Co., 1906), 114.
19. Richard Harding Davis, *Cuban and Porto Rican,* 166.
20. Freidel, *Splendid Little War,* 107.
21. James Rankin Young and J. Hampton Moore, eds., *Reminiscences and Thrilling Stories of the War by Returned Heroes* (Chicago: Providence Publishing Co., 1899), 191.
22. Edward Marshall, *Story of the Rough Riders,* 118; TR, *Rough Riders,* 89.
23. Stallman and Hageman, *War Dispatches of Stephen Crane,* 159.
24. Dodge, *Report of Commission,* 5:2261.
25. Freidel, *Splendid Little War,* 103.
26. Bonsal, *Fight for Santiago,* 93.
27. Leonard Wood, "Las Guasimas," 11.
28. Westermeier, "Teddy's Terrors," 126.
29. Leonard Wood, "Las Guasimas," 13.
30. *New York Herald,* June 25, 1898.
31. Azoy, *Charge!,* 91.
32. Leonard Wood, "Las Guasimas," 22.
33. Ibid.
34. Edward Marshall, "Santiago Campaign," 273.
35. Brown, *Correspondents' War,* 319.
36. *Albuquerque (N.M.) Morning Democrat,* Aug. 27, 1898; *Hero Tales of the American Soldier and Sailor,* 315.
37. *Hero Tales of the American Soldier and Sailor,* 315.
38. Virgil Carrington Jones, *Roosevelt's Rough Riders,* 128.
39. Leonard Wood, "Las Guasimas," 23, 24.
40. *Chicago Record's War Stories,* 68.

41. Richard Harding Davis, *Cuban and Porto Rican,* 164.
42. TR, *Autobiography,* 256.
43. Pringle, *TR: A Biography,* 184.
44. Richard Harding Davis, *Cuban and Porto Rican,* 169.
45. Dodge, *Report of Commission,* 5:2261.
46. Bonsal, *Fight for Santiago,* 93.
47. Dyer, *"Fightin' Joe" Wheeler,* 352.
48. Dodge, *Report of Commission,* 5:2262.
49. Ibid., 2261.
50. Herner, *Arizona Rough Riders,* 116.

Chapter 15. Body Count at Las Guasimas
1. *New York World,* June 25, 1898.
2. Leonard Wood to Louise Wood, June 27, 1898, LC.
3. Whitney, "Santiago Campaign," 801.
4. *New York Herald,* June 28, 1898; *New York Journal,* June 26, 1898.
5. Whitney, "Santiago Campaign," 801.
6. W. Nephew King, *The Story of the Spanish-American War* (New York: P. F. Collier and Son, 1900), 160.
7. Edmund Morris, *Rise of TR,* 646.
8. *New York World,* June 26, 1898.
9. *New York Times,* June 27, 1898; Leonard Wood, "Las Guasimas," 12.
10. Hall, *Fun and Fighting,* 141.
11. James Rankin Young and Moore, *Reminiscences and Thrilling Stories,* 191.
12. Richard Harding Davis, *Notes of a War Correspondent* (New York: Charles Scribner's Sons, 1912), 55.
13. Miley, *In Cuba with Shafter,* 82.
14. Steele, *American Campaigns,* 597; Chadwick, *Relations of the U.S. and Spain,* 71.
15. Trask, *War with Spain,* 199.
16. José Muller y Tejeiro, *Battles and Capitulation of Santiago de Cuba,* trans. U.S. Navy Department, Office of Naval Intelligence, Information from Abroad (Washington, D.C.: U.S. Government Printing Office, 1898), 43.
17. Ibid., 5 and 6.
18. Ibid., 45.
19. Ibid., 46.
20. Trask, *War with Spain,* 201.
21. Muller y Tejeiro, *Battles and Capitulation,* 47; Moss, *Memories of the Campaign,* 23f.
22. Sargent, *Campaign of Santiago de Cuba,* 2:53.
23. *New York Journal,* June 25, 1898; Sargent, *Campaign of Santiago de Cuba,* 2:69.
24. Leonard Wood, "Las Guasimas," 1.
25. Leech, *In the Days of McKinley,* 245.

Chapter 16. Preparing to Fight Again
1. *Albuquerque (N.M.) Morning Democrat,* Aug. 27, 1898.
2. Leonard Wood to Louise Wood, June 27, 1898, LC.
3. McIntosh, *The Little I Saw of Cuba,* 77.

4. E. E. Morison, *Letters of TR*, 2:844.
5. *New York Herald*, June 27, 1898.
6. *Spanish-American War Described by Eye Witnesses*, 102; Hall, *Fun and Fighting*, 161.
7. *New York Herald*, June 27, 1898.
8. Hall, *Fun and Fighting*, 162.
9. *Chicago Record's War Stories*, 99.
10. Edward Marshall, *Story of the Rough Riders*, 162.
11. *Leslie's Weekly*, Aug. 25, 1898.
12. Leonard Wood, Diary, June 25, 1898, LC.
13. Brown, *Correspondents' War*, 330; Brooks, *Story of Our War*, 179.
14. Moss, *Memories of the Campaign*, 274.
15. *Chicago Record's War Stories*, 70; *New York Journal*, June 26, 1898.
16. Charles Belmont Davis, *Adventures and Letters of Richard Harding Davis*, 254; *New York Herald*, June 27, 1898.
17. Herner, *Arizona Rough Riders*, 117; Moss, *Memories of the Campaign*, 27f.
18. McIntosh, *The Little I Saw of Cuba*, 77.
19. Leonard Wood, "Las Guasimas," 22.
20. Leonard Wood to Louise Wood, June 27, 1898, LC.
21. Alger, *Spanish-American War*, 112.
22. Richard Harding Davis, *Cuban and Porto Rican*, 132.
23. Ibid.; *New York Times*, June 30, 1898.
24. Bonsal, *Fight for Santiago*, 103.
25. Dodge, *Report of Commission*, 7:3251.
26. Beer, *Stephen Crane*, 189.
27. Charles Belmont Davis, *Adventures and Letters of Richard Harding Davis*, 254.
28. Ibid., 252.
29. Ibid.
30. Ibid.
31. Keenan, *Conflict with Spain*, 281.
32. Pringle, *TR: A Biography*, 181.
33. Virgil Carrington Jones, *Roosevelt's Rough Riders*, 118.
34. Charles Belmont Davis, *Adventures and Letters of Richard Harding Davis*, 252.
35. G. Edward White, *Eastern Establishment*, 153.
36. James Rankin Young and Moore, *Reminiscences and Thrilling Stories*, 429.
37. Kennan, *Campaigning in Cuba*, 99.
38. Lewis L. Gould, "Theodore Roosevelt and the Spanish-American War" (4 unpub. letters to President William McKinley), *Theodore Roosevelt Association Journal* (n.p., n.d.), 18.
39. Lodge, *Selections from the Correspondence*, 315.
40. *New York Times*, June 28, 1898.
41. Kennan, *Campaigning in Cuba*, 100; E. E. Morison, *Letters of TR*, 2:843.
42. Hagedorn, *Roosevelt Family*, 52.
43. Hall, *Fun and Fighting*, 164; F. Allen McCurdy and J. Kirk McCurdy, *Letters from Two Rough Riders*, 10.
44. Chadwick, *Relations of the U.S. and Spain*, 56.
45. Keller, *Spanish-American War*, 141.
46. F. Allen McCurdy and J. Kirk McCurdy, *Letters from Two Rough Riders*, 10.

47. Cosmas, *Army for Empire*, 209.
48. F. Allen McCurdy and J. Kirk McCurdy, *Letters from Two Rough Riders*, 10.
49. Freidel, *Splendid Little War*, 119.
50. John Bigelow, Jr., *Reminiscences of the Santiago Campaign*, 97.
51. Vivian, *Fall of Santiago*, 122; Charles Belmont Davis, *Adventures and Letters of Richard Harding Davis*, 252.
52. Vivian, *Fall of Santiago*, 122.
53. Musgrave, *Under Three Flags in Cuba*, 271.
54. Richard Harding Davis, *Notes of a War Correspondent*, 77; Hall, *Fun and Fighting*, 164.
55. E. E. Morison, *Letters of TR*, 2:843.
56. Dodge, *Report of Commission*, 5:2263.
57. Ibid.; Virgil Carrington Jones, *Roosevelt's Rough Riders*, 149.
58. Stallman, *Stephen Crane*, 382.

Chapter 17. March to El Poso

1. Moss, *Memories of the Campaign*, 27f.
2. Dodge, *Report of Commission*, 1:225.
3. Brooks, *Story of Our War*, 182.
4. John Dollard, *Fear in Battle* (New Haven, Conn.: Institute of Human Relations, Yale University, 1943), 58.
5. McIntosh, *The Little I Saw of Cuba*, 117.
6. Ibid.
7. Shafter, "Capture of Santiago de Cuba," 614.
8. Alger, *Spanish-American War*, 123.
9. Miley, *In Cuba with Shafter*, 98.
10. Cosmas, *Army for Empire*, 189.
11. Shafter, "Capture of Santiago de Cuba," 614.
12. Musgrave, *Under Three Flags in Cuba*, 271.
13. Steele, *American Campaigns*, 601.
14. Sargent, *Campaign of Santiago de Cuba*, 2:42.
15. Keenan, *Conflict with Spain*, 308.
16. *New York Journal*, July 1, 1898.
17. Sargent, *Campaign of Santiago de Cuba*, 2:97.
18. Ibid.
19. Henry C. McCook, *The Martial Graves of Our Fallen Heroes in Santiago de Cuba* (Philadelphia: George W. Jacobs and Co., 1899), 25.
20. *New York Times*, July 12, 1898.
21. Shafter, "Capture of Santiago de Cuba," 622.
22. Ibid.
23. John Black Atkins, *War in Cuba*, 121.
24. Wagner, *Report of the Santiago Campaign*, 84; Sargent, *Campaign of Santiago de Cuba*, 2:93.
25. Richard Harding Davis, *Notes of a War Correspondent*, 79.
26. Sargent, *Campaign of Santiago de Cuba*, 2:95.
27. Alger, *Spanish-American War*, 130.
28. Miley, *In Cuba with Shafter*, 102.
29. Sargent, *Campaign of Santiago de Cuba*, 2:95.

30. Leech, *In the Days of McKinley,* 248.
31. Ibid.
32. McClernand, "Santiago Campaign," 287.
33. Sargent, *Campaign of Santiago de Cuba,* 2:95.
34. Ibid.
35. Ibid., 2:95, 2:101.
36. Richard Harding Davis, *Cuban and Porto Rican,* 188.
37. Dodge, *Report of Commission,* 5:2263; *Harper's Weekly,* June 30, 1898.
38. Richard Harding Davis, *Cuban and Porto Rican,* 188.
39. Vincent, *Theodore W. Miller,* 132.
40. TR, *Rough Riders,* 113.
41. Virgil Carrington Jones, *Roosevelt's Rough Riders,* 163.
42. Hall, *Fun and Fighting,* 175; *New York Journal,* July 1, 1898.
43. "Spanish-American War Survey," Royal A. Prentice, "Scrapbook: A Rough Rider Looks Back," ch. 4, p. 56.
44. Hall, *Fun and Fighting,* 175.
45. *Spanish-American War Described by Eye Witnesses,* 115; *New York Herald,* July 3, 1898.
46. *Spanish-American War Described by Eye Witnesses,* 116.
47. TR, Diary of War, June 30, 1898, TRC.
48 Hall, *Fun and Fighting,* 176.
49. *Spanish-American War Described by Eye Witnesses,* 116.
50. Hall, *Fun and Fighting,* 176.
51. TR, *Rough Riders,* 115.
52. *New York Herald,* July 3, 1898.
53. Ibid.; *New York Journal,* July 1, 1898.
54. *New York Herald,* July 3, 1898.
55. Herner, *Arizona Rough Riders,* 125.
56 McClernand, "Santiago Campaign," 288.
57. Hall, *Fun and Fighting,* 176.
58. TR, *Autobiography,* 261.
59. Virgil Carrington Jones, *Roosevelt's Rough Riders,* 163.
60. TR, *Rough Riders,* 116.
61. James Rankin Young, *History of Our War with Spain* (N.p.: J. R. Jones, 1898), 511.
62. *Spanish-American War Described by Eye Witnesses,* 107.
63. Cashin, *Under Fire with the Tenth Cavalry,* 204.

Chapter 18. The Correspondents' War

1. Brown, *Correspondents' War,* vii.
2. W. A. Swanberg, *Citizen Hearst* (New York: Charles Scribner's Sons, 1961), 154.
3. James Creelman, "My Experiences at Santiago," *American Monthly Review of Reviews* 18 (1898): 542–46.
4. *New York Herald,* July 2, 1898.
5. Alger, *Spanish-American War,* 151.
6. James Creelman, *On the Great Highway* (Boston: Lathrop Publishing Co., 1901), 196.

7. Alger, *Spanish-American War,* 154.
8. Musgrave, *Under Three Flags in Cuba,* 294.
9. Trask, *War with Spain,* 225.
10. Ranson, "British Military," 33.
11. Creelman, *On the Great Highway,* 196; Creelman, "My Experiences at Santiago," 542.
12. *Harper's Weekly,* July 14, 1898, p. 722.
13. Brown, *Correspondents' War,* 341.
14. Musgrave, *Under Three Flags in Cuba,* 291.
15. Ranson, "British Military," 47, 48.
16. Post, *Little War,* 211; Musgrave, *Under Three Flags in Cuba,* 294.
17. *New York Sun,* July 15, 1898.
18. *New York Times,* July 19, 1898.
19. Trask, *War with Spain,* 233.
20. *New York Herald,* July 2, 1898.
21. *New York Times,* Aug. 13, 1898.
22. Chadwick, *Relations of the U.S. and Spain,* 71.

Chapter 19. Starting Toward San Juan

1. Hall, *Fun and Fighting,* 179.
2. Brown, *Correspondents' War,* 344.
3. Hall, *Fun and Fighting,* 179.
4. Richard Davis, *Cuban and Porto Rican Campaigns,* 196.
5. Musgrave, *Under Three Flags in Cuba,* 287.
6. McIntosh, *The Little I Saw of Cuba,* 120.
7. Ibid.
8. TR, *Rough Riders,* 267.
9. Musgrave, *Under Three Flags in Cuba,* 287.
10. Hall, *Fun and Fighting,* 179.
11. Herner, *Arizona Rough Riders,* 128.
12. Muller y Tejeiro, *Battles and Capitulation,* 57–105.
13. *New York Sun,* Aug. 3, 1898.
14. Dodge, *Report of Commission,* 5:2264.

Chapter 20. The Best of a Bad Situation

1. McClernand, "Santiago Campaign," 288.
2. Ibid., 290.
3. Alger, *Spanish-American War,* 152.
4. Dodge, *Report of Commission,* 8:469.
5. Hall, *Fun and Fighting,* 187.
6. *Prescott (Ariz.) Weekly Journal-Miner,* Dec. 14, 1898.
7. Miley, *In Cuba with Shafter,* 106.
8. Leonard Wood, Diary, July 1, 1898, LC; Bonsal, *Fight for Santiago,* 115.
9. McClernand, "Santiago Campaign," 290.
10. Brown, *Correspondents' War,* 353.
11. *New York Sun,* July 15, 1898.
12. McClernand, "Santiago Campaign," 291; Alger, *Spanish-American War,* 154.
13. Hall, *Fun and Fighting,* 187.

14. Nelson A. Miles, *Annual Report*, 370; Dodge, *Report of Commission*, 8:471.

15. Dodge, *Report of Commission*, 5:2264.

16. Alger, *Spanish-American War*, 154.

17. *Prescott (Ariz.) Weekly Journal-Miner*, Dec. 14, 1898.

18. Leonard Wood, Diary, July 1, 1898, LC.

19. Wagner, *Report of the Santiago Campaign*, 81.

20. Ripley Hitchcock, *Decisive Battles of America* (New York: Harper and Brothers, 1909), 365.

21. Hall, *Fun and Fighting*, 189.

22. Ibid.

23. Nelson A. Miles, *Annual Report*, 684.

24. Ibid., 369.

25. Ibid.

26. Richard H. Titherington, *A History of the Spanish-American War of 1898* (New York: D. Appleton and Co., 1900), 242, 243.

27. Ibid., 243.

28. Ibid., 244.

29. Ibid., 237.

30. John Black Atkins, *War in Cuba*, 121.

31. Azoy, *Charge!*, 110.

32. Rynning, *Gun Notches*, 166.

33. Webb, "Arizonans in the Spanish-American War," 64.

34. Nelson A. Miles, *Annual Report*, 686.

35. Herner, *Arizona Rough Riders*, 137.

36. Nelson A. Miles, *Annual Report*, 686.

37. Richard Harding Davis, *Cuban and Porto Rico*, 204.

38. John C. Hemment, *Cannon and Camera* (New York: D. Appleton and Co., 1898), 180.

39. Richard Harding Davis, *Cuban and Porto Rican*, 204.

40. "Spanish-American War Survey," U.S. Army Military History Institute, Carlisle Barracks, Pa., Arthur F. Cosby, "Scrapbook: A Rough Rider Looks Back," ch. 7, p. 104.

41. Stallman, *Stephen Crane*, 390.

42. Wagner, *Report of the Santiago Campaign*, 84.

43. Azoy, *Charge!*, 126.

44. E. E. Morison, *Letters of TR*, 2:852.

45. "Spanish-American War Survey," U.S. Army Military History Institute, Carlisle Barracks, Pa., Philip Hoffman, "Scrapbook: A Rough Rider Looks Back," ch. 1, p. 9.

46. Richard Harding Davis, *Notes of a War Correspondent*, 92; TR, *Autobiography*, 262.

47. Hermann Hagedorn, "Notes" (n.d.), TRC, 86.

48. Freidel, *Splendid Little War*, 157; Hall, *Fun and Fighting*, 190.

49. Edward Marshall, *Story of the Rough Riders*, 156; Hemment, *Cannon and Camera*, 180.

50. Richard Harding Davis, *Cuban and Porto Rican*, 213.

51. Hagedorn, "Notes," TRC, 11.

52. TR, *Rough Riders*, 126.

53. Eric Fisher Wood, *Leonard Wood: Conservator*, 91.
54. McClernand, "Santiago Campaign," 291.
55. *Prescott (Ariz.) Weekly Journal-Miner*, Dec. 21, 1898.
56. Bonsal, *Fight for Santiago*, 115.
57. Titherington, *History of the Spanish-American War*, 249.

Chapter 21. Making Ready to Charge

1. Post, *Little War*, 181.
2. Hall, *Fun and Fighting*, 194; TR, *Rough Riders*, 127.
3. Joseph Wheeler, "Introduction," in *Photographic History of the War with Spain* (Baltimore, Md.: R. H. Woodward Co., 1898).
4. "Spanish-American War Survey," Cosby, "A Rough Rider Looks Back," ch.7, p. 104.
5. E. E. Morison, *Letters of TR*, 2:852; McCaleb, *Theodore Roosevelt*, 81.
6. Dodge, *Report of Commission*, 5:2264.
7. Hall, *Fun and Fighting*, 189.
8. Herner, *Arizona Rough Riders*, 138.
9. J. O. Wells, *Diary of a Rough Rider* (Privately printed, 1900), 49.
10. Ibid.
11. Letter from Henry Anson Barber to TR (as president), Mar. 27, 1902, TRPP.
12. J. T. Dickman, ed., *The Santiago Campaign* (Richmond Va.: Williams Printing Co., 1927), 421.
13. Letter from Henry Anson Barber to TR (as president), Mar. 27, 1902, TRPP.
14. Titherington, *History of the Spanish-American War*, 249.
15. *Prescott (Ariz.) Weekly Journal-Miner*, Dec. 14, 1898.
16. TR, *Address and Papers from the National Guard*.
17. Keenan, *Conflict with Spain*, 309.
18. *New York Herald*, July 15, 1898.
19. Shafter, "Capture of Santiago de Cuba," 622.
20. McClernand, "Santiago Campaign," 290.
21. Letter from Wheeler to TR (as president), Mar. 9, 1909, TRPP.
22. Alger, *Spanish-American War*, 157.
23. Miley, *In Cuba with Shafter*, 110.
24. Hagedorn, *Boys' Life of TR*, 173.
25. Hagedorn, "Notes," TRC, 39.
26. Ibid., 39, 48.
27. Ibid., 37.
28. Nelson A. Miles, *Annual Report*, 684.
29. Ibid., 686; Hagedorn, "Notes," TRC, 1; Cashin, *Under Fire with the Tenth Cavalry*, 238.
30. Sargent, *Campaign of Santiago de Cuba*, 2:110.
31. Letter from Henry Anson Barber to TR (as president), Mar. 27, 1902, TRPP.
32. Nelson A. Miles, *Annual Report*, 704.
33. Letter from Capt. Eugene Dimmick to TR (as president), Apr. 6, 1909, TRPP.
34. *Army and Navy Journal*, Sept. 17, 1898.
35. Letter from Henry Anson Barber to TR (as president), Mar. 27, 1902, TRPP.
36. Ibid.; Nelson A. Miles, *Annual Report*, 704.
37. John Bigelow, Jr., *Reminiscences of the Santiago Campaign*, 124.

38. *Prescott (Ariz.) Weekly Journal-Miner,* Dec. 21, 1898.
39. *New York Herald,* July 5, 1898.
40. Lord Moran [Charles McMoran Wilson], *The Anatomy of Courage* (Boston: Houghton Mifflin Co., 1967). 11.
41. *New York Herald,* July 3, 1898.

Chapter 22. Charge at San Juan

1. Alger, *Spanish-American War,* 157.
2. *Chicago Record's War Stories,* 78.
3. Ibid., 85.
4. W. H. Carter, *From Yorktown to Santiago with the Sixth U.S. Cavalry* (Baltimore, Md.: Lord Baltimore Press, 1900), 295.
5. Hagedorn, "Notes," TRC, 54.
6. Ibid., 58.
7. Richard Harding Davis, *Cuban and Porto Rican,* 227.
8. Cashin, *Under Fire with the Tenth Cavalry,* 204; Stallman, *Stephen Crane,* 389.
9. Keenan, *Conflict with Spain,* 343.
10. Herner, *Arizona Rough Riders,* 146; *New York Journal,* July 5, 1898.
11. *New York Herald,* July 14, 1898.
12. Robinson, *My Brother, Theodore Roosevelt,* 177.
13. *New York Journal,* July 4, 1898; *Hero Tales of the American Soldier and Sailor,* 122.; Virgil Carrington Jones, *Roosevelt's Rough Riders,* 184.
14. Hagedorn Notes, "Notes," TRC, 75.
15. Ibid., 53.
16. Virgil Carrington Jones, *Roosevelt's Rough Riders,* 183.
17. Dickman, *The Santiago Campaign,* 421; *Leslie's Weekly,* Nov. 3, 1898, p. 324.
18. *New York Times,* July 28, 1898.
19. Hagedorn, "Notes," TRC, 74.
20. *New York Journal,* July 4, 1898; *Hero Tales of the American Soldier and Sailor,* 122.
21. *Spanish-American War as Described by Eye Witnesses,* 107.
22. Richard Harding Davis, *Cuban and Porto Rican,* 218.
23. *Leslie's Weekly,* Sept. 8, 1898, p. 172.
24. Ibid.
25. McCook, *Martial Graves,* 140.
26. Letter from J. T. McBlain to TR (as president), no date, TRPP.
27. Hagedorn, "Notes," TRC, 58.
28. Chadwick, *Relations of the U.S. and Spain,* 96.
29. TR, *Rough Riders,* 131.
30. *Albuquerque (N.M.) Morning Democrat,* July 26, 1898.

Chapter 23. First to the Top

1. Caster, *TR and the Rough Riders,* 138.
2. Chadwick, *Relations of the U.S. and Spain,* 91.
3. Hagedorn, "Notes," TRC, 37.
4. E. E. Morison, *Letters of TR,* 2:855.
5. F. Allen McCurdy and J. Kirk McCurdy, *Letters from Two Rough Riders,* 25.
6. Hagedorn, "Notes," TRC, 5.

7. Herner, *Arizona Rough Riders*, 140.
8. Edmund Morris, "Teddy's Charge Up San Juan Hill—to the Presidency." *Esquire*, Apr. 24, 1979, pp. 25–43.
9. *New York Sun*, Aug. 3, 1898.
10. E. E. Morison, *Letters of TR*, 2:851.
11. Dodge, *Report of Commission*, 8:472.
12. Hagedorn, "Notes," TRC, 48.
13. *New York Herald*, Sept. 16, 1898.
14. *Prescott (Ariz.) Weekly Journal-Miner*, Dec. 21, 1898; Nelson A. Miles, *Annual Report*, 327.
15. Nelson A. Miles, *Annual Report*, 704.
16. Dyer, *"Fightin' Joe" Wheeler*, 358.
17. Dodge, *Report of Commission*, 8:469.
18. Sargent, *Campaign of Santiago de Cuba*, 2:108.
19. Dodge, *Report of Commission*, 8:469; "Spanish-American War Survey," Royal A. Prentice, "Scrapbook: A Rough Rider Looks Back," ch. 4, p. 62.
20. *Chicago Record's War Stories*, 171.
21. Sargent, *Campaign of Santiago de Cuba*, 2:118; Titherington, *History of the Spanish-American War*, 250.
22. Titherington, *History of the Spanish-American War*, 250.
23. McCook, *Martial Graves*, 142.
24. Dodge, *Report of Commission*, 8:469.
25. Musgrave, *Under Three Flags in Cuba*, 299.
26. TR, *Rough Riders*, 134.
27. Sargent, *Campaign of Santiago de Cuba*, 2:110.
28. Musgrave, *Under Three Flags in Cuba*, 299; Titherington, *History of the Spanish-American War*, 251.
29. Hagedorn, "Notes," TRC, 16.
30. Ibid., 77.
31. Ibid., 56.
32. TR, *Address and Papers from the National Guard*.
33. Miley, *In Cuba with Shafter*, 114.
34. Hagedorn, "Notes," TRC, 80.
35. Ibid., 10.
36. Azoy, *Charge!*, 138.
37. Henry Watterson, *History of the Spanish-American War* (N.p: C. B. Denaple, 1898), 236.
38. Ibid.; TR, *Address and Papers from the National Guard*.
39. Nelson A. Miles, *Annual Report*, 685.
40. Hagedorn, "Notes," TRC, 37.
41. *Hero Tales of the American Soldier and Sailor*, 267; "Spanish-American War Survey," Royal A. Prentice, "Scrapbook: A Rough Rider Looks Back," ch. 4, p. 59.
42. *Prescott (Ariz.) Weekly Journal-Miner*, Dec. 21, 1898.
43. Hagedorn, "Notes," TRC, 48.
44. Ibid., 77.
45. Nelson A. Miles, *Annual Report*, 704.
46. Hagedorn, "Notes," TRC, 37, 82.

47. Edmund Morris, "Teddy's Charge up San Juan Hill," 43.
48. Vincent, *Theodore W. Miller,* 135.
49. Ibid.
50. Hagedorn, "Notes," TRC, 37.
51. "Spanish-American War Survey," Royal A. Prentice, "Scrapbook: A Rough Rider Looks Back," ch. 5, p. 64.
52. Hagedorn, "Notes," TRC, 85.
53. Edward Marshall, *Story of the Rough Riders,* 195.
54. Nelson A. Miles, *Annual Report,* 327; TR, *Rough Riders,* 139.
55. Bonsal, *Fight for Santiago,* 134.
56. Hagedorn, *Boys' Life of TR,* 176; Cashin, *Under Fire with the Tenth Cavalry,* 184.
57. TR, *Rough Riders,* 138.
58. Hagedorn, "Notes," TRC, 1.
59. E. E. Morison, *Letters of TR,* 2:851.
60. Wechter, *Hero in America,* 378; Sylvia Jukes Morris, *Edith Kermit Roosevelt,* 181.

Chapter 24. Ending the Charge

1. Hagedorn, "Notes," TRC, 9.
2. Halstead, *Life of TR,* 99; TR, *Autobiography,* 264.
3. "Spanish-American War Survey," Royal A. Prentice, "Scrapbook: A Rough Rider Looks Back," ch. 5, p. 64.
4. Carter, *From Yorktown to Santiago,* 295.
5. Wells, *Diary of a Rough Rider,* 50.
6. TR, *Rough Riders,* 140.
7. Hagedorn, "Notes," TRC, 87.
8. Ibid., 32.
9. Ibid., 73.
10. Hall, *Fun and Fighting,* 199.
11. Wells, *Diary of a Rough Rider,* 51; Nelson A. Miles, *Annual Report,* 686.
12. TR, *Rough Riders,* 143.
13. Ibid.; Trask, *War with Spain,* 244.
14. *Prescott (Ariz.) Weekly Journal-Miner,* Jan. 11, 1899.
15. *New York Sun,* July 15, 1898.
16. Titherington, *History of the Spanish-American War,* 258.
17. *Prescott (Ariz.) Weekly Journal-Miner,* Jan. 18, 1899.
18. Bonsal, *Fight for Santiago,* 115.
19. Titherington, *History of the Spanish-American War,* 258; *Prescott (Ariz.) Weekly Journal-Miner,* Dec. 14, 1898.
20. John H. Parker, *History of the Gatling Gun Detachment, Fifth Army Corps, at Santiago* (Kansas City, Mo.: Press of the Hudson-Kimberly Publishing Co., 1898), 141.
21. *New York Sun,* n.d.
22. Captain Wester, *The Battles around Santiago as Observed by a Swedish Officer* (n.p.: 1900), 1.
23. Sargent, *Campaign of Santiago de Cuba,* 2:129, 2:130.
24. Titherington, *History of the Spanish-American War,* 258.

25. TR, *Autobiography,* 264.
26. James Rankin Young and Moore, *Reminiscences and Thrilling Stories,* 215.
27. Nelson A. Miles, *Annual Report,* 685.
28. Ibid., 686.
29. Sargent, *Campaign of Santiago de Cuba,* 2:131.
30. Chadwick, *Relations of the U.S. and Spain,* 101; James Rankin Young and Moore, *Reminiscences and Thrilling Stories,* 459.
31. Trask, *War with Spain,* 244; Muller y Tejeiro, *Battles and Capitulation,* 60.
32. Keenan, *Conflict with Spain,* 331; "Spanish-American War Survey," Royal A. Prentice, "Scrapbook: A Rough Rider Looks Back," ch. 5, p. 64.
33. Sargent, *Campaign of Santiago de Cuba,* 2:134.
34. Muller y Tejeiro, *Battles and Capitulation,* 41.
35. Post, *Little War,* 213.
36. Ranson, "British Military," 49.
37. Sargent, *Campaign of Santiago de Cuba,* 2:118.
38. TR, *Address and Papers from the National Guard.*
39. James Rankin Young, *History of Our War with Spain,* 619.

Chapter 25. The Legend of Teddy

1. Charles G. Washburn, *Theodore Roosevelt* (Boston: Houghton Mifflin Co., 1916), 198.
2. Lodge, *Selections from the Correspondence,* 331.
3. TR, *Rough Riders,* 168.
4. Cowles, *Letters from TR to Anna Roosevelt Cowles,* 218.
5. *Cartoons of the War of 1898* (Chicago: Belford, Middlebrook and Co., 1898).
6. Lewis Einstein, *Roosevelt: His Mind in Action* (Boston: Houghton Mifflin Co., 1930), 73; Poultney Bigelow, *Seventy Summers,* 280.
7. Langford, *Richard Davis Years,* 222.
8. Poultney Bigelow, *Seventy Summers,* 286; Ernest Crosby, *Captain Jinks, Hero* (New York: Funk and Wagnalls Co., 1902), 81.
9. George Haven Putnam, *Memories of a Publisher,* 143.
10. Crosby, *Captain Jinks, Hero,* 81.
11. Creelman, *On the Great Highway,* 174.
12. Crosby, *Captain Jinks, Hero,* 77, 79.
13. *New York Herald,* July 14, 1898.
14. McIntosh, *The Little I Saw of Cuba,* 117.
15. Stallman, *Stephen Crane,* 397.
16. Ibid., 390.
17. Richard Harding Davis, *Cuban and Porto Rican,* 227.
18. Brown, *Correspondents' War,* 361.
19. Harbaugh, *Power and Responsibility,* 105.
20. Brown, *Correspondents' War,* 363.
21. TR, July 6, 1898, Military Archives, AGO file 104879, NA.
22. Brown, *Correspondents' War,* 361.
23. Ibid., 368.
24. McIntosh, *The Little I Saw of Cuba,* 131.
25. Musgrave, *Under Three Flags in Cuba,* 317.
26. Leech, *In the Days of McKinley,* 250.

27. Poultney Bigelow, *Seventy Summers*, 283.
28. *New York Journal*, July 5, 1898.
29. *Life*, July 28, 1898.
30. *Hero Tales of the American Soldier and Sailor*, 75.
31. Crosby, *Captain Jinks, Hero*, 237.
32. Westermeier, *Who Rush to Glory*, 146–68.
33. Millis, *Martial Spirit*, 217.
34. Blum, *National Experience*, 495.
35. Moran, *Anatomy of Courage*, 4.
36. Busch, *TR: The Story*, 129.
37. E. E. Morison, *Letters of TR*, 2:851.

Chapter 26. Alone in Cuba

1. William Draper Lewis, *Life of TR*, xiii.
2. John J. Leary, Jr. *Talks with Theodore Roosevelt* (Boston: Houghton Mifflin Co., 1919), 164.
3. Beer, *Hanna*, 223; John A. Garraty, *The American Nation* (New York: Harper and Row, 1966), 655.
4. Busch, *TR: The Story*, 6; Mason, *Remember the Maine*, 140.
5. Steffens, *Autobiography*, 346.
6. Langford, *Richard Davis Years*, 276; Roberts, "Strenuous Life," 1.
7. Roberts, "Strenuous Life," 52.
8. Dunn, *From Harrison to Harding*, 265.
9. *New York Times*, July 8, 1898.
10. *New York Herald*, July 5, 1898.
11. Rynning, *Gun Notches*, 176.
12. *New York Herald*, Aug. 3, 1898.
13. Ibid., July 22, 1898.
14. Alexander S. Bacon, *The Woolly Horse* (New York: N.p. ["37 Liberty Street"], 1909), n.p.
15. *New York Herald*, Jan. 29, 1900; E. E. Morison, *Letters of TR*, 3:95.
16. Annie Riley Hale, *Rooseveltian Fact and Fable* (New York: Broadway Publishing Co., 1908), 16.
17. Poultney Bigelow, *Seventy Summers*, 283.
18. Herner, *Arizona Rough Riders*, 151.
19. M. A. DeWolfe Howe, ed., *John Jay Chapman and His Letters* (Boston: Houghton Mifflin Co., 1937), 423; James Rankin Young and Moore, *Reminiscences and Thrilling Stories*, 226.
20. Bacon, *Woolly Horse*, n.p.
21. *New York Herald*, Aug. 28, 1898.
22. Abbott, *Impressions of Theodore Roosevelt*, 201.
23. Ibid., 260.
24. Hale, *Rooseveltian Fact and Fable*, 19.
25. Poultney Bigelow, *Seventy Summers*, 284; E. E. Morison, *Letters of TR*, 3:13.
26. McCook, *Martial Graves*, 141.
27. Bacon, *Woolly Horse*, n.p.
28. John J. Pershing, *My Experiences in the World War* (New York: Frederick A. Stokes Co., 1931), 1:22.

29. Leonard Wood to Adjutant General, July 6, 1898, Military Archives, AGO file 104879, NA.
30. Charles Collins to Sen. T. C. Platt, Oct. 6, 1898, Military Archives, AGO file 104879, NA.
31. Gen. Corbin to TR, Dec. 3, 1898, Military Archives, AGO file 104879, NA.
32. TR to Gen. Corbin, Dec. 7, 1898, Military Archives, AGO file 104879, NA.
33. Gen. Corbin to TR, Dec. 10, 1898, Military Archives, AGO file 104879, NA.
34. Corbin to TR, Dec. 19, 1898, Military Archives, AGO file 104879, NA.
35. Leonard Wood to Adjutant General, Dec. 30, 1898, Military Archives, AGO file 104879, NA; Capt. R. Howze to Adjutant General, Dec. 17, 1898, Military Archives, AGO file 104879, NA.
36. C. J. Stevens to Adjutant General, Jan. 4, 1899, Military Archives, AGO file 104879, NA.
37. Dunne, *Mr. Dooley Remembers*, 272.
38. Ibid., 186.
39. Ibid.
40. Rixey, *Bamie*, 151.
41. Brough, *Princess Alice*, 97.

Chapter 27. The Cravenette Man

1. *New York Herald*, Aug. 28, 1898.
2. *Chicago Record's War Stories*, 113.
3. Halstead, *Life of TR*, 145.
4. *New York Herald*, Aug. 16, 1898.
5. Gilman, *Roosevelt the Happy Warrior*, 174; Pringle, *TR: A Biography*, vii.
6. Leary, *Talks with TR*, 70.
7. *New York Times*, Aug. 15, 1898.

Bibliography

A, B. *Life of Roosevelt.* Washington D.C.: N.p., May 1, 1904.

Abbott, Lawrence F. *Impressions of Theodore Roosevelt.* New York: Doubleday, Page and Company, 1919.

Abramson, Harold A. *Psychological Problems in the Father-Son Relationship.* New York: October House, 1969.

Adams, Henry. *The Education of Henry Adams.* New York: Modern Library, 1946.

Albuquerque (N.M.) Morning Democrat. Apr. 28–Nov. 1, 1898.

Albuquerque (N.M.) Weekly News. Apr. 13–Sept. 10, 1898.

Aldrich, C. Knight. *An Introduction to Dynamic Psychiatry.* New York: McGraw-Hill, 1966.

Alger, R. A. *The Spanish-American War.* New York: Harper and Brothers, 1901.

Allen, Douglas. *Frederic Remington and the Spanish American War.* New York: Crown Publishers, 1971.

Allen, Gardner Weld, ed. *Papers of John Davis Long.* Boston: Massachusetts Historical Society, 1939.

Allen, Henry T. "Mounted Cavalry in the Santiago Campaign." *Journal of the U.S. Cavalry Association* 12, no. 44 (Dec. 1899).

Amos, James E. *Theodore Roosevelt: Hero to His Valet.* New York: John Day Company, 1927.

Archibald, James F. J. "The Day of the Surrender of Santiago." *Scribner's Magazine* 24 (Oct. 1898): 413–16.

———. "The First Engagement of American Troops on Cuban Soil." *Scribner's Magazine* 24 (Aug. 1898): 177–82.

Armstrong, LeRoy. *Pictorial Atlas Illustrating the Spanish-American War.* Chicago: Souvenir Publishing Company, 1898.

"The Athletic Meeting." *Harvard Advocate* 27, no. 4 (March 28, 1879): 39. Clipping in Theodore Roosevelt Collection, Houghton Library, Cambridge, Mass.

Atkins, Edwin F. *Sixty Years in Cuba.* New York: Arno Press, 1980.

Atkins, John Black. *The War in Cuba: The Experiences of an Englishman with the United States Army.* London: Smith, Elder and Company, 1899.

Austin, Mary. *Earth Horizon.* Boston: Houghton Mifflin Company, 1932.

Azoy, A. C. M. *Charge! The Story of the Battle of San Juan Hill.* New York: Longmans, Green and Company, 1961.

Bacon, Alexander S. *Seventy-First at San Juan.* 2d ed. New York: Cortlandt Press, [ca. 1900].

———. *The Woolly Horse.* New York: N.p. ["37 Liberty Street"], 1909.

Bangs, Francis Hyde. *John Kendrick Bangs, Humorist of the Nineties.* New York: Alfred A. Knopf, 1941.

Barry, David S. *Forty Years in Washington.* Boston: Little, Brown, and Company, 1924.

Beale, Howard K. *Theodore Roosevelt and the Rise of America to World Power.* Baltimore, Md.: Johns Hopkins University Press, 1956.

Beasley, Norman. *Frank Knox, American.* Garden City, N.Y.: Doubleday, Doran and Company, 1936.

Beer, Thomas. *Hanna.* New York: Alfred A. Knopf, 1929.

———. *The Mauve Decade.* New York: Alfred A. Knopf, 1926.

———. *Stephen Crane.* New York: Alfred A. Knopf, 1923.

Beisner, Robert L. *Twelve Against Empire.* New York: McGraw-Hill Book Company, 1968.

Bennett, J. W. *Roosevelt and the Republic.* New York: Broadway Publishing Company, 1908.

Bent, Silas. *Newspaper Crusaders.* New York: McGraw-Hill Book Company, 1939.

Benton, Elbert J. *International Law and Diplomacy of the Spanish-American War.* Baltimore, Md.: Johns Hopkins University Press, 1908.

Berge, William H. "The Impulse for Expansion." Ph.D. diss., Vanderbilt University, 1969.

Berningause, Arthur F. *Brooks Adams: A Biography.* New York: Alfred A. Knopf, 1955.

Berryman, John. *Stephen Crane.* New York: William Sloane Associates, 1950.

Bigelow, John, Jr. *Reminiscences of the Santiago Campaign.* New York: Harper and Brothers, 1899.

Bigelow, Poultney. *Seventy Summers.* New York: Longmans, Green and Company, 1925.

Bishop, Joseph Bucklin. *Theodore Roosevelt and His Time.* New York: Charles Scribner's Sons, 1920.

———, ed. *Theodore Roosevelt's Letters to His Children.* New York: Charles Scribner's Sons, 1919.

Black's Medical Dictionary. Edited by William A. R. Thomson. 32nd ed. New York: Harper and Row, 1979.

Blum, John M. *The National Experience.* New York: Harcourt, Brace, and World, 1963.

Bonehill, Ralph. *When Santiago Fell.* Rahway, N.J.: Mershon Company, 1899.

Bonsal, Stephen. *The Fight for Santiago.* New York: Doubleday and McClure Company, 1899.

———. *Heyday in a Vanished World.* New York: W. W. Norton and Company, 1937.

Bowers, Claude G. *Beveridge and the Progressive Era.* Cambridge, Mass.: Houghton Mifflin Company, 1932.

Brandenburg, Broughton. "The Rough Riders Ten Years Afterward." *New York Tribune Sunday Magazine,* pt. 3, Feb. 9, 1908.

Britton, Edward E. "The Battles Around Santiago as Observed by a Swedish Officer." *Journal of the Military Service Institution of the United States* (May 1900).

Brooks, Elbridge S. *The Story of Our War with Spain.* Boston: Lothrop Publishing Co., 1899.

Brough, James. *Princess Alice: A Biography of Alice Roosevelt Longworth.* Boston: Little, Brown, and Company, 1975.

Brown, Charles H. *The Correspondents' War.* New York: Charles Scribner's Sons, 1967.

Burton, David H. "The Influence of the American West on the Imperialist Philosophy of Theodore Roosevelt." *Arizona and the West* [University of Arizona Press, Tucson] 4, no. 1 (Spring 1962): 5.

———. *Theodore Roosevelt.* New York: Twayne Publishers, 1972.

Busch, Noel F. *T. R.: The Story of Theodore Roosevelt and His Influence on Our Times.* New York: Reynal and Company, 1963.

Cammann, William C., ed. *The History of Troop "A," New York Cavalry, U.S.V.* New York: R. H. Russell, 1899.

Carlson, Oliver. *Brisbane.* New York: Stackpole Sons, 1937.

Carlson, Paul H. *"Pecos Bill": A Military Biography of William R. Shafter.* College Station: Texas A&M University Press, 1989.

Carnes, Cecil. *Jimmy Hare: News Photographer.* New York: Macmillan Company, 1940.

Carroll, John M., ed. *The Black Military Experience in the American West.* New York: Liveright Publishing Corporation, 1971.

Carter, William H. *From Yorktown to Santiago with the Sixth U.S. Cavalry.* Baltimore, Md.: Lord Baltimore Press, 1900.

———. *The Life of Lieutenant General Chaffee.* Chicago: University of Chicago Press, 1917.

Cartoons of the War of 1898. Chicago: Belford, Middlebrook and Company, 1898.

Cashin, Herschel V. *Under Fire with the Tenth Cavalry.* New York: F. Tennyson Neely, 1899.

Caster, Henry. *Teddy Roosevelt and the Rough Riders.* New York: Random House, 1954.

Chadwick, French Ensor. *The American Navy.* Garden City, N.Y.: Doubleday, Page and Company, 1915.

———. *The Relations of the United States and Spain.* 2 vols. New York: Charles Scribner's Sons, 1911.

———. *The Relations of the United States and Spain—Diplomacy.* New York: Charles Scribner's Sons, 1909.

Chamberlin, Joseph Edgar. "How the Spaniards Fought at Caney." *Scribner's Magazine* 24 (Sept. 1898): 278–82.

Chambers, John Whiteclay. *Draftees or Volunteers.* New York: Garland Publishing, 1975.

Chanler, Mrs. Winthrop. *Autumn in the Valley.* Boston: Little, Brown, and Company, 1936.

———. *Roman Spring.* Boston: Little, Brown, and Company, 1935.

Chapman, John Jay. *Causes and Consequences.* New York: Charles Scribner's Sons, 1898.

Charnwood, Lord. *Theodore Roosevelt*. Boston: Atlantic Monthly Press, 1923.

Chessman, G. Wallace. *Governor Theodore Roosevelt*. Cambridge, Mass.: Harvard University Press, 1965.

The Chicago Record's War Stories. [By staff correspondents in the field.] Chicago: Chicago Record, 1898.

Chidsey, Donald Barr. *The Spanish-American War*. New York: Crown Publishers, 1971.

Christy, Howard Chandler. "An Artist at El Poso." *Scribner's Magazine* 24 (Sept. 1898): 168–78.

Church, James Robb. *The Doctor's Part*. New York: D. Appleton and Company, 1918.

Church, John A. "The Siege and Capture of Santiago." *American Monthly Review of Reviews* 18 (1898): 168–78.

Churchill, Allen. *The Roosevelts: American Aristocrats*. New York: Harper and Row, 1965.

Clemens, Will L. *Theodore Roosevelt the American*. London: F. Tennyson Neely, 1899.

Cobb, William T. *The Strenuous Life*. New York: William E. Rufge's Sons, 1946.

"Collegiate Sparring." *Boston Globe*, March 23, 1879.

Collins, Michael L. *That Damned Cowboy: Theodore Roosevelt and the American West, 1883–1898*. New York: P. Lang, 1989.

Cosmas, Graham A. *An Army for Empire*. Columbus, Mo.: University of Missouri Press, 1971. 2d ed., Shippensburg, Pa.: White Mane Publishing Company, 1994.

———. "San Juan Hill and El Caney." In *America's First Battles, 1766–1965*, ed. Charles E. Heller and William A. Stofft. Lawrence: University Press of Kansas, 1986.

Coston, W. Hilary. *The Spanish-American War Volunteer*. Middletown, Pa.: Published by the author, 1899.

Cowles, Anna Roosevelt, ed. *Letters from Theodore Roosevelt to Anna Roosevelt Cowles*. New York: Charles Scribner's Sons, 1924.

Crane, Stephen. *Wounds in the Rain*. New York: Stokes, 1900.

Creelman, James. "My Experiences at Santiago." *American Monthly Review of Reviews* 18 (1898): 542–46.

———. *On the Great Highway*. Boston: Lathrop Publishing Company, 1901.

Croly, Herbert. *Marcus Alonzo Hanna*. New York: Macmillan Company, 1923.

Crosby, Ernest. *Captain Jinks, Hero*. New York: Funk and Wagnalls Company, 1902.

Cutright, Paul Russell. *Theodore Roosevelt the Naturalist*. New York: Harper and Brothers, 1956.

Daughters of the American Revolution. *Second Report, 1897–1898*. Washington, D.C.: U.S. Government Printing Office, 1900.

Davis, Charles Belmont, ed. *Adventures and Letters of Richard Harding Davis*. New York: Charles Scribner's Sons, 1917.

Davis, Oscar King. *Released for Publication*. Boston: Houghton Mifflin Company, 1925.

Davis, Richard Harding. "The Battle of San Juan." *Scribner's Magazine* (Oct. 1898).

———. *Cuba in War Time*. New York: R. H. Russell, 1899.

———. *The Cuban and Porto Rican Campaigns*. New York: Charles Scribner's Sons, 1898.

———. "In the Rifle-Pits." *Scribner's Magazine* 24 (Dec. 1898): 644–58.

———. "The Landing of the Army." *Scribner's Magazine* 24 (Aug. 1898): 184–86.

———. *Notes of a War Correspondent*. New York: Charles Scribner's Sons, 1912.

———. *A Year from a Reporter's Note-Book*. New York: Harper and Brothers, 1897.

Dennis, Alfred L. P. *Adventures in American Diplomacy, 1896–1906*. New York: E. P. Dutton and Company, 1928.

Depew, Chauncey M. *My Memories of Eighty Years*. New York: Charles Scribner's Sons, 1922.

Dickman, J. T., ed. *The Santiago Campaign*. Richmond, Va.: Williams Printing Company, 1927.

Dictionary of American Biography. New York: Charles Scribner's Sons, 1937.

Dierks, Jack Cameron. *A Leap to Arms*. Philadelphia: J. B. Lippincott Company, 1970.

Dollard, John. *Fear in Battle*. New Haven, Conn.: Institute of Human Relations, Yale University, 1943.

Donovan, Frank. *The Medal*. New York: Dodd, Mead and Company, 1962.

Donovan, Mike. *The Roosevelt that I Know*. New York: B. W. Dodge and Company, 1909.

Douglas, George William. *The Many-Sided Roosevelt*. New York: Dodd, Mead and Company, 1907.

Downey, Fairfax. *Portrait of an Era*. New York: Charles Scribner's Sons, 1936.

———. *Richard Harding Davis and His Day*. New York: Charles Scribner's Sons, 1933.

Drake, Herbert A. "Anglo-Saxon Administration: Anglo-Saxon Dominance." [May 1899?] Theodore Roosevelt Presidential Papers, Library of Congress.

Draper, Andrew S. *The Rescue of Cuba*. Boston: Silver, Burdett and Company, 1899.

Dulles, Foster Rhea. *America's Rise to World Power*. New York: Harper and Brothers, 1954.

Dunbar, Flanders. *Mind and Body*. New York: Random House, 1955.

Dunn, Arthur Wallace. *From Harrison to Harding*. New York: G. P. Putnam's Sons, 1922.

Dunne, Finley Peter. *Mr. Dooley's Philosophy*. New York: Harper and Brothers, 1900.

Dunne, Philip. *Mr. Dooley Remembers*. Boston: Little, Brown, and Company, 1963.

Dyer, John P. *"Fightin' Joe" Wheeler*. Baton Rouge: Louisiana State University Press, 1941.

Einstein, Lewis. *Roosevelt: His Mind in Action*. Boston: Houghton Mifflin Company, 1930.

Ellis, Edward S. *From the Ranch to the White House*. Chicago: Albert Whitman and Company, 1906.

Emerson, Edwin. *Adventures of Theodore Roosevelt*. New York: E. P. Dutton and Company, 1928.

Emerson, Edwin, Jr. *A History of the Nineteenth Century Year by Year*. New York: P. F. Collier and Son, 1901.

———. "Life at Camp Wikoff." *Munsey's Magazine* 20 (1898): 256–72.

Emmett, Chris. *In the Path of Events*. Waco, Tex.: Jones and Morrison, 1959.

———. "The Rough Riders." *New Mexico Historical Review* 30, no. 3 (July 1955): 177–89.

Evans, Robley D. *A Sailor's Log.* New York: D. Appleton and Company, 1901.

Everett, Marshall. *Complete Life of William McKinley.* N.p., 1901.

Flint, Grover. *Marching with Gomez.* Boston: Lamson, Wolffe and Company, 1898.

Foner, Philip S. *The Spanish-Cuban-American War.* New York: Monthly Review Press, 1972.

Ford, John. "Theodore Roosevelt's Feet of Clay." *Current History* (Aug. 1931): 678–85.

Freidel, Frank. *The Splendid Little War.* New York: Bramhall House, 1958.

Gaer, Joseph, ed. *Frank Norris.* New York: Burt Franklin, 1935.

Gardner, Joseph L. *Departing Glory.* New York: Charles Scribner's Sons, 1973.

Garraty, John A. *The American Nation.* New York: Harper and Row, 1966.

———. *Henry Cabot Lodge.* New York: Alfred A. Knopf, 1953.

Gilman, Bradley. *Roosevelt the Happy Warrior.* Boston: Little, Brown, and Company, 1921.

Gosnell, Harold F. *Boss Platt and His New York Machine.* New York: AMS Press, 1969.

Gould, Lewis L. "Theodore Roosevelt and the Spanish-American War." Four unpublished letters to President William McKinley. *Theodore Roosevelt Association Journal.* N.d.

———, and Richard Greffe. *Photojournalist: The Career of Jimmy Hare.* Austin: University of Texas Press, 1977.

Graff, Abraham. Military substitute for the senior Theodore Roosevelt during the Civil War, including "Declaration of Substitute," "Record of Death and Interment," "Company Muster-in and Descriptive Roll," and "Company Muster Roll." Records of the Adjutant General's Office, 1780s–1917, RG 94, National Archives, Washington, D.C.

Graham, George Edward. *Schley and Santiago.* Chicago: W. B. Conkey Company, 1902.

Grenville, John A. S. "American Naval Preparations for War with Spain, 1896–1898." *Journal of American Studies* 2, no. 1 (1968): 33–47.

Grenville M. Dodge Commission. *Report of Commission Appointed by the President to Investigate the Conduct of the War Department in the War with Spain.* 56th Cong., 1st Sess., Sen. Doc. no. 221. 8 vols. Washington, D.C.: U.S. Government Printing Office, 1900.

Gurley, C. D. *National Rough-Rider Military Encampment.* Shenandoah Valley, Colo., 1900.

Gwynn, Stephen. *The Letters and Friendships of Sir Cecil Spring Rice.* Boston: Houghton Mifflin Company, 1929.

Hagedorn, Hermann. *The Boys' Life of Theodore Roosevelt.* New York: Harper and Brothers, 1918.

———. *Leonard Wood: A Biography.* New York: Harper and Brothers, 1931.

———. "Notes." N.d. Theodore Roosevelt Collection, Houghton Library, Harvard University, Cambridge, Mass.

———. *The Roosevelt Family of Sagamore Hill.* New York: Macmillan Company, 1954.

———. *Roosevelt in the Bad Lands.* Boston: Houghton Mifflin Company, 1930.

———. *The Rough Riders.* New York: Harper and Brothers, 1927.

Hale, Annie Riley. *Rooseveltian Fact and Fable.* New York: Broadway Publishing Company, 1908.

Hall, Tom. *The Fun and Fighting of the Rough Riders.* New York: Frederick A. Stokes Company, 1899.

Halstead, Murat. *Full Official History of the War with Spain.* Chicago: Dominion Company, 1899.

———. *The Life of Theodore Roosevelt.* Chicago: Saalfield Publishing Company, 1902.

———. *The Story of Cuba.* Chicago: Werner Company, 1896.

Harbard, James G. "A Volunteer Cavalry Regiment." *Journal of the U.S. Cavalry Association* 12, no. 44 (Dec. 1899).

Harbaugh, William Henry. *The Life and Times of Theodore Roosevelt.* New York: Oxford University Press, 1975.

———. *Power and Responsibility.* New York: Farrar, Straus and Cudahy, 1961.

Harper's Pictorial History of the War with Spain. 2 vols. New York: Harper and Brothers, 1899.

Harper's Weekly. Jan. 1898–Dec. 1899.

Harvard Crimson. Harvard University, Cambridge, Mass. 1906.

"Harvard's Athletic Contest." *New York Times,* March 23, 1879.

Hastings, Hugh. *New York and the War with Spain.* Albany, N.Y.: Argus Company, 1903.

Hawthorne, Julian. *The History of the United States.* New York: P. F. Collier and Son, 1910. 3:1059–1151.

Hazen, Charles Downer, ed. *The Letters of William Roscoe Thayer.* Boston: Houghton Mifflin Company, 1926.

Healy, David. *U.S. Expansionism.* Madison: University of Wisconsin Press, 1970.

Hecker, Frank J. *Recollections and Experiences in the Spanish-American War.* Detroit, Mich.: Privately printed, 1913.

Heller, Charles E., and William A. Stofft, eds. *America's First Battles, 1776–1965.* Lawrence: University Press of Kansas, 1986.

Hemment, John C. *Cannon and Camera.* New York: D. Appleton and Company, 1898.

Hening, H. B., ed. *George Curry.* Albuquerque: University of New Mexico Press, 1958.

Henry, Will [Henry Allen]. *San Juan Hill.* New York: Random House, 1962.

Herner, Charles: *The Arizona Rough Riders.* Tucson: University of Arizona Press, 1970.

———. "Arizona's Cowboy Cavalry." *Arizoniana: The Journal of Arizona History* 5, no. 4 (Winter 1964).

Hero Tales of the American Soldier and Sailor. N.p.: A. Holloway, 1899.

"High Tides." *New York Times,* Oct. 26, 1858.

Hill, Robert T. *Cuba and Porto Rico.* New York: Century Company, 1898.

Hinsie, Leland E., and Robert Jean Campbell. *Psychiatric Dictionary.* 4th ed. New York: Oxford University Press, 1970.

Hitchcock, Ripley. *Decisive Battles of America.* New York: Harper and Brothers, 1909.

Hoar, George F. *Autobiography of Seventy Years.* New York: Charles Scribner's Sons, 1903.

Hofstadter, Richard. *Social Darwinism in American Thought.* Philadelphia: University of Pennsylvania Press, 1945.

Holme, John G. *The Life of Leonard Wood*. Garden City, N.Y.: Doubleday, Page and Company, 1920.

Howe, M. A. DeWolfe. *John Jay Chapman and His Letters*. Boston: Houghton Mifflin Company, 1937.

Hudson, William C. *Random Recollections*. New York: Cupples and Leon Company, 1911.

Hughes, David L. "A Story of the 'Rough Riders.'" Unpublished paper, Arizona Historical Society, Tucson.

Iglehart, Ferdinand C. *Theodore Roosevelt: The Man as I Knew Him*. New York: Christian Herald, 1919.

Jacobs, Bruce. *Heroes of the Army*. New York: Norton, 1956.

Johnson, Robert Underwood. *Remembered Yesterdays*. Boston: Little, Brown, and Company, 1923.

Johnson, Virginia W. *The Unregimented General*. Boston: Houghton Mifflin Company, 1962.

Johnson, Willis Fletcher, ed. *Addresses and Papers of Theodore Roosevelt*. New York: Unit Book Publishing Co., 1909.

Johnston, William Davison. *TR: Champion of the Strenuous Life*. New York: Farrar, Straus, and Cudahy, 1958.

Jones, Virgil Carrington. "Before the Colors Fade, Last of the Rough Riders." *American Heritage* 20, no. 5 (Aug. 1969): 42.

———. *Roosevelt's Rough Riders*. Garden City, N.Y.: Doubleday and Company, 1971.

Jones, William. *United Spanish War Veterans*. Chicago: H. L. Ruggles and Company, 1920.

Josephson, Matthew. *The President Makers*. New York: Harcourt, Brace and Company, 1940.

Karsten, Peter. "The Nature of 'Influence:' Roosevelt, Mahan and the Concept of Sea Power." *American Quarterly* 4 (1971): 585–600.

Katz, William Loren. *The Black West*. Garden City, N.Y.: Doubleday and Company, 1971.

Keenan, Henry F. *The Conflict with Spain*. Philadelphia: P. W. Ziegler and Company, 1898.

Keithley, Ralph. *Buckey O'Neill*. Caldwell, Id.: Caxton Printers, 1949.

Keller, Allan. *The Spanish-American War*. New York: Hawthorne Books, 1969.

Kennan, George. *Campaigning in Cuba*. New York: Century Company, 1899.

———. "The Psychology of Mr. Roosevelt." *North American Review* 203 (May 16, 1916): 790–94.

King, W. Nephew. *The Story of the Spanish-American War*. New York: P. F. Collier and Son, 1900.

Kipling, Rudyard. *Verse*. Garden City, N.Y.: Doubleday and Company, n.d. "Definitive edition."

Kohlsaat, H. H. *From McKinley to Harding*. New York: Charles Scribner's Sons, 1923.

Krech, David, et al. *Elements of Psychology*. New York: Alfred A. Knopf, 1969.

LaFeber, Walter. *The New Empire*. Ithaca, N.Y.: Cornell University Press, 1963.

Lane, Anne Wintermute, and Louise Herrick Wall, eds. *The Letters of Franklin K. Lane*. Boston: Houghton Mifflin Company, 1922.

Lane, Jack C. *Armed Progressive: General Leonard Wood.* San Francisco: Presidio Press, 1978.

Lang, Lincoln A. *Ranching with Roosevelt.* Philadelphia: J. B. Lippincott Company, 1926.

Lang, Louis J., ed. *The Autobiography of Thomas Collier Platt.* 1910. Reprint, New York: Arno Press, 1974.

Langford, Gerald. *The Richard Harding Davis Years.* New York: Holt, Rinehart and Winston, 1961.

Lash, Joseph P. *Eleanor and Franklin.* New York: W. W. Norton and Company, 1971.

Lawrence, William. *Memories of a Happy Life.* Boston: Houghton Mifflin Company, 1926.

Leach, Jack Franklin. *Conscription in the United States.* Rutland, Vt.: Charles E. Tuttle Publishing, 1952.

Leary, John J., Jr. *Talks with Theodore Roosevelt.* Boston: Houghton Mifflin Company, 1919.

Lee, Arthur H. "The Regulars at El Caney." *Scribner's Magazine* 24 (Oct. 1898): 403–13.

Leech, Margaret. *In the Days of McKinley.* New York: Harper and Brothers, 1959.

Leslie's Weekly. Aug. 4–Dec. 29, 1898.

Letters about Marshall. In Theodore Roosevelt Collection, Harvard College Library, Harvard University, Cambridge, Mass.

"Letters Concerning the Rough Riders." Record and Pension Office Document File no. 536595. RG 94, National Archives, Washington, D.C.

Lewis, Henry Harrison. "The Santiago Battlefield as It Is Today." *Munsey's Magazine* 20 (1899): 857–72.

Lewis, William Draper. *The Life of Theodore Roosevelt.* N.p.: United Publishers, 1919.

Lidz, Theodore. *The Person—His Development Throughout the Life Cycle.* New York: Basic Books, 1968.

Life. Jan. 6–Dec. 29, 1898.

Linderman, Gerald F. *Embattled Courage.* New York: Free Press, 1987.

———. *The Mirror of War: American Society and the Spanish-American War.* Ann Arbor: University of Michigan Press, 1974.

Lininger, Clarence. *The Best War at the Time.* New York: Robert Speller and Sons, 1964.

Lodge, Henry Cabot. "The Spanish-American War." 6 pts. *Harper's Monthly* 98 (Dec. 1898–May 1899): 449–846.

———, ed. *Selections from the Correspondence of Theodore Roosevelt and Henry Cabot Lodge.* 2 vols. New York: Charles Scribner's Sons, 1925.

Logan, Mrs. John A. *Thirty Years in Washington.* Hartford, Conn.: Adworthington and Company, 1901.

Long, Margaret, ed. *The Journal of John D. Long.* Rindge, N.H.: Richard R. Smith Publishers, 1956.

Longworth, Alice Roosevelt. *Crowded Hours.* New York: Charles Scribner's Sons, 1933.

Lorant, Stephen. *The Life and Times of Theodore Roosevelt.* Garden City, N.Y.: Doubleday and Company, 1959.

Lundberg, Ferdinand. *Imperial Hearst.* New York: Equinox Cooperative Press, 1936.

Lynk, Miles V. *The Black Troopers.* New York: AMS Press, 1971.

Mabie, Hamilton Wright. *Our Country in Peace and War.* Philadelphia: J. H. Moore Company, 1898.

McCaleb, Walter F. *Theodore Roosevelt.* New York: Albert and Charles Boni, 1931.

McClernand, E. J. "The Santiago Campaign." *U.S. Infantry Journal* 21, no. 3 (Sept. 1922): 280–302.

McClintock, J. H. "Arizona in the Cuban Campaign." *Forward Arizona.* KTAR (the Arizona Republic's Electrical Equipment Company's Radio Station), Jan. 14, 1931. Arizona Historical Society, Tucson.

———. "The Arizona Rough Riders in Cuba." *Forward Arizona.* KTAR (the Arizona Republic's Electrical Equipment Company's Radio Station), Jan. 7, 1931. Arizona Historical Society, Tucson.

———. "Organization of the Rough Riders." *Forward Arizona.* KTAR (the Arizona Republic's Electrical Equipment Company's Radio Station), Dec. 31, 1930. Arizona Historical Society, Tucson.

McCook, Henry C. *The Martial Graves of Our Fallen Heroes in Santiago de Cuba.* Philadelphia: George W. Jacobs and Company, 1899.

McCullough, David. *Mornings on Horseback.* New York: Simon and Schuster, 1981.

McCurdy, F. Allen, and J. Kirk McCurdy. *Letters from Two Rough Riders.* New York: F. Tennyson Neely, 1902.

McCurdy, Harold Grier. *The Personal World.* New York: Harcourt, Brace and World, 1961.

McIntosh, Burr. *The Little I Saw of Cuba.* London: F. Tennyson Neely, 1899.

Mahan, Alfred T. *Lessons of the War with Spain.* Boston: Little, Brown, and Company, 1899.

Mairet, Philip, ed. *Alfred Adler.* New York: Harper and Row, 1964.

Manners, William. *TR and Will.* New York: Harcourt, Brace and World, 1969.

Marden, Orison Swett. *Little Visits with Great Americans.* New York: Success Company, 1905.

Marshall, Edward. "The Santiago Campaign: Some Episodes: A Wounded Correspondent's Recollections of Guasimas." *Scribner's Magazine* 24 (Sept. 1898): 273–77.

———. *The Story of the Rough Riders.* New York: G. W. Dillingham Company, 1899.

Marshall, Edwin [Edward]. Letters about Pension. Pension File no. SC923, 192, Records of the Veterans Administration, RG 15, National Archives, Washington, D.C.

Mason, Gregory. *Remember the Maine.* New York: Henry Holt and Company, 1939.

May, Ernest R. *Imperial Democracy.* New York: Harcourt, Brace and World, 1961.

Mayo, Lawrence Shaw, ed. *America of Yesterday.* Boston: Atlantic Monthly Press, 1923.

A Memorial to Theodore Roosevelt. Albany, N.Y. N.p., Feb. 21, 1919.

Merrill, James M. *Spurs to Glory.* Chicago: Rand McNally and Company, 1966.

Meyers, Robert C. V. *Theodore Roosevelt, Patriot and Statesman.* N.p., 1902.

Miles, Nelson A. *Annual Report of the War Department for the Fiscal Year Ending June 30, 1898: Report of the Major-General Commanding the Army.* 55th Cong., 3rd Sess. (1898), House Doc. no. 2. Washington, D.C.: U.S. Government Printing Office, 1898.

————. "Introduction." In *Harper's Pictorial History of the War with Spain.* New York: Harper and Brothers, 1899.

————. *Serving the Republic.* New York: Harper and Brothers, 1911.

Miley, John D. *In Cuba with Shafter.* New York: Charles Scribner's Sons, 1899.

A Military Album Containing Over One Thousand Portraits of Commissioned Officers Who Served in the Spanish-American War. New York: L. R. Hamersly Company, 1901.

Miller, T. W. *Theodore W. Miller, Rough Rider.* Akron, Ohio: Privately printed, 1899.

Millet, Frank D. *The Expedition to the Philippines.* New York: Harper and Brothers, 1899.

Millis, Walter. *The Martial Spirit.* Cambridge, Mass.: Literary Guild of America, 1931.

Moers, Ellen. "Teddy Roosevelt: Literary Feller." *Columbia University Forum* (Summer 1963): 10–16.

Moran, Lord [Charles McMoran Wilson]. *The Anatomy of Courage.* Boston: Houghton Mifflin Company, 1967.

Morgan, H. Wayne. *America's Road to Empire.* New York: John Wiley and Sons, 1965.

————. *William McKinley and His Administration.* Syracuse, N.Y.: Syracuse University Press, 1963.

Morgan, James. *Theodore Roosevelt the Boy and the Man.* New York: Macmillan Company, 1907.

Morison, Elting E. *Cowboys and Kings.* Cambridge, Mass.: Harvard University Press, 1954.

————, ed. *The Letters of Theodore Roosevelt.* 2 vols. Cambridge, Mass.: Harvard University Press, 1951.

Morison, Samuel Eliot. *The Oxford History of the American People.* New York: Oxford University Press, 1965.

Morris, Charles. *The War with Spain.* Philadelphia: J. B. Lippincott Company, 1899.

Morris, Edmund. *The Rise of Theodore Roosevelt.* New York: Coward, McCann and Geoghegan, 1979.

————. "The Saga of Teddy." *Newsweek,* August 6, 1979.

————. "Teddy's Charge Up San Juan Hill—to the Presidency." *Esquire,* Apr. 24, 1979, pp. 25–43.

Morris, Sylvia Jukes. *Edith Kermit Roosevelt.* New York: Coward, McCann and Geoghegan, 1980.

Moss, James A. *Memories of the Campaign of Santiago.* San Francisco: Mysell-Rollins Company, 1899.

Muller y Tejeiro, José. *Battles and Capitulation of Santiago de Cuba.* Translated from Spanish by U.S. Navy Department, Office of Naval Intelligence, Information from Abroad. Washington, D.C.: U.S. Government Printing Office, 1898.

Murdock, Eugene Converse. *Patriotism Limited.* Kent, Ohio: Kent State University Press, 1967.

Musgrave, George Clarke. *Under Three Flags in Cuba.* Boston: Little, Brown, and Company, 1899.

Musick, John R. *Cuba Libre.* New York: Funk and Wagnalls Company, 1900.

National Archives. File of letter of appointment, information about service of unit, and recommendations for Medal of Honor for Theodore Roosevelt. RG 94. U.S. Adjutant General's Office, Doc. File 104879.

Needham, Henry Beach. "Theodore Roosevelt—An Outdoor Man." *McClure's Magazine* 26, no. 3 (Jan. 1906): 231–52.

Neely's Panorama of Our New Possessions. New York: F. Tennyson Neely, 1898.

Nevins, Allan. *Henry White.* New York: Harper and Brothers, n.d.

Norris, Frank. *The Surrender of Santiago.* San Francisco: Paul Elder and Company, 1917.

Norvell, S. T. "Las Guasimas." *Journal of the U.S. Cavalry Association* 12, no. 44 (Dec. 1899): 351.

Núñez, Sévero Gómez. *The Spanish-American War: Blockades and Coast Defense.* Translated from the Spanish. U.S. Navy Department, Office of Naval Intelligence, War Notes no. 6, Information from Abroad. Washington, D.C.: U.S. Government Printing Office, 1899.

"Old Letters Shed New Light on Roosevelt." *New York Herald Tribune,* Dec. 1924.

Old War Songs and New and Old Patriotic and National Songs to Comrades of the G.A.R. and the Spanish War. Syracuse, N.Y.: J. C. O. Redington, n.d.

Older, Mrs. Fremont. *William Randolph Hearst, American.* New York: D. Appleton-Century Company, 1936.

Otero, Miguel Antonio. *My Nine Years as Governor of the Territory of New Mexico, 1897–1906.* Albuquerque: University of New Mexico Press, 1940.

Otis, James. *The Boys of '98.* Boston: Dana Estes and Company, 1898.

Paine, Ralph D. *Roads of Adventure.* Boston: Houghton Mifflin Company, 1922.

Parker, John H. *History of the Gatling Gun Detachment, Fifth Army Corps, at Santiago.* Kansas City, Mo.: Press of the Hudson-Kimberly Publishing Company, 1898.

Parsons, Frances Theodora. *Perchance Some Day.* N.p.: Privately printed, 1951.

Paullin, Charles Oscar. *Paullin's History of Naval Administration.* Annapolis, Md.: U.S. Naval Institute, 1968.

Perrigo, Lynn I. *Las Vegas and the Rough Riders.* Las Vegas, N.M.: Museum Board of the City of Las Vegas, 1961.

Pershing, John J. *My Experiences in the World War.* 2 vols. New York: Frederick A. Stokes Company, 1931.

Pierce, Frederick E. *Reminiscences of the Experiences of Company L.* Greenfield, Mass.: E. A. Hall and Company, 1900.

Post, Charles Johnson. *The Little War of Private Post.* Boston: Little, Brown, and Company, 1960.

Pratt, Julius W. *Expansionists of 1898.* Baltimore, Md.: Johns Hopkins University Press, 1936.

Prentice, Royal A. "The Rough Riders." *New Mexico Historical Review* 26, no. 4 (Oct. 1951): 261–76; and 27, no. 1 (Jan. 1952): 29–50.

Prescott (Ariz.) Journal-Miner Weekly. Apr. 1898–Dec. 1899.

Price, Willadene. *Gutzon Borglum.* McLean, Va.: EPM Publications, 1974.

Pringle, Henry F. *Theodore Roosevelt: A Biography.* New York: Harcourt, Brace and Company, 1931.

Putnam, Carleton. *Theodore Roosevelt: The Formative Years.* New York: Charles Scribner's Sons, 1958.

Putnam, George Haven. *Memories of a Publisher.* New York: G. P. Putnam's Sons, 1915.

Quesada, Gonzalo de. *The War in Cuba.* N.p.: Liberty Publishing Company, 1896.

Quick, John. *Dictionary of Weapons and Military Terms.* New York: McGraw-Hill Book Company, n.d.

Rachman, S. J. *Fear and Courage.* San Francisco: W. H. Freeman and Company, 1978.

Randall House catalog. Rare Books IX, no. 160. San Francisco, 1980.

Ranson, E. "British Military and Naval Observers in the Spanish-American War." *Journal of American Studies* (Great Britain) 3, no. 1 (July 1969): 33–56.

Rayburn, John C. "The Rough Riders in San Antonio, 1898." *Arizona and the West* 3, no. 2 (Summer 1961): 113–28.

Remington, Frederic. *Done in the Open.* New York: P. F. Collier and Son, 1903.

———. "With the Fifth Corps." In *The Collected Writings of Frederic Remington,* ed. Peggy and Harold Samuels, 338–48. Garden City, N.Y.: Doubleday, 1979.

Rhodes, Charles Dudley. "Foreword." In *The Santiago Campaign,* ed. J. T. Dickman. Richmond, Va.: Williams Printing Company, 1927.

Rhodes, James Ford. *The McKinley and Roosevelt Administrations.* Port Washington, N.Y.: Kennikat Press, 1927.

Rickover, H. G. *How the Battleship* Maine *Was Destroyed.* Washington, D.C.: U.S. Department of the Navy, 1976.

Riis, Jacob A. "Roosevelt and His Men." *Outlook* 60, no. 5 (Oct. 1, 1898): 287–93.

———. *Theodore Roosevelt the Citizen.* New York: Outlook Company, 1904.

Rixey, Lilian. *Bamie.* New York: David McKay Company, 1963.

Roberts, Gerald F. "The Strenuous Life." Michigan State University, Department of History, 1970.

Robinson, Corinne Roosevelt. *My Brother, Theodore Roosevelt.* New York: Charles Scribner's Sons, 1921.

Roosevelt, Anna Eleanor. *Hunting Big Game in the Eighties.* New York: Charles Scribner's Sons, 1933.

Roosevelt, Eleanor B. *Day Before Yesterday.* Garden City, N.Y.: Doubleday and Company, 1959.

Roosevelt, Kermit. *The Long Trail.* New York: Review of Reviews, 1921.

"Roosevelt March." Chicago: McKinley Music Company, 1910.

Roosevelt, Nicholas. *Theodore Roosevelt: The Man as I Knew Him.* New York: Dodd, Mead and Company, 1967.

Roosevelt, Theodore. *Address and Papers Taken from the Proceedings of the Convention of the National Guard Association of the State of New York, February 8, 1900.* Albany, N.Y.: Weed-Parsons Printing Company, 1900.

———. *An Autobiography.* New York: Macmillan Company, 1913.

———. *Diaries of Boyhood and Youth.* New York: Charles Scribner's Sons, 1928.

———. Diary of the Spanish-American War. Theodore Roosevelt Collection, Harvard College Library, Harvard University, Cambridge, Mass.

———. *The Foes of Our Own Household.* New York: George H. Doran Company, 1917.

———. *Good Hunting.* New York: Harper and Brothers, 1907.

———. *The Great Adventure.* New York: Charles Scribner's Sons, 1919.

———. "Kidd's 'Social Evolution.'" *North American Review* 161 (1895): 94–109.

———. Letters to Charles Stedman Hanks. Letters concerning Edith and Ted, 1897, 1898. Letters to Ted. Letters concerning the *Maine,* Navy. Letters on the ranch.

Letters about taxes on Oyster Bay property. All in Theodore Roosevelt Presidential Papers, Library of Congress.

———. Letters to children during the Spanish-American War. Theodore Roosevelt Collection, Harvard College Library, Harvard University, Cambridge, Mass.

———. Private diaries, 1879 to 1881. Theodore Roosevelt Presidential Papers, Library of Congress.

———. *Ranch Life and the Hunting Trail.* New York: Century Company, 1901.

———. *The Roosevelt Policy.* New York: Current Literature Publishing, 1908.

———. *The Rough Riders.* New York: Charles Scribner's Sons, 1899.

———. *Stories of the Great West.* New York: Century Company, 1921.

———. *Theodore Roosevelt Cyclopedia.* 2d ed. Oyster Bay, N.Y.: Meckler Corp., 1989.

———. *The Wilderness Hunter.* New York: G. P. Putnam's Sons, 1893.

Roosevelt, Theodore II. *All in the Family.* New York: G. P. Putnam's Sons, 1929.

Roosevelt's Rough Rider Association. New York: N.p., July 1, 1912. In Library of Congress.

Rosenbault, Charles J. *When Dana Was the Sun.* New York: Robert M. McBride and Company, 1931.

Rugoff, Milton. *Prudery and Passion.* New York: G. P. Putnam's Sons, 1971.

Rynning, Thomas H. *Gun Notches.* New York: Frederick A. Stokes Company, 1931.

St. Louis, Private [pseud.]. *Forty Years After.* Boston: N.p., 1939.

Samuels, Peggy, and Harold Samuels. *Frederic Remington: A Biography.* New York: Doubleday and Company, 1982.

Sargent, Herbert H. *The Campaign of Santiago de Cuba.* 3 vols. Chicago: A. C. McClurg and Company, 1907.

Satterlee, Herbert L. *J. Pierpont Morgan.* New York: Macmillan Company, 1939.

Schley, Winfield Scott. *Forty-Five Years Under the Flag.* New York: D. Appleton and Company, 1904.

Schneer, Henry I. *The Asthmatic Child.* New York: Harper and Row, 1963.

Schott, Joseph L. *Above and Beyond.* New York: G. P. Putnam's Sons, 1963.

Schriftgiesser, Karl. *The Amazing Roosevelt Family.* New York: Wilfred Funk, 1942.

———. *The Gentleman from Massachusetts: Henry Cabot Lodge.* Boston: Little, Brown, and Company, 1944.

"Scrapbook: The Rough Riders Look Back." In "The Spanish-American War Survey." U.S. Army Military History Institute, Carlisle Barracks, Penn.

Sears, Joseph Hamblen. *The Career of Leonard Wood.* New York: D. Appleton and Company, 1919.

Seitz, Don C. *Joseph Pulitzer.* New York: Simon and Schuster, 1924.

Shafter, William R. "The Capture of Santiago de Cuba." *Century Magazine* 57, nos. 80–81 (Feb. 1899): 612–30.

Sheldon, Charles M. "The Horrors of War." *Leslie's Weekly,* August 18, 1898.

Sigsbee, Charles D. *The Personal Narrative.* New York: Century Company, 1899.

Sinkler, George. *The Racial Attitudes of American Presidents.* Garden City, N.Y.: Doubleday and Company, 1971.

Smith, Albert E. *Two Reels and a Crank.* Garden City, N.Y.: Doubleday and Company, 1952.

The Spanish-American War: The Events of the War Described by Eye Witnesses. Chicago: Herbert S. Stone and Company, 1899.

Spears, John R. "Afloat for News in War Times." *Scribner's Magazine* 24 (Oct. 1898): 501–504.

Springer, Frank. *Theodore Roosevelt Memorial Service*. Santa Fe, N.M.: Museum of New Mexico, Feb. 9, 1919.

Stallman, R. W. *Stephen Crane*. New York: George Braziller, 1969.

———. *Stephen Crane: A Critical Bibliography*. Ames: Iowa State University Press, 1972.

Stallman, R. W., and E. R. Hagemann, eds. *The War Dispatches of Stephen Crane*. New York: New York University Press, 1964.

Steele, Matthew Forney. *American Campaigns*. Washington, D.C.: United States Infantry Association, 1935.

Steffens, Lincoln. *The Autobiography of Lincoln Steffens*. New York: Harcourt, Brace and Company, 1931.

———. "The Real Roosevelt." *Ainslee's Magazine* 2 (Dec. 1898): 478–84.

Stein, Harry H. "Theodore Roosevelt and the Press: Lincoln Steffens." *Mid-America* (Apr. 1972): 94–107.

Storer, Mrs. Bellamy. "How Theodore Roosevelt Was Appointed Assistant Secretary of the Navy." *Harper's Weekly*, June 1, 1912.

———. *Theodore Roosevelt the Child*. Privately printed, 1921.

Stratemeyer, Edward. *American Boys' Life of Theodore Roosevelt*. Boston: Lee and Shepard, 1904.

Street, Julian. *The Most Interesting American*. New York: Century Company, 1916.

Sues, Otto L. *Grigsby's Cowboys: Third United States Volunteer Cavalry, Spanish-American War*. Salem, S.D.: James E. Patten, 1900.

Sullivan, Mark. *Our Times*. Vol. 2. New York: Charles Scribner's Sons, 1927.

Sumner, William Graham. *War and Other Essays*. New Haven, Conn.: Yale University Press, 1911.

Swanberg, W. A. *Citizen Hearst*. New York: Charles Scribner's Sons, 1961.

Szurek, S. A., and I. N. Berlin. *Psychosomatic Disorders and Mental Retardation in Children*. Palo Alto, Calif.: Science and Behavior Books, 1968.

Taylor, Charles C. *The Life of Admiral Mahan*. London: John Murray, 1920.

Thayer, William Roscoe. *The Life and Letters of John Hay*. Boston: Houghton Mifflin Company, 1929.

———. *Theodore Roosevelt: An Intimate Biography*. Boston: Houghton Mifflin Company, 1919.

Thomas, Augustus. *The Print of My Remembrance*. New York: Charles Scribner's Sons, 1922.

Thompson, Albert W. "I Helped Raise the Rough Riders." *New Mexico Historical Review* 14, no. 3 (July 1939): 287–99.

Titherington, Richard H. *A History of the Spanish-American War of 1898*. New York: D. Appleton and Company, 1900.

Trask, David F. *The War with Spain in 1898*. New York: Macmillan Company, 1981.

Turner, Don. *A Plea for the Heroes: T.R. and the Rough Riders*. Texas: Humbug Gulch Press, 1971.

Tyler, John W. *The Life of William McKinley*. Philadelphia: P. W. Ziegler and Company, 1901.

U.S. Congress. House of Representatives. *Message of the President of the United*

States. 55th Cong., 2d Sess. (1898), House Doc. no. 405, Apr. 11, 1898. Washington, D.C.: U.S. Government Printing Office, 1898.

U.S. Congress. Senate. *Report of the Committee on Foreign Relations, Relative to Affairs in Cuba.* 55th Cong., 2d Sess., Report no. 885, Apr. 13, 1898. Washington, D.C.: U.S. Government Printing Office, 1898.

U.S. Navy Department. Office of Naval Intelligence. *Sketches from the Spanish-American War,* by Commander J. Washington, D.C.: U.S. Government Printing Office, 1899.

U.S. Works Progress Administration. *New Mexico: A Guide to the Colorful State.* New York: Hastings House, 1940.

"Uncle Sam's Best Fight." *London Graphic,* March 26, 1887.

Viereck, George Sylvester. *Roosevelt.* New York: Jackson Press, 1920.

Vincent, George E., ed. *Theodore W. Miller, Rough Rider.* Akron, Oh.: Privately printed, 1899.

Vivian, Thomas J. *The Fall of Santiago.* New York: R. F. Fenno and Company, 1898.

Vorpahl, Ben Merchant. *Frederic Remington and the West.* Austin: University of Texas Press, 1978.

———. *My Dear Wister.* Palo Alto, Calif.: American West Publishing Company, 1972.

Wagner, Arthur L. *Report of the Santiago Campaign.* Kansas City, Mo.: Franklin Hudson Publishing Company, 1908.

Walker, Dale L. "Bucky O'Neill and the Rough Riders." *Montana: The Magazine of Western History* 21, no. 1 (Jan. 1971): 60–71.

———. "'Bucky' O'Neill Died with 'Rough Riders'." *El Paso Times Sunday Magazine,* Apr. 12, 1970, pp. 2 and 3.

———. *Death Was the Black Horse.* Austin, Tex.: Madrona Press, 1975.

———. "Last of the Rough Riders." *Montana: The Magazine of Western History* 23, no. 3 (July 1973): 40.

———. "The Next to the Last Man." *Nova* (University of Texas at El Paso) 6, no. 2 (Feb.–Oct. 1972): 1–4.

———. "94 and Going Strong." *New Mexico Magazine* 50, nos. 9–10 (Sept.–Oct. 1972): 33–35.

Ward, Margaret. *Cimarron Saga.* N.p.: Privately printed, n.d.

Washburn, Charles G. *Theodore Roosevelt.* Boston: Houghton Mifflin Company, 1916.

Watterson, Henry. *History of the Spanish-American War.* N.p: C. B. Denaple, 1898.

Webb, A. D. "Arizonans in Spanish-American War." *Arizona Historical Review* (Jan. 1929): 50–68.

Wechter, Dixon. *The Hero in America.* New York: Charles Scribner's Sons, 1941.

Weems, John Edward. *The Fate of the* Maine. New York: Henry Holt and Company, 1958.

Welling, Richard. "Theodore Roosevelt at Harvard." *Outlook* (Oct. 27, 1920): 366–69.

Wells, J. O. *Diary of a Rough Rider.* N.p.: Privately printed, 1900.

Werstein, Irving. *Turning Point for America.* New York: Julian Messner, 1964.

Westermeier, Clifford P. "Teddy's Terrors: The New Mexican Volunteers of 1898." *New Mexico Historical Review* 27 (Apr. 1952): 107–36.

————. *Who Rush to Glory.* Caldwell, Id.: Caxton Printers, 1958.

Wheeler, Joseph. "Introduction." In *Photographic History of the War with Spain.* Baltimore, Md.: R. H. Woodward Company, 1898.

————. *The Santiago Campaign.* Philadelphia: Drexel Biddle, 1899.

White, Andrew Dickson. *Autobiography.* New York: Century Company, 1906.

White, G. Edward. *The Eastern Establishment and the Western Experience.* New Haven, Conn.: Yale University Press, 1968.

White, Leonard D. *The Republican Era, 1869–1901.* New York: Macmillan Company, 1958.

White, Trumbull. *Our New Possessions.* Philadelphia: J. H. Moore Company, 1898.

White, William Allen. *Autobiography.* New York: Macmillan Company, 1946.

————. *Masks in a Pageant.* New York: Macmillan Company, 1928.

Whitney, Caspar. "The Santiago Campaign." *Harper's Monthly* 97 (Oct. 1898): 799–813.

Wilcox, Marrion, ed. *Harper's History of the War in the Philippines.* New York: Harper and Brothers, 1900.

Wilhelm, Donald. *Theodore Roosevelt as an Undergraduate.* Boston: John W. Luce and Company, 1910.

Wilkerson, Marcus. *Public Opinion and the Spanish-American War.* Baton Rouge: Louisiana State University Press, 1932.

Williams, Ames W., and Vincent Starrett. *Stephen Crane: A Bibliography.* New York: Ben Franklin, 1948.

Willis, Jack [John]. *Roosevelt in the Rough.* New York: Ives Washburn, 1931.

Willner, Ann Ruth. *The Spellbinders.* New Haven, Conn.: Yale University Press, 1984.

Winkler, John K. *W. R. Hearst.* New York: Simon and Schuster, 1928.

Winter, John G., Jr. "The Fight of the Rough Riders." *Outlook* 60 (Sept. 1898): 19, 20.

Wisan, Joseph E. *The Cuban Crisis as Reflected in the New York Press (1895–1898).* New York: Columbia University Press, 1934.

Wister, Owen. *Roosevelt: The Story of a Friendship.* New York: Macmillan Company, 1930.

————. "Theodore Roosevelt The Sportsman and the Man." *Outing* 38, no. 3, (June 1901): 243–48.

Wood, Eric Fisher. *Leonard Wood: Conservator of Americanism.* New York: George H. Doran Company, 1920.

Wood, Frederick S. *Roosevelt as We Knew Him.* Philadelphia: John C. Winston Company, 1927.

Wood, Leonard. Diary. Library of Congress.

————. "Las Guasimas." *Century Magazine* (June 1898).

————. Letters to Louise Wood [wife]. Library of Congress.

Wooster, Robert. *Nelson A. Miles: The Military in the Twilight of the Nineteenth Century.* Lincoln: University of Nebraska Press, 1993.

Wormser, Richard. *The Yellowlegs.* Garden City, N.Y.: Doubleday and Company, 1966.

Wright, Marcus, ed. *Leslie's Official History of the Spanish-American War.* N.p., 1899.

————. *The Official and Pictorial Record of the War with Spain.* Washington, D.C.: n.p., 1902.

Wyeth, Betsy James. *The Wyeths*. Boston: Gambit, 1971.

Young, Art. *On My Way*. New York: Horace Liveright, 1928.

Young, James Rankin. *History of Our War with Spain*. N.p.: J. R. Jones, 1898.

Young, James Rankin, and J. Hampton Moore. *Reminiscences and Thrilling Stories of the War by Returned Heroes*. Chicago: Providence Publishing Company, 1899.

Ziff, Larzer. *The American 1890s*. New York: Viking Press, 1966.

Zipf, Walter. "High, Wide and Handsome." *Arizona Highways* 24, no. 6 (June 1948): 20.

Index

Note: Pages with maps and photographs are indicated by italics.